FAIRNESS IN PRACTICE

OXFORD POLITICAL PHILOSOPHY

*GENERAL EDITOR: SAMUEL FREEMAN,
UNIVERSITY OF PENNSYLVANIA*

Oxford Political Philosophy publishes books on theoretical and applied political philosophy within the Anglo-American tradition. The series welcomes submissions on social, political, and global justice, individual rights, democracy, liberalism, socialism, and constitutionalism.

N. Scott Arnold
Imposing Values: An Essay on Liberalism and Regulation

Peter de Marneffe
Liberalism and Prostitution

Iris Marion Young
Responsibility for Justice

Paul Weithman
Why Political Liberalism? On John Rawls's Political Turn

Aaron James
Fairness in Practice: A Social Contract for a Global Economy

FAIRNESS IN PRACTICE

A Social Contract for a Global Economy

Aaron James

UNIVERSITY PRESS

Oxford University Press is a department of the University of Oxford.
It furthers the University's objective of excellence in research, scholarship,
and education by publishing worldwide.

Oxford   New York
Auckland   Cape Town   Dar es Salaam   Hong Kong   Karachi
Kuala Lumpur   Madrid   Melbourne   Mexico City   Nairobi
New Delhi   Shanghai   Taipei   Toronto

With offices in
Argentina   Austria   Brazil   Chile   Czech Republic   France   Greece
Guatemala   Hungary   Italy   Japan   Poland   Portugal   Singapore
South Korea   Switzerland   Thailand   Turkey   Ukraine   Vietnam

Oxford is a registered trade mark of Oxford University Press
in the UK and certain other countries.

Published in the United States of America by
Oxford University Press
198 Madison Avenue, New York, NY 10016

© Oxford University Press 2012

First issued as an Oxford University Press paperback, 2013.

All rights reserved. No part of this publication may be reproduced, stored in a retrieval
system, or transmitted, in any form or by any means, without the prior permission in
writing of Oxford University Press, or as expressly permitted by law, by license, or under
terms agreed with the appropriate reproduction rights organization. Inquiries concerning
reproduction outside the scope of the above should be sent to the Rights Department,
Oxford University Press, at the address above.

You must not circulate this work in any other form
and you must impose this same condition on any acquirer.

Library of Congress Cataloging-in-Publication Data
James, Aaron.
Fairness in practice : a social contract for a global economy / Aaron James.
    p.   cm.
ISBN 978-0-19-984615-3 (hardcover : alk. paper); 978-0-19-934456-7 (paperback)
1. Fairness. 2. International economic relations. 3. Globalization. I. Title.
BJ1533.F2J36   2012
337.1—dc23   2011030223

9 8 7 6 5 4 3 2 1

Printed in the United States of America
on acid-free paper

For Marshall,
who mixed philosophy and public affairs

Contents

Preface ix

    1 MAIN IDEAS 3

SOCIAL FOUNDATIONS
    2 ECONOMIC SKEPTICISM 35
    3 HOBBESIAN SKEPTICISM 77
    4 THE MORAL PROBLEM OF ASSURANCE 103

BASIC FAIRNESS
    5 STRUCTURAL EQUITY 131
    6 THE BENCHMARK OF EQUALITY 165
    7 PRINCIPLES OF EQUITY 203

FAIRNESS ISSUES
    8 FINANCIAL CRISES 249
    9 THE LEVEL PLAYING FIELD: INTELLECTUAL PROPERTY 285
    10 EXPLOITATION, DEGRADATION, AND OTHER MORAL CONCERNS 305

Works Cited 335
Index 355

Preface

The global economy is not fair. This bald claim seems plainly true, and yet it is far from obvious what fairness in the global economy would mean. What would it be for the global economy to be fair?

If we cannot plausibly answer that philosophical question, there will be a good case for skepticism about our initial sense of unfairness. Any perversity we find in the systems of trade, money, and finance will have to be explained in some other register of value; perhaps the global economy is inefficient or sub-optimal or dysfunctional, but not unfair per se. This book defends the opposite conclusion: our initial sense that the global economy is unfair, or unfairly arranged, can be vindicated. We can characterize fairness in the global economy, in an attractive general way, as fairness in a social contract for an economy of global size.

If the idea of fairness initially seems obscure, we have a relatively good grasp of why we should want a global economy in the first place. As economists have explained for over two and a half centuries since Adam Smith, by removing barriers to trade, societies fruitfully expand the division of labor. Goods and services become more various and abundant, standards of living rise, and poverty is steadily reduced. We thus augment the wealth of nations. We can therefore welcome the historical emergence of a robust economy in the postwar era. That is not to say, however, that we can be sanguine about unfairness in its organizing terms. The stakes are extraordinarily high. As the early twenty-first-century global financial crisis has made painfully clear, the organization of the global economy is of the first practical significance for lives, countries, and regions of the world. Perhaps only war and peace, basic human rights, and catastrophic global climate change are of comparable moment for human life.

It should therefore come as little surprise that arguments about fairness have become a major currency of public debate in world economic politics. We now hear a dizzying array of appeals to "fair trade," "unfair protectionism," "equitable growth," "level playing fields," "unfair competition," "exploitation," "special and differential treatment," or "unfair risk," often alongside, or even in place of, appeals to welfare or basic rights and freedoms. Fairness *itself* is assumed to have far-reaching practical implications—for domestic trade and social policy; for the multilateral system of trade (the World Trade Organization [WTO]); for standards in labor, the environment, competition, and intellectual property; for the terms of developing country integration; for monetary and financial arrangements; for the management of financial crises; and, ultimately, for the extent of poverty and inequality within and among nations.

And yet, slogans aside, we lack a good understanding of what fairness would be in a global economy. Plausible examples of *un*fairness are easy enough to find in the morning news: lavish rich-country farm subsidies impoverish millions of poor farmers in the developing world; low-skilled workers in advanced countries are displaced by more cheaply produced foreign goods and left to fend for themselves; a government must deeply cut services to its citizens because foreign investors demand budgetary reassurance when a financial crisis has spread from the other side of the world. But such examples do not by themselves explain what our implicit fairness assumptions are, what those assumptions more generally require, and why they even apply in a global economy in the first place. While the examples resonate in our inchoate sense that something is very wrong, the question is then what, more exactly, is wrong and why, from a fairness point of view. It is precisely here that answers may elude our grasp. When pressed to voice our concerns, the temptation is to fall back on other ideas—of welfare, poverty, basic freedoms, or human rights—in a way that leaves the status of fairness unclear.

Economic, legal, and political theory has provided at least the beginning of wisdom about many fairness concerns. Yet no purely descriptive claims, about economics, law, or political trends, will settle a *moral* question about what fairness is, what it requires, and what *ought* to be done in its name. Such questions are for political philosophy, and indeed only political philosophy has the resources to frame the moral or normative relevance of empirical findings in a disciplined, principled way. John Rawls's landmark *A Theory of Justice* laid the foundations for decades of study of fairness in domestic society,[1] and global justice is now high on political philosophy's agenda. Yet the idea of fairness in a global economy remains poorly understood. Political philosophy has only begun to address the idea as a topic of interest for its own sake.[2]

In particular, political philosophy has only begun to "reach down" far enough to firmly grasp the hands of economists, lawyers, and political theorists who are "reaching up." This book takes up fairness in the global economy in its own right as a work of political philosophy. Yet we view moral justification through a constructivist methodological lens that hopes for synthesis with the work of social scientists. If social scientists can ask political philosophy for normative foundations, we in turn ask for help, not only in determining matters of fact, but in characterizing the social and economic realities that ground our conception of fair practice.

Our main goal is to forge a new path. We criticize rival views and address objections to our proposals, but mainly for purposes of developing our constructivist approach. Many potential objections and further possibilities are thus left for another day. The reader is invited to help elaborate how the approach might go on issues or territory which we fail to explore.

The book has an overarching progression—from social foundations, to basic principles, to substantive applications. Because each chapter offers a largely self-contained argument, the chapters may be read in an order suited the reader's own interest and expertise (perhaps starting with the overview in Chapter 1).

This book was written with the generous support of the American Council of Learned Society's Burkhardt Fellowship at the Center for Advanced Study in the Behavioral Sciences, Stanford University. I am grateful to Iris Litt, Robert Scott, Linda Jack, Cynthia Pilch, and the entire Center staff for their assistance during the 2009–2010 academic year, when much of the book was drafted.

My greatest debt is to T. M. Scanlon, for both his intellectual influence and his warm and gracious mentorship. Less obvious

---

1. Rawls, 1971.
2. Discussions by philosophers of trade or trade-related issues include James 2005b, 2006, forthcoming; Moellendorf, 2005, 2009; Sreenivasan, 2005; Risse, 2007, 2008, 2012; Miller, 2007, manuscript; Barry and Reddy, 2008; Brock, 2009; Ronzoni, 2009; Miller, 2010; de Bres, 2011; Hassoun, 2012. Homage must also be paid to seminal but more broadly concerned works such as Beitz, 1979, and Pogge, 1989, 2002.

from the text of the book is the influence of Christine Korsgaard, who has deeply shaped my understanding of philosophy, constructivism, and Rawls. (With Scanlon, Korsgaard supervised my Harvard dissertation, completed in 2001, on the topic of constructivism and objectivity.) For extended discussion of the material of this book, including extensive comments on numerous chapter drafts, as well as for friendship and support, I am especially grateful to Marshall Cohen, A. J. Julius, and Leif Wenar. I also thank Nicole Hassoun, Michael Howard, and Doug Woodward for our ongoing exchanges.

I thank many others for helpful comments or relevant discussions, including Arash Abizadeh, Ben Alaire, Kenneth Arrow, Kyle Bagwell, Christian Barry, Charles Beitz, Christina Bicchieri, Clara Brandi, William Bristow, Gillian Brock, Bruce Brower, Justin Bruner, Christine Chwaszcza, Carl Cranor, G. A. Cohen, Joshua Cohen, Stephen Darwall, Peter de Marneffe, Liran Einav, Frank Garcia, Varun Gauri, Gerald Gaus, David Gauthier, Margaret Gilbert, Judith Goldstein, Claire Finkelstein, Samuel Freeman, Barbara Fried, Nathan Fulton, Casey Hall, Pamela Hieronymi, Louis-Philippe Hodgson, Nicholas Jolley, Ruth Kelly, Louise Kleszyk, Niko Kolodny, Rahul Kumar, Christopher Kutz, C. L. Lim, Sharon Lloyd, John Linarelli, Ben McKean, Violet McKeon, Allegra McLeod, Darrell Moellendorf, Sophia Moreau, Stephen Munzer, Thomas Nagel, Chris Naticchia, James Nickel, Kieran Oberman, Daniel Pilchman, Thomas Pogge, Douglas Portmore, Maura Priest, Priya Ranjan, Arthur Ripstein, Mathias Risse, Faviola Rivera, Miriam Ronzoni, Immanuel Saez, Andrea Sangiovanni, Debra Satz, Tamar Schapiro, Daniel Speak, Wayne Sumner, Margaret Summers, Kok-Chor Tan, David Tannenbaum, Sergio Tenenbaum, Fernando Teson, Chantal Thomas, Philippe Van Parijs, Rob Reich, Diego Von Vacano, R. J. Wallace, Ernest Weinrib, Stephen White, Nicholas White, and Andrew Williams.

I am also grateful to audiences at Arizona State University Law School; the American Philosophical Association, Pacific Division; the American Society of International Law, Washington D.C.; the Center for Advanced Studies in the Behavioral Sciences, Stanford University; Florida State University; the National Autonomous University of Mexico; the Southern California Law and Philosophy Group; Tulane University and the Murphy Institute; UC Berkeley; the University of Cape Town; the University of Pennsylvania; the University of Southern California; the University of

Toronto; the University of Utah; the University of Washington; San Diego State University; Sheffield University; Stanford University (the political theory/global justice workshop and Ethics at Noon); Westmont College; and the 23rd World Congress of Philosophy of Law and Social Philosophy, Krakow.

I thank Robin Risque for copyediting help at a crucial stage of the project. Finally, for her patience and support, I thank Secil Artan.

FAIRNESS IN PRACTICE

CHAPTER ONE

Main Ideas

A philosophical account of fairness in the global economy should answer three central questions. First, the question of *applicability*: In what sense, if at all, does fairness apply in the global economy? Second, the question of *significance*: What might fairness require, in principle and in practice, and how significant is it for economic and social institutions? Third, the question of *justification*: How, from a moral point of view, is an appropriate conception of fairness to be justified?

We will offer the following answers. As for applicability, fairness in the global economy is fairness in a social practice. The global economy is constituted, in a fundamental sense, by an international social practice in which societies mutually rely on common markets. This shared practice raises a general issue of "structural equity," that is, equity in how different countries and their respective classes are treated within the common market reliance relationship.

As for potential significance, structural equity places significant egalitarian demands upon nonmarket institutions. In a world of "free trade," nonmarket institutions must, in fairness, regulate how the global economy distributes its benefits and burdens across societies and their respective social classes. Fairness requires strong social insurance schemes, international capital controls, policy flexibility for developing countries, development assistance, and more. The cost of such measures is to be shared by all trading countries, as the "fair price" of free trade.

As for justification, the demands of structural equity arise as emergent responsibilities, in virtue of the global economy's organizing social practice, quite apart from concerns with the general welfare, efficiency, basic freedoms, human rights, or other forms of justice. Fairness demands arise, in their own right, as though from a "social compact" for an economy of global size, akin to a promise made but as yet unfulfilled. They arise, that is to say, by way of a practice-based, constructive method of justification, which is inspired by the social contract tradition of Hobbes, Locke, Rousseau, Kant, and (in our own day) Rawls and Scanlon.

1. Skepticism About Fairness

Our argument begins from skepticism about fairness in international trade, especially as it arises in serious economic and political theory. In economic theory, the standard case for free trade can initially seem to leave little place for claims to fairness; talk of "fair trade" can seem little more th an inefficient and unwise "protectionism." In political theory, "realists" since Hobbes urge that fairness has no place in anarchic international relations. Given the absence of an assurance-providing political authority at the global level, policy is and ought to be set by the "national interest" rather than fair play.

We will suggest that such arguments become far less forceful once we view international trade in its proper light, as an established, distributively consequential social practice. Chapter 2 shows that this conception is fully consistent with economic theory, and, indeed, implicit in much of classical and recent trade theory itself. Chapter 3 argues that the stable continuance of the trading system, for over half a century now, itself shows that a centralized political authority is not required for governments to have the assurances needed for obligations of fairness to apply. We thus build the foundations of our account of fairness, not in spite of skepticism, but from its basic concerns.

Skepticism also can come in various more practical forms. When a country's currency collapses, causing mass unemployment and protests in the streets, or when trade flows steadily rout a country's familiar industrial or agricultural base, it can seem odd, even comical, to ask whether this is fair. Moreover, even if fairness does in some sense apply, it is routinely abused, as a thin veil for mere commercial self-interest or national egoism. Fair is foul, and foul is fair, as the witches of international relations might say. Fairness discourse may therefore seem untrustworthy and better replaced by a moral vocabulary better suited to guide public deliberation and choice. Finally, even if we seek to render a fairness judgment, we face the global economy's daunting complexity. Even experts struggle to fully understand the numerous, interdependent, ever-changing, and profoundly influential social and economic forces at work. Furthermore, the complexity is also moral: our age of globalization cannot be readily judged as good or bad without a gross oversimplification of the moral issues in play. The global economy bears on a wide variety of moral values in conflicting ways, and there is no obviously correct moral perspective by which to balance the different values at stake. There is no obviously correct way to say what is "fair."

We will answer these concerns chiefly by developing a positive conception of fairness that begins from highly plausible basic ideas. After all, in the deepest sense, the bare applicability of fairness is not especially controversial. Everyone will at least agree that the global economy is unfair in the sense that "life is unfair," in the cosmic sense potentially beyond all human control. When a country's currency collapses, perhaps because a banking crisis has spread from the other side of the world, people usually do not deserve the hardships that ensue. Most will also accept that the global economy is in one way or another *unfairly set up*, that is, unfairly organized by institutions and practices that human beings have created and continue to sustain and shape over time. Far-reaching commerce occurs only because of the mundane, regularized interaction enabled by organizing nonmarket institutions—the state system, international economic law and practice, domestic capitalist institutions, and innumerable decisions to free trade, or at least make trade freer than before. And even zealous advocates of laissez-faire will often accept "formal" or "procedural" fairness requirements for how such institutions are designed: the rule of law, stable property rights, conditions of "fair competition," and perhaps even of "fair opportunity."

Others will point out that the systems of trade, money, and finance are extraordinarily consequential for how almost every country and their citizens fare over time. They will ask whether we can fairly leave the distributional chips where they fall, with little or no concern for relative inequality, so long as formal ideals of "same treatment" or "equal opportunity" are realized. Is not fairness also "substantively" concerned with how the institutions of the global economy distribute wealth around the world? There will be real disagreement at this point, to be sure. But the disagreement is substantive; it assumes that fairness is applicable and potentially of great significance for the way institutions are arranged, depending on what appropriate fairness principles require. The central question is what those principles are.

We will defend the view that distributional equity is of significant practical moment, but in a way that takes skepticism seriously. Our guiding aim is to make a lot from a little: to show how substantial principles follow from what Rawls calls "widely accepted but weak premises"—in this case, a set of independently modest claims about the social structure of the global economy and what fair practice requires. If we can first agree on the nature of our basic social relation, and on the general kind of fairness issues it poses, the idea goes, we can then get traction—and perhaps even agreement—in more specific areas of dispute. If all goes well, we reach significant principles from modest normative grounds. We "construct" fairness for the global economy, by a constructivist methodology (to be explained later in this chapter), from more basic social and moral materials. The claim of this book is that this leads to significantly egalitarian results.

2. Fairness in International Political Morality

If we look to the philosophical literature on global justice for guidance, we are offered an unattractive choice between nationalistic or parochial egalitarian views and fully "cosmopolitan" viewpoints. The choice is unattractive because both approaches seem at best incomplete. Neither perspicuously addresses a distinctive set of fairness arguments often made about the structure of the global economy. Our aim is to offer a fresh approach that better captures this politically important class of fairness concerns.

The arguments in question share the following general features: (1) they concern socioeconomic outcomes; (2) they are essentially comparative, or concerned with the relative gains or losses, advantages or disadvantages, to different parties (countries or their respective social classes); (3) they take the general framework of domestic and international political relationships and responsibilities more or less for granted; and (4) they are presented as non-utopian, practical demands, in light of accessible policy or structural change, perhaps despite obvious lack of moral agreement and political will. Let us call this class of arguments, so defined, *relative socioeconomic fairness in international political morality*.

Examples include the following familiar (often implicit) appeals to what is fair. (Attend for now not to their merits but their common form.)

Farm subsidies. Advanced countries lavishly subsidize agribusiness and thereby impoverish millions of developing-country farmers who would otherwise profit from their ability to more cheaply produce cotton, sugar, or corn. Although some rich country farmers will lose under freer commodities trade, rich countries can well afford to compensate them for this. It is therefore only fair to abolish the subsidies.[1]

Fair development flexibility. Current World Trade Organization (WTO) law forbids industrial policies (e.g., export subsidies and infant industry protection) that have been instrumental for industrial "self-discovery" in most development success stories. Fairness requires relaxing (or not enforcing) economic law, as required for developing countries to trade to their "dynamic" (rather than "static") comparative advantage (e.g., by promoting high-revenue industry, such as high-tech, rather than low-revenue production, such as raw materials and agriculture).[2]

Unfair labor competition. Advanced countries should protect their low-skilled workers against "unfair competition" from cheap labor in developing countries. They can fairly impose tariffs on developing-country goods, or insist that developing countries adopt labor standards that "level the playing field."[3]

Unfair insurance burden. Most advanced societies in the postwar era have established social insurance schemes that partially compensate and retrain workers displaced by trade. Yet social safety nets have become difficult to pay for in a world of high capital mobility. Domestic taxation may trigger capital flight, and international capital markets may (e.g., in a crisis) demand fiscal austerity, whatever the social cost. Although high-income citizens handsomely profit from globalization, low-skilled workers see scant wage and income gains, even as many in effect bear the tax burden of their own social protection. Fairness therefore requires more progressive domestic taxation and aggressive

---

1. E.g., Wolf, 2004, p. 216.
2. E.g., Rodrik, 2007, ch. 4; Stiglitz and Charlton, 2006, pp. 29–30; Mangabeira, 2007.
3. E.g., Sabina Dewan, 2010, of the Center for American Progress, defends Obama administration actions against Colombia under CAFTA in part by arguing that "Enforcement ensures that American workers can compete on a level playing field." For general discussion, see Leary, 1996; Bhala, 1990; Howse and Trebilcock, 1996. For our reply to this general kind of argument, see Chapters 5.9, 9.3–9.5, and 10.6.

8   FAIRNESS IN PRACTICE

international tax cooperation (an international "Tobin tax," regulation of offshore banking, the end of bank secrecy, etc.)[4]

Unfair crisis risk. The recent (post-1970) style of international capitalism—liberalized controls on capital movements and high capital flows across borders—has led to hundreds of enormously destructive financial crises. Because developing countries do not see substantial growth gains from capital liberalization, it is fair for them to adopt capital controls (e.g., inflow taxes) that protect them against excessive debt and foreign financial contagion—even controls that dramatically worsen the value of trade for the rest of the world.[5]

On a natural reading, each of these arguments is in its own way about relative socioeconomic fairness in international political morality. Each answers "yes" to the general question, Does the global economy, roughly as now constituted in international relations, generate practically significant demands of socioeconomic fairness in its own right, independent of humanitarian concerns, human rights, or other forms of justice? The question might be refined as follows. To what extent, we may ask, are moral or fairness issues "internal" to the global economy, roughly as it is now organized and understood? Many "external" evaluative concerns do not essentially depend on the existence of a global economy. Humanitarian values and basic human rights and freedoms, for example, would apply in much the same way even if no global economy existed. But suppose that we temporarily set these issues aside, assuming, by stipulation, that there are no such external values. We may then ask, Would any basis for concern about fairness remain? Does the global economy, organized roughly as we now know it, generate responsibilities of fairness in and of itself, given its consequences for different countries and their respective classes?

This question will not seem open if we mistakenly assume that a global economy is a fixed fact of international life. Economists often warn that "globalization" is fragile, and that trade and capital

---

4. Rodrik, 1997, ch. 4, suggests this point in light of an observed correlation between increasing "external risk" and increasing public support for welfare institutions in the postwar era.
5. See, e.g., Bhagwati, 2004, ch. 13, and Eichengreen, 2004a. Krugman, 2010, suggests that China has, however, crossed an important line.

flows reached comparable levels before the world wars and interwar years brought them to a halt. This view reflects a more general political reality: in a global economy parceled out among sovereign states, each government can in principle choose economic self-sufficiency over integration into a global marketplace. If every government did so this year, by imposing prohibitive border controls on goods, services, and capital flows, the global economy as we know it would be more or less shut down. Governments are not about to do this, of course: they continue to self-consciously allow regional or global markets to exist and profoundly shape domestic and international social life, and they will in all likelihood do so for the foreseeable future. The question, then, is what moral responsibilities of fairness we incur from this enormously consequential decision, and what those responsibilities mean for social and economic policy, law, and politics. Again, the arguments enumerated earlier each suggest what might be required in practical terms.

Neither of the two standard approaches mentioned—parochial egalitarianism and cosmopolitanism—provides an especially perspicacious characterization of this general fairness concern. While we cannot offer sustained critique of either view, we will mention several general reasons for wanting an alternative.

Parochial egalitarianism. According to parochial egalitarianisms (or related nationalist views), we should confine our concerns of relative socioeconomic distribution *within* domestic society. Across societies, we consider only a humanitarian or human rights minimum, international political fairness, or overall welfare, with little or no intrinsic concern for the fact that different societies often face quite different relative prospects in a common global economy.[6]

This approach emphasizes the distinctively *international* character of the global economy. It takes for granted that the global economy is still—and may always be—partitioned across distinct political authorities, within a system of states. But the approach arguably makes too much of political borders: when an objection to *relative* socioeconomic inequality *across* different societies is proposed, we cannot take it at face value. The objection will count

---

6. The approach comes in very different forms and degrees. The rough family includes Rawls, 1999; Blake, 2001; Nagel, 2005; Freeman, 2006, chs. 8–9; Sangiovanni, 2007; Miller, 2007; Miller, 2010; Risse, 2012.

as mistaken, or must have a different, noncomparative basis, for instance, in the fact that absolute poverty is at stake, or that the socioeconomic inequality is *instrumentally* bad (e.g., because of untoward consequences for international politics). Parochial egalitarianism thus leaves us either (1) with a reductive explanatory project—which may "explain away" as much as it explains—or (2) in need of a supplementary account that characterizes the fairness arguments on their own terms.[7]

This is so because it can seem insufficient to claim that inequality across borders is of little or no intrinsic significance. The persistence of relievable absolute poverty is indeed the great moral challenge of our time. But it is also a *fairness* consideration that bears, for example, on the terms of integration offered to developing countries. And as the various arguments we have outlined suggest, the fairness issue is not in every case simply about bringing people above a specified absolute poverty threshold and the sacrifice that can be expected of rich countries (or the rich in poor countries) for that specific end. Indeed, the fairness issues at stake are often of a kind that could equally arise in a future world without material destitution, say, in a world in which all countries have developed and everyone lives high above the current one dollar and two dollar per day poverty lines. In a future world of advanced societies, we could, for example, still aptly pose all of the following fairness questions: When, if ever, would it be fair for a certain government to impose tariffs on imported goods, despite the costs they impose on exporters and national income in a trading partner? When are export subsidies, preferential taxes, industrial policies, or other "behind the border" policies fair or unfair, given the way they substantially affect the flow and the value of trade for all countries involved? How should the cost of preventing and addressing financial crises be shared, within and across societies? Do investors have any reasonable complaint against aggressive global systemic risk management, even when it cuts deeply into their expected returns? Should countries that slight prudent banking supervision bear larger costs of crisis mitigation than countries that keep their financial markets tightly regulated? Is labor unfairly asked to pay for its own social insurance

---

7. Some approaches do offer means of further supplementation. I merely sketch what they share in common.

because investors threaten to fly and because free capital mobility fails to give labor real wage returns over time?

Parochial egalitarians can speak to some of these concerns, say, in terms of domestic distribution and unfair imposition of harms abroad. The pressure, however, will be to move beyond discrete transactions or policies and toward systemic interdependencies, and this will invite more encompassing concerns for relative gains or losses over time.[8] Nor can it plausibly be said that each sovereign government bears sole responsibility for its national decision to engage in free trade. The global economy is now largely unavoidable, and the lines of national responsibility cannot be sharply drawn. What any government does is already too dependent not only on the policies of other particular governments but also on economic law and the government policy practice (e.g., liberalization) prevailing in a given regulatory era.

Cosmopolitanism. The cosmopolitan approach, in contrast, readily admits issues of relative fairness across societies. Indeed, it asks us to look beyond international relations, to how each individual of the world fares by comparison with every other. Principles of relative distribution apply directly across all individuals.[9] The rough model for cosmopolitanism is domestic society: there we can consider how each citizen, from every social class, is treated under a common set of domestic social, political, legal, and economic institutions, which deeply shapes the relative (and absolute) life prospects of each of its subjects. Likewise, on the cosmopolitan approach, we might view the global economy as merely one part of a larger "global basic structure" that now determines the relative fates of everyone. (On some versions, no such common structure is required; any disparity in relevant prospects, among any two people, is unfair, however it comes about.)[10] Crucially, however, the *international* nature of the global economy—the fact that people and commerce are organized within a system of states—does not bear on what basic principles are justifiable but

---

8. For our full argument, see Chapter 3.
9. Beitz, 1979; Pogge, 1989, 2002; Goodin, 1988, 2010; Sen, 1992; Held, 1995; Barry, 1999; Buchanan, 2000; Moellendorf, 2002 2009; Tan, 2004; Nussbaum, 2006; Caney, 2006; Abizadeh, 2007; Brock, 2009. Cosmopolitan positions not intrinsically concerned with distribution include Singer 1972 and Nozick 1974.
10. E.g., Sen, 2009; Nussbaum, 2006; Caney, 2006.

only on how best to *implement* what justice independently requires. The state system itself needs to be justified according to what will best advance the right global distribution of wealth among all the individuals of the world.[11]

This, however, renders concerns of relative socioeconomic inequality across societies more puzzling than they should otherwise seem. At least on structurally sensitive versions, the argument turns on whether there is a "global basic structure" that strongly determines the life prospects of every person of the world in much the way domestic institutions do. This arguably overstates or at least oversimplifies the global economy's real importance.[12] It is quite true that recent globalization has supported unprecedented reduction in poverty in developing countries, and that colonialism and other evils of history partly explain persistent underdevelopment. Yet trade and capital flows—and even financial crises—are hardly the whole story of why countries grow rich or remain poor. Institutional quality arguably matters as much if not more.[13] Mere fair trade will hardly bring the millennium. A fair global economy will not replace, and may to a large extent depend on, justice in domestic society.

If those are controversial claims, the point is that concerns of relative socioeconomic fairness in international political morality do not depend on whether stronger claims about the global economy's scope and influence can ultimately be sustained. We can confine ourselves to the global economy's real influence, whatever it in fact is (where social scientists will tell us what that amounts to), and still pose relative fairness questions of enormous practical significance. It is not especially controversial to say that the global economy is of great and growing significance for social life, for good and for ill, even as that significance is manifested primarily through international channels. To remind ourselves of this, we need only observe that domestic fiscal prospects substantially limit what any society can sustainably make of itself, in terms of

---

11. Some cosmopolitans, such as Tan, 2004, and Brock, 2009, allow appeals to national values and partiality.
12. For critical discussion of appeals to a "global basic structure" in light of relevant empirical debates, see Risse, 2005.
13. The vast relevant empirical literature includes Rodriguez and Rodrik, 2001, Sachs, 2003, and Rodrik et al., 2004. Institutional quality is significantly influenced by the structure of the global economy, but arguably not wholly or even largely determined by it.

short- and medium-term public services as well as longer-term prospects for progressive reform, and that almost every country's fiscal plight is now substantially tied to the flow of trade and capital as it is shaped by the trade, currency, and fiscal policies of governments in other parts of the world.

A deeper limitation of cosmopolitan approaches is that they obscure the distinctively international structure of the central class of fairness arguments of our concern. Those arguments take the basically international form of global-sized cooperation largely for granted, in a way that supports strong, non-utopian demands for how the organizing international relationship is institutionally expressed. But because a cosmopolitan approach justifies principles in a way that abstracts away from the international nature of the global economy, it is not then tracking central features of the social context from which fairness responsibilities seem to emerge. It is a basic social fact that the global economy is embedded within the state system; government decisions on trade and currency policy, and international arrangements (or the lack of arrangements) for the coordination of those national decisions, are not only the primary regulator of economic interdependence but a *constitutive* condition of its very existence.[14] By abstracting away from the embedding international form of the global economy, cosmopolitan approaches obscure the question of how a distinctive class of fairness responsibilities could emerge from that kind of social relationship. Thus the non-utopian character of many fairness demands. When people stand up and *demand* the abolition of impoverishing farm subsidies, or crisis-prone capital markets, or development-inhibiting WTO rules, as protesters now regularly do, they feel right in doing so in part because they aren't asking for the moon. They aren't simply invoking one part of a worthy ideal future toward which history might move, over generations, in a gradual revolution away from the state system. They are laying claim to what they or others are owed, in fairness, right away, given the global economy as we *already* know it in its basically international form.

None of this is to reject cosmopolitan views per se. Indeed, cosmopolitans can welcome an account of economic fairness in international political morality as part of the "morality of transition" to something better, as part of "non-ideal" rather than "ideal" theory.

---

14. Polanyi, 1971, and Ruggie, 1982. See also Chapter 2.1-2.2 and 2.5.

Although much of our project may indeed be cast in these terms, Chapter 4 resists this interpretation in light of "moral assurance problems" inspired by Hobbes and Rousseau. Problems of moral assurance, which arise from the human condition itself, mean that we cannot abstract away from our basically international system of global cooperation even as a matter of "ideal theory." This is true so long as we are concerned with our responsibilities of social justice as a matter of what we call "normative political philosophy." Our account of fairness in international political morality is as a fundamental, "ideal theory" conception within that centrally important moral domain. The status of cosmopolitan versions of "ideal theory," by contrast, is at best unclear. In that sense, a cosmopolitan approach is far from inevitable once we move away from parochial egalitarian views. Our conception of fairness in international political morality presents a distinctive "third way."

3. Proposals

Our distinctive approach begins from a general question of moral justifiability. When the stakes are as high as they are in global economic life, people are inclined to ask: Is my country, or my class, or, more specifically, am I, being given fair terms? Can we, or I, find our shared, international arrangements reasonably acceptable, given the costs I am being asked to bear? Can I embrace them, or should I take to the streets? Asked as a question of *fairness* rather than of mere self-interest, the answer is implicitly about how *others* fare by comparison. The question then becomes, Can each country, and each of their respective classes, feel they are being treated fairly by the rules, practices, and institutions that shape their relative prospects? How must the global economy be set up so that it distributes advantages and disadvantages in a way that is reasonably acceptable to all? Or in T. M. Scanlon's terms, the crucial issue is how prospects for different people compare in the light of regulative principles for global economic affairs that "no one can reasonably reject."[15]

That is the *start* of a fairness question, but it does not yet say how we are to evaluate any particular set of market relations. The issue

---

15. Scanlon, 1998. See Chapter 5.1–5.4 for discussion.

cannot be addressed, in the first instance, as a matter of interpersonal morality. Too much of the global economy is largely beyond the control of any particular person or state. Were we to limit ourselves to what each individual agent (whether a person or a state) could be reasonably expected to do, given his or her quite limited information and powers, much of the global economy would have to be regarded as the result of purely impersonal forces, as mere workings of fate.[16] We avoid this implication by taking a structural approach: we address the large-scale patterns of distribution chiefly at issue by evaluating the social institutions and practices that produce them.[17] The special concern of *social* justice, we may say, is not the conduct of individuals, at least not in the first instance, but rather the justifiability of collectively sustained social institutions and practices, in light of their large-scale distributive consequences. Even if no person, official, or state is in a position to unilaterally change social structures of any scale, we can still pose the question of what *collective* responsibilities arise among those who sustain and regulate larger social and institutional forms.[18]

But how then should we approach economic relations? While Rawls offers little guidance on the global economy (and indeed suggests a parochial egalitarianism), we can follow his focus on social structures: we assess market relations, as fair or unfair, in light of their embedding social relationships. Social justice is not justice in a state of nature, or justice in discrete market transactions, but justice in the shared, ongoing social relations that organize economic life. Accordingly, any assessment of economic relations must be sensitive to going practice. In general, that means setting aside the supposedly "natural" pro-capitalist property

---

16. Indeed, it is unclear why the state should be justified if Scanlon's contractualism is understood as a strictly interpersonal theory. While Hobbesian, Lockean, or Kantian arguments against the philosophical anarchist can be recast within Scanlon's framework, the theory itself offers no such account of the conditions of society and politics, let alone of global economic structure. Scanlon's "principle of established practices" is relevant (1998, p. 339) but does not specify which social practices are ultimately justifiable. The matter is left open.
17. Our model, in this respect, is Rawls's social contract theory, which takes existing basic social practices and institutions largely for granted (James, 2005a). It sees no need to somehow derive principles for practices and institutions from principles of personal or interpersonal conduct. Such principles are relevant, but a distinct concern.
18. See Chapter 3.5.

rights and liberties of Locke as well as the anti-capitalist property rights and liberties of Marx.[19] What rights and liberties we have are justified *for* the market relations in question, on the basis of a conception of fairness not grounded in independent rights and liberties. Moreover, on a Rawlsian approach, justification must be sensitive to differences in social forms; it should let each social thing be the thing it is and not another thing, to appropriate Butler's dictum.[20] Much as we cannot readily judge a modern capitalist market economy by generalizing from a small-scale relationship such as a firm, we can't readily generalize from a domestic economy to an economy of global size. Even an argument from analogy will offer an uncertain guide to a world parceled into distinct territorial states.[21] Or at least we will have to address the global economy anew in any case to decide whether or not the proposed analogy is valid.

The basic question, then, is *how* we might consider the global economy in its own right, in light of the kind of social relationship it is or involves. How should we address its distinctive and especially puzzling features? Or as the problem is sometimes expressed, how should we think about a world in which economics is global but politics is local, a world in which integration readily crosses borders but political authority does not?[22]

Our methodological answer is as follows. Tentatively setting the standard menu of options aside, we work out a conception of fairness for, and in part from, the social practice that organizes the global economy as we know it. We assume the basic circumstances of global social life more or less as we know them, subject to idealizations appropriate for matters of moral principle (we ignore rank selfishness,

---

19. Likewise as regards Lockean views such as Nozick, 1974, and Marxist views such as Cohen, 2002. Cohen, 1995, emphasizes that he and Nozick share a fundamental idea of property (of self-ownership) and differ simply over what it takes to own further worldly things.

20. Rawls's version of the dictum (1971, p. 29) is, "The correct regulative principle for anything depends on the nature of each thing."

21. See, e.g., Beitz, 1979, to which I am greatly indebted, even as I depart from Beitz's strong conclusion that Rawls's domestic principles apply globally. Our argument is consistent with the weaker version of Beitz's argument suggested in the Afterword to the 1999 edition.

22. For the general problem, see the "impossible trinity" of capital mobility, fixed exchange rates, and monetary autonomy, or the "open economy tri-lemma," in, e.g., Obstfeld and Taylor, 1998. See also the "political tri-lemma of the world economy" in Rodrik, 2007, ch. 7.

total lack of concern for justice, and so on). We then set the sociological stage by way of moralized "constructive interpretation" of the global economy's embedding social structure. We engage in moral reasoning about what fairness substantially requires, as a matter of principle, but we do so as framed by our best understanding of the identified practice's distinctive structure and organizing aims.

On the basis of this methodology, we will argue that the global economy is organized by a distinctive kind of international social practice, a social practice in which countries mutually rely on common markets. If we take seriously this practice's basic economic aim—the augmentation of national income—this leads to a distinctive normative position. The national income gains of trade are the fruit of international social cooperation, the joint product of the social practice of mutual market reliance. In that case, fairness bears on distribution both within and across societies, in contrast with parochial egalitarian views. Yet because principles govern the *national* income gains of *international* trade, they retain a fundamentally international basis and structure, in contrast with fully cosmopolitan conceptions. We thus capture in general terms the specific concerns of relative fairness in international political morality. We do that by showing that the global economy *itself* generates a distinctive set of emergent egalitarian responsibilities, quite independently of other moral or justice concerns which might equally apply in the global economy's absence.

Principles of equity. More specifically, we will argue that such emergent responsibilities can be characterized as three principles of equity. Each principle governs a specified set of socioeconomic outcomes typically created by relations of international trade and economic interdependence.

The first principle concerns the harms of trade, such as unemployment, wage suppression, income volatility that diminishes lifetime savings, and the costs of financial crises. According to

> *Collective Due Care*: trading nations are to protect people against the harms of trade (either by temporary trade barriers or "safeguards," or, under free trade, by direct compensation or social insurance schemes). Specifically, no person's life prospects are to be worse than they would have been had his or her society been a closed society.

The second and third principles concern the "gains of trade," roughly as understood in economic theory. Chiefly, these include national (average or aggregate) income gains from productivity-enhancing specialization in the division of labor, economies of scale, and the spread of technology and ideas. According to

> *International Relative Gains*: gains to each trading society, adjusted according to their respective national endowments (e.g., population size, resource base, level of development) are to be distributed equally, unless unequal gains flow (e.g., via special trade privileges) to poor countries.

And according to

> *Domestic Relative Gains*: gains to a given trading society are to be distributed equally among its affected members, unless special reasons justify inequality of gain as acceptable to each (as, e.g., when inequality in rewards incentivizes productive activity in a way that maximizes prospects for the worst off over time).

These principles are limited in important general ways. They apply only to the benefits and burdens that international economic integration *creates*, and so not to conditions that exist or would exist independently of the trade relationship. Nor do they admit of "cosmopolitan" comparisons of the relative gains of any two individuals of the world. Once no one is harmed by trade, relative gains are compared either among compatriots or among societies as wholes. Even so restricted, however, we will argue that these basic principles place significant demands upon nonmarket institutions, provided plausible empirical and policy assumptions. Such demands of fairness arise, moreover, quite apart from appeals to welfare, human rights, or freedoms, or more general requirements of justice. They arise simply in virtue of responsibilities that emerge from the distinctive kind of social relationship that the global economy in fact is.

For better or worse, then, our argument is hostage to empirical fortune. We have to take a position on what the global economy is in fact like, though not in ways that are entirely beyond the political philosopher's provenance. Social scientists often develop aspects of social life which they (implicitly) take to be of moral or normative relevance. Philosophers are well situated to explicitly examine and develop those assumptions in light of the assumed moral and normative concerns. Undaunted, then, we ground our argument in the following main interpretive/moral theses.

The nature of trade. The basic subject of fairness in the global economy is the existing *international social practice of market reliance*, the practice whereby countries rely, mutually, on common markets (in goods, services, or capital) for the sake of mutual economic gain. This general practice is to be distinguished from several other things often called or associated with "trade," including particular market transactions, transactional flows across borders, as well as from particular government policies that influence transactional flows (tariffs, quotas, safeguards, subsidies, etc.). A chief function of the larger market reliance practice is the regulation of government trade and trade-related policies, according to both formal trade law (e.g., WTO rules) and informal understandings of how the market/state balance is to be struck (e.g., the postwar "embedded liberalism compromise"). Such rules or understandings represent *substantial market reliance expectations*, the terms upon which governments and the societies they represent participate in the larger market reliance practice. The practice itself, and the basic subject of fairness, is the underlying social fact that countries do comply, more or less, with some system of market reliance expectations (concerning trade, finance, and money), in order to mutually benefit from the national income gains of trade.

The fairness issue. The basic and central fairness issue in the global economy is *equitable treatment in the structure of a social practice,* specifically, in the structure of the international practice of mutual market reliance. This concern—what we will call *structural equity*—is not with unequal outcomes per se, but with the way the international market reliance practice treats the different countries it affects, where "treatment" is assessed in light of how the practice distributes the advantages and disadvantages it creates among countries and their respective classes. The general test of distributive arrangements is whether each party affected could find associated regulative principles reasonably acceptable in the light of its consequences for them.

The structural equity issue is *basic* because it applies to the social practice without which the global economy as we know it would not exist. As we will explain in Chapter 5.9, the issue is also *central* because it organizes a wide range of appeals to fairness aired in world politics—"fair trade," "the level playing field," "fair play," and so on.

Fair Division. Our argument's central normative thought is that the gains of trade present a problem of fair division. The gains of trade over autarky, once adjusted for background endowments, are essentially the fruit of international social cooperation within the common market reliance practice. The default fair division is equality of gain, not because equality is fair as such, but because trading countries are (1) equal in moral status, (2) similarly interested in augmented national wealth, and yet (3) lack special entitlements to any particular level of gain. In that case, the default fair division is equality of (endowment-adjusted) gain. Equality of gain is required, unless special reasons can be given why gains should be distributed unequally.

Substantive argument. That presumption is not yet a set of principles that appropriately regulate the market reliance relationship, since special reasons for inequality of gain would still need to be accounted for. Our proposed three principles of structural equity follow from further considerations of when such considerations arise. Collective Due Care follows on the grounds that it is unfair for many to benefit while some are made substantially worse off, overall, for life in an open economy. The Domestic and International Relative Gain Principles follow from considerations of the national character of the gains of trade and of the acceptability of unequal gain given background conditions of poverty.

Practical conclusions. By way of both applying and explicating our proposed principles, we will pay special attention to several key policy recommendations. If none are especially novel, our distinctive thesis is that they are grounded in *emergent* fairness responsibilities, which arise quite independently of humanitarian, human rights, or other justice requirements.

> *Social insurance*: The removal of trade barriers ("free trade") can be fair, but only if each trading society maintains a robust social insurance scheme, which compensates people for the harm they suffer as a result. The cost of social insurance is the collective responsibility of all countries engaged in the common economic practice (as discharged, e.g., by an international social insurance organization, which provides assistance or low-interest loans) (Chapters 2.6 and 7.1–7.3).
>
> *Capital curbs*: Due Care requires measures to dramatically reduce the risks of financial crises, such as securities taxes that curb short-term capital flows (Chapter 8).
>
> *Regulation of long-term gain*: Domestic and International Relative Gains support the regulation of long-term inequalities in the endowment-adjusted national gains of trade, for example,

by appropriate corrections in industrial or competition policy, or, if necessary, direct compensatory payments (Chapter 6.4).

Intellectual property exemption: Fairness supports granting developing countries an unlimited grace period to comply with WTO intellectual property standards. Developing countries should, in fairness, be free to have any or no intellectual property system, as suits their development goals (Chapter 9).

Industrial policy exemption: Fairness supports an exemption from WTO industrial policy rules that forbid the policies of "self-discovery" needed to trade to "dynamic" (rather than "static") comparative advantage (e.g., export subsidies and infant industry protection) (Chapters 5.6 and 7.8).

Labor standards: Fairness requires international "linkage" measures that promote labor standards improvement in developing countries (e.g., through trade incentives rather than trade sanctions). It also requires governmental and transnational measures of firm accountability and influence through supply chains) (Chapter 10.4-10.5).

4. The Global Economy as We Know It

According to Rawls, "Conceptions of justice must be justified for the conditions of our life as we know it or not at all."[23] We will follow this thought (and defend it in Chapter 4) by seeking to justify a conception of fairness for the global economy as we know it, that is, for the global economy as it roughly is now and seems likely to be for the foreseeable future. It will matter how this problem space is understood, so we should state our main framing assumptions up front. We will assume at least three key general realities: politics is decentralized, economic integration is partial, while political and economic forces intermix. These are as follows.

Political decentralization. The global economy is embedded within a state system that lacks a centralized political authority. Authority is parceled over distinct territorial states, and economic relations across state borders are governed or regulated in various decentralized ways: in diplomatic relations, bilateral or multilateral talks, trend-setting state or coalition action, international organizations (e.g., the WTO, the International Monetary Fund

---

23. Rawls, 1971, p. 398.

[IMF], the World Bank, the International Labor Organization [ILO], the Organization for Economic Cooperation and Development [OECD], the Group of 20 [G20]),[24] formal and informal governance networks,[25] transnational firms and associations,[26] and accountability from global civil society.[27] While state authority is dominant, established international institutions and networks constitute a relatively autonomous sphere of global administrative law.[28] As we explain in Chapter 4, we take the state system for granted for lack of a feasible, reasonably well-assured alternative for the management of global affairs.

Partial economic integration. The "global economy" is not a well-integrated market akin to advanced-country economies, and, for all we now know, it may never become one. Despite increasingly efficient communications and transportation, state borders dramatically curb trade and factor flows. Even among quite similar and relatively open industrialized economies such as Canada and the United States, there is still more goods and services trade between any two provinces of Canada than between those provinces and equidistant states within the United States.[29] Such "border effects" are even more influential across dissimilar countries and are likely to persist, especially with respect to labor. While "liquid capital" is highly mobile across borders, labor is not, and will never be, mobile to a remotely comparable degree.[30] Even where the free movement of people is legally allowed, as in the

---

24. For discussion of international organizations, see Keohane and Nye, 2002.
25. Slaughter, 2004.
26. On the government-like functions of many firms and associations, see Cutler, 2002, and Sassen, 1996, 2002.
27. Wapner, 1995; Keck and Sikkink, 1998; Ruggie, 2003, 2004.
28. Kingsbury et al., 2005; Cohen and Sabel, 2005.
29. McCallum, 1995.
30. Indeed, in his classic treatise on political economy, J. S. Mill, 1848 (reprinted 1987), explains that labor immobility is central to the gains of international trade. The gains of exchange between England and Portugal "could not happen between adjacent places" such as the north and south banks of the Thames river, for if producers suffered a significant market disadvantage as compared to competitors on the opposite side of the river, they would simply move to the other side. This is not the case, however, "between distant places, and especially between different countries," since "persons do not usually remove themselves or their capitals to a distant place without a very strong motive" (p. 575).

European Union, people overwhelmingly remain in their country of birth.[31]

Politico-economic structural interdependence: Political authority both shapes and is shaped by economic activity and relationships. Contrary to marxist-structuralism, the state system is not a mere "superstructure" of global economic relations.[32] State choices are "productive" of the global economy: trade and capital flows occur only to the extent that states choose to remove or withhold trade barriers—something they may or may not decide to do.[33] On the other hand, insofar as governments do substantially liberalize trade, especially in fast-moving private capital flows, they often have weak powers to regulate market outcomes. The need for inter-governmental policy coordination becomes especially acute but also difficult to establish or maintain in a world of decentralized politics.[34]

In addition to these three features, we also make a fourth, "ideational" assumption, about what is generally assumed. *Presumed legitimacy*: It is generally assumed that international trade is by and large legitimate, in the sense that governments are not morally required simply to shut it down. (This counts as "assumed" either because enough people in fact accept it, or because enough people believe that most others assume it, whether or not the attributed view is in fact widely held.) The global economy is thus seen as unlike activities and practices such as murder and slavery that are to be abolished outright, as well as distinct from the "black markets" that comprise major components of the global economy. Slave trading, sex trafficking, arms dealing, and the drug trade are simply to be curbed or minimized. But governments are *not* similarly required, absent further considerations, to impose prohibi-

---

31. Flanagan, 1993, p. 184. Also, many migrants return home. On the EU, see Pollard et al., 2008. Migration from developing to advanced countries is of course a different, perhaps special kind of case. Four in ten Mexicans report willingness to migrate to the United States if permitted to do so, according to Suro, 2005, p. 13. I take it, however, that even dramatically liberalized immigration would not radically change fundamental labor mobility patterns, at least not permanently. I thank Kieran Oberman for the above references.
32. Pace Marx (1859), 1968, and Wallerstein, 1979.
33. Waltz, 1970, 1979. But see also Keohane and Nye, 2001, and Keohane, 2002.
34. See Chapter 8.6.

tive controls on mundane trade in rice, corn, wheat, bananas, shrimp, oil, textiles, shoes, telephones, computer chips, automobiles, airplanes, consumer services, legal help, insurance policies, and much, much more.

We will also assume limitations imposed by the human condition.[35] These include conditions of moderate scarcity and limited altruism—David Hume's "circumstances of justice"—which make social and economic cooperation both possible and necessary.[36] For without a modicum of abundance and amenability to forgo immediate self-interest, cooperation becomes impossible—as in Thomas Hobbes's state of nature.[37] And yet without a modicum of scarcity and self-interest, the familiar rationales for economic cooperation lose their point. In a world of material abundance, there is no need to refine ever further the division of labor, in order to eke out still greater productive gains. And in a world without reliable self-interest, we cannot count on the butcher, the brewer, or the baker, in Adam Smith's famous examples, to inadvertently contribute to the public good by seeking private gain. If political philosophy has extensively explored the upshot of such conditions for domestic society, our basic, less well-understood concern is how they bear on the global economy, as marked by the political and economic circumstances outlined above.

If these are very abstract formulations, we should emphasize that they are fully consistent with enormous further complexity. For example, if advanced countries of North America and Western Europe have become similar, developing countries vary widely. Some surpass economic expectations (South Korea, Singapore, China, India, Vietnam). Others excel but have yet to include much of the rural or suburban population in the economic life of the cities (South Africa, Brazil). Still others have suffered dearly for efforts to "globalize" (Argentina, Mexico). Many of the least-developed countries (Ivory Coast, Burkina Faso, Gabon) face per-

---

35. Cohen, 2008, would deny that any resulting principles are fundamental. See Chapter 4 for discussion.
36. Hume (1896), 1975; Rawls, 1971.
37. Hobbes (1652), 1996, ch. XIII, says the state of nature is terrible in part because of lack of trade: the life of man is "solitary, poore, nasty, brutish, and short," not simply because of "continuall feare, and danger of violent death," but because "there is no place for industry; because the fruit thereof is uncertain . . . [nor] Navigation, nor use of the commodities that may be imported by Sea."

sistent social ills—civil war, dictatorial rule, geographical misfortune, and rampant disease—which will never be resolved by mere market-friendly reforms and trade.[38] Despite such important complexities, we refer to "developing countries" as a class (with "middle income" and "least-developed" countries as subgroups) under no pretense that specific moral or fairness issues come to the same thing in each case. General issues can be refined as specific cases require.

5. Constructive Method

The overall structure of our argument can be put this way: we move from this very general understanding of the global economy to the more substantial conception of fairness expressed in the three principles outlined. The bridge is our constructivist methodology. The constructive method bears some similarity to the "social constructivisms" of sociology, political theory, and international relations except that we treat it as a method of substantive moral justification. The method is part of the special moral domain of "what we owe to each other," in Scanlon's sense, but supplemented with a Rawlsian approach that takes independently identified social structure as a point of departure.[39]

On this approach, we settle the question of structural equity in light of the nature of the social practice of our concern. It would therefore be a mistake, for instance, to *simply* ask what principles would be accepted for the global economy from behind a Rawlsian "veil of ignorance." On one version of this question, for example, we assume that people have an interest in both the benefits of life in an open society as well as protection against its insecurities. We then ask what form of international trade self-interested, uncertainty-averse people would agree to live under, in light of these interests, not knowing their actual social positions—not knowing, that is, whether they are low-skilled or high-skilled workers, whether they are born into a higher or a lower class, or whether their country of origin is rich or poor. Once the veil of

---

38. On several "poverty traps," see Collier, 2007.
39. On such practice-dependence, see James, 2005a; Sangiovani, 2008; Meckled-Garcia, 2008; Beitz, 2009; Ronzoni, 2009; Valentini, 2011.

ignorance is so constructed, one could argue that the parties would insist on our three principles, specified earlier. Yet on the present approach, this argument is premature; it assumes too much that is properly controversial about how the veil of ignorance thought experiment is best run. Why not pose the question in a different way, with different interests or levels of ignorance? Why not construe the veil of ignorance a la John Harsanyi, in which case rational optimizers with an equal probability of being anyone choose not our principles but the principle of average utility?[40] Why assume an international system? Why not favor a "global original position," in which each individual of the world is represented and the basic form of global association is left open?

According to Rawlsian methodology, we answer these questions according to an independent characterization of the trade context's organizing social structure and a specified set of relevant interests and claims.[41] The argument against alternative constructions, in other words, is only as good as the positive argument for the grounding, independent characterization of the social context in which the fairness issues in question arise.[42] Ultimately, then, we justify principles for, and in the light of, an independently identified social practice, on the basis of (1) morally informed "constructive interpretation" of the organization and aims of the social practice in question, (2) explication of the morally relevant interests at stake, and (3) reasoning about what organization is reasonably acceptable to each person affected, as far as those relevant interests are concerned.

40. Harsanyi, 1975.
41. For this practice-sensitive account of Rawls's original position, see James, 2005a.
42. The answer to Harsanyi is that the fairness situation in trade is not appropriately framed as a voluntary gamble by rationally self-interested optimizers; the appropriate framing, rather, is acceptable risk under uncertainty (without known probabilities), within a not fully voluntary, international practice of market reliance and in the light of each person's basic morally significant interest in both the benefits of the global economy and protection against its vicissitudes. The answer to the "cosmopolitan" framing is that while a "global original position" would be appropriate if the global order were akin to a single domestic society, fairness in the global economy as we know it is best understood in international terms, given the realities of decentralized governance and partial economic integration.

Because the approach has *both* social and moral elements, it offers a "middle way" between the following two methodologies of justification:

> *Pure moralism*: Principles are justified by *purely moral argument*, in the abstract, for abstractly specified circumstances. Although abstract principles must be *applied* to an activity or practice by interpretive judgments (that any relevant applicability conditions are met), this is not required for their very justifiability. They are fully justified, as bona fide principles, even in the abstract.[43]
>
> *Pure interpretivism*: Principles are justified *by purely interpretive argument* as "constitutive" of, or otherwise assumed within, an independently identified practice; without the putative principles, the practice would not be the kind of practice it is.[44]

In contrast with pure interpretivism, the constructive method assumes that moral principles cannot be justified by mere social interpretation. Morality is not a function of what people happen to implicitly assume or explicitly accept; what principles are justifiable is ultimately settled only by substantive moral reasoning. But in contrast to pure moralism, principles cannot be justified wholly in the abstract. They have to be justified specifically for, and from, an *independent conception of the practice* in which the principles are to have a regulative, governing role.[45]

To arrive at an "independent conception" of a practice, we proceed by way of three main steps.[46] (The order is irrelevant within

---

43. Cohen, 2008, defends an especially clear version of this kind. Which other views qualify will depend on how the necessary degree of "abstractness" is specified. According to Ripstein, 2009, abstract principles must have some determinate institutional realization or other. Even so, I believe he would say that abstract principles are fully fledged. They lack "circumstances" that shape their abstract content, as in Hobbes, Rousseau, Hume, or Rawls.
44. Examples of pure interpretivist approaches include Fuller, 1964, Walzer, 1983, Koskenniemi, 1989, Wendt, 1992, and Weinrib, 1995.
45. A moralized interpretivist could reject our focus on regulation. We take this to flow from our assumed contractualist moral theory, which is essentially concerned with self-governance and how it bears on the relation each bears to each other (James 2011).
46. See the three stages of constructive interpretation in Dworkin, 1986, pp. 65–66. We do not, however, assume his "protestant" view that shared understandings are relevant only as initial data. For discussion, see Postema, 1987.

a holistic "reflective equilibrium" methodology, as long as each step can be fully justified in its appropriate way.)

> *Identification.* Identify a social practice in relatively uncontroversial, sociological terms, much in the way legal interpretation points to given statutes, or literary interpretation points to a certain text, as its object of interpretation.
>
> *Moralized characterization.* Characterize the general purposes, aims, or nature of the practice as independently identified. The characterization can use moral concepts, and draw from and emphasize moral elements.[47] This must (at this stage) answer to canons of *interpretation* rather than of pure moral judgment (roughly, it could be accepted by an amoralist anthropologist). Moral considerations must be credibly regarded as (perhaps deep) presuppositions of moral concepts or conceptions that are explicitly recognized or implicitly assumed.
>
> *Moral assessment.* Engage in substantive moral reasoning about what structural organization is reasonably acceptable to each party affected, as framed by the underlying (perhaps moralized) conception of the practice and the interests that are morally relevant in the context in question.[48] We reach principles by comparing different potential objections to proposed principles for the regulation of the practice, grounded in these relevant interests.

To comment on each stage: the goal of the pre-interpretive, identification stage is to single out the object that different interpretations are each proposed interpretations *of*. We aren't then *simply* making a moral recommendation but also a claim about what is required of a practice independently there. A range of features can be cited as pre-interpretive "data" in order to both individuate the practice in question and pose the question of how it is to be understood. How much of the data must be explained, and in what ways, is a separate question of how the merits of rival interpretations compare.

---

47. In his theory of domestic justice, for example, Rawls, 1993, p. 109, n. 15, mentions H. L. A. Hart's "minimum content of natural law" from Hart, 1961, pp. 189–95, as well as the strong moral requirements for a legal system defended by Soper, 1984. See also Rawls, 1999, p. 66, n. 5.
48. We speak vaguely of "framing" because there is no bright line and indeed interplay between interpretive explication of deep moral presuppositions and independent moral judgment.

As for the canons of interpretation themselves, they assign no controlling significance to original intent, voiced majority opinion, the latest polls, official or informal pronouncements, or any particular shared understandings. Any of these may turn out to be inconsistent with the aim or structure of the practice as best understood. The best interpretation is the characterization that, in comparison to alternative interpretations, yields the most consistent, coherent, comprehensive, illuminating interpretation of its various elements as a whole.

In interpreting a practice, the aim is to consider whether or how a practice can, in some form, ultimately be justified. In some cases (e.g., "the practice of slavery") the practice will count as illegitimate and to be abolished, because it cannot take on any defensible form (as a system of property), even if deeply revised. In general, a wrongful action cannot be justified *simply* by making a practice of it. On the other hand, the regularization of conduct can in various ways change the nature or consequences of an act, presenting a fresh occasion of justification to be addressed on its own terms. In assessing a practice on its own terms, we seek to cast it as far as possible as both the kind of practice it generally is, and yet as having a morally legitimate purpose such that it might, if suitably organized, count as fair in light of the interests relevant in a context of the relevant kind.[49]

The final stage, of moral assessment, is to justify principles that tell us how existing versions of the practice would have to be reformed if they are to be justifiable. Here our reasoning is substantive: we consider what principles for the regulation of the practice no one could reasonably reject, in light of different potential objections raised on each affected party's behalf.[50] Yet moral principles remain practice-sensitive, in the dual sense that they are justified *for* a relevant social practice and in part *from* its implicit understandings. They are not "internal" to a practice in the

---

49. In Rawls's domestic theory, for example, the object of interpretation is the "basic structure" of "modern constitutional democracies." In his international theory, it is "international law and practice" concerning assistance and the use of coercion and force. In both cases, Rawls offers a further moralized interpretation of the relevant subject's nature. Modern constitutional democracies are a cooperative scheme for reciprocal advantage among free and equal citizens. International law and practice is a society of self-determining peoples. See James, 2005a, p. 300.

50 See Chapter 5.1–5.4.

strict sense that they are extracted directly from it, as according to pure interpretivism. Moral reasoning and judgment are essential. Yet neither are principles fully justified in the abstract and merely applied to a practice, as according to pure moralism. Any principles that do in fact apply would not have been applicable had the practice not existed or taken an essentially different form (which is not to say that no other principles would have applied, depending on the fresh social or interpersonal situation at hand).

In these terms, our main fair division argument may be put as follows. The argument is not an exercise in pure moral reasoning and judgment. It begins from an independent conception of the trade relation. As a matter of sociology, the global economy is socially embedded within both the state system and an international market reliance practice. As an "ideational" matter, the market reliance practice has what is presumed to be a morally legitimate aim—the mutual augmentation of national income—in contrast with presumed illegitimate "black markets." Furthermore, implicit in both economy theory and actual international practice is the idea that the market reliance practice is a form of international cooperation, for mutual national advantage, and so open to a fairness assessment according to how it distributes the gains and losses from trade over time.

By a further moralizing step—still within the bounds of constructive interpretation—we tentatively accept the practice's assumed goal (mutual national income augmentation) as legitimate, if still subject to the demands of fairness. In light of that assumption, and now by way of moral assessment, we then find appropriate the idea that participating countries, seen as moral equals, have similar claims to the fruit of international social cooperation. Absent special reasons that the gains of trade should be unequal, then, equal distribution of gains is the justificatory default. The three principles of structural equity then result from both interpretive clarification of the nature of the gains of trade and substantial reasons for inequality, as informed by substantive moral reasoning. This substantive reasoning compares rival principles for the trade context, in light of what is reasonably acceptable, and either absorbs their insights or finds them open to crucial objections.

The constructive method of course raises deeper questions about why social practices should have distinctive importance for political philosophy. Although we touch upon answers (especially in Chapter 4), our chief aim is not to defend the method but to use it, or rather to defend it by showing it to be fruitful. It sheds light upon an exceedingly important area of social life. It yields a significant and non-obvious normative position. And it does so by giving us traction in the rough terrain where principle and practice meet. Overall, it suggests how we might rise to political philosophy's most challenging task: the task of bringing principle to bear on major issues in practical life, without compromising either the key realities of practice or the highest intellectual standards for moral thought.

PART I

Social Foundations

CHAPTER TWO

Economic Skepticism

Economists and economics-minded observers are often skeptical about talk of "fairness" in trade. Sometimes the concern is simply of a practical nature, that talk of fairness is open to abuse or even pernicious—a mere pretext for "protectionism" and a threat to liberal order of trade. It is in this connection, for example, that eminent trade economist Jagdish Bhagwati complains that the idea of "fair trade" is a "Pandora's box" which has "grown out of hand."[1] We will return to such practical skepticism and suggest that it does not call fairness into question once it is properly understood. Our focus in this chapter will be a different kind of skepticism that is less readily disposed of and that potentially strikes to the heart of our proposed conception of fairness itself. Answering this skepticism will unearth the social foundations of fairness and set the stage for the rest of this book.

We are proposing that fairness in the global economy be seen as (1) equity in the structure of a kind of international *social practice*, where (2) equity is assessed in light of that practice's *distributional* consequences, within and across societies. But both of these claims can seem founded on bad economics, for reasons arising from nothing less than the standard case for free trade, as understood since Adam Smith.

This is for two main reasons. First, the economic argument for free trade is said to be *unilateral*: each country has sufficient reason to free trade of its own accord, regardless of what other counties do, whether or not a general practice of freeing trade is established. The standard reasoning is as follows. Trade augments national income, because imports free up resources for more productive uses. Exports mainly pay for imports. In that case, however, the gains of trade can be reaped by freeing trade regardless of whether other countries do likewise; imports are still beneficial even if other countries protect their markets. If in reality governments

---

1. Bhagwati, 1993, pp. 582–83. See also 1991, p. 14.

show reluctance to free trade, this only shows that trade law and practice can be a useful remedial measure: it helps governments do what national prudence dictates in any case. As Paul Krugman forcefully puts the point, in criticizing trade negotiations for their misguided preoccupation with "mutuality" and "reciprocity":

> Anyone who has tried to make sense of international trade negotiations eventually realizes . . . they are a game scored according to mercantilist rules, in which an increase in exports—no matter how expensive to produce in terms of other opportunities forgone—is a victory, and an increase in imports—no matter how many resources it releases for other uses—is a defeat.[2]

On the contrary, Krugman explains,

> If economists ruled the world, there would be no need for a World Trade Organization. . . . [G]lobal free trade would emerge spontaneously from the unrestricted pursuit of national interest.[3]

And as it is with formal law it may be with mere practice as well. Trade will flower, provided only sufficient national prudence, whether or not *mutuality* in informal practice is ever established.

Second, even if international trade is a social practice, it is often said that our basic reasons to free trade make no essential reference to distributional concerns. The rationale for free trade lies in considerations of productive efficiency and aggregate national income. Moreover, it is suggested, if societies are concerned with the domestic "losers" from trade, they can simply be compensated with some portion of the gains to national income. Distributional fairness therefore does not support reluctance about more or less complete trade liberalization. As Nobel Laureate economist John Hicks famously counsels, in a similar vein, "If measures for efficiency are to have a fair chance, it is extremely desirable that they should be freed from distributive complications as much as possible."[4]

---

2. Krugman, 1997a, pp. 113–14.
3. Ibid, p. 113.
4. Quoted in Hausman and McPherson, 1996, p. 95.

Upon closer examination, however, neither of these arguments undermines our proposed conception of trade as a shared, distributively consequential social practice. For one thing, however strenuously these points have been voiced by politically embattled economists, neither follows from serious economic theory as applied to real world trade. As all economists will agree, economic theory is strictly speaking the study of trade-offs. It implies no verdict about what we conclusively ought to do without some further judgments about what objectives we ought to pursue, which economic theory is not itself suited to justify. By itself, then, economic theory is neither skeptical nor supportive of fairness as a guide for policy. Economists have nevertheless weighed into public debate for over two hundred years with a more or less conclusive judgment in favor of free trade, often while voicing skepticism about whether considerations of fairness should have any role in that policy choice. But this, we will claim, reflects a *philosophical* position that is readily open to doubt. To the extent the standard argument for free trade can be plausibly made, its most defensible form is fully *consistent* with our proposed conception of fairness, and indeed *depends* on considerations of mutuality and distribution that are part and parcel of fairness issues of structural equity. In this way, we find grounds in favor of our basic approach from *within* standard free trade argument itself.

1. Trade as a Practice

A central claim of this book is that the global economy is constituted and organized by an *international market reliance practice*, a social practice, created and sustained by nations, wherein nations each mutually rely on common markets. This practice, we want to suggest, raises the global economy's central fairness question, the question of "structural equity": What form must the practice of market reliance take if it is to distribute its advantages and disadvantages in a way that is reasonably acceptable to each country and class it affects?

To elaborate, let us say that a *social practice* exists when the following (sufficient) conditions hold:

1. the behavior of two or more agents is coordinated over time (in contrast with an intrapersonal practice involving the same

agent at different times, for example, brushing one's teeth each day);
2. coordination is maintained by generally if not universally understood behavioral expectations (in contrast with purely accidental or unknown regularities in conduct);
3. expectations are governed, if only by decentralized means (unlike an angry mob which has gotten out of control); and
4. expectations are set or adjusted, despite potentially divergent interests, according to a shared organizing purpose or aim (in contrast with coordination by pure force, backed by no publicly available or coordinating rationale, or coordination that bears little or no rational relation to a goal to which lip service is paid).

Social practices, in this sense, can take very different forms. They may be informal and of small scale, as with a household division of labor; the use of common resources, in irrigation, fisheries, or forestry; or the procedures of a deliberative body in an association or firm. Or they may be formalized and large enough to include strangers, as with the system of institutions that make up the modern state system, or a practice of mutual aid on the open seas. Social practices may also vary in underlying "social ontology." A practice may reflect "shared agency," as when agents coordinate by way of their mutually referential commitments or intentions (e.g., each of several agents acts from a commitment or intention to *dance salsa together*).[5] Alternatively, in "ideational" cases, a group may organize around an aim that its members generally attribute to enough of its other members, whether or not any shared intentions or commitments can be attributed individually and severally to its members. Even if most dancers in a room would prefer to salsa "on two,"[6] for example, all may nevertheless dance "on one" because most assume (mistakenly) that most of the others intend or are committed to this. Similarly, a large group, such as a set of nations, may coordinate around a "shared purpose or aim" by forming and adjusting rationally related expectations

---

5. Quite different accounts of this are offered, e.g., by Gilbert, 1989, 2006; Searle, 1995; or Bratman, 1999, chs. 5–8.
6. This is a way of timing the first step of the basic salsa dance pattern according to the music.

of conduct, because enough of its members believe that enough other participants (perhaps implicitly) endorse that aim or purpose for the group as legitimate and worthwhile.[7]

What, then, of the global economy, as chiefly constituted by relations of international trade in goods, services, and capital? We might answer by ruling out several senses of "international trade" that cannot be said to organize the global economy as we know it, in the general sense specified in Chapter 1.4. Most obviously, the unilateral removal of trade barriers by a single country would not suffice, for the simple reason that other countries must open or have opened their borders as well. In at least that sense, trade depends on de facto coordination of government action; borders must be open at the same time. Nor will open borders and minimal exchanges qualify as "trade" in a sense that organizes the global economy as we know it. Trade flows must rise to the level at which the societies become substantially economically interdependent (even if only partially integrated); the pattern of exchanges must at least affect the division of labor and overall structure of production. Moreover, even substantial trade flows will not be sufficient, in themselves, if they cannot be said to have a recognizably legitimate social purpose. Although socially unproductive "black markets" are in fact a large part of global trade flows, they exist largely because governments are unable to close borders down. By contrast, international trade, in the relevant organizing sense, is generally assumed to have the presumptively legitimate social purpose of augmenting national wealth, by creating a shared, ever-refined division of labor, and ever-greater productive efficiency. The choice to maintain policies of open trade is, as we might put it, a kind of *market reliance*, in the sense that governments each choose, on behalf of their citizens, to rely on a common market as an organizing part of social life, by allowing routine and sustained cross-border exchange, for the sake of augmenting national wealth.

---

7. It may nevertheless be true that *stable* practices, which have a disposition to last, usually require *actual widespread endorsement* and not just the general assumption thereof. Many social practices founded on mistaken assumptions are prone to sudden reversal, as when a dictatorial regime is suddenly overthrown, or when equity markets crash in a "Minsky moment." Even here an ideational structure may last a long while (years go by without revolution or while the equity bubble grows).

In sum, then, we have "international trade," in the organizing sense of our concern, only when several different countries become relatively integrated, because their respective governments choose to rely on common markets, for the generally assumed purpose of mutual national economic gain. This plausibly satisfies our fourfold definition of a social practice.

As for condition (1), the multiple agents in question are countries as represented by their respective governments. Government trade policies are coordinated over time, in the sense that each government concurrently maintains policies needed for a common market to exist. These include forbearance in the use of "border measures" such as tariffs and quotas but also in "behind the border measures" such as subsidies, internal taxes, or preferential rules that undercut the effect of opened borders.

As for condition (2), such policy coordination is not a mere de facto behavioral regularity but an undertaking that is sustained on the basis of generally understood market reliance expectations. Beyond minimum expectations of the trade policies needed for a common market to exist, participation includes compliance with expectations regarding the form that market reliance takes. These are publicly specified by formal treaty rules (e.g., a rule forbidding quotas, binding tariffs, or limiting subsidies) or as emergent informal understandings about how each country is to strike the balance between market and state (e.g., the postwar "embedded liberalism compromise").

As for condition (3), market reliance expectations are set and adjusted in several decentralized ways: by formal multilateral negotiations within the WTO; informal multilateral negotiations (e.g., within the OECD or the G20); formal bi-lateral or regional negotiations (within the European Union [EU] or North American Free Trade Agreement [NAFTA]); and informal bi-lateral influence (though diplomatic or governance network suasion). In addition to such "official" forms of governance, there is the significant role of public pressure, including advocacy by nongovernmental organizations (NGOs) and special interest groups (e.g., aid or trade organizations, unions, multinational firms).

As for condition (4), market reliance expectations are so governed, despite potentially divergent interests in using trade policy for "beggar-thy-neighbor" gains (discussed later in the chapter), according to the shared organizing purpose specified in over two hundred years of international economic argument since Adam

Smith: the aim of augmenting national (average or aggregate) income. Governments presumably often choose to free trade for their own sakes, partly as a matter of national prudence, for the expected increase in national income. Even when this is not the reason that government officials behave as they do (some seek to advance special interests or their own careers), the goal of national income gain is part of the ideational structure of trade practice: it is generally assumed that governments usually endorse the goal of national income augmentation as a legitimate and worthwhile aim of expanding market relations.

That suffices to make trade a social practice in our fourfold sense. We also claim, as a further thesis of constructive interpretation, that the organizing aim of market reliance is *mutual* national income gain. Although formal trade negotiations do often take the form of a policy swap based in national egoism, as in "I'll cut such-and-such tariffs if you cut yours," the more general rationale for trade practice, in light of economic theory, is better put this way: "We both know that cutting such-and-such tariffs is win-win."

2. Is Trade an Exceptional Case?

We might put our conception of the trade relation in sociological terms: all markets are "embedded" within nonmarket institutions or social practices, and international trade is no exception. The global economy is embedded not only within the underlying state system but also within an international social practice of mutual market reliance.

To elaborate, let us say that a market of some scope and kind is *constitutively embedded* within some nonmarket institutions when the *very existence* of a market of that scope and kind depends upon the establishment and maintenance of those nonmarket institutions. The standard Arrow-Debreu model of a competitive market,[8] for example, presupposes a well-defined system of property and contract rights, as well as any necessary security, judicial, and political institutions. A market is *functionally embedded* within nonmarket institutions, by contrast, when the institutions

---

8. Arrow and Debreu, 1954.

are needed so that the market meets some functional standard, such as efficient allocation. The difference between constitutive and functional embedding emerges when the supposed nonmarket institutions are absent. A "market failure" (e.g., a monopoly, negative externality, or information asymmetry) that calls for functionally embedding institutions (anti-trust measures, externality taxes, or transparency laws) may amount to nothing more than a market *dysfunction*. When constitutively embedding institutions break down, however, we don't have a "market failure," an "inefficient market," or a market dysfunction but rather fail to have a market at all. When property rights disintegrate and there is no "yours" and "mine" to exchange, we have not a *market*, in the relevant standard sense, but rather bartered exchange, chaos, war, or in any case a different kind of social thing. True laissez-faire is, in this sense, pure fiction. There could be no such thing as a purely self-organizing, self-sustaining, self-correcting market system of individual choices and exchanges (in this standard sense) without some constitutively embedding institutions or other.[9]

Put in these terms, our thesis is that even perfectly free international trade is, and can only be, *constitutively* embedded within an international market reliance practice. But for a practice wherein countries each rely, mutually, on common markets, international commerce would not and could not go on in anything like the extensive way it does (residual "black markets" aside). Even complete "free trade" is but one *version* of market reliance—indeed, a version only somewhat more "free" than the relatively liberal market reliance practice that governments now sustain.[10]

Many economists will only partially grant this picture. Most will perhaps admit the constitutive role of the state system. If we are not considering distinct political authorities each deciding to free, or not to free, cross-border exchange, then we are not quite

---

9. On the role of the state in creating free markets, see Polanyi, 1971, and North, 1990, 2005. According to Irwin, 1996, ch. 10, Adam Smith and many other classical theorists took the social nature of markets largely for granted, although trade theory would only decisively and self-consciously break its association with pure laissez-faire in the 1940s and 1950s debate associated with Manoilescu's wage differential argument for protection (see "Wage differentials" later in the chapter).
10. On the diversity of versions of market/state mixes, see Rodrik, 2007, and Unger, 2007.

considering *international trade*, but something rather different. Otherwise, however, many economists otherwise seem to regard international markets as without need of constitutively embedding institutions. We have already suggested why economists see the case for free trade in unilateral terms (imports free resources to do more productive things, even if foreign governments protect their markets). The picture is further reinforced by neo-classical models of trade (e.g., the Heckster-Ohlin-Samuelson model) that show net national income gains without cooperative law or practice of any kind. Reality, it is suggested, would approximate the models if only countries could get the economics straight and pull the levers of power according to national prudence (being free from confusion, special interest pressures, faintness of heart, and so on).[11]

Here a first line of reply is to argue that, for our purposes at least, this picture makes little difference. So long as a trading system does already exist, it may be said, we *do* have a market reliance practice that can be assessed as having an equitable or inequitable structure—even if its origins lie in national imprudence. The case, one might argue, is much like discriminatory law enforcement: if one racial group is much more likely than others to be prosecuted under established laws against murder, with no actual group difference in murder rates, then the charge of structural inequity is appropriate. And that will be true even if such laws are rooted in the imprudence of people—that is, even if, in a world of perfect prudence, no one would commit murder given the risks of personal injury, reputation costs, harm to one's soul, and so on. So long as laws against murder do exist, discriminatory enforcement is an important kind of structural inequity, which a society would have decisive reasons to reform.

---

11. As Krugman, 1997a, pp. 113–14, puts the point: "Never mind that the 'concessions' trade negotiators are so proud of wresting from other nations are almost always actions these nations should have taken in their own interest anyway. . . . The economist who wants to influence policy, as opposed to merely jeering at its foolishness, must not forget that the economic theory underlying trade negotiations is nonsense—but he must also be willing to think as the negotiators think, accepting for the sake of argument their view of the world." A similar choice between the unilateral case for free trade and mere considerations of unilateral political economy is suggested in Krugman, 1993, and Irwin, 2002, pp. 166–68.

Likewise, even if the WTO system is born of national imprudence, this does not preclude structural equity assessment of how it distributes any advantages and disadvantages that it in fact creates. Structural inequities may even be of the first moral importance.

This is, however, a pyrrhic victory. Although structural equity concerns would not be *wholly* out of place, their scope would remain sharply limited. So long as the standard economic picture remains unchallenged, international economic cooperation might help nations help themselves, but it would otherwise have a limited role in explaining the outcomes that actually ensue from trade. The major economic consequences of trade (for unemployment, or national income) are not then attributable to international cooperation per se. They are less the result of an international joint enterprise than something akin to climate management: each government adapts to its local weather, for good or for ill, but the goods or bads received do not ultimately reflect its participation in a common practice with essentially social fruit.

We therefore mount a stronger line of reply: a mutual market reliance practice is an essential enabling condition for most any trade relationship that could qualify as the centerpiece of the global economy as we know it. The practice is essential, not as a necessary remedy for national imprudence, but because of problems of uncertainty and risk that arise among distinct agents in virtue of the human condition. In that deep and practically relevant sense, economic reality cannot approximate neo-classical models in the absence of a constitutively embedding market reliance practice. The gains of trade, in the most basic sense, are neither pure self-help nor akin to local climate management. They are by their very nature socially created through international cooperation, and thus within the proper ambit of international structural equity.

To see why this is so, observe the grain of truth in the standard picture. According to economic models, free trade is to each country's unilateral advantage, whatever other countries do, when (1) governments care only about maximizing national income, and so are indifferent to domestic distribution (at least as far as trade policy is concerned), and (2) no country is able to impose an externality upon the others, for example, by altering the "terms of trade" (i.e., the buying power of exports for imports). We may happily grant that such circumstances arise in certain special situations (e.g., a "small" country integrating into a larger economy, with an ample tax base and solid compensation schemes). But the central question is whether the model is representative of the global economy as we know it. And, in fact, it isn't especially representative, for general and fundamental reasons.

For one, almost every country, always and everywhere, cares about domestic distribution (if only because of special interest pressure, but often for fairness reasons as well). And this is as it should be. As we will see, the standard free trade argument *depends* on sensitivity to domestic distribution (e.g., on whether "losers" will in fact be compensated).

Moreover, "mutuality" and "reciprocity" in trade are, in a very basic sense, unavoidable in any trade relationship. We see this in important recent work in the political economy of trade, according to which terms-of-trade (or other) externalities are themselves substantial enough to justify "mutuality" or "reciprocity" in trade agreements.[12] Indeed, much of the existing multilateral system can be plausibly explained in game-theoretic terms, as a way of escaping what Bagwell and Staiger call a "terms-of-trade prisoner's dilemma."[13]

Such work offers only a partial defense of "mutuality," however. If nothing else is said, the standard picture outlined here may simply take a more qualified form: even if *formal* agreements, such as the WTO, can be required to optimize trade gains, *informal practice* is still not in any fundamental sense required. We will see, however, that recent game-theoretic accounts do not fully develop their own fundamental insight, which is not essentially about formal arrangements. It is common practice, whether formal or informal, that is essential: virtually any lasting trade relation depends on the establishment of a shared social practice of trade marked by (perhaps implicit) mutuality. A practice of trade is essential for the resolution of basic problems of assurance that arise from the human condition itself.

---

12. This is emphasized in Bhagwati, 2002a, 2002b, p. 102.
13. Bagwell and Staiger, 1990, 2002, 2009; Milner and Rosendorff, 2001.

3. The Standard Case for Free Trade

For this argument to be at all convincing, it must be clear that we are taking the standard economic case for free trade very seriously. To that end, as well as to review the case for non-specialist readers, we pause to reconstruct the standard case in detail.[14]

Why should countries trade? Or more specifically, why should the governments of different countries remove trade barriers—quotas, tariffs, duties, subsidies, controls, and so forth—and so allow transactional flows in goods, services, or capital to cross their borders? They should do so, according to standard economic theory, because each country thereby augments its national income, taken in the aggregate. One of Adam Smith's signal advances over mercantilist thought (which called, e.g., for export promotion and import minimization to protect jobs) was the benchmark of national income.[15] Economists have since sounded a common refrain: imports free productive resources to do other things. Exports mainly pay for imports. The losses that imports create are more than outweighed, in the aggregate, by the resulting productivity gains.[16]

Productivity gains result for several reasons. First, specialization and exchange allow countries to benefit from differences in their "natural" endowments. As Smith argued, trading countries mutually take advantage of their differences in ease of production: "If a foreign country can supply us with a commodity cheaper than we ourselves can make it, better to buy it of them with some part of the produce of our own industry employed in a way in which we have some advantage."[17] While Smith suggested that a country look to its "absolute advantage"—what it does better than other countries—Robert Torrens, David Ricardo, and James Mill explained that a country does better still to trade to its "comparative advantage"—specializing in what it produces best

---

14. Our presentation closely follows the invaluable history in Irwin, 1996, which cites and helpfully contextualizes many of the historical references later in the chapter.

15. See Irwin, 1996, p. 76, on Smith's appeal to the "annual produce" of a whole country in Smith, 1776, as well as Irwin's discussion of English mercantilist thought in Ch. 2.

16. For a canonical statement, see Krugman and Obstfeld, 2003, pp. 3–4, 54–57.

17. Smith (1776), 1976, IV.ii.12.

relative to its *own productive options*.[18] Thus, even a country that might produce everything more efficiently than every other country—it has an absolute advantage in everything—does still better to do what it does best and trade, to comparative advantage, for what it does relatively less well from abroad.

Second, specialization has inherent economic advantages, even among countries similarly endowed. When labor is divided, people tend to produce more than they otherwise would, even with the same resources (if only because the mind then focuses on a single task). Given trade, the division of labor can be ever-further refined. As the scale of production expands, costs of production fall, and output is further increased ("economies of scale").

Third, trade brings a variety of indirect economic and political benefits: it improves the variety and quality of goods; it undercuts price fixing and other anti-competitive practices; and it undermines special political interests that divert benefits away from the larger population. Perhaps most important, it spreads embedded technology, research and design, know-how, and ideas, which further spur innovation, reduce production costs, release productive resources, and promote economic growth. If classical trade theory developed each of these insights, neo-classical economics has rigorously modeled how the gains of trade arise (e.g., in the Heckscher-Ohlin-Samuelson model)[19] and confirmed the predicted gross domestic product (GDP) gains in empirical studies (mainly for advanced rather than developing countries).[20]

The basic economic case argues that trade is "better for the nation" than self-sufficiency. It also claims that the removal of almost any barrier to trade—whether "at the border" (e.g., a tariff) or "behind the border" (e.g., an export subsidy)—makes a country richer than it would be if the barrier is retained. National income is optimized under completely free trade—except in a handful of cases that admit of a prima facie case for market protection. These exceptional cases are as follows.

In a first class of cases, a government measure can be used to maximize national income. This may be true for several reasons.

---

18. Torrens, 1815; Ricardo (1817), 1951; Mill, 1821.
19. Far less important is the Ricardian "two by two" model, which predicts the "pattern of trade" but does not account for internal distribution.
20. Irwin, 2002, surveys some of this evidence, along with a thorough and sympathetic presentation of the standard economic arguments.

Terms of trade. A judiciously set tariff, against a backdrop of free trade, can increase national income by increasing the international purchasing power of a country's exports for imports. The resulting trade surplus (in a large country) leads to monetary adjustments, which lead to higher domestic prices, wages, and profits. The country thus buys more imported goods for the same amount of exported goods.[21]

Infant industries. A temporary tariff or subsidy can optimize a country's income by insulating its firms from otherwise debilitating foreign competition. This enables them to acquire necessary knowledge, know-how, and capital.[22]

Increasing returns. National income may be optimized by a permanent tax on industries marked by "decreasing returns" (i.e., an increasing scale of production leads to increased costs), or by a permanent subsidy to increasing returns industries. The tax or subsidy diverts labor toward industries that contribute to greater national gains.[23]

Wage differentials. A tariff in a developing country may optimize national income by shifting labor from low-productivity, low-wage industries (such as agriculture) to high-productivity, high-wage industries (such as manufacturing).[24]

Strategic trade. Government policy (e.g., an export subsidy) can promote the national advantage by shifting profits from foreign to domestic firms. When firms are interdependent (the pricing, investment, and output decisions of one firm affect others), and competition is imperfect (firm rivalry is insufficient to normalize profit level), the subsidy helps domestic firms capture greater international market shares (yielding gains larger than the cost of the export subsidy).[25]

A second class of prima facie reasons for market protection concerns national income distribution. Economists readily admit that even as trade maximizes aggregate income, it creates both "winners" and "losers." This is for any of several reasons.

21. Torrens, 1844; Mill, 1844; Edgeworth, 1894; Kaldor, 1940; Johnson, 1950.
22. Mill (1848), 1909.
23. Graham, 1923; Panagariya, 1981.
24. Manoilescu, 1931; Ohlin, 1931; Haberler, 1936.
25. Brander and Spencer, 1985; Cournot (1838), 1927; Dixit and Kyle, 1985; Krugman, 1987.

Consumer loss. Trade changes "relative prices" within a society, as the relative scarcity of goods or services is altered. While some, previously (relatively) scarce goods become cheaper, others previously abundant become more expensive. One may be made worse off, on balance, if more goods in one's consumption basket become more costly, or if certain essential goods (e.g., food) become more expensive.

Wage loss. Wages in advanced countries may decline or stagnate as trade with developing countries makes labor more abundant.[26] Declining or stagnating wages may not be compensated by gains in cheaper goods or services, due to consumer loss (see *Consumer loss*).

Job loss. Workers in import-competing industries will often lose their jobs as a result of trade and be unable, for lack of skill, information, or opportunity, to procure jobs being created in export-oriented industries.[27]

Underemployment. When resources are not fully employed (due, e.g., to a crisis of confidence, insufficient demand, or immobile factors/workers), trade barriers may increase overall employment levels, productive output, and net national income, at least in the short run.[28] (This argument may make reference to both national income and the distribution of gains and losses.)

The standard argument for free trade does not dispute any of these economic grounds for market protection in principle, in appropriate circumstances. It urges instead either that (1) protection is unadvisable in practice for reasons of political economy, or that (2) trade measures are less good than other policy remedies. According to (1), the *political-economy argument*, the relevant circumstances for justified protection are usually too difficult to reliably identify in practice. As often as not, officials will get the

---

26. Stopler and Samuelson, 1941; Krugman, manuscript. Wages in developing countries may also fail to rise as "factor price equalization" would predict, because of imperfect competition or incomplete risk markets (Newbery et al., 1984).
27. Torrens, 1821; Brigden, 1925; Brigden et al. 1929; Sidgwick, 1883; Stopler and Samuelson, 1941; Samuelson, 1981a; Kletzer, 1998a, 1998b, 2001, 2005; WTO, 2003.
28. Keynes, 1936; Robinson, 1937; Samuelson, 1964. Trade liberalization can also contribute to vulnerability to external shocks which reduce national income (Easterly et al., 2001).

delicate parameters wrong, erasing the potential gain and perhaps doing more harm than good. (This is argued, e.g., for terms of trade,[29] increasing returns,[30] and strategic trade[31]). Moreover, protection risks retaliation from other countries and a mutually destructive trade war. According to (2), the *optimal remedy argument*, trade barriers are usually more disruptive of economic activity than more direct policy responses to the relevant condition.[32] In the cases of consumer loss, wage loss, and job loss, for example, it is admitted that trade creates winners and losers but suggested that the best remedy is simply to "compensate the losers" directly with some portion of the net income gain—for example, through cash payments or a social insurance scheme.[33] (Different remedies are optimal in the cases of infant industries,[34] wage differentials,[35] and underemployment.[36])

Notice that the optimal remedy argument has a conditional character: trade barriers are sub-optimal *when, but only when*, more direct policies are available. In many countries, we can expect that the losers from freer trade will *not* in fact be compensated, either for lack of political will or, as in many developing countries, for lack of funds or feasible supporting institutions. But what then should be done? Should barriers be removed anyway? Or should freed trade wait for more favorable political or institutional circumstances? Though economists often advocate going

---

29. Edgeworth, 1908.
30. Knight, 1924; Chipman, 1965; Viner, 1937; Markusen, 1990.
31. Grossman, 1986; Dixit and Grossman, 1986; Carmichael, 1987; Krugman, 1992.
32. Bhagwati, 1971, 2004.
33. As J. S. Mill, 1825, p. 399, put it, "It would be better to have repeal of the Corn Laws, even clogged by compensation, than not to have it at all; and if this were our only alternative, no one could complain of the change, by which, though an enormous amount of evil would be prevented, no one would lose." Similar optimal remedy arguments have been made in what I am calling "job loss" cases. See Taussig, 1893; Viner, 1929; Metzler, 1949.
34. Meade, 1955; Baldwin, 1969.
35. Ohlin, 1931; Meade, 1955; Bhagwati and Ramaswami, 1963.
36. Economists came to favor flexible exchange rates instead of trade barriers, e.g., Friedman, 1953. Even so, Keyensian fiscal stimulus was widely supported by economists during the 2008–2009 crisis, when monetary policy measures had been exhausted.

forward with freed trade anyway, economic theory is ambiguous about this.

According to the Kaldor-Hicks compensation criterion, trade counts as "good for the nation" simply insofar as compensation could *hypothetically* be provided.[37] Actual compensation is not required, in which case a country should move ahead with free trade even when it is clear that *many people will in fact be made worse off* than they would have been had trade barriers not been removed.

Pareto efficiency, perhaps the more commonly invoked efficiency conception, does require that losers be compensated: freed trade is Pareto efficient (leads to a "Pareto improvement") just in case it leaves some better off and no one worse off.[38] Hence, when compensatory arrangements are not likely to be set up, *protective barriers are Pareto efficient*. Because there will be "losers," free and efficient trade must wait for circumstances favorable for compensation. To put the point in more general terms, the probability that freed trade will be efficient in a given society, over some period of time, will always be no greater than the probability that adequate compensation will in fact be arranged, over that period of time. (Some economists confusingly offer a "hypothetical Pareto criterion," which has the same status for our purposes as Kaldor-Hicks efficiency).

4. Mutuality in Trade Agreements

Having rehearsed the standard case for free trade, we return to our main line of argument. Contrary to the initial picture presented thus far, it is not strictly true that agreements between countries have no proper function beyond getting nations to do what national prudence requires in any case. Agreements marked by "mutuality"—as in "I'll cut such-and-such tariffs if you do likewise"—can be required even by prudent nations *in order to* wholly free trade. The fly in the ointment, as economists have long recognized, is that a country can often adopt *beggar-thy-neighbor* policies, that is, policies that generate real gains for it at some cost to its trade partners.

---

37. Kaldor, 1939; Hicks, 1939.
38. Pareto, 1894; Samuelson, 1939, 1962; Kemp, 1962.

A judiciously set trade barrier can (for terms-of-trade or strategic trade reasons) optimize national income at the equal or greater expense of other countries. Or to take a prominent contemporary example, a "competitive" devaluation of the currency (e.g., of Chinese renminbi relative to U.S. dollars) may cheapen domestic imports and optimize national gains (for China) while making imports more expensive for other countries (the United States). (Countries trading in a third currency may also lose out—for example, African or Latin American country firms are less competitive in the United States against Chinese exports—or have reduced entrepreneurial incentives). The question of national prudence is whether or to what extent to remove trade barriers given that each trading country may be in a position to both impose and be subjected to beggar-thy-neighbor policies, in the short run and down the road.

What we called the "optimal remedy argument" offers no counsel against taking beggar-thy-neighbor gains at the expense of one's trading partners, so long as the gains optimize national income. The "political-economy argument" does, by contrast, suggest why countries might withhold beggar-thy-neighbor policies, and on purely unilateral grounds. Again, the required "optimal tariff" (or other measure) is easy to get wrong. But this is hardly a firm foundation for free trade doctrine. After all, why not invest heavily in the science and practice of getting it "right" more often than not? Why presume, against technology and innovation, that the science and practice cannot be adequately developed, or even perfected? Perhaps for such reasons, the political-economy argument often shifts to a multilateral perspective. We also should consider the consequent choices of other governments: the disadvantaged countries will likely respond in kind, either by barriers of self-protection or by escalation into full trade war, leaving both countries worse off. In that case, however, the ultimate argument for free trade is based in *reciprocity*.

While the most celebrated neo-classical models obscure this, it was quite explicit in classical trade theory. When J. S. Mill settled the terms-of-trade debate (in favor of Robert Torrens's view that tariffs could be optimal), he not only emphasized the unilateral political-economy argument that "the benefits of such a tax [are] always extremely precarious," "even on the most selfish principles," he also suggested that the case for free trade depends on "considerations of reciprocity."

A country cannot be expected to renounce the power of taxing foreigners, unless foreigners will in return practice towards itself the same forbearance.[39]

Mill suggests this must be done by a kind of social contract, involving the "common consent of nations":

> Until, by the common consent of nations, all restrictions are done away, a nation cannot be required to abolish those from which she derives a real advantage, without stipulating for an equivalent.[40]

Accordingly, national prudence counsels not only against short-term gains at the expense of trading partners but in favor of *cooperative mutual forbearance* over the longer haul. As Irwin explains, in surveying the history of economic debate:

> The analysis of strategic trade policy, like the terms of trade argument, illustrated the possible unilateral advantages of deviating from free trade to exploit one's trading partners. . . . But the real implication . . . is not so much that . . . trade interventions can be potentially beneficial. Rather, these theories reinforce the notion that trade is a form of economic interdependence. If each country ignored others and pursued policies that were apparently to its unilateral advantage, most countries would likely be worse off in the end. Cooperative agreements between countries, in which all agree to forgo the use of such policies, could potentially make each of them better off.[41]

As suggested, recent game-theoretic work has developed this insight into an impressively robust rational reconstruction of the GATT/WTO (General Agreement on Tariffs and Trade/World Trade Organization) system.[42] The leading idea is that terms-of-trade (and perhaps other) externalities present countries with a prisoner's dilemma, which can be overcome only by making a reciprocal agreement. If a narrow exchange of "market access" is

---

39. Mill, 1844, pp. 25, 28–29.
40. Ibid, pp. 31–32.
41. Irwin, 1996, p. 216.
42. Bagwell and Staiger, 2002, 2009.

arguably unnecessary, a more "relaxed" form of reciprocity is mutually beneficial.[43]

Although we have no qualms with this argument, it is important for our purposes that it concerns only the potential gains of *formal* agreements. The useful benchmark, in that case, is not autarky but whatever mix of tariffs and liberalization it would be rational for countries to choose (according to government preferences) given the decisions made by other governments. Specifically, the benchmark is the Nash equilibrium in the absence of a formal agreement: each country adopts the trade policies that are best for it given the policies that other governments adopt, in which case no government has reason to change its policies so long as other governments do not change theirs. The question, in this approach, is whether making a formal agreement might move to an improved equilibrium situation. The move, in short, is from (somewhat) freed to even freer trade.

When our concerns are the fundamental social basis for the gains of trade, however, the game-theoretic situation is not fully captured in these terms. Prisoner's dilemma situations surely arise, but they leave out the basic, unavoidable reality of uncertainty and risk. As we will see presently, the "stag hunt" or "assurance game," which highlights these features, more aptly represents the fundamental social situation. This will show that the gains of trade are fundamentally inseparable from international cooperation, whether as a matter of formal agreements *or* of informal social practice.

5. The Unavoidablity of Mutuality

Our main thought might be put as follows. Insofar as our concern is to understand how a significant global economy could in fact emerge, the one-shot prisoner's dilemma is of little help: it rules out cooperation by definition. If we move to a repeated prisoner's dilemma model, however, and now suppose that countries adjust trade policy in light of the shadow of the future, the basic situation (given plausible assumptions) becomes equivalent to Rousseau's

---

43. Bhagwati, 2002a.

"stag hunt"[44] or the game theorist's "assurance game."[45] Even among the most prudent of nations, and in the best of circumstances, the general facts of uncertainty and risk in cooperative activity mean that free (or freer) trade will be reasonable only within a common practice that provides *assurances* to each country of sufficient benefit over the longer haul.

Unlike the prisoner's dilemma, the essential tension in an assurance game is between mutual benefit and risk. That is, suppose two or more players ("you" and "I") can each either hunt hare or hunt stag. We will each eat something if we separately hunt hare, but we will eat best if we work together to hunt stag. Cooperation is thus a (Nash) equilibrium: hunting stag is best for me if you also hunt stag, and hunting stag is best for you if I also hunt stag. Yet because neither of us knows what the other will do, we each face certain risks. If you decide to hunt hare, and I am left hunting stag on my own, I'll get nothing, eating less than I would if I simply hunted hare from the start. And the same goes for you as regards me. Thus non-cooperation is also an equilibrium option: hunting hare is best for me if you hunt hare, and hunting hare is best for you if I hunt hare. Given our uncertainty, the non-cooperation equilibrium becomes the "risk dominant" choice.[46] The risk averse won't miss out on the easy gains of hunting hare. But even the moderately cautious will forgo greater, risky cooperative gains for the smaller, safer benefits of acting alone.

The case of trade is similar. Even nations that would happily forgo "opportunistic" gains at their trading partners' expense will

---

44. Rousseau (1754), 1997, part 2, par. 9, writes: "This is how men may imperceptibly have acquired some crude idea of mutual engagements and of the advantage of fulfilling them, but only as far as present and perceptible interest could require.... If a Deer was to be caught, everyone [would] clearly sense that this required him faithfully to keep to his post; but if a hare happened to pass within reach of one of them, he will, without a doubt, have chased after it without a scruple and, after catching his prey, have cared very little about having caused his Companions to miss theirs."
45. Skyrms, 2004, p. 5. Among the required assumptions are that the game is in each case more likely to be repeated than not. As Skyrms elaborates, ibid, p. 125, "If the probability of repetition is low enough, the repeated game is still a prisoner's dilemma. If the probably of repetition is high enough, the stag hunting equilibrium becomes risk dominant."
46. On "risk dominance," see Harsanyi and Selton, 1988.

be concerned to reap some goodly measure of national gain. They will therefore require certain assurances about the uncertain conduct of other nations if trade is to be foreseeably worthwhile. Absent a relatively assured market reliance practice, sufficient benefits cannot be taken for granted. Wise nations will require confident expectations of benefit, over the longer haul, in order to justify expected and "known unknown" (1) terms-of-trade losses, (2) tariff revenue losses, (3) adjustment costs, including the foreseeable cost to workers and other losers, and (4) any other losses from foreign beggar-thy-neighbor policies—all of which may arise in the near future or down the road.[47] (There is also uncertainty about whether future governments in the same country will adopt "beggar-myself" policies, but leave these aside.) Questions of confidence thus loom: How committed will current and future governments be to freed trade, given political change, bureaucratic dynamics, special interest pressures, and so on? Will they opt for beggar-thy-neighbor gains at our expense? And how good is our evidence on any or all of these matters? In principle, such uncertainty is all it takes for a government to face risks that imperil any move toward freer trade. Without the shadow of an assured future, free trade may well be unwise.

Fortunately, the governments of the world have converged upon a basic solution: mutuality—that is, a mutual market reliance practice that offers assurances of longer-term benefit on all sides. Very roughly, mutuality marks the difference between the distrustful, destructive interwar years and the hugely successful postwar GATT system, which induced trust through a deft mix of constraint and flexibility (discussed later). Our present point is that some such "agreement," whether formal, informal, or both, is the *only* way the basic assurance problem can be realistically overcome—even among wise nations that fully embrace the economic theory of trade.

As briefly suggested earlier, the most fundamental reason this is so is not clearly represented by a prisoner's dilemma. Let us say, for example, that each government seeks to optimize its national

---

47. To be sure, short-term adjustment or beggar-thy-neighbor costs may sometimes be outweighed by short-term gains. But wise nations still require evidence that this will in fact come about in order to justify the risk of loss.

interest. Because each lacks confidence about the longer haul, however, each considers only short-run expectations. Both nations do best, taken collectively, to jointly free trade (to "cooperate"). But each does best, taken individually, to block trade (to "defect") if the other cooperates. For, let us say, if the other cooperates, freeing trade, each country will do best to impose an "opportunistic," beggar-thy-neighbor tariff, in order to reap terms-of-trade gains (the countries, then, are not "small" and so unable to affect world prices). And if the other defects, keeping barriers up, then each country does best to defect as well, avoiding the cost of the other's beggar-thy-neighbor gain. Hence the self-interestedly rational choice for both nations is to defect *whatever* the other chooses: if the other nation defects, defection is best; if the other cooperates, defection is still best. Defection is the *sole* equilibrium outcome. Now notice that this situation makes no reference to *risk given uncertainty about the conduct of others*. From the point of view of pure national interest, defection is the equilibrium outcome *even when the choice of the other (e.g., to cooperate) is known*. In an assurance game, by contrast, there is a stable *cooperative* equilibrium. What keeps the players from getting to it is simply the *risks* of cooperation, that is, the expected opportunity cost of going alone, given *uncertainty* about what the other agent, facing similar risks, will do.[48]

If uncertainty is the basic issue, however, then we cannot start out assuming an equilibrium state of substantially freed trade and then ask whether an emergent social practice might lead to mutual improvement. The basic issue is not the move from freed

---

48. The repeated prisoner's dilemma might still be appropriate for many purposes, including explanation of the emergence of cooperation (e.g., Axelrod, 1985). Our claim is that it obscures basic issues of uncertainty and risk in the present context. For appeals to the prisoner's dilemmas in order to suggest the need for cooperation, see Trebilcock and Howse, 2005, p. 7. The multiple equilibrium tariff game in Bagwell and Staiger, 1990, 2002, is closer to the assurance game analysis but does not highlight the role of uncertainty and risk. (Kyle Bagwell suggested in personal communication that assurance game modeling would likely also work for his purposes.) Closer still is the model incorporating "political uncertainty" offered by Milner and Rosendorff, 2001. For discussion of the limitations of prisoner's dilemma situations, see Koremenos, Lipson, and Snidal, 2001.

to freer trade, but any move away from autarky. The Nash equilibrium is the situation in which each government adopts the policies that are of the greatest expected benefit to it given the *known* fact that other governments are adopting the policies best for them. But uncertainty about this is the crucial issue. Sufficient uncertainty and aversion to risk under uncertainty ("risk dominance" rather than "payoff dominance") is all it takes, in principle, to push all countries into autarky. That is not to say that modest trade levels cannot at all emerge without a shared practice. There was indeed limited trade in the interwar years. But that is consistent with our claim that a social practice is required for a global economy as we know it, which involves substantial (if partial) integration far beyond minimal interwar year levels.

This basic predicament is a fundamental feature of virtually all human social interaction. It is a general feature of the human condition, especially as far as intentional coordination of action is concerned, that the agents face uncertainty about what the other agents will do. Indeed, this is part of what it means for the agents to be numerically distinct: they lack the sort of direct knowledge of and control over the intentions and conduct of others that they (usually) have over themselves. So insofar as an agent acts with reference to others at all, it is with some measure of uncertainty about their conduct and thus, often, under conditions of risk. Even in quite prosaic circumstances, and especially when the stakes are high, agents can only act together or in agreement, in any intentionally coordinated way, provided certain assurances—the assurances provided when the pattern of coordination becomes established in a public, jointly available way.

This is so even under the best of circumstances for cooperation. Compare, for example, the "coordination game" played by David Hume's rowers ("you" and "I"). You and I row together, each with the aim of crossing the lake without wasted effort or great risk of hitting things. We each thus have an interest in rowing in rhythm, at any steady rate, and we know this about each other, and so readily cooperate. Even so, according to Hume we do so out of a "common sense of interest . . . *known* to both [which] produces a suitable resolution and behavior" in which "the actions of each . . . have a reference to those of the other, and are preferred on the *supposition* that something is to be preferred upon the other part."[49] The "common sense of interest" here is not simply that people *in fact* have common interests, but that each has *good evidence* of this—in Hume's terms, each "knows" or "supposes" that certain interests are shared. What is crucial, in other words, is not what happens when we row but how things look to each of us as we approach the boat. If you don't *look* like you wish to go across the lake (perhaps you are taking a nap, waiting for a fellow rower), I may lack the evidence I need for it to make sense to forgo rowing alone or walking on to look for another partner. Indeed, you may *in fact* be careful but simply look to me like the careless type; whatever the reality, you may not seem to share my interest in uneventful passage. If the matter is sometimes easily cleared up, the fog can also persist—as when we lack a common language, or we can't read each other's gestures, or cannot quite feel trusting, because of differences in culture, mannerisms, or temperament.

Such uncertainties multiply in international trade. Distances are great; communication fails; domestic politics presses; officials or bureaucracies send mixed signals, are confused, or seek war—not to mention inevitable uncertainty about the economics of the case. Even if both of two countries are firm in their commitment to mutual gain over the long haul, this must be evident to both and cannot simply be presumed. Without appropriate evidence, and especially when there is (perhaps misleading) evidence to the contrary, the expected and potential costs of market openness will not justify uncertain gains in purely prudential terms. Prevailing uncertainties might be readily overcome. Even so, the only basic way nations have of overcoming them is to display willingness to establish a practice of mutual market reliance that will last, to confirm this over time in routine mutually beneficial commerce, and to constructively address new sources of uncertainty as they arise with diplomatic and policy assurances. Trade and mutuality in the practice of trade are inseparable from a practical point of view.[50]

---

49. Hume (1896), 1975, p. 490, italics mine.
50. "Mutuality" in the present sense is not yet the stronger idea, suggested earlier, that the aim of trade practice is *mutual or reciprocal benefit*. The practice of trade could be sustained, for instance, from pure national prudence by firmly established threats of exclusion (although even this would have to overcome problems of assurance). The stronger interpretation is already perhaps suggested by the passage from Mill, 1844, and Irwin, 1996, quoted in the text above. We provide further reasons for it in Chapters 3.3 and 6.8.

6. The Unavoidablity of Distribution

We mentioned that governments inevitably care about domestic distribution, and that economic theory happily admits that there will always be "winners" and "losers" from freer trade. We also noted that economic theory is ambiguous about what significance distributional outcomes might have for the free trade argument (again, Pareto efficiency requires *actual* compensation, Kaldor-Hicks efficiency does not). We will now argue that the basic case for free trade, understood as a more or less conclusive practical judgment, *depends* on appropriate sensitivity to distribution, in much the way fairness would require. While economists happily grant that free trade is *compatible* with social insurance schemes that compensate the "losers" from trade in each country, the crucial, often overlooked (or perhaps suppressed) point is that social insurance is *required* if free trade is to be fair. Social insurance is the fair price of free trade.

If that is to take a purely domestic point of view, we will also suggest that the standard case for free trade depends on sensitivity to international distribution. Countries will gain from trade to different degrees, depending on underlying economic factors (e.g., their differential endowments), but also depending on the extent to which different countries liberalize. Beggar-thy-neighbor policies and terms-of-trade effects will shape relative gains. And even when a country is better off wholly freeing trade of its own accord, it is better off still if its trading partners do likewise, under reciprocal liberalization. Failure for one country to liberalize can mean that its trading partners gain less than they otherwise would.[51]

Why, then, aren't economists pretty concerned about distribution? The main thought is perhaps this: if trade might make each country and each person in each country better off, why worry about how gains compare in size? Each country or person would have a powerful reason to prefer freer trade to market protection, however the relative gains fall out. This is plausible enough in itself, but no reason to think that fairness in relative distribution is unimportant, or even that the case for free trade is wholly independent of distributional concerns. Let us concede that the general case for free trade should not be *wholly dependent*

---

51. Bhagwati, 2002a.

upon ultimate questions of what distributions are desirable or fair; a move toward freer trade can be a legitimate policy move and leave specific distributional questions somewhat open or unsettled. It may be legitimate, a wise step forward, but not as yet fully fair. But it is quite another matter to suppose that a free trade argument can or should be *wholly or largely insensitive* to how the benefits and burdens of free trade fall out. Few would say that distribution should *not* be regulated if societies happen to prefer this. But for all this says, the main reasons governments have to free trade *do not at all depend* on such distributional concerns.[52]

In fact, however, we will now see that the case for free trade cannot wholly avoid distributional concerns, at least not if the argument is (1) for a more or less conclusive policy recommendation, and (2) justified on relatively modest or uncontroversial grounds. Indeed, how could the principled basis for the argument be *wholly insensitive* to distribution and *also* modest or uncontroversial? Would it not *just for that very reason* be properly controversial indeed? Economists often suppose that the idea of "efficiency" can have this complex role. We will now see why this is a mistake. The familiar conceptions of efficiency are either relatively uncontroversial but of inconclusive force; of conclusive force but highly controversial; or of conclusive force and relatively uncontroversial but *sensitive* to distribution.

Why, again, should governments open their markets? Strictly speaking, economic theory implies only that trade barriers have an opportunity cost: net national income is not as great as it would be under freer trade. That is *some* reason to be interested in freer trade, but not necessarily a conclusive reason, let alone a conclusive reason for completely free trade. For why not favor substantial trade up to some liberalization threshold, for the gains over self-sufficiency, but forgo further national income gains to protect would-be losers from harm, or to slow the breakneck pace of historical change? (If the "revealed preferences" of actual governments indicate what societies prefer, then such cases are common;

---

52. There is a venerable tradition in economics of suppressing mention of distributive considerations. Ricardo famously ignored losses to landowners in repealing the Corn Laws, and we have noted John Hicks's famous counsel to suppress distributional concerns as far as possible. If that could be taken as a mere point of political persuasion, some serious theory is consciously insensitive to distribution, e.g., Meade, 1995.

many societies do not seem to prefer optimized national income at any social cost, since many sub-optimal trade barriers remain.) If some appeal to "efficiency" is supposed to answer this question, what version, exactly, would do the job?

Mere instrumental efficiency. Economic theory insists, often convincingly, that such trade-offs do not arise as often as it is believed. We often can free trade *and* compensate any losers, for instance. Does economics say more than this? Many economists will admit that true economic science does not tell governments or societies what ends to have in the first place, or how to balance values, should they conflict. The "argument" for free trade only makes *instrumental* claims about the means to given ends; the "oughts" it offers are mere "hypothetical imperatives," whose force depends on some aims having already been set. In that case, when we raise the question of final ends—"To what extent should we favor national income over other values?" or "Should we prefer market protection to stabilize prospects for the low-skilled, least well-off, despite the economic opportunity cost?"—the case for free trade must remain silent, at least until some ends are set.

This is not, however, the "argument" for free trade that has been zealously advocated over two hundred years in public debate. It is not the argument that has become a virtual orthodoxy in the economics profession, and, indeed, a test of faith for whether one is serious about social science and its bearing on policy. Or, at any rate, we will consider the argument for free trade that urges, as a more or less conclusive policy recommendation, that countries ought to free trade and sort out the rest afterward or otherwise. Our question is, What principled grounds, if any, could plausibly support this position?

One normative principle would be as follows: governments ought to optimize net national income, whatever the cost to other values. Yet even Adam Smith sensibly rejects this particular view: if forced to choose, national security trumps opulence.[53] The question, then, is whether some more plausible normative principle might be offered instead. And notice that plausibility is crucial. No normative principle, about what one *ought* to do, can be a verdict of science, since it cannot be established by mathematical reasoning, direct observation, or an explanatory inference from

---

53. Smith (1776), 1994, IV.2.24.

observations. If classical trade theorists such as Smith, Ricardo, and Mill were unbothered about scientific scruple, freely blending economics with advocacy and moral and political philosophy, the scientific aspiration of modern economics requires that it be more circumspect. If a proposed principled basis for free trade is highly or properly controversial (e.g., the principle stated earlier that Smith rejects), then free trade argument is more of a piece with political advocacy or political philosophy than with social scientific inquiry. Accordingly, modern economics has favored modesty: the now standard view is that normative assumptions are fine, and at least not *unscientific*, so long as they are *relatively or appropriately uncontroversial*.[54]

Efficiency as preference satisfaction. Some conceptions of efficiency are indeed relatively uncontroversial, yet quite insufficient to support a more or less conclusive argument for free trade. Economists happily concede that a society whose "social welfare function" includes concern for relative gains or inequality might make redistributive arrangements as it sees fit (with a larger pie, under free trade, to share around). Distributive arrangements are then "efficient" in the sense that they answer to a society's preferences. Yet the question is whether or how the argument for freer trade can be made on relatively uncontroversial grounds *without* addressing such distributional concerns. If no such grounds are available, the case for free trade is *sensitive* to distribution.

Inefficiency as waste. Other relatively uncontroversial conceptions also lack the requisite conclusive force. When a valuable resource already exists but goes unused or spoils, we find it a shame to let it "go to waste" when someone could have benefited instead. We say this, however, only when someone could benefit, when the cost of maintenance and future use is low, and when there are no undesirable side effects. As costs rise, the issue becomes a less uncontroversial matter of what is "too expensive" to maintain rather than a matter of mere waste. Trade barriers that forgo national income gains are not "inefficient" in this sense. No existing valuable resource goes to waste since the goods and services that would be produced under freer trade have yet to be created. Nor is the failure to remove trade barriers clearly a

---

54. For discussion of how welfare economics settled on this view, see Irwin, 1996, p. 184.

"wasted opportunity." The cost of taking the opportunity is often not low, so the issue is a properly controversial matter of *expense* rather than waste.

Utilitarianism. Other conceptions of efficiency have sufficient force but are properly controversial. According to utilitarianism, for example, law and policy (conclusively) ought to maximize welfare in the aggregate, relative to the available options. This principle is wholly insensitive to distribution, as a matter of principle: relative gains and losses have no intrinsic importance. The welfare of everyone is to be counted equally—everyone counts for one, and no more than one, in Bentham's phrase—but particular distributions can only be required as effective *means* of optimizing utility, in the aggregate. So insofar as free trade can be shown to maximize welfare overall, where the welfare of everyone in the world is counted, it follows that free trade ought to be adopted as an all-things-considered conclusion.

However, utilitarianism leads to conclusions quite at odds with commonsense morality *and* the basic argument for free trade, precisely because distribution is assigned no significance in principle. Freed trade would count as justifiable, and indeed morally required, even if many people would be severely and irreparably harmed (e.g., unemployed and destitute for the long haul), so long as this is necessary to provide a greater sum of benefits to other people. The benefits may be small to any given person (e.g., slightly cheaper luxury goods) as long as the beneficiaries are sufficiently numerous. Indeed, free trade will be acceptable even if *most* people in a society are made worse off, so long as this is unavoidable and large enough welfare gains go to a lucky few. The beneficiaries may well live abroad, leaving everyone in a society worse off for freed trade, so long as this is indeed necessary to optimize welfare in the global aggregate.

Such cases are perhaps unlikely, but not inconceivable. Perhaps a single-industry developing country will suffer massive unemployment for many years as its chief source of productivity is destroyed; perhaps its limited infrastructure and weak government exacerbate the difficulties; perhaps terms-of-trade effects further worsen the outcome; perhaps net gain is not received for decades, leaving a generation of workers on balance worse off over the course of their lives. According to utilitarianism, the imagined country will be required to self-sacrificially free trade, knowing the domestic cost, so long as this is necessary for an aggregate welfare improvement via benefits to foreigners. The benefits to foreigners may be small (e.g., slightly cheaper tuna fish), so long as the number of beneficiaries is correspondingly large (millions eat fine sushi more cheaply). Or to take a slightly more realistic example: suppose, in globalizing China and India, that dramatic poverty reduction in urban areas (where most of the gains in fact accrue) somehow, as a result of trade, dramatically worsened poverty in rural areas. We would not regard this as a huge success—a case of free trade living up to its promise—even if the net aggregate utility gain turned out to be positive.

Under appropriate circumstances, utilitarianism can equally require radical trade barriers. Suppose that advanced countries could maximize poverty reduction globally by trading exclusively with India and China, given that they together contain much of the world's population and much of the world's poor. Perhaps they erect high trade barriers against the rest of the developing and less developed world. Or perhaps, because Latin America is relatively populous, advanced countries include it and block only Africa. Yet even the most vigorous advocates of global free trade assume that the poor countries of Latin America and Africa are supposed to have a chance to benefit from access to global markets. In that case, utilitarianism is not the assumed normative basis of the argument.

Utilitarians will hasten to add that free trade is not in fact likely to have such consequences. (For the rule utilitarian, it will be said that a practice of trade diversion will tend on balance to be suboptimal.) While such empirical claims may (or may not) in fact be true, the essential point, for present purposes, is that utilitarianism is hardly the modest normative basis the free trade argument requires. If it is the *only* reason in principle why governments should free trade, then free traders should give up any pretext of scientific scruple and defend their view as the extremely controversial normative doctrine it would then be.

Kaldor-Hicks efficiency. Kaldor-Hicks efficiency would not ask a country to choose free trade if it would be worse off on the whole, or if the gains of trade were of insufficient size to hypothetically compensate its losers. Yet, again, like utilitarianism, Kaldor-Hicks efficiency is otherwise insensitive to how the gains are distributed, at least as a matter of principle. It is enough that the aggregate gain is large enough to fully fund a *hypothetical* compensation scheme, regardless of whether compensation is ever actually paid.

This is consistent with all or most of the gains of trade being distributed to a lucky few, leaving most people no better off. Indeed, it is consistent with all or most of the gains flowing to a lucky few, leaving many people *much* worse off; the gains to beneficiaries need only be large enough.

Here we might grant that augmented national income is itself a good thing, other things being equal. If in a given case we do not know what distribution will result, and we have no evidence that a compensatory scheme cannot or will not be set up, the possibility of such gains is still presumably *some* reason to free trade. But, again, the free trade argument requires a *conclusive* normative principle. In that case, the present suggestion must be that countries have conclusive reason to free trade even when we can expect the gains to flow to very few people, rather than being, in some sense, broadly shared. But this principle is hardly a modest or properly uncontroversial basis for free trade. Would any reasonable society allow a potentially large portion of its members to be made significantly worse off, or even no better off but with greater risk of harm, just to benefit what may be a small minority? Surely it is at least reasonable to forgo free trade under such circumstances.

Economic theory usually assumes that this will not (ever?) happen: the gains of trade tend to flow broadly, across the population, and indeed will usually weaken monopoly or special interest control and "rent-seeking" behavior. The idea that gains are broadly shared is not, however, a well-established empirical generalization from careful case studies over a range of countries and long periods of time. Empirical studies largely measure GDP gains, which are insensitive to distribution per se. To the extent we seem to observe broadly shared gains in practice, they often reflect compensatory institutions already established—hardly an independent basis for *determining* whether such institutions are required for the gains of trade to be in some sense broadly shared. The idea that trade yields broad-based gains is, rather, largely a theoretical conjecture.[55]

---

55. As Paul Samuelson, 1981b, p. 227, explains, there is merely a "vague presumption that the law of large numbers will obtain" when numerous "quasi-independent" sectors are exposed to different gains and losses. "Any random person will be on balance benefited . . . even though any one of the events may . . . [be] less favorable [for some]." Quoted and discussed in Driskill, manuscript.

This is important, not because the conjecture isn't often plausible, but because of what it shows about the case for free trade. If free traders would not endorse free trade under all of the conditions consistent with Kaldor-Hicks efficiency, then they either do not accept that efficiency principle, or they accept it in a *specifically distribution-sensitive form*, that is, in a form that is applicable *only* when the gains of trade are, in some sense, broadly shared. If the latter, then the case for free trade is indeed sensitive to distribution, much in the way considerations of structural equity are.[56] Indeed, we could then see the case for free trade as requiring a good measure of structural equity in how the gains of trade are shared. Free trade would be justified only insofar as it is sufficiently fair.

Pareto efficiency. Many economists instead appeal to Pareto efficiency, which does require that losers from trade be compensated. Even so, our present point holds, in much the same way. Pareto efficiency is consistent with any of the following adverse distributional outcomes, both domestic and international:

> *Domestically*: most people neither gain nor lose, or are only slightly better off, while a relatively small number of people reap large gains. In the limit, so long as no one is worse off, a single person reaps all of the gains.
>
> *Internationally*: most nations are neither better nor worse off, on the whole, or only slightly better off, while a few nations reap large gains. In the limit, nearly all countries are no better off, while one country reaps all the gains of trade.

As earlier, it will be said that these adverse distributional outcomes do not usually come about. But if economists will not conclusively recommend free trade under the conditions consistent with Pareto efficiency, then they either do not accept the proposed principle, or they accept it in a *specifically distribution-sensitive form*, which applies only when the gains of trade are, in some sense, broadly shared. The latter position is fine, but it also suggests

---

56. It may be said that broad sharing is more a matter of *numbers* of beneficiaries, rather than distribution. Even so, international distribution remains at stake. If numbers matter within countries, we have already seen why countries might not endorse national self-sacrifice for the sake of broadly shared gains abroad.

that Pareto efficiency *assumes* a good measure of structural equity in how the gains of trade are shared. Fairness would require not only compensating the losers from trade, but also that the gains are, in some sense, broadly shared. The operative principle, we might say, is not Pareto efficiency but Pareto efficiency *cum* structural equity.

7. Fairness Concerns

We close this chapter by briefly addressing a range of further concerns that economics-minded observers often voice about fairness in trade. These are of three main kinds.

First, *redundancy*. In some cases, appeal to fairness is said to be redundant; the appeal can be rephrased without loss in purely economic terms. For example:

1. Some "unfair subsidies" (e.g., rich country subsidies of corn, sugar, or cotton) are productively inefficient, because other countries (developing countries, rich in both labor and land) have a comparative advantage in the subsidized goods.[57]
2. Some "unfair dumping" (i.e., selling goods in a foreign market below the cost of production, in order to put competing firms out of business) amounts to predatory behavior inconsistent with the idea of a competitive market.[58]

Second, *obscurity*. In some cases, if appeal to fairness is not clearly objectionable, it is at least questionable. We may ask,

3. What could a "fair price" or "fair wage" be if not simply the market price[59] (perhaps constrained at some level, e.g., by minimum wage laws)?
4. Why should "losers" from trade be compensated if we do not compensate "losers" from domestic technological change?

---

57. Wolf, 2004.
58. Cass and Boltuck, 1996.
59. For this claim about wages and exploitation, see Robinson, 1933.

Why should the losses from trade be special simply because they have an external source?

5. What is special about the job destroyed by imports given that an export-industry job is equally created? In advanced countries, trade under normal conditions does not change to the total number of jobs, so a trade barrier deprives people of gainful work as much as it protects it. What is fair about that? Why isn't the person in a protected job collecting unfair rent, at the expense of the would-be worker and the consumers that would see cheaper goods from freer trade?

Third, *objectionable*. In still further cases, appeal to fairness is simply objectionable, for economic or political reasons. So, for example,

6. U.S. steel might argue that a protective tariff is fair on the grounds that the United States is the most efficient steel producer in the world. In a system of international trade to *comparative* advantage, however, a U.S. absolute productive advantage in steel, relative to other countries, is beside the point. If U.S. high tech is still more efficient, the country does better to specialize in high tech and import steel from abroad.
7. Low-skilled workers in rich countries commonly complain that trade exposes them to "unfair competition" with low-wage, poor country laborers. But cheap labor is precisely where developing-country comparative advantage lies. To suggest a need for a more "level playing field" is simply to fail to appreciate the point of international trade.[60]
8. Insofar as trade negotiations seek concessions on "market access," in the name of fairness as "reciprocity," fairness assumptions depend on long-debunked mercantilist mistakes about the point of trade (see the Krugman passage quoted earlier).
9. From a more general perspective, the prevalence of talk of "fairness" may seem not only objectionable but on balance pernicious. As with the routine abuse of anti-dumping "fair trade" laws, appeal to fairness often thinly veils pure self-interest, empowers special-interest lobbies, and encourages

---

60. Bhagwati, 1993; Howse and Trebilcock, 1996.

protectionism born of political expedience—all of which may threaten to bring down the liberal trading system.[61]

None of these concerns impugn fairness as structural equity, however. They at most bear on how structural equity is best understood.

Redundancy? Even if some appeals to fairness can be rephrased in economic terms, this is not to say considerations of fairness are not also at work. Economic considerations may make implicit fairness assumptions, as we argued for Pareto and Kaldor-Hicks efficiency. Or the issue may simply be overdetermined. Parallel reasons of fairness may have separate normative force, requiring different forms of argument and perhaps even different policy measures.

In case (1) above, we can agree that rich country farm subsidies are a failure to trade to comparative advantage. They are also arguably a failure of several other kinds: a failure of WTO commitments, a humanitarian disaster, and grossly unfair. Each of these charges is different and requires argument of a quite different kind from bare comparative advantage considerations. For instance, many poor people in developing countries (e.g., "net food importers") benefit from rich country farm subsidies, especially the urban poor, who see cheaper food. If comparative advantage and aggregate income considerations side firmly against the farm subsidies anyway, the full structural equity argument against them is more complicated: it requires justifying the resulting losses to the urban poor. A good case can be made; one can argue that rural farmers tend to be poorer still, in which case it is fair for them to see the gains they reap under more competitive commodities trade. But an argument of this different kind is required.

Moreover, mere considerations of comparative advantage and aggregate income would not necessarily imply that rich-world farmers should be compensated if the subsidies are dropped. But

---

61. As Bhagwati, 1991, p. 14, expresses the concern: "fair trade is a two-faced creature: Once face is friendly to free trade; the other . . . seeks to devour it . . . [as] new definitions of widening scope, of what constitutes unfair, 'unreasonable', unacceptable trade, can be invented in unending improvisations." For similar fears, see Bhagwati, 1993, Hudec, 1990, and Finger, 1992.

insofar as the fairness argument must account for the cost to rich-world "losers" as well, the implication may be that freer agricultural trade *requires* the social insurance scheme to be established or, if existing but minimal, beefed up. Free trade can't *simply* be "efficient"; it must also be fair.

Likewise in case (2). If "dumping" can amount to predatory behavior inconsistent with the idea of a competitive market, a further question is how far this can be part of a structurally equitable market reliance practice. Usually the problem is that "anti-dumping laws" are used for unfair retaliation against normal market competition. Still, it could well be that proper dumping is required for a developing country to reap sufficient gains from the larger trade relation. That is, if developing countries were not gaining as much as they should (by some as yet unspecified fairness criteria), and "dumping" seemed the only effective measure available, then temporary dumping practices might be akin to perfectly legal "safeguards." Advanced countries might, in fairness, forgo legally permitted anti-dumping duties, to "look the other way."

Obscurity? We can grant that a good deal of fairness talk is questionable, and explain why this is so. In case (3), we can grant that the "fair price" is normally that set by the market, at least when the market is fully embedded within nonmarket institutions of property and contract that ensure against various forms of transactional unfairness—coercion, duress, deception, manipulation, exploitation (of monopoly pricing power, or of extraordinary circumstances, etc.). Use of the market to set prices can be part of a larger market reliance practice, domestically among fellow citizens and internationally through relations of trade. Fairness, we may say, is not micro but macro, at least in the first instance: it is not a matter of particular transactions and their outcomes, or the behavior of particular individuals or firms in the market, but rather the larger-scale outcomes that markets, embedded within nonmarket institutions, tend to produce over time.

As for case (4), trade is both different from and much the same as general technological change. In principle, losses people suffer *through the trade relationship* (via the changing structure of production, embedded technology, or otherwise) are the responsibility of the international market reliance practice. Roughly, without that practice the losses in question would not have occurred. If people may also or anyway lose from purely domestic technological innovation, this may be a different, perhaps purely domestic concern, but similar in several respects. It may also be an issue of fairness, of domestic structural equity over time, and call for similar remedies: not compensation on a technology-by-technology basis, but an effective social insurance scheme that ensures an appropriate level of benefit over the longer haul. The scheme may be much like that needed for fairness in trade, but this is only to say they have a dual function, on distinct fairness grounds.[62]

Our focus on macro rather than micro policy suggests that, in case (5), there is nothing necessarily unfair about the job destroyed by imports when an export industry job is equally created. Everything depends on how things are made to work out over time. Job loss *may* be perfectly fair if the larger nonmarket institutions, including the social insurance scheme, *do in fact* ensure overall benefit to the unemployed worker over the course of his or her life. When this condition is not met, however, there is an unfairness case to make. It is insufficient simply that "losers" could, hypothetically, be compensated; they must *actually be compensated* if trade is to be fair to them. Suppose the unemployed worker is severely and irreparably harmed, being afforded no way to restore anything close to the income trajectory he or she would otherwise be on, through no real fault of his or her own; the opportunities are just not there, and not arranged. And suppose the higher-skilled worker whose position is improved by the newly created export-industry job is only slightly better off, while a small number of consumers see only small gains (e.g., slightly cheaper big-screen TV sets). We do not otherwise think it is fair to harm one person simply in order to benefit another, especially if the harm is severe,

---

62. Rodrik, 2011, pp. 59–60, discusses several further reasons that technological change does not suggest the naturalness of laissez-faire as regards outcomes of trade. We not only already regulate technological progress (e.g., in nuclear engineering and genetic engineering), but government regulation often drives technological development (e.g., auto emissions regulations, or subsidized research). Moreover, the regulatory needs are different. The burdens of technological change generally fall upon different groups over time, but the burdens of trade tend to hit the same, uneducated, low-skilled, and immobile people again and again. And while technological change offers sustained and ongoing benefits, the gains from removing trade barriers diminish as trade becomes freer and freer.

the benefit slight, and the beneficiaries few. We would not regard "free trade" as a structurally equitable market reliance practice if the resulting employment restructuring were generally like this— if many people were routinely, irreparably harmed for the sake of very small benefits to a huge number of people.

Objectionable? Nothing we have said in the name of structural equity is objectionable for the economic or political reasons cited above. We can agree in case (6) that captains of industry in U.S. steel have no claim of fairness to competitive advantages against foreign firms: this is inconsistent with the comparative advantage rationale for trade. The structural equity issue chiefly concerns what will happen to the "losers" as the United States specializes in high tech instead, as the steel industry is eroded or destroyed. Do U.S. nonmarket institutions ensure that displaced workers will ultimately gain from life in an open economy over the course of their lives? If not, then structural equity requires that appropriate arrangements be made, for instance, by strengthening the social insurance scheme. When the arrangements are not established, free trade is unfair.[63]

Likewise in case (7). When low-skilled workers in rich countries complain that trade exposes them to "unfair competition" with low-wage, poor country laborers, the complaint is ill-framed. Because cheap labor is precisely where developing countries have a comparative advantage, the demand for a "level playing field" indeed fails to appreciate the point of international trade. But the underlying fairness concern is real: will the low-skilled worker really be better off overall for life in an open society, or does this come at his or her expense? Would he or she have been better off had his or her society been closed to trade over the course of his or her life, or will his or her society make the arrangements needed to ensure that trade is to everyone's overall gain, or at least no one's overall loss?

Turning to politics, we can also agree in case (8) that it is a mistake for trade negotiators to seek concessions on "market access" from other countries, being prepared to "give up" only as much access as is received. This seems unobjectionable only when we focus too much on the trade deal on the bargaining table, instead of on what trade negotiations can and ought to be about: how to

---

63. See Chapter 3.1–3.4 on who the "losers" are.

make the common market reliance practice mutually beneficial, on structurally equitable terms. Insofar as "reciprocity" often means quid pro quo bargaining over gains *measured against the status quo*, this may have little relation—directly or as a general rule—to structural equity in the market reliance practice being shaped by any new rules or institutions agreed to.

For example, in the 1994 Uruguay Round "grand bargain," rich countries asked developing countries for concessions on services and intellectual property in exchange for concessions on agriculture. As we see further in Chapter 9, the intellectual property agreement was damaging to developing countries (e.g., the patent rules would mean higher prices for essential medicines), as well as largely unnecessary, except for increased enforcement powers (the World Intellectual Property Organization already existed).[64] This may have seemed fair as a matter of narrow reciprocity: rich country negotiators felt it was fair not to give something up without getting something in return. But if we consider the common market reliance practice as a whole, the grand bargain was clearly a raw deal. Structural equity already required agricultural and textile liberalization and so it is not a "concession" that could be fairly used to extract reciprocal benefits.

No especially exotic moral judgment was needed for this conclusion; it followed pretty clearly from standing trade law. GATT was founded on ideas of non-discrimination (the most-favored nation and national treatment norms) and reciprocity in market access. But it had also from its inception in 1947 acknowledged, in word if not deed, the special needs of developing countries. Article 36(3), for instance, mentions a "need for positive efforts designed to ensure that less developed contracting parties secure a share in the growth in international trade commensurate with the needs of their economic development." It was only in 1979, during the Tokyo Round, that the rule of non-discrimination was formally waved for developing countries; the Generalized System of Preferences (GSP) provided special tariff reductions, by specified developed countries, for developing-country exports. The understanding was clearly that the liberalization of agriculture and textiles, areas where many less developed countries enjoy

---

64. Irwin, 2002, p. 184, and Bhagwati, 2004, pp. 182–85.

comparative advantage, needed to be provided if the system of trade was to be fair, in the minimal sense of being worth their while. Thus concessions in agriculture and textiles in the Uruguay Round would have made the structure of trade fairer, even if rich countries got nothing in return. A narrowly "unfair bargain" (assessed as a departure from the then-status quo) was *required* for structural equity in trade. (The point equally applies to, and partly motivated, the development-focused Doha Round.)

Finally, we can also agree in case (9) that "fairness" talk is routinely abused, and indeed, that this may often be pernicious—if only because such abuse often leads to substantial structural inequities.[65] That is not to say the *concept* of fairness itself is best left out of trade policy, however.[66] Nor is it to say that fairness concepts and principles are more open to abuse than any other moral concepts that bear in other policy contexts (e.g., domestic judicial or tax systems). The way forward is not to disregard or disparage moral or fairness language—throwing the baby out with the bathwater—but rather to clarify its proper structure, content, and basis, so that abusive language can be more readily seen for what it is.[67]

---

65. Section 301 of the U.S. Trade Act of 1974 is often seen as a locus of protectionist abuse. However, Abbot, 1996, plausibly analyzes a long history of its use under a family of implicit "fairness norms": the norm of adherence to international commitments and law; of nullification and impairment; of non-discrimination; of reciprocity (including "specific reciprocity," "equal access," "national reciprocity," "sectoral reciprocity," "equal outcomes and measurable results,"); and "the norm of the free market," as well as issues of "structural unfairness" and "mercantilist claims." This suggests that a potentially legitimate set of fairness notions is being abused rather than fabricated whole cloth for political advantage.
66. Howse, 2002, argues that "political" appeals to moral and social values have always been part and parcel of the trading system, even before a more recent turn to supposedly value-free governance.
67. This is, e.g., the aim of Howse and Trebilcock, 1996, for a range of moral values (excluding ideas of "fair competition").

CHAPTER THREE

Hobbesian Skepticism

We now turn from economics to politics, from economic skepticism to the political skepticism inspired by Thomas Hobbes. The global economy as we know it is politically decentralized; there is no sovereign power capable of regulating international trade in the way each government regulates its own national economy. According to many social scientists and political theorists, this political reality undercuts the idea of fairness in international relations, or at least opens its applicability or practical significance to serious doubt. In the prevailing condition of "anarchy," the idea goes, each sovereign government is left to set and negotiate its own trade policy in a competitive "self-help" system, a system in which relative bargaining power rules and compliance with trade rules is motivated by national interest rather than fair play. Because nations can have no assurance that concerns for fairness will be reciprocated, talk of fairness and unfairness is out of place. Things are much as Hobbes says: In such a "warre of every man against every man . . . nothing can be Unjust. . . . Where there is no common Power, there is no law: where no Law, no Injustice."[1] Fairness in trade can still be a domestic obligation—perhaps the "losers" from trade should still be compensated. But it has no application *across* borders, whether in domestic trade policy that shapes relative gains between trading partners or in bargaining over market access in trade negotiations.

The Hobbesian argument is particularly forceful because it can happily grant our challenge to economic skepticism in Chapter 2. That is, even if we aren't skeptical about morality or fairness generally, the Hobbesian can insist that the practice of market reliance nevertheless is not governable in the appropriate way. So long as there is no centralized sovereign authority capable of providing assurance that trade rules and expectations will be generally followed, what we call "international law and practice" is not

---

1. Hobbes (1651), 1996, ch. XIII [63], p. 90.

genuine law. And if international law and practice generates no duty to obey, neither does structural equity. Even if structural equity does "apply" as a worthy ideal goal, it fails to "apply" in any sense that *obliges* nations to trade other than according to the perceived national interest. (In Hobbes's terms, it binds not *in foro interno*, but *in foro externo*—only "to a desire that they should take place," but not necessarily "to the putting them in the act.")[2] In short, to the extent there is "unfairness" in trade, no one is responsible for it.

We will see that this position is difficult to maintain for the global economy as we know it. The Hobbesian argument is strongest when a practice is yet to be set up, or exists but threatens to unravel. But the global economy is not in this precarious situation; the market reliance practice that organizes the global economy is well established and, in its basic outline, well assured. The situation is a political but *not* a social "state of nature." But in that case, we will argue, Hobbes's assurance-based argument fails to get traction: one cannot cite lack of assurance as a general excuse for failing the responsibilities of "fair play."

A further question is whether or to what extent this conclusion is of practical consequence. We will see that it weighs against the prevailing norm of "reciprocity" in trade negotiations, understood as quid pro quo bargaining over market access. To bargain in accord with the prevailing balance of power is inconsistent with broadly *legislative* responsibilities arising from the common market reliance practice being shaped. Fairness requires fair bargaining, which requires governments to negotiate toward distributional structural equity.

1. Duties of Fair Play

According to Hobbes, mere international practice does not bind. Covenants without the sword, in Hobbes's terms, are but mere words. But why, exactly, should this be so? When states are involved in a practice of mutual market reliance, why aren't they obliged, in the name of fairness, to abide by and negotiate toward structurally equitable terms of economic cooperation? Hobbes himself offered a principled answer to this question, but it has

2. Ibid., ch. XV.

little relevance in the contemporary global economy. Contemporary neo-realists suggest that the Hobbesian view remains relevant, but they do not offer adequate principled reasons for why responsibilities of fairness should generally fail to apply.

To sharpen the issue, consider two potential *duties of fair play*.

Absent special justification, countries that voluntarily accept benefits from the cooperative activity of others in a common market reliance practice have the following moral obligations:

1. a *duty of fidelity* to comply with established terms of market reliance in good faith (e.g., follow tariff rules, forgo banned subsidies);[3] and
2. a *duty of fair governance* to negotiate toward structurally equitable terms (e.g., in decentralized negotiations, or in trend-setting unilateral action).[4]

In both cases, the "special justification" clause is intended to admit circumstances in which the duty does not apply. For instance, the duty of fidelity might not apply when some market reliance expectation is reasonably seen as grossly unfair (e.g., certain banned exports subsidies are crucial for development). That is, compliance in "good faith" would normally require full compliance with prevailing expectations, interpreted in light of their understood rationale and applicable requirements of structural equity (perhaps as informed by the good faith provisions of public international law). But when a rule, or system of rules, is grossly and manifestly unfair, partial or limited compliance, or even outright disobedience, may be justified. For example, developing countries might adopt illegal pro-development export subsidies, or under-enforce or ignore grossly unfair WTO intellectual property rules (see Chapter 9).

If this case invokes a "special justification," for special circumstances, other cases involve extenuating circumstances of general

---

3. Since GATT/WTO signatories have each explicitly agreed to the treaty, they count as accepting the benefits of the practice, in a way that obligates one to share in its burdens (see also "fair play" in Chapter 5.9).
4. For further discussion, see Chapter 5.9 as well as Chapter 10 on the nature of exploitation.

scope. Suppose trading countries lacked assurance of widespread compliance with the general market reliance practice, as, for example, during the interwar years. Then they may have no duty of fair governance (or of fidelity) to do other than what best serves their own economic goals. In negotiations, they can simply exploit to the hilt whatever bargaining power they have. Hobbes offers a version of this challenge, which cites *lack of assurance, weighed in the scales of self-preservation*. He explains:

> If a Covenant be made, wherein neither of the parties performe presently, but trust in one another; in a condition of meer Nature (which is a condition of Warre of every man against every man,) upon any reasonable suspition, it is Voyd; But if there be a common Power set over them both, with right and force sufficient to compel performance; it is not Voyd. For he that performeth first, has no assurance the other will perform after; because the bonds of words are too weak to bridel mens ambition, avarice, anger, and other passions. . . .[5]

Of course, a mere "reasonable suspition" of non-compliance would not normally render an agreement "Voyd"; if I promise you a ride to the airport from your house, but then hear from a friend that you *might* not be home in time for some reason, I'm still obligated to show, even if I now reasonably suspect that you won't be there (I might be reasonably mistaken, because you are home in time). Hobbes's argument therefore seems to turn on an implausibly lax theory of extenuating circumstances.

The argument is also open, however, to a more charitable reading. Mere "reasonable suspicion" excuses only because life and death is at stake. When "performing first" in a covenant will "expose [one] to Prey,"[6] one is thrown back upon one's right of self-defense (the "Right of Nature") to preserve one's life. Indeed, the point stands even if we further constrain self-defense, requiring, for instance, that the threat be credible and imminent. So long as the imagined situation of uncertainty is sufficiently dark and grave, even if merely unfortunate, Hobbes points to circumstances in which a duty of fair play would generally not apply.[7]

---

5. Hobbes (1651), 1996, ch. XIV [68], p. 96.
6. Ibid., p. 92.
7. For further discussion of assurance and self-defense, see Chapter 4.1.

2. Contemporary Practice

Does this argument let contemporary trading nations off the hook? Whatever was true in Hobbes's day, we saw in Chapter 2 that the basic assurance problem in trade has long been overcome, despite the absence of global sovereign rule. The liberal order of trade is now well established. Every country of the world can safely assume that it will endure for the foreseeable future. The GATT system was extraordinarily successful in freeing trade, in contrast with the ill-assured interwar years, partly because it offered assurances in several ways: the "discipline" imposed by the non-discrimination norms (the most-favored nation and national treatment norms) reduced concerns of arbitrariness in trade policy; various "opt outs" and "escape clauses" (safeguards, anti-dumping measures, exemptions, etc.) provided assurance that trade protection would be available for social purposes if need be; and a background of shared values offered confidence that trade protection would be used only for mutually agreeable reasons (e.g., social protection, in light of common moral values).[8] The WTO reforms added further grounds for confidence. The system is now an "all or nothing" agreement, with an enhanced dispute resolution system enforced by a reciprocal sanctioning system. It is now widely believed that no country involved can afford to quit the system, and that no country can afford not to join. If further assurances are wanted, observe that even the global financial crisis of 2008–2009 testifies to the resilience of the liberal order of trade. Not only did governments substantially (if imperfectly) coordinate fiscal and monetary policies but they also largely avoided trade barriers—despite the fact that they offer desperately needed and readily available shorter-term gains. Finally, trade now rarely creates national security risks (unlike in the interwar years). Threats of world war have given way to security problems of smaller scale—terrorism, regional crises, genocide, and civil war—and there is no manifest reason to think this security situation will change dramatically.

If "assurance game" situations still arise in economic policy, our claim is that they have largely become localized within the broader framework of economic law and practice. There is, in

---

8. On the role of values, see Ruggie, 1982, and Howse, 2002. On the stabilizing role of "opt outs," see Rodrik, 2007, ch. 7.

fact, sufficient (if not universal) compliance for duties of fair play to apply. Government decision making is at least substantially shaped by prevailing rules and understandings, even when lack of assurance informs the application of vaguely specified expectations to concrete policy issues. The shaping role is seen as governments consider litigation risks, reputational costs, or ways they or their relationships may be injured when other governments follow suit. If the specific extent and nature of these roles is subject to substantial debate among theorists of international law and politics, our point is about the broad social context and its tendencies. Few if any countries can entertain "reasonable suspicion" that most other countries are not cooperating in the overall economic practice, or that cooperation would create any new grave threats to national security.[9] It is at best unclear, then, how Hobbes's proposed "special justification" could still apply.[10]

3. The "National Interest"

A Hobbesian argument might of course be updated, and the Hobbesian perspective on international relations is indeed well represented in the contemporary theory of international relations. Do such "neo-realists" offer principled rationale for governments to generally have an appropriate "special justification" for setting aside duties of fair play? The suggestions tend to revolve around different conceptions of "national interest." We will suggest that no conception of "national interest" offers an excusing rationale of a general, principled kind.

---

9. If an assurance-providing sovereign has thus not historically been necessary, it also wasn't necessarily *sufficient*, or at least wouldn't have been sufficient in the unstable interwar years. As Ruggie, 1992, p. 392, explains: ". . . efforts to construct international economic regimes in the interwar period failed not because of the lack of a hegemon. They failed because, even had there been a hegemon, they stood in contradiction to the transformation in the mediating role of the state between market and society, which altered fundamentally the social purposes of domestic and international authority."
10. The same points apply to Hans Morgenthau's realism, e.g., in Morgenthau, 1946, which loses any real resonance absent the grave existential security threats of his day.

In some of its uses, the notion of the "national interest" is trivial or empty, as when it refers to *whatever in fact motivates* nations to do what they do (i.e., to their "revealed preferences.") The claim that "nations always act in the national interest" is then a tautology and fully consistent with robust *moral* national motivation. Suppose developing countries are "given a break," in fairness, by rich countries, as they arguably did in agreeing to the Doha Round, which focused on agricultural liberalization (ignore for the moment the fact that rich countries have failed to follow through). In that case fairness is, *by definition*, in the rich countries' "national interest," even when they suffer major economic costs.

In distinct but similar cases, talk of the "national interest" is not empty but open to moral content in any case. "Social constructivists" emphasize that a state's "identities" define its interests. In many cases, national security interests will not appear to be threatened by military or economic power abroad, simply because the foreign power is identified as a "friend."[11] The same might be true in trade: a potential beggar-thy-neighbor gain would not be in the "national economic interest" because the foreign countries it burdens are counted as "partners" or "fellow participants" in a relationship of mutual benefit.[12]

Some neo-realists assert a more substantial national psychological egoism. On one such view, national officials are always or chiefly motivated by what they regard as benefits specifically to the country or countrymen they represent, even at what is regarded as a great expense to foreigners.[13] Such motivation no doubt exists. But of course the mere fact that it does exist, or even that it is prevalent, by itself provides no reason to think national officials should not be bound by a duty of fair play. The report, "I usually look out for my own," simply fails to address the challenge: "Don't you think you ought to play fair?" The ready reply is: "I'm not saying you do in fact play fair, but that you *ought* to." We need a *rationale* for why the putative motivational facts undercut a duty of fair play if they are to be of any relevance.

---

11. Milner, 1991; Wendt, 1992; Ruggie, 1998.
12. For a sample of the emerging global economic "constructivist" literature, see Abdelal et al., 2010.
13. Psychological egoism can have several bases: Hobbes, on some readings (especially in *De Cive*), sees it as a general psychological truth, even if also within each agent's Right of Nature to self-preservation.

We would have such a rationale if nations were by and large *incapable* of anything but national egoism (in the sense specified earlier). An agent cannot reasonably be asked to do what he or she is incapable of, so no duty of fair play would apply. But this strong claim is empirically doubtful. Moral considerations arguably have *some* historical role in motivating restraint in war, humanitarian assistance and intervention, and human rights practice.[14] Likewise, international economic relations arguably involve the occasional if not infrequent concessions in the name of fairness. Compare individual persons. There is considerable evidence that people worldwide respond to fairness considerations for their own sake. They tend to refuse a personal benefit in the "ultimatum game," for example, because the proposed split seems too unfair.[15] Citizens will presumably have similar preferences for how their government relates with foreign countries (I personally know many people who do). Likewise with national officials (who are of course people too): they are at least open to similar motivations, perhaps in part by recognition that the citizens they represent have them. In that case, the present incapacity thesis would have to insist that officials somehow become wholly incapable of fairness motivation once they have assumed their national roles. But why would mere assumption of a role wholly disable certain motivations (as opposed to simply recommending against them)? Empirical evidence for such a phenomenon has never been provided and seems unlikely to emerge. Indeed, there is an empirical case to make that fairness considerations in fact motivate trade negotiation behavior.[16]

Kenneth Waltz's structural realism at least provides a general rationale that would explain why nations and their officials might be drawn into policies of national "self-help," even despite their altruistic wishes: the very structure of the international system induces such motivation. As Waltz explains:

> Structures encourage certain behaviors and penalize those who do not respond to the encouragement.... In an unorganized realm each unit's incentive is to put itself in a position to be able to take care of itself since no one else can be counted on to do so. The

---

14. Goldstein, 1988.
15. Henrich et al., 2001, 2002.
16. Chan, 1985; Finger et al., 1999.

international imperative is "take care of yourself"! Some leaders of nations may understand that the well-being of all of them would increase through their participation in a fuller division of labor. [Yet] [s]tates do not willingly place themselves in situations of increased dependence. In a self-help system, considerations of security subordinate economic gain to political interest.[17]

For our purposes, everything depends on what sort of "encouragement" or "incentive" to self-help the international system provides. The issue is not simply a matter of psychological tendency; we find a principled excuse or justification for self-help only when we consider, in a moral or normative key, what reasons for action nations thereby have, regardless of what reasons actually motivate them to act. (The duties of fair play purport that there are such reasons, and so must be answered in kind.) So the crucial question is not, Do the suggested structural incentives give nations *some* reason to avoid anything like "increased dependence"? The question is rather, Do nations thereby have *sufficient* reasons, which appropriately silence any and all other considerations, even of the mutual benefits of trade? For if nations merely have *some* reason to watch their backs, the strength of that reason may vary in strength across contexts and may sometimes or often be appropriately outweighed by more powerful reasons to expand the division of labor for the sake of the gains of trade. Waltz's account needs to show that this is never or rarely or not normally the case. But it is hard to see how it could show this without stepping beyond its descriptive and explanatory aims into the domain of substantive moral and prudential doctrine.

Even so, let us presume, for the sake of argument, that nations more or less do what they have reason to do, in which case their "revealed preferences" indicate their real reasons for action. Waltz's model still does not seem to capture much of emergent law and practice. The two world wars once made it credible to hold that nations are preoccupied with relative economic gains, especially as they shape the balance of international power and perceived national security interests.[18] Yet the steady emergence

---

17. Waltz, 1979, pp. 106–7.
18. Neo-realists, e.g., Grieco, 1988, generally place special emphasis on relative gains from a national security perspective. For criticism of neo-realism as unrealistic about existing threats, see Keohane, 1993.

of "regimes," such as the GATT agreement, has suggested that nations are also susceptible to more cooperative motives.[19] According to neo-liberal institutionalist accounts of the trend, nations have learned to worry less about relative gains, especially over the short run, for the sake of mutually beneficial cooperation into the further future.[20] (This is said to be true despite an assumption of national egoism, made for the sake of argument.) Even prominent neo-realists have become concessive, suggesting only that competitive motivation still has an important, often underappreciated explanatory role to play.[21]

Competitive motivation is surely common in international affairs. But even that would not imply that fairness as mutuality or reciprocity is rarely what motivates foreign economic policy, let alone that states are incapable of acting for the sake of fairness. Different social contexts and different international relationships can cue different motivational reactions. Indeed, once it is granted that nations at least in many cases value *jointly beneficial cooperation*, we are a short step to the morally inclusive sense of "national interest" that assigns value to *reciprocal benefit alongside national gain*. It is then a still shorter step to motivation by *fairness as reciprocity*. Nations, like people generally, may offer fair return to others for their cooperation without any very specific sense of how doing so is justified in purely self-interested terms.[22] While it could in theory be shown that such motivation is never or rarely to be found—because nations are, after all, pure egoists— a conclusive empirical argument for this is not likely to emerge.

To be sure, nations do horrible things. They are often less than resolute in their commitment to fairness, especially when it comes

---

19. For general reasons to doubt that coercion (of the sort a centralized authority might exercise) plays much of a role in explaining why governments comply with international agreements, see the "process" or cooperative view of sovereignty in Chayes and Chayes, 1995.
20. Keohane, 2002.
21. Waltz, 1986, p. 329. As one leading neo-realist, Joseph Grieco, 1993, p. 302, explains, "In general, realists have argued that cooperation is possible under anarchy, but that it is harder to achieve, more difficult to maintain, and more dependent on state power than is appreciated by the institutionalist tradition."
22. See Gibbard, 1991, on reciprocity, as distinct from both full impartiality and mere mutual advantage. Rawls, 1993, p. 17, agrees with Gibbard that his concern is with this "intermediate" idea.

at a substantial cost. Like individuals in the "ultimatum game," they make and accept "exploitative" offers, that is, offers which, though not grossly unfair, are not clearly fair, either—not, say, what both parties would agree to with more equal bargaining power. But, again, this is not to say nations are incapable of fairness, or that they have overwhelming reasons of self-interest, and so it is not to give a "special justification" for why a duty of fair play does not apply. The fact that nations are horrible and less than resolute about fairness does not show that they have no reason, or insufficient reasons, to be less horrible or more resolute about offering fair terms.

4. Barganing Without Assurance

A further line of Hobbesian argument is more plausible because it is limited to the bargaining table. Beyond certain political constraints (e.g., the rule of consensus in WTO negotiations), tough negotiations and relative bargaining power often hold sway in international economic politics.[23] Structural equity is often not foremost on the trade negotiator's mind. Even if the bargaining culture could be otherwise, the bare fact of tough negotiations may be all it takes for Hobbesian reasons of self-defense to apply.

To see this, suppose the situation could indeed be otherwise: let us say that any given officials are disposed to negotiate toward a structurally equitable practice, as understood by whatever consensus there is, *provided assurances that other officials would do likewise*. Even so, as long as uncertainty about the negotiating behavior of others prevails—if only because tough bargaining is commonly the order of the day—why isn't political self-defense justified? Why should a duty of fair governance apply? If a well-intentioned official negotiated toward structurally equitable terms anyway, without assurances that others will do so as well, he may, in Hobbes's terms, simply "expose himselfe to Prey" by officials with less high-minded concerns. At best, it may then be argued, nations should follow the going rule of "reciprocity" in negotiations, not in the name of fairness, but as shrewd bargaining strategy: each country concedes only as much as it gets (by whatever measure of

---

23. On bargaining power, see Caporaso, 1978, and Harsanyi, 1965, 1969.

"national interest" is in play) so to ensure that it is not taken advantage of.

Such circumstances clearly do arise, interwar negotiations being a plausible case in point.[24] But are contemporary trade negotiations like this? In the interwar years, the main task was to see whether nations could get a mutual market reliance practice up and running. As explained, this problem is long overcome. The task of contemporary negotiations is merely to *modify* the terms of cooperation that is already going on. The function of negotiations, in other words, is not *constitutive*—not to set up, stabilize, or reestablish a practice—but *legislative*: to set or shape the specific terms of market reliance upon which cooperation will very likely proceed. Why, then, shouldn't negotiators be obliged to do what they can to negotiate toward a structurally equitable practice? Why wouldn't the choice to simply exploit one's bargaining advantages to the hilt just then be a *failure* of fair play, which is to say that the duty of fair governance is violated and so *applies* in trade negotiations?

Notice that fair governance will *not* require setting the perceived "national interest" aside. The case need not be like a hyper-cooperative group of friends, or a community of saints, who cannot make a decision because no one is willing to express a firm preference. Structural equity will involve mutual national benefit over time, and we may presume that officials of a given country are usually in the best position to know what rules or policies would be most beneficial to it. Making claims in the name of the "national interest" can thus be a form of *cooperation* in negotiations.

So, indeed, can "hard bargaining." Countries with limited bargaining power (that is, most developing and less developed societies, perhaps with exceptions such as China) can *cooperatively*

---

24. As an influential 1942 League of Nations report described the interwar period, ". . . trade was consistently regarded as a form of warfare, as a vast game of beggar-my-neighbor, rather than as a cooperative activity from the extension of which all stood to benefit. The latter was the premise on which the post-war conferences based their recommendations—a premise accepted by all in theory but repudiated by almost all in practice. It was repudiated in practice because, as the issue presented itself on one occasion after another, it seemed only too evident that a Government that did not use its bargaining powers would always come off second-best." League of Nations, *Commercial Policy in the Interwar Period: International Proposals and National Policies* (Official No.: 1942.II.A.6). Quoted in Hudec, 1975, p. 6.

"exploit" what bargaining advantages they have to ensure that their interests are *adequately* represented when those interests will otherwise, in all likelihood, be slighted. This may involve various bargaining tactics, including threatening an inconvenient trade war (that may have implications for other issue-areas, such as security, where the less dependent parties may have greater power, or at least be able to bring more powerful countries to the bargaining table);[25] threatening partial or issue-specific retaliation without wholly ceasing trade; increasing the costs of retaliation by banning together bargaining coalitions (as the "BRIC" countries—Brazil, Russia, India, China—now do); increasing trade with one another in order to reduce dependence that empowers rich countries (an emerging trend); formally legitimizing the specified retaliation by seeking rulings in local, foreign, and international courts (as Brazil has in the WTO against U.S. cotton subsidies); using moral suasion with the support of international civil society (e.g., Oxfam's crusade against rich country farm subsidies); and so on.

Most important, when developing countries so negotiate, it will not follow that rich countries have a corresponding right of self-defense. Insofar as the duty of fair governance binds, their corresponding responsibility is to *not* fully exploit their superior bargaining position but rather to use it to guide negotiations toward structurally equitable terms. They can of course bring their perceived "national interests" to bear, insofar as they are relevant to structural equity. What they cannot do, consistent with the duty of fair governance, is advocate the "national interest" at the *expense* of structural equity in the overall market reliance practice, as they arguably did, for example, in insisting on intellectual property rules in the Uruguay Round (see Chapter 9).

To be sure, like many parties to negotiations that enjoy superior bargaining power, rich countries are prone to overestimate the force of their own fairness claims. This is one reason that hard bargaining by developing countries can be required if a structurally equitable practice is to emerge. And lack of clarity about what structural equity requires may also encourage countries to err on

---

25. This can work because trade involves *mutual but asymmetric dependence*, not complete dependency by one party and domination by the other. See Caporaso, 1978, and Keohane and Nye, 2001.

the side of self-interest. But this shows only that there is no substitute for high-quality policy analysis and supportive political culture (e.g., in international civil society) informed by appropriate fairness principles. We offer no such empirical analysis, but will (in Chapter 7) propose principles that might have this regulative role.

Accordingly, the rule of "reciprocity" may often be *inconsistent* with cooperative negotiations, at least when "gains" and "concessions" are measured by the status quo. There is then no reason to think quid pro quo bargaining will yield an overall structurally equitable market reliance practice.[26] There's no reason to presume that the overall practice at a particular time (e.g., the start of the Uruguay Round) is fair, so it is not an appropriate baseline from which fair deals can be struck. A norm of "reciprocity" which is *not* essentially sensitive to the status quo might have some useful instrumental role: it may, in some form or other, stabilize negotiations over time, limit the painful structural adjustments governments must manage at a given time, or create a desirable balance of special interest groups.[27] But most likely, multilateral trade governance needs to be supplemented, for instance, with a mechanism to induce unreciprocated trade barrier reductions where they are fair. If the least-developed WTO member countries are owed unreciprocated market access, for example, the WTO secretariat might adjudicate the deal as the first phase of each negotiating round, as a condition for moving forward with normal bargaining. The "transfer round" might be finalized only after normal negotiations had concluded, so that least-developed countries gain in initial bargaining power without being able to wreck the whole process.[28] But whatever the merits of such proposals, the present point is that the appropriate form of trade governance is largely if not entirely an *instrumental* matter: everything depends on what is most likely to induce reforms in the direction of structural equity in the trade practice overall.[29]

---

26. Keohane, 1986, distinguishes between "specific" reciprocity, concerned with exchange of items of equal value, and "diffuse" reciprocity, which, because less well defined, requires a sense of cooperative obligation and trust. See also Kapstein, 2006.
27. Brown and Stern, 2007.
28. Collier, 2007, pp. 171–72.
29. But see also the "procedural" concerns discussed in Chapter 5.9.

5. Negotiation as Legislation

In other words, the true task of negotiations is legislative, not constitutive: what is being negotiated, ultimately, is not the deal on the table but the overall scheme of economic cooperation. Here talk of "legislation" is more than a philosophically suggestive metaphor. Our argument might be put in a legislative key as follows. The absence of centralized political authority means not that a stable, mutually assured market reliance practice is impossible or impractical or unlikely, but only that trading nations are at once the subjects and the authors of economic law, with no legislative intermediary. At least in some basic sense, there is no fundamental difference between trade negotiations and the workings of a domestic legislature, where moral legislative responsibilities of fair governance presumably clearly apply.

Compare rule by a single absolute monarch: the law is given by the decrees of a single human agent, expressing a single human agent's state of mind. But proper legislatures can also be collectives, personified.[30] In domestic law, conscientious judges routinely view the varying minds of a congress or parliament as a personified author of law. At the national level, we often personify varying and opposed members of different branches of government as constituting a single authority. So why not personify in trade? This would be inappropriate if the agents involved were wholly unorganized, or were organized but unable to conceptualize and regulate larger patterns of behavior. But trade negotiators are not in this position; they are often socially coordinated by largely shared purposes, if only those commonly understood as the basic purposes of the overall market reliance practice itself. Trade talks are not and need not be tightly constrained by established procedural rules, in the way procedural rules unite branches of government or a legislative house. Yet they do normally proceed, in negotiation rounds, under the auspices of previously formulated and agreed upon negotiation goals. These are set by a range of broadly normative concerns present in the background political culture, and they may and often do include considerations of structural equity in trade. The

---

30. Dworkin, 1986, p. 167ff.

suggested analogy with domestic government is perhaps closest when state legislators are at political war—when procedural rules become fluid, and laws emerge more than usual as mere creatures of political bargaining advantage. Even so, we routinely personify such a legislature as being of one mind. If that can be appropriate, then the difference between state government and trade negotiations is largely a difference in degree rather than a difference in kind.

Political responsibility no doubt differs across these and other contexts in various important ways. For our purposes, the essential general thought is that organization as social practice, as specified in Chapter 2.1, generates (non-distributive) *collective* governance responsibilities for regulating the practice as structural equity requires. Collective responsibility, in this non-distributive sense, is a two-stage affair: it is assigned in the first instance to the organized group as a whole, for how the common practice is organized, and only secondarily to particular agents, according to their position within the practice, given their political circumstances and governance powers.

The case is thus unlike those in which responsibility falls without remainder to each or many members of a group and not to the group as a collective (e.g., a diffuse mob, or co-religionists spread around the world). The collective bears responsibility in the first instance.[31] But neither do we assume that a randomly collected group of agents might be responsible as a collective in the present sense.[32] There may be no specifically collective fault when several agents fail to organize themselves because of unfavorable conditions, insufficient assurance, or sheer lack of willingness; fault may need to be assigned to each agent, individually, or not at all. We can assume that a background of prior organization among the agents is required, though we can sidestep delicate questions about what the minimum necessary organizational conditions

---

31. Such collective responsibilities are also distinct from responsibilities that merely *concern* a group, such as the Hart/Rawls principle of fair play (see Chapter 5.9). The suggested principle concerns the group of agents organized as the practice in question; when someone takes a free ride, any participant can complain on the group's behalf. But this is not to say that a genuinely (non-distributive) collective responsibility is at work. The responsibility not to "free ride" may fall only to individuals.
32. As argued by Held, 1970.

are.³³ It is enough, for our purposes, that organizing into a mutual market reliance practice *suffices* to generate collective governance responsibilities for the set of nations involved, much as organization as a domestic legislature does for its officials and democratic society does for its citizens.

Accordingly, the duty of fair governance, as characterized earlier in this chapter, is assigned in the first instance to the set of nations participating in the economic system as a collective, and only secondarily to particular nations according to their particular political circumstances and governance powers. The diverging negotiation responsibilities of rich and poor countries as outlined reflect such secondary responsibility assignments, according to their relative political positions and bargaining power.

The idea, in other words, is that there are two quite different contexts in which an agent might be tempted to "throw up his or her hands" in the face of unruly politics. The first reflects mere tragic coordination failure. The second reflects unfairness and social injustice. In the first kind of case, agents fail to be organized in desirable ways merely because of unfortunate or unavoidable circumstances. Perhaps pervasive distrust hobbles meaningful cooperation for a time, as it did in the interwar years. Indeed, the parties may even be *morally* motivated but lack reasonable assurances about what other morally motivated agents will do, simply as bad evidential luck (see Chapter 4.1). Even if such situations involve tragic "cosmic unfairness," no one may be responsible for it. The situation is quite different, on the other hand, when governable social practice exists and is relatively assured and yet the agents involved fail to adopt feasible improvements required for structural equity. Even if there is little each particular agent can do for effective change in the direction of greater structural equity, taken by himself or herself, it is not appropriate to say that no one is responsible. To the extent the practice stands structurally inequitable, the organized group remains collectively responsible to move in the direction of equity. And while the group bears responsibility in the first instance, many or most of the parties involved will own a share of the blame.³⁴

---

33. Examples from the large relevant literature include Feinberg, 1968; Dworkin, 1986; pp. 167–75; Kutz, 2000; and Miller, 2004.
34. What share of responsibility each bears and why is a further question of the "ethics of complicity," in light of each agent's circumstances, costs of action, role in or relation to the practice, and so on.

6. Sovereignty, Coercion, and Justice

We have yet to comment on the relation between fairness in trade and *social or socioeconomic distributive justice*. For broadly Hobbesian reasons, recent "coercion-based theories," defended in different forms by Michael Blake, Thomas Nagel, and Matthias Risse, would not classify fairness in mutual market reliance as an issue of socioeconomic distributive justice. According to such views, that special kind of moral issue is triggered only under a sovereign's rule (Nagel), or at least under a coercive legal order of the sort found only or mainly in the coercive state (Blake and Risse).[35] That is not to say that morality has no scope: humanitarian duties, human rights, or even (for Risse) collective resource ownership still apply. But we do not, it is suggested, find issues of socioeconomic distributive justice across societies of the same strong egalitarian kind that arise within each domestic state.

From a practical point of view, the issue of moral classification may seem purely academic: If nations are subject to moral duties to advance structural equity in the global economy, what turns on calling this a matter of "justice" or "socioeconomic distributive justice"? What's in a name? Nevertheless, political philosophy is concerned with understanding general differences within the moral domain, both for their own sake and because they potentially bear on what forms of justification are appropriate and on what trade-offs between moral values may be made in practice and institutional design. Our emerging conception of global economic fairness represents an alternative to coercion-based theories without moving to a fully "cosmopolitan" position that is largely insensitive to associational forms and the distinctive forms of power they exercise. It is therefore worth developing the contrast with coercion-based views, in order to suggest how the relation between justice and structural equity in trade might be understood, as well as to further pursue relevant Hobbesian themes.

Nagel's version is particularly uncompromising. Beyond basic humanitarian or human rights requirements, which do not govern relative distribution as such, the special egalitarian demand of justice to "eliminate arbitrary inequalities" arises only given an exercise of authority of the direct kind found within domestic law. Domestic law is a directive system that tells individuals what to

---

35. Blake, 2001; Nagel, 2005; Risse, 2012.

do by orders backed by force. If this is not to be "pure coercion," but rather a legitimate exercise of *authority*, then the law must "claim our active cooperation" and so implicitly give us "standing to ask why we should accept" the social system it organizes and any arbitrary inequalities it generates.[36] According to Nagel,

> ... it is this complex fact—that we are both putative joint authors of the coercively imposed system, and subject to its norms, i.e., expected to accept their authority even when the collective decision diverges from our own personal preferences—that creates the special presumption against arbitrary inequalities in our treatment by the system.[37]

By contrast, international law and institutions are only indirectly related to the lives of individuals, as mediated by the domestic state.

> They are set up by bargaining among mutually self-interested sovereign parties. International institutions act not in the name of individuals, but in the name of the states or state instruments and agencies that have created them. Hence the responsibility of those institutions toward those individuals is filtered through the states that represent and bear primary responsibility for those individuals.[38]

Nagel takes the "filter" of domestic institutions to make all the difference. It means that

> [international institutions] are not collectively enacted and coercively imposed in the name of all the individuals whose lives they affect; and they do not ask for the kind of authorization by individuals that carries with it a responsibility to treat all those individuals in some sense equally.[39]

Nagel seems quite right about the general form of international economic rules. Trade rules addressed, say, to the officials setting tariff schedules will not require anything of producers or

---

36. Nagel, 2005, p. 129.
37. Ibid., pp. 128–29.
38. Ibid., p. 138.
39. Ibid., p. 139.

consumers per se, even as the change in tariffs changes relative prices and so the incentives of each. It is partly for such reasons that we have treated the global economy as organized by a fundamentally international relationship, by a practice in which the primary participants are whole societies rather than individuals. But why should this mean that questions of fairness about its organizing structure cannot count as questions of socioeconomic justice? Even if they are less profound for individual prospects than domestic institutions, the systems of international trade, finance, and money remain highly consequential, over time, for how the world's wealth is distributed around the globe. Very large sums of money are involved, and their flow systematically affects relative prospects for both countries and their respective social classes. The concern need not be with profound outcomes or "arbitrary" inequalities as such, but rather the inequalities generated specifically by the internationally organized global economic relationship. The concern with "arbitrariness" is simply that inequalities must arise for appropriate reasons if the larger social practice is to be justifiable to all. In what sense, we may ask, is this not a socioeconomic justice concern?

Nagel suggests that the international system is not implicitly asking for my authorization, as an individual person, simply in directing the conduct of my country and its officials, and that this makes all the difference. Much as in the case of illegal immigrants facing guns at the border, "since no acceptance is demanded..., no justification is required... It is sufficient... that the polices do not violate... prepolitical human rights."[40] But even if *one* issue of legitimate authority does not present itself, it is unclear why questions of justification about relative distribution are therefore out of court. The basic question, we may say, is not what the international system does or does not implicitly ask of me, but what I might ask of it: Does the going practice of market reliance treat me or my country fairly? Do the relative advantages and disadvantages that result, across countries and within their respective classes, arise for the right reasons—reasons that every one affected, if reasonable and well-informed, could find acceptable if they thought about it?

Nagel claims that "obligations of justice and presumptions in favor of equal consideration" "will not emerge merely from

---

40. Ibid., p. 130.

cooperation and the conventions that make cooperation possible."[41] The reason, presumably, is that "cooperation" could in principle be fully voluntary and shaped entirely by self-interested negotiations in a way that generates procedural constraints on transactions and deal-making—limitations on deception, coercion, manipulation, and so on—and nothing more. But we can admit that something more is required without insisting on sovereign rule. We have argued that the global economy is organized by a collectively sustained social practice, which is governed, not on a transaction-by-transaction basis, but within a political and social framework that sets rules and expectations that shape the structure of economic production and the distribution of wealth within economies and around the world. The absence of centralized rule does not imply an absence of authority, we have suggested, but only that trading nations are at once the subjects and the authors of economic law, with no legislative intermediary. They are collectively responsible for the international structure and profound outcomes that result—responsible, that is, to comply with and negotiate toward structurally equitable terms. Can we not aptly say that the global economy is *unjustly* organized—that its organizing market reliance practice is socially unjust—when nations fail to live up to this responsibility?

Nagel emphasizes the role of self-interested bargaining, but we have already suggested that this is consistent with a collective responsibility of structural equity. Indeed, it supports one plausible way of treating the question of structural equity as a question of social justice. Structural equity, we may say, is about whether the practice of market reliance embodies the influence of arbitrary bargaining advantages. The idea that a practice can "embody" the arbitrary exercise of bargaining power is the negative corollary of Rawls's well-known thesis that a free agreement in fair conditions (from behind a veil of ignorance) necessarily gives rise to a fair practice (or rather principles which, when followed, make for fair practice). That is, if a practice is a *mere* function of relative bargaining advantage, then this can only mean the practice treats those it affects on arbitrary terms. For there is no general reason to suppose that any or all of the many factors that in fact influence

---

41. Ibid., p. 143.

bargaining advantage at a particular time and place are other than *irrelevant* to the question of whether the practice is fair or justified. It would be different if there were some reason to suppose the various determinants of bargaining advantage tracked considerations relevant to what could be justified to all those involved. But there's no reason to suppose this is the case in the world as we know it, not least in international relations.

Blake's coercion-based theory is potentially more inclusive than Nagel's. The trigger for distinctive egalitarian requirements is not an implicit request for authorization, but rather a coercive legal order's more general, inevitable role both in maintaining and potentially threatening the autonomous functioning of individuals. This permits some scope for insisting on the distinctiveness of the coercive state while also evaluating international institutions in the register of socioeconomic justice. According to Blake:

> No matter how substantive the links of trade, diplomacy, or international agreement, the institutions present at the international level do not engage in the same sort of coercive practices against individual moral agents.... [I]nternational practices can indeed be coercive—we might understand certain sorts of exploitative trade relationships under this heading, and so a theory concerned with autonomy must condemn such relationships or seek to justify them. [Yet] only the relationship of common citizenship is a relationship potentially justifiable through equality in distributive shares.[42]

As for what the relevant "exploitative trade relationships" are, Blake does not say. A plausible example (from finance rather than trade) would be international bank loan conditionality. In the 1990s, Bolivia was pressured to privatize water rights, as a condition of much needed loans, even as many Bolivian citizens were unable to meet their basic water needs (and so were less "autonomous" or "lacking in reasonable options" in that very basic regard). Such cases arguably raise important questions of socioeconomic justice, in part because autonomy is infringed, perhaps at both personal and national levels.[43] Yet the case is arguably unlike domestic coercive law; the form of "coercion" or "exploitation"

---

42. Blake, 2001, p. 265.
43. See Hassoun, 2012, for development of this theme.

involved in international loan conditionality has a different, less direct, or even lesser significance.[44]

We may happily grant that domestic and international institutions have important moral differences that should be noted and preserved. As a rule, we should "lump" social realities together only when we have a clear rationale for this, and otherwise let each thing be the moral thing it is, and not another moral thing. Blake means to suggest, however, that autonomy-infringing coercion is a general *necessary* condition for socioeconomic justice questions of "relative deprivation," and that international economic institutions do not qualify. This suggestion is harder to see.

As noted in Chapter 2 and further discussed in Chapter 9, WTO intellectual property standards were adopted largely because advanced countries unfairly exploited their superior bargaining position in the Uruguay Round negotiations. Developing countries accepted intellectual property expectations, which largely hinder their development prospects, as part of a "grand bargain" for agricultural liberalization that was arguably owed to them in fairness anyway. The unfairness does not lie clearly in threats to individual autonomy. Under the required intellectual property systems, developing-country actors have weaker incentives to appropriate foreign ideas or technology, because royalties must be paid. But this is not obviously objectionable as an infringement upon autonomous functioning, at least not any more than other taxation. Moreover, insofar as the rules do imply a loss of commercial opportunity for market actors, it is not clear why the unfairness must count as a threat to autonomy simply for it to be aptly named a social injustice. The injustice can consist of the fact that developing country-prospects are significantly disadvantaged for the sake of benefits to the relatively rich bearers of intellectual property rights, mainly in advanced countries. The net distributive effect is a transfer from poor countries to rich ones. Although the structural inequity is perhaps not quite the same as an unfair (e.g., highly regressive) domestic tax system, it seems not only an issue of relative socioeconomic distribution across societies, but highly consequential.

There are many cases of this kind, within trade law and general practice. The larger argument of this book, again, is that the structural equity issue arises, with substantial (albeit limited) egalitarian

44. Risse, 2012.

upshot, for the international market reliance practice that organizes the global economy as a whole. We may even regard the general issue of structural equity as related to the conditions for "coercion" or "exploitation," at least in a broad sense. The WTO and larger global economy represent a "voluntary association" in the formal sense that sovereign states are legally free to leave or never join. But they are not "voluntary" in any sense that legitimates any market outcomes that happen to result. Nowadays no country can afford not to participate. Formal rules in the WTO come "all or nothing," and they are enforceable by judicial rulings and coordinated reciprocal sanctions. Even in the relatively free-wheeling case of capital liberalization there are powerful market and social pressures to integrate as conventional wisdom dictates (e.g., to liberalize or adopt only certain limited capital controls). Although the richest countries enjoy huge advantages in bargaining power over what is agreed to or enforced, the power relation is not one of dominance but rather of asymmetric dependence. Developing countries (e.g., the BRIC countries) have become increasingly assertive partly in recognition of this fact. Rich countries cannot credibly threaten to "walk" from the overall market-reliance relationship and so can be at least weakly "coerced" into arrangements that may not particularly favor them, even as they enjoy considerable scope for "exploiting" their lesser dependence on reaching any particular agreements. Still, none of this is to say that the general question of fairness or socioeconomic justice in the global economy should be framed and settled in narrow terms of when "coercion" or "exploitation" is justified. These issues may generally pose and complicate questions of fairness, and we may see all social justice issues as fundamentally issues about the exercise of collective power (discussed later). But the general question of fairness in the global economy is simply what a structurally equitable market reliance practice would be.

Risse's more limited appeal to coercion seeks only to account for the "normative peculiarity of the state." Domestic coercion has greater "immediacy" than coercion in international relations, though international relationships, too, are one among several significant "grounds of justice."[45] This brings coercion-based theory ever closer to our own approach, though our concern is less the comparison between domestic and international spheres than

45. Ibid.

with whether and to what extent international economic institutions might generate substantial egalitarian demands.[46] Risse's pluralism does suggest some need at least to indicate what the scope of social justice includes. We should take up the task on our own terms in light of the suggestions made previously.

As suggested in Chapter 1, our general concern is with "what we owe to each other," in Scanlon's sense.[47] What ultimately matters are relations of "recognition" between people, as realized in the ways individual or collective agents conduct themselves, rather than the mere impersonal desirability of states of the world.[48] Regulative principles do not apply simply because the world contains undesirable or "cosmically unfair," unlucky, or (in that sense) "morally arbitrary" states of affairs, even if we are sometimes or often in a position to mitigate such outcomes. If this is an important concern of morality or justice, it is of a fundamentally different kind from what we owe to each other.

Our concern, however, is institutional rather than interpersonal. Most of what goes on in the global economy is beyond the regulative powers of individuals taken simply as such. Social coordination, especially of any scale, nearly always depends on the choices of many agents, precious few of which (save special cases of manipulation and mind control) will be in any one individual's control to regulate by careful planning or any momentary act of will. In most social settings, no individual, as such, has power over the structure of a social practice of the sort they have over their attitudes and bodily movements. When officials or leaders enjoy special powers, they are empowered only by organization and patterns of authority or deference. At the same time, it will often be a mistake to regard social forms a brute fact of life, as though responsibility rests solely with God, Nature, or the Hand of Fate. In many cases collective responsibility can be assigned, to a group of agents that can, through cooperation, regulate the arrangements they share, according to regulative principles justified in light of the group's collective governance powers.

---

46. Risse's account of fairness in trade, in 2007, 2012, and Kurgjanska and Risse 2008 is compatible with our account but deals with a narrower range of issues.
47. See also Chapter 5.1–5.2.
48. On the theme of recognition and why it implies independence from mere states of affairs, see James, 2011.

In sum, Chapter 2 argued that the global economy is constitutively organized by a kind of international social practice. While this practice, too, must be suitably "governable," we have argued as against Hobbesian skepticism that the decentralized trade politics qualifies. We have now also suggested that trade negotiations and the market reliance practice they shape exercise various forms of power. Interdependent nations in many important respects share a common fate, and yet their terms of economic cooperation are shaped by coercion, exploitation, and other arbitrary circumstances—circumstances, that is, which do not necessarily track the various reasons all parties have for organizing the common practice in one rather than another way. This poses a distinctive occasion of justification, not of what each owes to each, but what "we," as so organized, owe to each. We can ask how the common practice must be arranged if it is to be justifiable or reasonably acceptable to all involved. This is partly a question of structural equity, but also a question about the justifiability of collectively exercised power. Our question, in that sense, is a question of social justice.

CHAPTER FOUR

The Moral Problem of Assurance

Having just resisted Hobbes, we now argue that he has an important insight. Even if problems of assurance do not foreclose questions of global socioeconomic justice, as Hobbes claims, they do shape how those questions arise. For specifically *moral* reasons of assurance, questions of global socioeconomic justice properly take an *international* rather than "cosmopolitan" form.[1]

In general, agents face normatively significant problems of assurance because they have imperfect knowledge about the conduct of others and must therefore weigh consequent risks of action. The basic human device for their resolution, practically speaking, is for agents to form "agreements"—promises, conventions, social practices, or institutions—that reduce uncertainty and thus "assure" the parties involved. If Hobbes's problem arises among self-interested agents, we will see that problems of assurance equally arise among morally motivated agents. Given the risks of failing to advance purely moral ends, even morally motivated agents require the assurances provided by a publicly established social practice.

Political philosophers often relegate problems of assurance to "non-ideal theory" or the "morality of transition" to an independent "ideal theory" conception of a just social world. Although surprisingly little attention has been paid to what exactly "ideal theory" involves, the assumed thought is perhaps as follows. Insofar as our concern is the *fundamental* principles of justice, and not useful maxims of action or rules of thumb, we can surely abstract away from corruption, indifference, or ill-will. It would be perverse to allow morally culpable lack of concern for justice to itself limit what justice could require as a matter of basic principle. But if we can so help ourselves to a world of morally motivated agents, then it seems that problems of assurance will either

---

1. This chapter draws heavily from James, forthcoming(b).

not arise or be readily overcome: morally motivated people will work things out. "Ideal theory" can thus presume an open horizon of social possibility: its task is simply to formulate the ideal conception of justice upon which morally devoted agents would or should converge.

We will argue that this runs afoul of the truth in Hobbes: morally motivated agents will not necessarily work things out, for reasons arising from nothing less than the human condition itself.

We have already suggested in Chapter 2.5 that problems of assurance arise in virtue of the human condition, from the mere fact that agents are distinct individuals. Because they are distinct, each agent has limited knowledge of and control over the conduct of others and so must weigh consequent risks of action according to what others can be expected to do. It is in life much as it is in the "stag hunt" or "assurance game": uncertainty is all it takes to keep the players out of the cooperative equilibrium. It is for this reason, we argued, that a "cosmopolitan" world of spontaneously generated free trade is illusory. Because governments have limited knowledge about what other governments will do, they require the assurances provided by an international social practice of freeing trade if the consequent vulnerabilities are to be justified. The global economy as we know it depends on the historical emergence of public international market reliance practice marked by mutuality.

If we made this argument in the standard way, in terms of self-interested payoffs, we now develop a similar global-sized problem of assurance with morally concerned "players." The problem is general and fundamental, and properly limits abstraction within "ideal theory." So long as we expect political philosophy to be normative for us—so long as its aim is to justify basic principles of social justice that tell us what we conclusively ought to do—proposed principles must credibly address the available human means for the public resolution of problems of assurance. While such problems can arise even on a small scale, they become especially acute in matters of global size, when large numbers of very different people must relate over great distances with limited knowledge of what others are doing. We in fact have a basically international form of global cooperation. Our claim will be that if political philosophy is to be normative for us, it must begin from and credibly address our international political system, simply for lack of a well-assured alternative for the management of global-sized affairs.

"Cosmopolitan" views, as we will understand them, deny this: they hold that basic principles can and should be justified by abstracting away from our basically international forms of global governance. An international system is justified only insofar as it happens to best *implement* independently justified principles. Although our argument hardly refutes cosmopolitanism, it does show that it is not inevitable once we become dissatisfied with nationalistic or parochial egalitarian theories. Indeed, our argument shows that cosmopolitan views carry a heavy burden of justification: they must plausibly explain why the suggested methodology of abstraction should yield strongly normative global responsibilities of international political morality of the sort we seek to characterize.[2]

1. Fundamental Relevance

On one reading, leaving Hobbes's state of nature is analogous to Rousseau's stag hunt.[3] We each do best if we both seek peace; we each then enjoy the benefits of commodious living instead of constantly defending ourselves and struggling to survive. Yet we are each uncertain about what the other will do. If I seek peace while you conspire against me, I'll not only fail to see the benefits of commodious living but also miss a chance of protecting myself. And the same goes for you as regards me. So both cooperation and non-cooperation are equilibrium outcomes. Given our uncertainty about what the other will do, however, non-cooperation is the prudent, "risk-dominant" course.[4]

---

2. See Chapter 1.2 on what we call "relative socioeconomic fairness in international political morality."
3. Moehler, 2009, defends a version of this interpretation. We claim only that this reading is suggestive, not that it captures the whole or even the core of Hobbes's position.
4. As noted in Chapter 2.5, an assurance game is distinct from a prisoner's dilemma because there is a stable *cooperative* equilibrium. Accordingly, Hobbes makes only passing comments on the Foole: he'll suffer reputational costs, and he can't reasonably expected to cheat for long. So we can assume there to be few Fooles once a covenant gets made. The issue is rather one of risk in "performing first": each of us needs to know that the uncertain gains of cooperation are sufficiently likely for it to be wise to pass up the lesser but surer gains of acting alone.

The state of nature scenario shows how assurance and its lack could bear not just on the *implementation* of an independently justified and applicable principle or ideal but also on what basic principles of conduct could be said to apply in the first place. The essential thought is that any basic *normative* principles—principles concerned with what agents have (normally) sufficient reason to do[5]—depend on the *epistemic* circumstances agents are in (*in foro interno*, at least in a certain general sense). What agents have sufficient reason to do thus depends as much on the risks of action, given uncertainty, as on the size of potential or actual losses or gains. As a result, sufficient uncertainty about the conduct of others can justify what would be unacceptable given better knowledge.

Hobbes's position gains plausibility if we are assumed to be relatively certain that others will be coming after us. If they, like us, cannot but preserve themselves, doing whatever they happen to judge necessary for that end, then prudence arguably not only counsels but commands—and perhaps compels—anticipatory self-defense. Whether or not this is Hobbes's view, it overstates his case. It is quite enough for principled self-defense that each agent is sufficiently *uncertain* about what others will decide they must do to preserve themselves. Even if you are *in fact* no threat to me, so long as there is good enough (albeit misleading) evidence that you will attack me, I have some reason to strike first. And if you are in the same uncertain situation as regards me, then you of course have the same reason to try to get the jump on me. When the stakes are high, time short, and the options few, war can break out between us even if we are in fact both peace-loving people, just by a stroke of bad evidentiary luck: signals got crossed, one of us "looked at the other wrong," one or both of us happened to have a gun—and we lacked a common language or set of communicative signs by which to clear things up. Most important, though the result may be mutual destruction, we cannot necessarily conclude that the agents involved have failed to fulfill an independently justified principle of peaceful coexistence. Rather, no one may have been at fault, because there was, under the uncertain circumstances, no normative principle that tells

---

5. One could also call these "strongly normative" principles if one prefers to use the term "normative" for less-than-sufficient reasons for action as well. I use the stated terminology merely for ease of exposition.

anyone to do otherwise than they in fact did. (Consider, e.g., a case in which we encounter but cannot communicate with alien beings.)[6]

This point about epistemic sensitivity does not depend on Hobbes's unconditional view of self-defense. Contrary to the Right of Nature, evidentiary standards surely must inform one's judgment of what counts as a threat; the threat must be *highly credible*, quite aside from how one happens to judge one's own fears. Moreover, the evidence must be agent-specific: even if it is true in a state of nature that people mostly break their promises, I cannot reasonably cite this general fact as grounds for why I don't have to keep an appointment I made with you; I need evidence that *you* won't show. (This perhaps stands behind the rule of international law that preemptive self-defense requires a "credible and imminent" threat of attack. A country cannot preventively strike against threats "before they are fully formed," as the Bush Doctrine puts it, because they are not manifested to a degree required for them to be credibly attributed to the specific country or population attacked.) Still, our present point holds: if, simply by bad evidentiary luck, you or I present a credible and imminent threat to one another—even if we are *in fact* no threat at all—war may break out between us through no fault of our own. We may not have failed any principle of peaceful coexistence; under the uncertain circumstances, there may have been *no applicable principle that tells either of us to do otherwise than we did*.

These amendments represent a substantively moral conception of self-defense. We therefore have a specifically *moral* (rather than purely self-interested) assurance problem: what moral principles apply depends on circumstances of uncertainty and risk that can equally arise among morally motivated agents—in the present case, agents who are committed to act in self-defense only when it is strictly morally allowed. We cannot decide what normative principles apply in the imagined case by simply selecting an ideal outcome—peace for all involved. Even basic normative principles are epistemically sensitive; they have to take into account the uncertainty and risk that the agents in question actually face.

6. As, e.g., in Wendt, 1992, p. 405.

2. Moral Risks

Vivid as self-defense cases are, assurance problems have fundamental significance for what principles of conduct apply even among morally motivated, *non-defensive* agents. Such agents assess risks of action not in terms of expected self-interested costs but in terms of *opportunity costs to moral aims* they might have otherwise advanced.

To illustrate, consider global warming. Suppose I have limited my total greenhouse gas emissions to a degree my conscience accepts. Shall I go further still? I could spend all of my discretionary income to minimize carbon output by buying new energy-saving appliances and cars, first for myself, then for my friends, and then for my neighbors—until my money runs out. One reason *not* to do so is moral. Any money I spend on the fight against warming is money I will not be spending on direct poverty relief. And this opportunity cost may not be justifiable if I cannot expect the money I spend on warming to make a difference, while I *can* expect to help some poor person (if not the foreign distant poor, then perhaps someone down the street). But whether the proposed warming expenditure will indeed contribute something depends entirely on what others do. If global consumption and production proceeds unabated, at recent rates, my conservation efforts will make little difference. Unless I can be assured that I am *acting within a scheme of cooperation* which, in conjunction with similar choices of others, makes a dent in the warming problem, I'll have little justification for passing up the more certain chance of doing something for poverty relief.

Here it makes little difference if I assume that most everyone is morally motivated. We are each still balancing complex moral risks as well as we each can, and there is no necessary reason that our various uncoordinated judgment calls should combine in a way that steers humanity off its present course toward ecological ruin. Nor then is the problem that "Fooles" may "free ride" on the conservation efforts of others, or even that expectations of free riders may unravel or prevent an effective conservation scheme. Insofar as all parties involved are morally motivated, we can suppose this means each will do his or her fair share in any established scheme, whatever it happens to be. We can even imagine that everyone knows that everyone else will so comply. Yet the crucial form of uncertainty remains. Each may ask, Is any reasonably effective scheme in fact being jointly followed? The risk of action (e.g., the opportunity cost to poverty relief) can derive entirely from uncertainty about whether the various choices of morally motivated agents in fact combine into a common scheme that addresses the warming problem to some extent. They may or may not so combine. If people simply act from their own sense of what will help, from within their particular limited perspective, the combined effect of all such choices may still make no or little difference. The various choices will need to be combined in the right ways, into a common, more or less effective scheme, and everyone will need to know well enough that this is the case.[7]

For example: let us assume that global-sized environmental cooperation is a real possibility today. We can feasibly adopt an aggressive multilateral carbon tax or cap-and-trade system. If everyone were morally motivated, a stable more or less effective international agreement would arguably have already emerged. (Though of course no one really knows how effective an agreement might be; we may already be beyond an ecological "tipping point.") However, any such solution could only be of an *international* kind, a solution in which the citizens of each country will have their respective legally or socially mandated roles to play. The solution is available to us, that is, only because there already exists an international system, in which governments can work out and jointly follow an effective scheme, acting on behalf of their respective citizens,

---

7. While we mean to leave the scope of relevant "moral aims" open-ended, we are not here considering cases in which doing something is wrong (e.g., killing someone for fast cash) regardless of what other people are doing or how many people are cooperating. It is not a wrong against someone to admit carbon, per se, for example, because any consequences for people (e.g., dispossessed on the Bangladeshi flood plains) will result as cumulative effects of many, many carbon emission acts. Such particular acts are not properly conceptualized as wrongfully harmful unless they are part of larger consequential patterns of emissions choices. In other, "step-good" cases, when social production of the good (or relevant bad) requires only a critical mass of participants, one may lack sufficient reasons to cooperate when the number of assured cooperators is insufficiently low *or* sufficiently high. We generally focus on the first variation. The latter version invites familiar questions about self-interested free riders. These do not come up under our idealization of moral motivation, though we leave open whether moral opportunity costs might equally justify "moral free riding" in some cases. I thank Gerald Gaus for discussion of these complexities.

drawing their cooperation along in tow. It is hard to see, by contrast, how all or most of the individuals of the world could somehow *directly* establish an effective, publicly recognized, and mutually assured warming arrangement without the help of international relations. One reason for this is each person's sheer lack of reliable information about what millions or billions of other people are doing in places both far and near. Another is that any arrangement would have to make reference to each person's contribution to the problem, telling him or her in some sort of regulable terms what emissions to forgo, and at what cost to other important goals. Yet our respective emissions *as individuals* just cannot be conceptualized as contributions to the warming problem at that fine-grained level; it is only when we consider larger-scale collective emissions output (for the United States or for California) that consequential patterns emerge (which is not of course to say that smaller groups such as cities or families, or even individuals, would not do well to *try* to make some contribution). Any solution to the contemporary global warming assurance problem therefore cannot take a purely "cosmopolitan" form.

3. Hobbes's Basic Insight

Suppose for the moment that the self-defense and warming cases are representative of the basic issues of normative political philosophy—that is, political philosophy concerned with normative principles. In that case Hobbes and the social contract tradition he influenced is essentially right about the basic circumstances of justification. Any justification of principle would have to be addressed specifically to the conditions of human agency that give rise to uncertainty about the conduct of others and the agreement-forming devices we have for managing associated risks.

These circumstances cannot be readily set aside or abstracted away, at least not without compromising certain very basic features of human life. As we explained in Chapter 2.5, the basic conditions of agency in question arise for a single reason: human agents are distinct individuals, in which case we often cannot be expected to be or act in agreement unless this becomes established in a public, jointly available way. This is not to say "agreement" need always have the same form, notwithstanding

Hobbes's insistence on sovereign rule. In person-to-person cases, being in agreement may be as easy as exchanging a kind word, gesture, or other commonly known indicator of good will (unless, say, the alien beings we are encountering share no such signaling conventions, which is then a less straightforward kind of case). Our respective evidential circumstances then change, removing grounds of self-defense, allowing us take basic expectations of interpersonal morality for granted. Cases involving large numbers of people and uncertain patterns of conduct are more complicated and so still more uncertain, much as Hume explained. Even if morally motivated people will not require the strong assurance of a sovereign power, they cannot be expected to automatically converge on a common scheme by themselves. Matters of large scale are often too uncertain for that. There are too many cases like the global warming case, in which well-motivated and basically competent moral agents reach different moral judgments, and are known to reach different judgments, as a result of differences in position, complex information, and how situations are interpreted or principles applied. Thus even an assumption of universal moral motivation will not provide sufficient assurance in and of itself. It is only provided a public agreement, which selects, and is commonly known to select, certain large-scale patterns of conduct over others that the moral and other risks of action become justifiable.

The source of the problem is in part that moral reasoning, though not necessarily irredeemably fragmented, does often need the help of social circumstances to be unified in the form of principles suitable for the governance of collective life.[8] Justification of basic moral principles must, in those cases, take into account the nature of the relevant social circumstances and its implicit understandings. Otherwise, we have little assurance that proposed principles will be consistent with a stable cooperative equilibrium, as any principles that are supposed to regulate collective life must be.

Accordingly, Rawls, for example, justifies principles of "ideal theory" for independently identified and interpreted social practices and institutions, drawing bases for social agreement in part

---

8. For a related argument, see Kavka, 1995. We agree with his argument for the state, but focus on the similar but global-sized question about the state system.

from the practices or institutions themselves.[9] His idealizations are modest, being limited to assumptions of (1) the normal, "favorable conditions" under which a mutually assured practice has in fact emerged, and of (2) "full compliance" with its terms, so that no participant can cite free-riding Fooles as an excuse for non-compliance. In addition, Rawls imagines people as willing (to a normal degree) to abide by whatever governing principles are ultimately justified, lest sheer lack of concern for justice itself limit what justice could require. Otherwise, however, the basic features of the practice in question are assumed to hold sway over the question of what principles should govern the joint enterprise.

4. The Question of Global Justice

What import, if any, does any of this have for global justice? We have discussed global-sized examples to illustrate Hobbes's basic insight: again, any justification of normative principles, concerned with what agents ought to do, must be sensitive to the conditions of human agency that give rise to uncertainty about the conduct of others and the agreement-forming devices we have for managing associated risks. The challenge, then, is to discern what this implies.

Kant took moral reasons of assurance to imply a view much like Hobbes's, that a coercive political authority is necessary for people in a common world to "enter a rightful condition."[10] Yet it is not clear why formal legal rule should be the *only* way for nations to establish the necessary forms of public agreement once we moralize motivation. Well-defined *informal* social practices can also be reasonably well assured. Assuming that nations are morally motivated, and known to be so motivated, we could expect each to be more willing to take risks for expected moral gains as compared to our world of mixed national motives. The cost of failing to act together for the sake of shared moral ends would weigh on all more heavily than the smaller moral improvements a country

---

9. James, 2005a, pp. 286–98.
10. Kant (1797), 1996, ch. 1. On Kant, Ripstein, 2009, takes decentralized international law to be consistent with the required determinate, coercively assured political authority, given the possibility of domestic enforcement.

might achieve acting alone. Even nations averse to action under uncertainty would arguably take a chance on publicly established arrangements or understandings that advance clearly worthy moral aims better than unilateral action (as with climate change or poverty relief). This may be so, moreover, even if informal regulative expectations are not fully specified and are known to require good faith judgment to apply in practice. Morally motivated nations that have established a modicum of trust and common social purpose will tolerate divergence in the interpretation of expectations, especially when these are roughly consistent with common values or open to informal mutual accountability and adjustment on an ongoing basis. The postwar multilateral trading system is a case in point (even as its members presumably had mixed rather than morally pure motives).

We suggest that Hobbes's insight instead comes to this: questions of global justice are best understood as taking an international rather than a cosmopolitan form, because there are limits on *abstraction* within "ideal theory." There are general facts of global social life that idealization should not abstract away from, even as a matter of basic principle, given certain principled demands of *epistemic availability*, which we explain momentarily.

For our purposes, "cosmopolitanism" is the following view about *principles* of socioeconomic justice and how they are properly justified: such principles (1) allow us to directly compare the relative prospects of each individual of the world (according to a favored distributional criterion, e.g., sufficiency, equality, or priority for the worst off), (2) they can be justified independently of international political institutions (though perhaps assuming a "global basic structure" abstractly described), and yet (3) they give rise to responsibilities for action (e.g., by way of a general duty to promote whatever it is that basic principles of justice call for, such as a version of Rawls's Natural Duty of Justice).[11]

Let us assume for the moment that questions of global justice are questions of normative political philosophy, that is, questions about what various agents have normally conclusive reason to do (barring extenuating circumstances). In general, principles that answer to that kind of question cannot be justified by pointing to

---

11. Though the details vary, examples include Beitz, 1979; Moellendorf, 2002, 2009; and Caney, 2006. Pogge, 2002, appeals to a complicity-based rather than natural duty of justice.

114   FAIRNESS IN PRACTICE

desirable states of the world, even if the outcomes they require could well come about as a logical or even physical possibility. Rather, such principles have to be addressed as normative demands *to* specified agents and can only require forms of action or social cooperation that are "available" to them, given their regulatory powers. Although we can in theory address hypothetical normative principles to hypothetically situated and empowered agents (e.g., in a world of easy material abundance rather than our world of moderate scarcity), such hypothetical principles do not necessarily tell us anything about what justice requires in the circumstances of *actual* social and political life. So insofar as political philosophy seeks to address *us*—as normative political philosophy does—it must specifically address our actual world regulatory position. Otherwise, it does not tell us what justice requires of us.[12]

For all this says, one could argue that any physically and biologically possible states of affairs *are* "available" to us, in the relevant sense.[13] It is here, however, that the Hobbesian insight enters with particular force: availability, properly understood, is *epistemic* availability, in a sense that limits the basic form of human cooperation that justice could require.[14] As we will explain presently, there are reasons that our collective epistemic position leaves us without a viable alternative to an international system, even if in a deeply revised form.

Again, it is a basic fact of the human condition that we are distinct individuals who lack direct knowledge of or control over the minds of others. We therefore must interact in uncertainty about what those others will do. Given the unavoidable risks of cooperation (or what we hope will be cooperation), any principles must address this basic epistemic predicament. No one can be expected to be or act in agreement with others unless some expectations of

---

12. Implicit here is a weaker challenge: cosmopolitan views must deal with assurance problems that arise among any agents they seek to address, whether or not those agents are us. The point equally holds, that is, for merely hypothetical principles and agents in circumstances that may be very different from ours.
13. Elster, 1985, p. 201, argues for this, suggesting that perceived obligations can contribute to their historical feasibility.
14. Rawls, 1971, p. 398, similarly claims, "Conceptions of justice must be justified for the conditions of our life *as we know it* or not at all." Italics mine.

regulation become established in a public, jointly available way. There may then be no question of "global justice" beyond the question of what each individual is separately morally required to do, simply for bad evidentiary luck: unfortunate epistemic conditions may leave even morally motivated agents in an unorganized, global "state of nature."

When cooperation of certain kinds has been achieved, as in domestic society and in international relations, this is to *partially address*, rather than wholly overcome, our fundamental epistemic predicament. Established, mutually assured cooperation on one issue-area may leave other, localized "states of nature," where cooperative relations are not under way. In any cooperative practice, expectations of regulation are for a specified *type* of activity, which participants distinguish from other activity types, track over time, and associate with attached regulatory expectations in both momentary action and cross-temporal planning. Assurances that regulatory expectations are widely understood and complied with in one area do not then imply that adequate assurances are available in other areas. Even morally motivated agents require not just assurance, but assurance of certain specific sorts.

What goes for individuals also goes for the collectives that individuals form. Just as normative principles for the regulation of conduct must be sensitive to the regulatory position of individuals, including their respective epistemic situations, normative principles must be sensitive to the regulatory position of any collectives those individuals form, including their respective, collective epistemic circumstances. So, for example, any significant change in the structure of cooperation in a group will equally be a change in the regulatory expectations of (many of) its members. The wrong kind of change can destabilize or destroy assured public understandings, precisely Hobbes's chief concern with the English Civil War. But the concern can equally arise among the morally motivated: as assurance declines, the moral opportunity cost of unilateral action increases, potentially undermining a going cooperative equilibrium. But even when no such "constitutive threat" is in the cards, it is still true that the scope of reasonable change is subject to the common epistemic environment. A move toward a new (perhaps rough) cooperative equilibrium within an ongoing practice is equally sensitive to the general epistemic conditions that shape not only the risk assessments of particular agents but also the general regulatory expectations that could be jointly established and maintained.[15]

It follows from all of this that normative principles of global justice can only require cooperative arrangements that we can know—with reasonable confidence—that we can jointly establish and maintain, starting from our current agential situation. If "ideal theory" rightly abstracts away from lack of concern for justice, it cannot ignore our current, collective regulatory position without simply changing the subject, from normative principles of justice for us to something else.

What, then, is our regulatory position in contemporary global political life? We have already noted that epistemic problems become particularly acute at a global scale, and nothing in our globalizing world of transnational firms, civil society organizations, or governance networks changes that fundamental epistemic predicament. Matters of very large scale are highly uncertain, because even well-motivated and basically competent moral agents reach different moral judgments, and are known to reach different judgments, as a result of differences in position, complex information, and the way situations are interpreted or rules or principles applied. But notice, now, that these problems become especially sharp when we are considering very basic, ground floor forms of cooperation rather than mere adjustments within a more general framework of largely assured cooperative background. Even the French Revolution can be seen as a deep change within a continuous roughly shared conception of what a nation-state is. Similarly, we might clearly and credibly envisage deep reform in the state system. But the situation is quite different when we are considering revolution of the international order itself, even if by a stepwise and gradual route. As we will now suggest, our basic epistemic situation is that we simply do not know well enough what fundamental revolution might mean and how it might work.

---

15. Binmore, 1994, treats institutional reform as an assurance game, with the status quo as the relevant "state of nature" and the reformed state as a new potential cooperative equilibrium. We do not assume that this is an appropriate use of the assurance game as it is best understood. The standard cases, as discussed, involve not institutional change but rather agents who need uncertainty-reducing assurances for cooperation to be established or maintained. We are suggesting that the individual and collective cases are similar in important respects, even if the same model is not appropriate.

Even if it is logically or physically possible, it is presently unavailable to us.

It is a basic fact of global political life that the international order is the central publicly understood means for managing global-sized affairs. For all of its many flaws, it has, and is known to have, significant capacity to effectively address issues of global size (global security, the global economy, humanitarian aid and intervention, the environment, and so on). It does so, moreover, in a way that can in principle draw along the compliance of most every person in the world, seen as citizens of one or another national government. By contrast, as the case of global warming suggested, it is hard to see how the individuals of the world could ever *directly* arrange a coordinated response to global-sized problems, given the scale of the problems and the difficulties of coordination and communication. Transnational movements do have an important and growing influence on national and international policy, but this is still to say that specifically international relations have an indispensable role in world affairs. (Even if direct global coordination is indeed somehow possible, the difficulty of *readily conceptualizing* it would itself disable it as a generally understandable solution to an assurance problem. People who feel confused would expect that others are likewise confused, and so would lack assurance. Even those who felt clear might expect that enough others are confused (if clear about the general confusion and likewise be less than fully assured).

None of this implies that the international order is justifiable in anything like its present form, or that concerns of assurance must stand in the way of deep structural change. Morally motivated governments and their publics will be amenable to cooperation and require "general" compliance only up to some reasonable threshold. They will put great weight on the opportunity cost of failing to act collectively. In these terms, numerous substantial reforms are arguably available to us within the near and relatively near future. We can, for instance, adopt an aggressive carbon tax or cap-and-trade system along with large investments in green technology and mitigation efforts for those adversely affected by climate change; eliminate the international borrowing and resource privileges that incentivize poverty-creating corruption and civil unrest in developing countries;[16] establish maximally effective agencies for humanitarian aid and intervention; give an international

---

16. Pogge, 2002, pp. 155–58, 2005; Wenar, 2008.

criminal court robust enforcement powers; improve coordination and coherence between international organizations; strengthen the ability of civil society to hold national and international governments publicly accountable for applicable human rights standards; increase international labor mobility; improve public deliberation, accountability, and administrative functioning.[17] And we may add the numerous reforms to the global economy defended in this book. But while all this might cumulatively cut deeply into the current international order, it arguably would not change its basic international outline. It may retain, say, territorial borders and the presumption that each government has a default, special responsibility for the lives of people within its jurisdiction.

A deeply reformed international order could retain the basic assurance-providing roles it currently has. What is less clear, and indeed completely unknown, is whether any *fundamentally* distinct alternative global social form—a world state, or system of vertically dispersed agencies—could provide the necessary assurances; the answer is at best unclear, a highly speculative empirical matter.[18] Nor can we confidently expect our limited conceptual and epistemic situation to change in the foreseeable future. It might change, but it also might not. We cannot be sure, or even confidently expect substantially greater certainty on the matter.[19] As regards our most basic social forms, we have to admit that, in Keynes's honest words, "we simply do not know."[20]

The issue is not simply the current descriptive state of empirical knowledge, which is, after all, subject to deliberate alteration (e.g., by public investment in research). Moreover, what level of

---

17. Cohen and Sabel, 2005.
18. For suggestive accounts of radical (if gradual) global transformation, see Pogge, 1992; Held, 1995; Goodin, 2010. Such proposals are of deep interest and not clearly implausible. We merely point out their speculative nature.
19. A similar epistemological argument in Risse, 2012, makes the stronger claim that a fundamental alternative is *unintelligible* and not simply insufficiently credible.
20. Keynes, 1936, says: that "our knowledge of the world is fluctuating, vague, and uncertain renders wealth a peculiarly unsuitable topic for the methods of economic theory.... About these matters there is no scientific basis on which to form a calculable probability whatever. We simply do not know." Is fundamental global social revolution any *less* uncertain?

certainty and what kinds of assurances are "adequate" are normative questions. If one favors a very low standard of "adequacy," highly speculative arrangements might qualify as "available to us." Why then think the appropriate standard of adequacy should be high enough to limit our available institutional future to a fundamentally international system?

As we have already suggested, our answer appeals to both practical limitations of understanding and reasonable uncertainty-aversion. A fundamental alternative would have to be of a kind that people can generally understand, see the point of, and know how to uphold in their various social roles, despite the enormous difficulties of coordination on a global scale. And we would need evidence that most everyone in the world could actually be expected to come to this understanding in practice, over some appropriate time frame (again, assuming the good faith efforts available to morally motivated agents). More significant, the proposed arrangements would have to be known with reasonable confidence to be just as good, or indeed better, than any international order we have or could have. Otherwise, why risk the safer moral benefits of the existing or reformed international system for the sake of gains that may or may not be greater, and may or may not even be reaped? What is morally valuable about that?

We are suggesting that the appropriate evidentiary standard is "reasonable confidence," where that is understood to reflect familiar and reasonable *uncertainty-aversion.* At very least, that implies a substantial burden of evidentiary justification. Mere plausible speculation is insufficient. The issue is not, moreover, one of rational risk-taking when expected outcomes have known probabilities; our point is precisely that fundamental revolution is deeply uncertain even about probabilities, in which case still greater caution is required.[21] Nor do we endorse the familiar conservative claim that social change will usually be worse than the status quo because of unintended bad consequences. That view, we assume, forecloses changes about which we can indeed have reasonable confidence.

21. Uncertainty-aversion contrasts with risk-aversion, which involves preferences over outcomes with calculable probabilities. When even probabilities are unknown or very difficult to assign, people are generally cautious, especially when the stakes are high. Keynes, 1921; Ellsberg, 1961; Fox and Tversky, 1995. We are suggesting that this difference carries over for moral preferences, when prudential prospects are not the issue.

Although our argument is at best suggestive without a fuller specification of the appropriate burden of justification, we will not provide that here. We instead suggest how we might press the case against global revolution on several ways of assessing the stakes.

On one Hobbesian version of the argument, it would have to become clear that any radical alternative would leave people just as secure. A reformed international order arguably would do that; as suggested earlier, if the international borrowing and resources privileges were abolished, removing powerful perverse incentives for military coups, millions of people in underdeveloped African countries would be less likely to face the hell of civil war, with no security loss to advanced countries (and indeed potential gains in preventing terrorism). But it is far from clear that global *revolution* would do better or even equally as well as a deeply reformed international security system. We have little basis now for reasonable confidence that this would be so.

Indeed, there is cause for serious concern, as Rawls, following Kant, claims when he explains why he takes "international law and practice" largely for granted. Just before specifying his principles for international relations, Rawls says:

> These principles will . . . I assume, make room for various forms of cooperative associations and federations among peoples, but will not affirm a world-state. Here I follow Kant's lead in *Perpetual Peace* (1795) in thinking that a world government—by which I mean a unified political regime with the legal powers normally exercised by central governments—would either be a global despotism or else would rule over a fragile empire torn by frequent civil strife as various regions and peoples tried to gain their political freedom and autonomy.[22]

Rawls's worry of inducing either despotism or civil strife would be puzzling if "ideal theory" could *thoroughly* idealize circumstances

---

22. Rawls, 1999, p. 36. In footnote 40, Rawls quotes Kant. "Kant says in Ak: VIII: 367: 'The idea of international law presupposes the separate existence of independent neighboring states. Although this conditions is itself a state of war (unless federative union prevents the outbreak of hostilities), this is rationally preferable to the amalgamation of states under one superior power, as this would end in one universal monarchy, and laws always lose in vigor what government gains in extent; hence a condition of soulless despotism falls into anarchy after stifling seeds of good.'"

and motivation. In that case, we could simply assume all will happily comply with whatever global social order we think justice requires. Since this assumption is clearly not being made, the argument is best read as instead placing *limitations* on ideal theory according to what we know, and can be expected to learn, about how global politics will, or will not, work. It is fine to abstract away from the fact that agents often have morally irrelevant motives (e.g., they are selfishly self-interested). Given the present and expected state of human knowledge, however, we cannot expect even morally motivated agents to have security assurances comparable to those they have under a reformed international order. Even if there were a feasible transitional route to a revolutionary order, it would not be worth the security opportunity cost. (Again, this claim is consistent with the deep changes in the international system needed to give many developing countries security against despotic regimes and civil war.)

The same kind of argument can take a more clearly moralized form in terms of the opportunity cost to moral goals such as poverty relief. Not only are security and stable property rights conducive to economic development but the international system combined with regulated markets is the most successful engine for broad-based poverty reduction we know of. The point is not that global capitalism in its present form is justified because it has in fact reduced poverty on an unprecedented scale. The justifiability of global capitalism still depends on whether there are arrangements that are better still, and, as we've suggested, there is every reason to think that significant moral improvements are indeed possible. Beyond deep reform, however, we simply do not know that any fundamentally different alternative to the international system will do better or even just as well in terms of economic development. Economic science itself, moreover, is too limited to supply such knowledge. If anything, the major recent mistakes in development economics result from excessive idealization and a corresponding failure to take given institutional contexts seriously.[23]

This argument depends on claims about the current and foreseeable state of human knowledge of the possibilities of global-sized social coordination. The state of such knowledge might of course change. Our argument is that even if it eventually did become clear that a fundamental alternative will provide the

23. Rodrik, 2007.

needed assurances, normative political philosophy cannot assume that possibility until that time.

It bears emphasizing that none of this is to deny the importance of utopian speculation and localized institutional experimentation.[24] Such intellectual and practical projects may expose going assumptions about social possibility as false or weakly supported.[25] Even when such assumptions are fairly well grounded, speculation or experimentation may change our epistemic circumstances, widen the scope of available arrangements, and so change what justice requires of us. Justice is not then discovered, but rather specified, or further constructed. But neither compelling speculation nor local institutional success make such a difference in and of themselves; they imply a change within justice only when the appropriate evidentiary and organizational standards have been met. Our claim is that they are not met, and cannot now be expected to be fulfilled, for our most basic international social forms.[26]

---

24. We thus fully appreciate the "real utopias" discussed in Wright, 2010, including Wikipedia; participatory city building (as in Porto Alegre, Brazil); the Mondragon conglomerate of worker-owned enterprises in the Basque region of Spain; unconditional basic income (as expansions of the more generous welfare states, or the pilot program in Namibia). We also fully embrace Roberto Unger's focus (2007, pp. 36–44, 150–65, 179–93) on experimentation in modes of production as a means to self-transformation within the world economy. We offer fairness reasons for developing-country institutional flexibility in later chapters.

25. We may also grant a general weighty reason, or even a duty, to investigate and experiment in ways that potentially change our general epistemic situation. That, we might say, is the element of truth in utilitarianism: we should be on the lookout for ways of bettering people's lives beyond potentially outmoded conventional practice. We may have "first mover" responsibilities to initiate investigation and experimentation, as well as "bandwagon" duties to contribute to and uphold emerging practices, especially once a threshold of sufficient compliance is reached, but perhaps also in a more exploratory spirit.

26. Wright, 2010, p. 373, seems to agree when he admits our "ignorance about the future limits of possibility," cautioning only that this does not mean that "socialism is impossible." He elaborates: "We simply do not know what the ultimate limits to the expansions of democratic egalitarian social empowerment might be. The best we can do, then, is treat the struggle to move forward on the pathways of social empowerment as an experimental process in which we continually test and retest the limits of possibility and try, as best we can, to create new institutions which will expand those limits themselves."

5. Concessions

Our argument for internationalism is so far largely suggestive.[27] We now strengthen our case by offering several concessions.

For one, we grant what might be called *bare individualism*, the view that individual persons are the ultimate unit of moral concern. That is not to say how *principles* should be justified or the form they should take, so it is consistent with agnosticism about cosmopolitanism in the methodological sense defined above. Nor do we assume that justification can or must appeal to collectivist values of national identity or national self-determination which "cosmopolitans" often reject or deemphasize. We assume some special (defeasible) national responsibilities, but our argument can turn, as we have suggested, on values such as security and poverty relief.[28]

We have so far simply *stipulated* that questions of global justice are questions of normative political philosophy. This is hardly trivial. It means that, for all we have argued so far, one might simply insist that principles of *justice*, properly speaking, are not strongly normative in the sense specified, and so not constrained by contingent problems of uncertainty and assurance in the way we have suggested. Indeed, here we happily concede that some concepts naturally called "justice" are of this kind (e.g., "cosmic fairness"). Our argument, then, is perhaps not about the whole of justice, but limited to what we are calling "normative political philosophy," which by definition deals with basic "normative principles" concerned with what specified agents have normally sufficient reason to do. We insist only that normative political philosophy is a central and important part of political philosophy, if not also political life, and that its normative principles are *fundamental* within the general moral kind to which they belong.

---

27. Risse, 2012, addresses a range of further relevant historical and contemporary positions and objections.
28. We will argue, in Chapter 6.5, that the morally relevant interests of individuals include "societal interests" or certain stakes in the character of collective life (e.g., a security interest in living in a society free from external threats, or an economic interest in living a society that sees steadily rising standards of living). A "cosmopolitan" view (whether methodological or otherwise) may or may not reject such "societal interests of individuals."

It does seem that matters of justice, including global justice, cannot be wholly divorced from what agents have sufficient reason to do. It would be odd to say that certain conditions are not merely good but *required of us by justice* and yet admit that no one will ever in fact have sufficient reason to do anything about them. Moreover, political philosophy is presumably at least *centrally* concerned with what agents have sufficient reason to do, if not in the short run, when political will may be lacking, then at least over the medium to longer term. But in that case the Hobbesian problematique is unavoidable. A political philosophy of global justice must deal with basic facts of the human condition, including the reality of uncertainty and the feasible scope of assurance-providing agreements.

The cosmopolitan abstracts away from our basic way of handling matters of global scale and so leaves the normative status of its proposed principles at best obscure. The burden of justification, then, is to clarify the proposed governance role of the suggested principles in a sense that might justify and require fundamental revolutionary change rather than (perhaps deep) adjustments to our basically international system of cooperation. If the cosmopolitan instead means to justify principles of "justice" in a sense that is not normative in our sense, it bears the burden of specifying that sense and explaining why associated (perhaps weaker) "availability" conditions, if any, are in fact satisfied.[29]

G. A. Cohen would press a version of the present objection even on these terms. According to Cohen, normative principles cannot be *fundamental* principles of justice because they are not "fact-insensitive," that is, they are not valid whatever the facts (including facts about levels of uncertainty and assurance).[30] According to Cohen, assurance problems would at most bear on "principles of regulation" for social life, which are properly "fact-sensitive" but *not* fundamental. Such principles concern matters of wise social technology, including the implementation of justice, but not the fundamental nature of justice itself. Yet Cohen's

---

29. A cosmopolitan account might be addressed to hypothetical agents whose epistemic situation affords global institutions, such as a world state, which are unavailable to us. The burden of justification would then be to explain why this should have significance for us, beyond a mere potentially worthy aspiration.
30. Cohen, 2008.

argument fails: principles justified for or in the light of factual circumstances (e.g., of uncertainty or assurance) are trivially "fact-insensitive." Any principle P, justified for a set of facts F, trivially entails a conditionalized principle "If F, then P." That principle will be valid whatever the actual world facts—that is, regardless of whether facts F actually obtain. But Cohen nowhere explains why such trivially "fact-sensitive" principles cannot be fundamental principles of justice.[31]

Moreover, it is not hard to see how certain "principles of regulation" might be basic principles of justice. This follows straightforwardly if we regard justice as part of "what we owe to each other" in Scanlon's sense. The basic concern of morality, in that sense, is with whether agents govern themselves in ways that are justifiable to all, according to regulative principles essentially sensitive to the agent's contingent self-governance capacities, where such capacities include epistemic limitations and expected costs of action. So conditions of uncertainty and lack of assurance can shape what basic regulative moral principles apply, in just the way our earlier examples suggest. Scanlon's concern is interpersonal morality, but the same goes for collective life. Collectively sustained and governed social practices and institutions can have their own regulative principles, which need to be justified in the light of underlying conditions of uncertainty and the established and available forms of agreement that address them. (As argued in Chapter 3.6, the limited powers of individuals mean that principles of individual morality won't settle the collective responsibilities we incur through our essentially collective social forms. How the two classes of responsibility relate is a separate question.)[32]

Much as with principles for individuals, principles for social practices can be fundamental. They do not depend on principles of individual morality, or more general regulative principles of what we owe to each other, or any principles of their same moral

---

31. See "Deflating Fact-Insensitivity," available at my UC Irvine Philosophy Department Web site.
32. Insofar as international responsibilities *bear* on individual action, they do so indirectly—not, that is, without further principles, for individuals, which indicate how they are to relate to the state or international or other collectives in question, in light of assurance problems. We take Rawls's "natural duty of justice" (1971, pp. 115, 334) in this practice-sensitive way. See James, 2005a, p. 292.

kind. They depend only on the independent moral reasoning by which they are constructively justified (reasoning about what collective regulative principles no one could reasonably reject, given various grounds for personal objection—of which more in Chapter 5.1–5.4).[33]

A final objection might urge that the proper role of *fundamental* principles is to provide a plateau from which to stage a fundamental moral critique of the institutional status quo. In that case, we must abstract away from the global scene's prevailing international social and political structure to ask whether it is justified. Here we admit that if wholesale social critique is the goal, the pressure is toward greater abstraction for the sake of increased critical depth. For maximal depth, one would identify a favored distributional state of affairs among human beings taken simply as such (e.g., equal welfare for all), idealizing away even the human condition, which might also thwart the favored ideal. We, however, have different purposes of justification, which call for greater sensitivity to reality. Normative political philosophy seeks to address actual world agents with normally conclusive demands for action (strongly "normative" principles), so the pressure is toward specificity. For any such demands will apply only to the extent that they address the conditions the responsible agents are actually in. Instead of critical depth, our aims require credible normative address.

The tension arises within our practice-based constructive methodology. That approach seeks to justify principles of normative political philosophy for and in light of a social practice, under some description or other. A more abstract characterization of the general nature of a given practice will afford greater scope for criticism of its going institutional realization. But while a generally described practice might still provide a normative plateau from which to advocate revolution or otherwise radical structural change, a set of proposed principles may not credibly speak to our social forms as we understand them. A practice-based approach is already willing to forgo wholesale revolutionary critique (otherwise, why not just talk about bare distributional states of affairs?)

---

33. In Cohen's terms (2008, p. 238), justified principles *would* depend on any "methodological principles" that inform the justifying reasoning, but not on principles of the same kind.

for the sake of underwriting strong criticism of the conduct of particular governments from *within* a prevailing practice.[34] But a strong basis for criticism requires as much specificity as possible. For the more global revolution seems to be what is called for, the harder it is to convincingly argue that any particular course of action, here and now, is definitely required. We will perhaps have a vague responsibility to do something, somehow, at some point, for the cause of revolutionary change, but that won't be the strong basis for criticism and censure that a practice-based account is after.

The point also holds in degrees, even when revolution isn't in the cards: the more abstract the framing characterization of a practice, the weaker the argument for resulting conclusive obligations. The appropriate framing of a practice conception is in the role of a public regulative conception, which is supposed to guide different agents in grasping and following their resulting obligations. In that case, the more abstractly the practice is described in the framing characterization, the easier it is to slough off as not really in force, or not really applicable in a particular context of decision, especially when real costs are to be borne. Even morally motivated agents might generally lack sufficient assurance for the reasons we have described, in which case credible specificity is crucial.

To be sure, a philosophical theory can be only so specific, especially if it seeks generalities across policy areas. It is difficult to say where such limits lie in the abstract. We simply have to work out different approaches, at different levels of specificity, and weigh their relative merits. To find the right level of abstraction—not too general, and not too specific, but just right—is one of our central tasks in the positive account offered in the remaining chapters of this book.

---

34. But see James, 2005a, pp. 312–16, on the critical resources of a practice-based approach.

PART II

Basic Fairness

CHAPTER FIVE

Structural Equity

According to our argument so far, the internationally organized global economy generates a distinctive class of fairness responsibilities. The global economy as we know it is organized by a kind of international social practice, a practice of mutual reliance on common markets. By sustaining this practice, trading nations together incur a collective responsibility to work toward and uphold the arrangements needed for the practice to be organized in a structurally equitable way.

That is not to say what "structural equity" might require. So far, we have mainly posed the relevant question, namely, When does the international practice of trade take a form that every country, and each of their respective classes, could find reasonably acceptable, given how it distributes the advantages and disadvantages of global economic integration among them? We will answer this question, in Chapters 6 and 7, with three principles of equity. In this chapter, we further characterize the *issue* of structural equity, in ways that will frame and guide the more substantive arguments we offer later on. We discuss structural equity's appropriate forms of moral reasoning, its "deontological" normative force, its treatment of competing values, its wide scope of application in global economic life, and a wide variety of fairness ideas it helps to explain and organize.

1. Contours of Reasoning

In general, to claim that some form of the market reliance practice is *structurally inequitable* is to claim that it would be reasonable for some country or class to reject the way it is treated (or to reject a regulative principle that allows such treatment) in favor of some feasible alternative arrangement. To claim that a form of the practice is *structurally equitable* is to claim that no such reasonable objection can be mounted; no country or class is in a position to reasonably complain of the way it is treated under the practice. The market reliance practice is reasonably acceptable to all involved.

To illustrate, suppose a trade rule can be modified so as to prevent the substantial disadvantage of some country or its low-skilled workers. And suppose the modification would not make any other country, or any of its classes, worse off in any substantial respect (perhaps because "losers" can and will be compensated). The question of structural equity is, Can the disadvantaged parties reasonably object to the status quo and thus reasonably insist upon reform? The natural answer is that this would indeed be reasonable, given the relative inadequacy of other potential complaints. For if the others are no worse off, or if adequate compensation can and will be arranged, how could they reasonably complain of being asked to adjust? Any actual complaint would be founded on either ignorance of crucial facts or unreasonable self-interest.

If this example is abstract, it is roughly the standard argument against rich-world farm subsidies. The subsidies (especially in the United States and European Union) disadvantage millions of developing-country farmers (especially in Latin America and West Africa) who would otherwise benefit from lower costs of production. Developing-country farmers are poor, numerous, and laboring under fragile economic circumstances and stand to gain dramatically from small improvements in export markets. Rich country farmers will lose if subsidies are reduced, but they are increasingly few in number (large farms dominate) and by and large already very rich. And in any case advanced countries can afford to compensate them for any losses as needed (e.g., through paid retirement or retraining and other social support).[1] For these reasons, it is often concluded, the subsidies are grossly unfair, even inexcusable. In our terms, poor country farmers can reasonably reject the subsidies (or a principle that allows them). They suffer dearly under them, and, if they were abolished, rich country farmers could not reasonably mount a comparable complaint.[2]

---

1. Rich-world consumers also suffer dramatic health and environmental costs from over-production of certain favored crops such as corn. These also ground powerful complaints against existing subsidies.

2. Similar reasoning indicts persistent advanced-country barriers to manufactured goods from developing countries, often at levels much higher than from advanced countries (Hertel and Martin, 2000). Indeed, "tariff

To be sure, this argument cannot be quite so straightforward. As noted in Chapter 2.7, abolishing the subsidies would for the most part (with the exception of cotton) hurt poor urban consumers in *developing* countries, especially "net food importers." And would it really be fair to benefit poor rural producers at the expense of poor urban consumers who now benefit from cheap imported food? This arguably is fair, though to be minimized as far as possible. Poor rural producers and their families are poorer and more numerous, with scarce alternatives to farming, short of moving to the city. So the subsidies cannot be justified in the name of poverty relief, and there would seem to be no other significant reason they should be seen as fair. (But what if rural populations dwindle, while urban populations retain high concentrations of poverty?) The fair course, it would seem, is thus to liberalize agriculture as quickly as possible, and to differentiate among crops and countries in ways that have the largest positive effects on producers and the smallest adverse affects on developing-country consumers.[3]

This example shows that we have a basic sense of how to reason about what is "reasonably acceptable to each" in particular contexts. Such reasoning is neither wholly empty nor morally irrelevant. The example also highlights that any such reasoning will be invariably complicated when applied to practical issues of real consequence. And indeed the issue of farm subsidies is something of an *easy* case. Questions of whether the world should adopt a single global currency, despite unruly international monetary practice and the uncertainties of the euro experiment, or of how governments should coordinate fiscal policy in a time of tight budgets and weak growth, as during the Great Recession years, are vastly more complicated. What is initially needed, then, is some

---

escalation" and other barriers to manufactured goods are arguably more profoundly damaging to developing countries than farm subsidies: they slow developing-country diversification out of primary product production and into higher-skilled, higher-return industry. To mention a still further example (of perhaps many more), stringent "rules of origin" often prevent developing countries from benefiting from established tariff preferences. This not only deprives them of important benefits but it also undercuts prior agreements to provide them.
3. Stiglitz and Charlton, 2006 pp. 121–22.

way of getting complicated issues of these sorts under a modicum of intellectual control. What is needed, at least, is a *framework* of reasoning which gives us relative confidence about how to address substantial fairness questions, in specific areas and in broader terms.

To that end, we might look first to the general contours of moral reasoning. Because the question of structural equity is a *moral* question, our answer can freely abstract away from morally irrelevant features of the actual circumstances of politics. We need assign no special authority to what countries or their publics would *actually* accept, or have in fact accepted, perhaps under conditions of ignorance, error, social pressure, purely selfish motivation, or weak bargaining power. Although actual acceptance may offer a suggestive guide, a judgment about what is reasonably acceptable, in the morally relevant sense, is to be made on the merits of the case. As for how to make such a judgment, the moral domain of "what we owe to each other," as Scanlon defines it, tells us in a general way how to proceed. We reason on the merits of the case *from* the standpoints of different parties (countries or their respective classes) in at least the following three analytically distinct steps.

First, we identify the different interests of each party involved, specifically, some "generic" and "personal" interest that is morally relevant to the practice in question (in trade practice, e.g., the interest of each in greater productivity gains, or in lesser socioeconomic vulnerability). For now we remain open about who the morally relevant parties are; they may be persons, social classes, or countries or political communities, depending on the context in question. (We argue in Chapter 6.5 that trading societies do have claims to national income as collectives, given an appropriate relation to the interests of their individual members.)

Second, we consider the different objections that might be mounted on each party's behalf. We first fashion *potential* complaints or objections against a form of the practice, on the basis of each party's relevant interests. Working within the confines of feasibility, we imagine complaints or objections being raised, on a given party's behalf, to some regulative principles which, if followed in practice, would hinder the interests in question. A complaint or objection is well formed only when a feasible alternative principle is proposed.

Third, we compare different objections or complaints, proceeding *serially*, taking each party affected one by one. The aim is to reach a verdict, by our best moral lights, about when some country or class can, or cannot, "reasonably reject" the practice in some form, where such a verdict comes to nothing more than this: a judgment that the imagined objections or complaints are, or are not, sufficient to defeat other objections or complaints. Reasonable objections are the objections that defeat all contenders. Principles of structural equity are principles for the regulation of a social practice that no one can so rule out.[4]

2. Equity and Its Force

Structural equity is a species of *equity*. According to Hobbes, questions of "equity" or "just distribution" come up, and require equality of shares, when a trusted "arbitrator" is "said to distribute to every man his own."[5] This is plausible, except that Hobbes seems to overlook cases in which agents themselves set the terms of their relationship. (For Hobbes, that would presumably count as a state of nature, in which case the problem is not equity but war.) For if a question of equity arises anywhere, it arises in the following basic problem of fair division (which is central for our argument in Chapter 6). Two (or more) symmetrically situated moral equals are to divide some distributable good (e.g., $100). Each has the same interest in greater rather than lesser shares. Neither has any special claim of need, entitlement, or differential gain. The equitable division, all will agree, is equal shares.[6]

But why would equity require an equal division? A *consequentialist* view, as we will call it, simply identifies equity with an ideal distributional state of affairs (such as distributive equality), assigning it no special normative significance for reasons for action. To the extent that equity (as equality) is required, it is

---

4. Justification is therefore comparative in a deep sense. That is not to say that structural equity is always a simple matter of relative distribution as opposed to harm or simple benefit. We leave the nature of the "distributional" concern open for case-specific analysis.
5. Hobbes (1651), 1996, ch. XV [16]
6. People always choose equal division in playing some versions of the similar "divide-the-dollar" game (Nydegger and Owen, 1974).

required *only* because potentially more weighty considerations—of welfare or efficiency or liberty—happen not to be in play. When they are in play, we simply throw equity into the deliberative scales with other values, giving it no presumptive weight.

Hobbes's view, by contrast, is *deontological.* An equal division is required because it is required by an *independent* demand of equitable treatment, the demand that the arbitrator "distribute to every man his own." The demand, as we are putting the idea, is one of "what we owe to each other": when shares are divided unequally, the disadvantaged party is not treated as he or she is *owed*, but rather in a way that could not be justified *to* him or her, on any grounds that we could reasonably expect him or her to accept. The disadvantaged can reasonably object to getting less than half, since neither party has good reason to be treated differently from the other.

The deontological conception differs from the consequentialist reading in two main ways. First, equity is not equality of distribution by its very nature. The demand of equitable treatment requires equal division in some cases, but with no essential reference to an outcome of equal distribution per se. Second, the demand has presumptively *conclusive* normative force, whatever other considerations might be at stake, at least over some assumed range of "normal," non-extenuating circumstances. Equity is not "just another worthy value"; it is of decisive significance for action.

As regards the first feature, the natural question is how a requirement of equal distribution would arise if it does not make essential reference to equality of outcomes per se. This requires two further assumptions. The first is that the parties are moral equals, in the following minimal sense: they both enjoy the capacities required for full moral status, such that any difference in how they are treated (at least that a given party has some reason to care about) must have relevant, sufficient grounds.[7] Otherwise, differential treatment is subject to reasonable complaint by the disadvantaged party. The second assumption is that the parties are symmetrically situated in all morally relevant respects. They have the same interest in greater rather than lesser shares, at least as

---

7. If one party has no reason at all to care about the difference in treatment, then either any division is acceptable to him or no question of its acceptability to him comes up.

regards the kind of treatment in question—in the present case, the act of dividing gains. Short of a special justification for the difference in treatment—a justification which is, by stipulation, lacking in the case—there is no justifying ground for treating the parties differently in the decision of how to divide the gains. To walk off with the whole pie, or to take half and let the other go to waste, or to insist upon the lion's share (as is common in the ultimatum game)[8] is therefore either to deny the relatively disadvantaged party's status as a moral equal or to count his or her interests but give them insufficient weight.

The second feature of the deontological reading is that the agents in our fair division problem have *decisive* reason to divide shares equally, because differential treatment, in this case, is *wrongful*. When we are set to divide an unowned pie, and I simply walk away with it (I am stronger, and thus do so with impunity), you are wrongfully ignored: your interest in having something rather than nothing is disregarded, or the interest is noted and you are assumed simply not to count. I act as though might makes right and so fail to acknowledge you, in a morally basic sense. The moral failing is similar when I instead divide the pie but take the lion's share. Your interest in having *something* is recognized—otherwise I would take the whole pie—but you are not fully recognized as an equal: I favor myself on grounds that are in fact irrelevant to the force of our respective potential claims. I still act as though might makes right. When I do offer you an equal share, then, I am not necessarily promoting an ideal distributional state of affairs in which you happen to be involved. I am recognizing you, giving you your due, or respecting you, by treating your interests in the same way I treat mine.

Following Scanlon, we are characterizing this wrongful failure of recognition in terms of what one can reasonably accept or reject, and so what could or could not be justified to one. When someone asks, "How could you?" "Why is that supposed to be OK?" "What were you thinking?" or "How am I supposed to feel about that?" the idea is that it makes all the difference whether we can explain ourselves by producing the right sorts of reasons—reasons the person would have to accept, on pain of being unreasonable. If the person could mount a reasonable complaint, this seems to settle

---

8. Henrich et al., 2001, 2002.

the matter of whether our action or practice is permissibly done. By definition, there is nothing reasonable and of moral relevance to say on the other side.

Still, equity might not seem normatively decisive in the present case. People often tolerate an inequitable division for the sake of personal benefit; in the ultimatum game, for instance, people often refuse a 9/1 offer on grounds of egregious unfairness, and yet accept an offer of 7/3, well short of the equitable 5/5 split. Does this show that equity is less than decisive in the appropriate sense, or that equity should be simply balanced against other values after all? The answer is "no." We may instead conclude that people reasonably refuse to take a stand for fairness at any personal price. Which is not to say that the person making the offer in the first place had less than a decisive reason to offer equal shares: the unfair offer still should not have been made. Whether it should be accepted, once made, is a different question, which depends on the further matter of what costs it is sensible or reasonable to bear in the face of unfair treatment.

3. Equity Over Time

Our basic fair division problem is a case of *transactional* equity or inequity, in the sense that the parties divide a good, in a one-time transaction, and otherwise may have nothing to do with one another. The question of *structural* equity stretches across time: it arises only when people relate in a regularized way that constitutes an ongoing social practice (as defined, e.g., in Chapter 2.1).

A sustained practice will normally create and distribute advantages and disadvantages over time. In that case, the question of how those affected are justifiably treated often cannot be settled by standards of transactional equity that apply in the absence of the practice. In a temporally extended relationship, momentary relative disadvantages can often be compensated for later on and perhaps in different but acceptable terms. Some social arrangements such as slavery are simply *illegitimate*, because no such adjustments will render the practice even minimally acceptable to each over time. Other arrangements are potentially legitimate, because they can be adjusted in ways that are potentially acceptable to each involved, in light of the kind of relationship being sustained. A married couple, for example, might reasonably accept a division of labor that would be clearly unfair among friends, given other features of the more encompassing relationship. Friends might reasonably embrace an exchange of favors that would be clearly unfair among strangers. The friends, unlike the strangers, perhaps cheerfully assume that "everything will work out in the end." Similarly, market-oriented society is often defended in temporally extended terms, in light of dynamic production. Each member of society, it is said, should find it acceptable to forgo fairness claims on a transaction-by-transaction basis, leaving things to market relations, for the sake of fair shares of a more productive system of cooperation over time.

It is important that this temporally extended justification is hardly license for laissez-faire; structural equity may make significant and indeed egalitarian demands. A market-oriented society will have to adopt not only the constitutively embedding institutions needed to make a set of exchanges in a competitive market but also the functionally embedding social and political institutions needed to return structurally equitable levels of benefit to each person over the course of his or her life. And benefits cannot be deferred to the economist's "long run." In the long run, as Keynes famously quipped, we are all dead. Deferred benefits must accrue to each person *within* his or her own lifetime, appropriately distributed over the stages of life. In principle, structural equity may even require equality of lifetime shares, much as in our initial transactional problem of fair division. Rawls's Difference Principle for major domestic institutions is a highly (if not fully) egalitarian principle of this structural kind, for example (it permits inequality for reasons of dynamic production). In Chapter 6, we will argue that the global economy similarly presents a temporally extended fair division problem to which an "equal gains benchmark" is the structurally equitable solution. At the moment our point is more general: even as practice may change what is fair, transactional equity demands are not eliminated by market relations but rather shifted to the structural level. What was or would have been an issue of transactional fairness becomes a fresh question of structural equity. The transactional relations need only be sufficiently embedded within an ongoing practice.[9]

---

9. When do transactional relations (or a small social practice) become "sufficiently" caught up in a larger social practice? Answers do not seem

Although structural equity is a deontological idea, the *consequences* of a market economy therefore matter, but in a distinctive and especially important way. In the global economy, they reflect on whether its organizing market reliance practice treats different countries and classes as the moral equals they are. It is not enough that an outcome is a good or bad state of the world, since that may say nothing about how we *treat* one another (perhaps the outcome is beyond all human control). At the same time, what is chiefly in question is not the actions of individuals. The outcomes that matter are those attributable to a social practice, to the systemic upshot of regularized conduct over time. Examples are familiar from domestic society: a judicial system systematically prosecutes a minority racial group while consistently ignoring illegal conduct among a racial majority, or larger society systematically excludes the handicapped from opportunities for basic education and work. Our claim is that the consequences of the global economy matter in this general way: they matter because they reflect equitable or inequitable treatment in the structure of a social practice as it (perhaps unintentionally) operates over time.

4. The Force of Structural Equity

If outcomes therefore matter over time, our deontological conception of equity implies that they matter in a normatively decisive way: barring extenuating circumstances, those who bear the responsibility of structural equity have conclusive reason not to allow certain distributional outcomes to come about over an appropriate time frame—the medium to longer haul, perhaps, but before we are all dead.

Of course, tough trade-offs invariably accompany real-world decisions of policy or law. These might seem to present a dilemma: we either opt for intuitive balancing of different values, which each lack any special normative force, or we try in futility to specify a balancing rule that at once has plausibility and determinate implications for all or most questions of law or policy.

---

forthcoming when the question is posed at a high level of abstraction. Our constructive method, by contrast, is context specific: we need only say something sensible about the global economy in particular. We return to this later in the chapter.

A major methodological assumption of this book is that the latter task is indeed futile: no general rule of decision could yield plausible verdicts in the full range of contexts that might come up for consideration, at least not without implausible revisionism of significant fairness ideas. Nor is it wise to *insist* on some such rule all the same. As Aristotle famously counseled, we should not expect more determinacy than our subject matter will bear, whether in physics, economics, or political philosophy. Determinacy shouldn't trump plausibility.[10] But are we then left with intuitive balancing of worthy values, with little hope of justifying any principles of structural equity as conclusive responsibilities? Not necessarily. There is a third way: we can "weigh up" competing values within a framework of reasoning that guides us toward conclusive judgments, in part by allowing us to plausibly take competing values into account. The test of such a framework is not determinacy per se (certainly not at the cost of plausibility) but rather *relative confidence*: the test is whether we have greater confidence in our judgments of structural equity when they are made and adjusted within the proposed moral/interpretive framework than if they were made ad hoc.[11]

We have already begun to outline the general moral features of such a framework in a way that speaks to potentially competing

---

10. Utilitarianism has often been favored on these grounds, despite its well-known difficulties. Although it may lead to counter-intuitive or barely defensible results, it is thought, we can simply revise our intuitions accordingly: we at least have a determinate decision rule. But compare the analogous thought in mathematics: "We need a determinate decision rule for answering mathematical questions, even if it leads to intuitively incorrect results. We can simply revise our mathematical intuitions accordingly. At least we have a determinate decision rule." Even if a modicum of revisionism is ultimately needed, intuitive plausibility should have great weight.

11. The framework increases our confidence, we hope, in several ways: it delineates the relevant components of a fairness judgment and their specific moral roles; it makes fairness assessment at least *more* determinate than arbitrary stabs in the dark; it allows us to account for the manifest moral and social complexity of the global economy without feeling completely swamped; it gives us a general basis for isolating specific areas of dispute and adjudicating them with appropriate sensitivity to their relevant complexity; it narrows the plausible sources of disagreement on matters of practical concern; and, ultimately, it adds to our confidence in our own favored side of particular disputes.

values. Our personalistic conception of reasoning—we reason *from* different agential standpoints—rules out any direct appeal to "impersonal" considerations of how the world goes over time, from no particular person's point of view. Impersonal considerations qualify as relevant only when some relevant agents have *personal* reasons to be allowed to act on and advance impersonal values (e.g., the impersonal value of environmental protection might strengthen a country's personal objection to environmental degradation). This leaves no scope for utilitarianism as a fundamental moral doctrine; the mere fact that some action or policy would make the state of the world go better, on balance, by maximizing utility overall, has *no relevance at all*, per se, for structural equity. Yet this is not to deny all aggregation of benefits or burdens across persons, when it has a personalistic rationale. Aggregation may, for example, provide a "tie-breaking" consideration among benefits and costs of comparable significance (e.g., one person may be left to die in order to save five others from death or comparably serious injury).[12] While an aggregative cost-benefit analysis may therefore be appropriate in particular policy areas, the crucial point is that the case in a given area must be made, in terms of what is reasonably acceptable to every party involved, rather than by naked appeal to what is impersonally best overall.

It is hotly debated whether such personalism is sufficiently insensitive to aggregative or other impersonal concerns.[13] For our purposes, we should remain open to the possibility that such concerns sometimes have overriding importance. We therefore accept personalism as our methodological default, initially proceeding as though it is correct. But we admit impersonal concerns when, and only when, there is a clear and especially powerful case for them.

Impersonal concerns aside, there are several ways of accounting for competing values consistent with structural equity's normally conclusive significance. First, structural equity will remain normally conclusive for action, so long as we can plausibly treat the circumstances of conflict as extenuating circumstances. When forced to choose between better and worse structural inequities (perhaps due to moral corruption or lack of political will), we may

---

12. Kamm, 1993, pp. 116–17; Scanlon, 1998, p. 232.
13. See especially Parfit, 2011.

permissibly choose the lesser evil. More generally, insofar as our first concern is the normal general conditions of market reliance over the medium to longer haul, value conflicts over the short run can be treated as a secondary concern: they can be addressed in light of the long- or medium- to longer-haul responsibilities justified by temporarily setting the short run to one side.

Second, instead of abstracting away from value conflicts, we may also *absorb* apparently competing values as relevant fairness concerns. We suggested this for dynamic productivity gains: the inequalities of reward that incentivize risk-taking and effort may count as justifiable, not because we can justifiably *compromise* equity for the sake of efficiency or welfare, but because the inequalities are *equitable*, provided they remain in a form acceptable to each and to all.

Third, we may also partly absorb and partly challenge the force of competing values. Consider several examples. *Rights and liberties*. We assumed in Chapter 1.3 that rights and liberties have no general force independent of what terms of social cooperation are fair. We also argue, in Chapters 7–9, that they in some cases present morally relevant considerations that both shape and are shaped by other considerations of fairness. *Welfare*. While we admit *aspects* of welfare as relevant to fairness argument, we deny the relevance of welfare per se.[14] The rich man's preference for fine living isn't morally on a par with the poor man's preference to leave his condition of material destitution, or even the moderately well-off man's preference for limiting volatility in his wage prospects. Not all preferences should have equal moral weight, and some preferences (or aspects of welfare) simply don't count as relevant from a moral point of view (e.g., a preference for being the richest person in the world).[15] *Efficiency*. When we cannot simply absorb the force of efficiency concerns, fairness may trump efficiency. We shouldn't efficiently benefit some, even at no harm to others, if this would be unfair: if the others can lay reasonable claim to the benefit (e.g., because they are less well-off), it should go to them instead (perhaps at some cost to those better off). *The "greater good."* If aggregation across the lives of

---

14. Scanlon, 1998, ch. 3.
15. Scanlon, 2003, ch. 4.

different individuals is justified in some cases, it should in many cases be resisted. When overall utility is optimized by imposing severe burdens on some for the sake of trivial benefits to billions of others (e.g., poor-country farmers are rendered destitute by rich-world farm subsidies, but billions of consumers see slightly cheaper commodities), this seems unfair to the severely disadvantaged. This is a normally decisive reason not to adopt the policy, even if it in some sense advances the "greater good."

5. Internal and External Issues

We now descend from the intellectual clouds and wade into the muddy global economic terrain.[16] Much of our discussion in later chapters will assume a distinction between two general kinds of fairness issue. Let us say that a moral or fairness issue is *external relative to the global economy as we know it* (an *external issue*, for short) when the issue would not be fundamentally different if no properly global economy existed. A moral or fairness issue is *internal relative to the global economy as we know it* (an *internal issue*), by contrast, when it comes up *because* a global economy exists, with certain distinctive characteristics (those outlined in Chapter 1.4). If the global economy as we know it did not exist, or took a radically different form, internal moral or fairness issues would not necessarily arise or apply, at all or in the same basic ways.[17]

---

16. The remainder of this chapter draws heavily from James, forthcoming(a).
17. More generally, we may say that a moral issue, value, or principle is *internal relative* to a form of activity or practice P just in case it would not apply in the absence of P, and *external relative* to P just in case it would so apply. Thus, even among issues external to the global economy, issues may be either internal or external relative to other social forms. For example, even if human rights concerns are external relative to the global economy, they may be internal relative to international relations rather than purely natural rights (e.g., as according to Rawls, 1999; Nickel, 2007; and Beitz, 2009). Even central humanitarian obligations can be seen as having institutional preconditions. Rawls's duty of assistance is not a duty to individuals as such but rather to support "burdened societies." Other basic concerns of humanitarian obligations (e.g., to rescue a drowning child, as in Singer, 1972) are presumably fully external to any contingent social relationship.

Humanitarian values are clearly external: our reason to relieve human suffering does not depend on the existence or nature of the global economy, or indeed any established social practices or institutions. Likewise, if countries were more or less economically self-sufficient, but interacting for non-economic reasons, they would still have the same moral grounds for avoiding war, for advancing human rights, for protecting the global environmental commons, and so on. The class of internal issues is less open to clear-cut definition. In the first instance, it includes the straightforward socioeconomic benefits and costs *created* by economic integration—things such as greater wealth and higher standards of living, but also unemployment, wage suppression, increased risk of social and economic displacement, and so on. Consequences for other interests, such as security or health, might also be relevant, so long as their significance is not seen as settled by external principles but rather as an open, internal question of reasonably acceptable trade practice. Some values may mix internal and external elements. We consider exploitation and other values as mixed in this way in Chapter 10.

In order to focus on internal issues, we adopt the working stipulation that *there are no external issues*. We assume there are no underlying issues of human rights, poverty relief, environmental protection, or of any other external kind, until explicitly indicated otherwise. The main question of this book may then be put this way: Is anything left? There exists a global economy. What sorts of internal fairness issues, if any, does it bring up, simply in virtue of the kind of social reality it is and the difference in the world it makes?

To answer, it will be helpful to temporarily set aside (perhaps internal) questions of rectification—for example, for the evils of colonialism and innumerable other profoundly consequential past wrongs. Although this background deeply shapes the terms upon which many countries enter or participate in the global economy, we will focus, in the first instance, on relatively recent, current, or prospective internal fairness issues and factor rectification in separately. We do not assume that status quo holdings are justified, but only that, if they are objectionable, there are non-rectificatory grounds for fairness objection. Further arguments against status quo holdings and for rectificatory justice can be made on their own terms—perhaps with reference to any internal, prospective principles we identify by temporarily setting rectification aside.[18]

Because our question is whether *any* internal issues arise, we do not initially require any very precise delineation of the class of internal concerns. We can begin with the straightforward *socioeconomic* benefits and costs created by economic integration and consider less straightforward cases in light of proposed elaborations of the internal/external distinction. If the internal issues are few, we conclude that fairness issues in the global economy must be mainly of the external sort. If the internal issues are substantial, we seek to isolate and characterize them, factoring in other (perhaps equally or more important) external issues down the road. The upshot is *not* that external issues are secondary, less important, or less demanding, but that they are not the only issues of significance. The general aim is simply to delineate deeper joints in the structure of moral ideas and to say with clarity how moral or fairness issues may relate, conflict, or combine.

6. Internal Issues: Examples

Our main question, then, is, To what extent, if at all, do internal fairness issues arise? We now canvass a range of examples, offering stipulations about what is reasonably acceptable for purposes of suggestive illustration. Our main claim is that significant internal structural equity issues do seem to arise, in specific areas and for the international practice of market reliance as a whole.

Consider first an *unfair ruling*. WTO rules allow a member country to legislatively protect the environment or public health even if this restricts international trade to the detriment of its trading partners (see, e.g., GATT Article XX or the WTO Sanitary and Phytosanitary Agreement). Suppose this permission is one that no one can reasonably complain of, perhaps because it is reciprocally enjoyed. Or to take a purely economic case, consider

---

18. Past wrongful expropriation (through colonialism, or a dictator's theft of a country's resources) can also upset the legitimacy of initial holdings in a way that changes what structural equity requires. Our argument assumes only that the issue of structural equity is in principle separable from rectificatory and other moral issues.

the WTO Safeguard Agreement, which allows a member government to adopt industrial policies (e.g., infant industry protection) that disadvantage firms in other countries. Suppose the member country can reasonably insist on this (e.g., because it is essential for economic development). But now imagine, in either case, that a foreign member country files a legal complaint with the WTO on grounds of economic disadvantage, and that a dispute settlement panel erroneously rules against the trade restriction (perhaps on the grounds that it is a disguised and unnecessary form of protectionism).[19] The panel ruling, we may say, is not only mistaken jurisprudence but unfair: it has introduced a structural inequity into the shared market reliance relationship.

In other cases, a rule may seem not simply misapplied but itself an *unfair rule*. Many criticize the WTO's dispute settlement system on the grounds that developing member countries are not in a position to effectively rely on the WTO Dispute Settlement Understanding (DSU). According to the DSU, only the wronged party has a right of retaliation (if all other remedies fail).[20] That rule could be changed: third-party or collective retaliation could instead be permitted, which might help developing countries find support in enforcing their rights when they cannot do so by themselves. But as things stand, developing WTO members often have little capacity to effectively retaliate against the advanced members, with limited ability to negotiate for compensation. They do not enjoy the "fair value" of their rights under the DSU, as compared to richer or larger WTO members, who can take full advantage of the system. It would seem then that poorer WTO members can reasonably insist that third-party or collective retaliation be permitted. To the extent this isn't allowed, the DSU creates a structurally inequitable distribution of political and economic advantages and disadvantages in the legal system.

As this example suggests, we may also wish to speak of a fair or unfair *system* of rules. The centerpiece of trade law is its "non-discrimination" norms (the most-favored nation rule and the rule of national treatment): roughly, trade and trade-related policy is

---

19. One might think here of the famous Tuna/Dolphin cases, decided by GATT panels prior to the establishment of the current WTO dispute settlement system, which turned on a balance between economic and noneconomic factors. We mean to offer a stylized and so clearer-cut example.
20. WTO DSU, Art. 22.

not to discriminate between different trading countries and their firms.[21] But despite the prima facie fairness in the idea of "same treatment," it is now well recognized that developing countries require "special and differential treatment" provisions, in part for fairness reasons. Developing countries often need to take special discriminatory measures to protect highly vulnerable groups, to nurture infant industries, or to sustain fiscal solvency (e.g., through tariff revenues), in virtue of their less-developed infrastructure, institutional capacity, high unemployment, or poverty levels. To relate to developing countries under a blanket non-discrimination norm, without allowing special privileges of market protection, would be to ignore their special circumstances in a way they could reasonably complain of. They could so complain, we may say, because mutual benefit is the very point of the trading system, and because developing countries would be harmed or fail to benefit to a sufficient degree.

While current WTO practice is broadly sensitive to fairness in this way (e.g., in the Generalized System of Preferences), current practice arguably both allows unfair policies (e.g., rich-world farm subsidies) and bans fair policies (such as pro-development export subsidies). Developing countries are now expected to forgo infant industry protection, preferential taxes, and export subsidies aimed at industrial "self-discovery" and trade to "dynamic comparative advantage," even as these have historically been instrumental for rapid and successful development among peer countries.[22] In effect, developing countries are not allowed to benefit from trade in the way that best serves their development needs. This is facially contrary to structural equity as well as other parts of standing trade law.[23]

The inconsistency is only facial because the fairness issue is of a systemic kind. The onerous ban on pro-development infant

---

21. The "most-favored nation" rule concerns discrimination *between* different foreign countries, but not between its own economy and all foreign countries. The "national treatment" rule requires that foreigners be treated as nationals.
22. Rodrik, 2007; Stiglitz, 2006.
23. GATT Article 36.3 mentions a "need for positive efforts designed to ensure that less developed contracting parties secure a share in the growth in international trade commensurate with the needs of their economic development."

industry protection or export subsidies is unfair only because "corrections" are not made elsewhere in the system. In principle, an otherwise inequitable export subsidy in one country might be counterbalanced by otherwise inequitable anti-dumping duties in another country, with the longer-term result that relative advantages and disadvantages appropriately "balance out" over the longer haul. Likewise, even if developing countries have historically benefited from policies of industrial self-discovery, the prima facie inequity of now being precluded from taking such measures could well be counterbalanced by other measures, with the long-term result that currently developing countries perform in league with their historical peers. It is only because such "corrective" measures have not been adopted that the prima facie inequity is an inequity in fact.

This suggests that we should often speak of fairness or unfairness in an *overall practice*. Suppose similarly governed and endowed countries sustain trade relations over time, but with the result that one country (or set of countries) reaps substantially larger gains as compared to the others. Suppose we cannot plausibly attribute the divergence to any underlying difference in endowment (e.g., resource base, population size) or other general social arrangements (a culture of work versus leisure) that would be consistent with the economic rationale for trade. Indeed, suppose the disadvantaged country or countries in question reap minimal gains. In this case, we may say, the overall trade practice is structurally inequitable because of how its gains are distributed over time.

The scope of "overall trade practice" would seem to go beyond the "international system" narrowly construed. It includes bi-lateral and regional trade agreements, which are explicitly allowed under WTO law (provided that trade is freed) and which substantially "divert" the flow of trade. Overall trade practice would also seem to extend beyond negotiated government rules, as contrasted with domestic policies (beyond those regulated by the international rules). A wide range of domestic social or economic policies shape the value of trade for other countries (e.g., by shaping domestic cost of production and relative advantages or disadvantages of foreign importers or exporters). These seem quite open for fairness review.[24] The more difficult question is where to draw lines. If many domestic policies

---

24. On the unavoidability of "behind the border" fairness concerns, see Langille, 1996.

are *potentially* relevant, what we can say in general terms is that what would otherwise be a structural inequity in one part of the practice, taken by itself, might still be "corrected" (or exacerbated) by other domestic or international institutions. We perhaps often cannot assess any part of the practice without considering the practice as a whole.[25]

7. Capital Markets

We have so far focused on the multilateral system of trade. Does our inclusive conception of trade practice also extend to global financial and monetary markets that lie beyond the WTO's purview? They could in theory count a localized "state of nature" in which structural equity does not apply. In fact, however, they are plainly manifestations of the same market reliance practice that is expressed in the system of trade.

Capital markets are closely tied to goods and services trade in numerous ways. "Trade finance" for firms is crucial for well-functioning goods and services trade. Trade flows affect currency exchange rates, while currency valuation dramatically affects the value of goods and services trade. At the more general level of economic rationale, the comparative advantage argument for trading capital for labor, and vice versa, runs much as it does in the case of goods and services trade: advanced countries abundant in capital but scarce in labor can profitably trade with developing countries abundant in labor but scarce in capital. From a regulatory point of view, investment is addressed in trade agreements, in limited ways within the WTO, but more substantially in many bi-lateral or regional agreements. Taken aside from trade rules, financial transactions are highly regulated by domestic law and extraterritorial enforcement through international agreements. And even the current "non-system" for monetary policy and capital controls is substantially shaped by informal international practice as enforced by powerful social pressures emanating from central bank officials and international organizations such as the G20 and the IMF. To the extent

---

25. This is further reflected in "nullification or impairment" provisions of GATT/WTO law.

political authority remains divided, this is plausibily viewed as *mere* fragmentation of governance across monetary, financial, and trade rather than a number of fundamentally distinct economic forms. Whatever their final merits, calls for greater responsiveness between the IMF and the WTO or even for direct exchange rate regulation within WTO disciplines (especially given the profound influence of the Chinese currency peg on the value of trade most everywhere else) are perfectly appropriate. They are appropriate because capital markets and goods and services trade are aspects of one and the same international market reliance practice.

Of course, different economic realities could simply reflect an assortment of distinct and coincidentally related practices. Merely pointing a range of interconnections does not decisively suggest otherwise. History, however, clearly supports a more unified interpretation. In 1947, in the aftermath of two world wars, the major nations of the world banned together and self-consciously established a common practice of mutual market reliance. The GATT agreement on trade was but one element of the newly devised Bretton Woods system, which included several parallel arrangements, each with a different rationale within the overall system of economic cooperation. The roughly concurrent establishment of the IMF was intended to segregate trade policy from short-term balance of payments problems, so to stabilize the trading system. Governments could thus avoid, or at least delay, restrictions on trade, while the currency system (a dollar-mediated gold standard) would create monetary stability and deter the "competitive" currency devaluations commonly used during the interwar years.[26]

---

26. As Hudec, 1975, p. 10, explains: "Most of the inter-war restrictions on trade and payments had been justified as measures to deal with balance-of-payments problems. When payment deficits grew large enough to threaten a country's reserves of foreign currency and gold, governments usually had intervened in commercial transactions in order to reduce foreign expenditures and increase foreign receipts. The full catalogue of trade and monetary controls had been used to this end—tariffs, quantitative restrictions, export subsidies, and exchange controls. . . . The central idea of the IMF reform was to increase the reserves on which governments could draw in times of payment deficits. The increased reserves would allow governments to finance larger deficits and thus to avoid, or at least delay, restricting trade."

152   FAIRNESS IN PRACTICE

Under Bretton Woods, international currency and credit markets were part and parcel of the market reliance practice expressed in the multilateral system of trade as matter of conscious design. But even in the less coherent post–Bretton Woods era, the underlying practice of mutual market reliance is the same, but now expressed in a less regulated way. Much as with calls for policy coherence between the systems of finance and trade, it seems perfectly apt to call for a major reorganization of the dysfunctional systems of money and credit in the name of a more fair practice of economic cooperation overall. We do just this in Chapter 8.

8. The Question of Limits

Structural equity therefore has an inclusive scope. Along with the benefits and burdens of goods and services trade, concerns of structural equity will arise in any number of benefits and burdens created specifically by the systems of money and credit, including their consequences for growth, standards of living, development, and employment levels. While the measurement of such benefits and burdens is delicate, they in principle count as part of the "currency" of structural equity in the global economy. (Which is not to say that capital market reliance can be assessed in the same way as goods and services trade; Chapter 8 argues that the special hazards of capital markets raise special issues of fair risk imposition.)

The natural question, then, is what might *limit* the scope of structural equity concerns. We are temporarily postponing issues or values that mix internal and external elements. But we might also ask about purely internal issues related to the limits of the basic international market reliance practice itself.

History is again our guide. Compare the mutually destructive interwar years, when the practice of mutual market reliance was at best a sham.[27] The contemporary reliance practice, we may say, is roughly the difference between our world of economic globalization and the interwar years of fundamental distrust. We can set aside theoretically fascinating question of whether the late nineteenth- and early twentieth-century wave of globalization, organized by colonial rule, was of a fundamentally different

---

27. See the quoted passage in Chapter 3.4, note 24.

STRUCTURAL EQUITY 153

associative kind, or merely a very different version of the same general kind of practice. The contemporary world is not necessarily the same kind of beast. The world wars and interwar years fundamentally changed things, in conjunction with other trends such as the rise of democratic politics.

We can equally ask about the subject of structural equity in a prospective mode. The difference the practice will make is the difference between our expected future and the future as it would be if borders were sealed, at least for economic purposes. Or we may put the essential thought ahistorically: the going international market reliance practice as a whole stands in contrast to a hypothetical world of universal economic autarky, where there are no international trade deals, no trade flows across borders, and no economic gains or losses are to be had. The difference between that world and ours is the difference the market reliance practice makes and what its relevant scope includes.

This sphere of concerns corresponds to the scope of collective responsibility for a common economic practice. As suggested in Chapter 3.5, responsibility for the global economy's outcomes does not stop at each domestic government's borders, because integrated societies share responsibility for the outcomes their shared practice creates. Which is not to say the boundary of collective responsibility is very precise; it remains a hard question what domestic responsibilities result, and where international social responsibility leaves off. While there is perhaps no such demarcation in the abstract, this is also not to say that responsibility for the global economy swamps all of the responsibilities of domestic life. That responsibility extends no further than the global economy itself, and we continue to assume conditions of "partial integration" as outlined in Chapter 1.4. The consequences of the international market reliance practice remain meaningfully distinct from the consequences of different domestic economies taken by themselves. Sufficiently radical change in the underlying state system—for example, sufficiently deep economic and regulatory integration, over enough time—could of course obliterate any meaningful benchmark of comparison for identifying the benefits and burdens that market reliance practice creates. Yet our politically decentralized and partly integrated world is, and for the foreseeable future will be, safely short of this obliterating line. It is not clear that globalization will even gradually take us in the direction of full integration of the requisite kind. And even if it eventually does, our present question of international structural equity will be applicable and important for world politics for a century or two or three—or at any rate a good long while.

A question of limits might instead be asked at the international level. To what extent is the international market reliance practice separable from larger international relations? Our answer is mixed: it is separable in some ways, but not in others, but in any case separable enough to pose a distinctive question of fairness.

The embedding state system clearly does bear on internal structural equity in very basic ways, by defining property rights, for instance. Consider the problem of "clean trade." The current state system grants any ruling government, however illegitimate, the legal right to sell resources in its country's name. Yet it is also a basic requirement of fair market exchange that the seller must have title to what is sold. Insofar as illegitimate dictators lack resource ownership rights—the oil, or diamonds, or jute they sell belong to the people instead—it follows that international resource transactions with dictatorial regimes are not fair exchange, but trafficking in stolen goods.[28] A huge swath of world commodities market transactions—and what price isn't affected by tainted oil?—then counts as unfair, or illegitimate, on internal grounds. The issue is internal, unlike a bare concern for human suffering, because it would not equally come up in a world of universal economic autarky, and because it takes the form it does take in part because of the way commodities trade is situated within a system of international property rights (i.e., the people of each country together own the resources).

We are also suggesting, however, that the international practice of mutual market reliance is to a considerable extent separable, conceptually and practically, from larger international relations. Or at least it is not inseparable in any sense that prevents us from meaningfully posing our general question of structural equity about the global economy, taken in its own right. This is of course open to challenge. For example, given that countries routinely free trade in exchange for security services (e.g., Nimibia with South Africa, or with the United States), why say there is a distinct international economic practice? Are not security services

---

28. Wenar, 2008. Wenar proposes that importing governments raise tariff revenue to be held in a "clean hands" trust until it can be returned to the people under more a legitimate government.

that partly enforce property rights a precondition for mutually beneficial economic relations in any enduring form? While we cannot fully take up the matter here, our answer is that, as a general interpretive matter, the various relevant sources of law and practice point toward relative autonomy.

We may grant that security issues present special extenuating or short-run fairness concerns. Security guarantors may in some cases be fairly "paid" in augmented trade. Even so, the established international practice of mutual market reliance retains its own general rationale, which we presented in detail in Chapter 2. That rationale assumes a relatively stable international system but does not follow from it: a stable international system is consistent with universal economic autarky. Moreover, the relative autonomy of economic fairness seems well reflected in world political argument. The core issues are often assumed to be largely economic; complaints are made and conceded often without reference to security issues. Accordingly, to the extent the costs of security services do raise fairness issues, it is natural to suppose that they can be settled as special concerns.[29]

So the global economy can be evaluated as a kind of sub-system of larger international relations. But how, then, is that consistent with the inclusive conception of economic practice suggested earlier? Why shouldn't we assess, say, WTO intellectual property rules on their own terms, in just the way the larger international economic practice is to be assessed separately from the larger set of international relations? Our answer is holistic. We offer a range of interpretive considerations that point toward relative economic autonomy, but no fully general theory of embedding that somehow directly yields a division of fairness domains. Bearing in mind that social interpretation is an inherently messy affair, we simply work out the best available interpretation of an extraordinarily complex set of relations, by comparing alternative interpretations and evaluating them on the merits overall.

---

29. Suppose, for example, that security gains motivate a small government to open itself further to trade, and that the security guarantor expects certain economic advantages. This might bear on our assessment of the terms upon which the small country entered and began to participate in the international practice of market reliance. But it need not change our basic sense of what terms of participation will be fair over time, especially as economic and security conditions evolve.

156   FAIRNESS IN PRACTICE

9. Internal Fairness Concerns

We close this chapter by canvassing a range of seemingly loose and sundry fairness ideas. Bringing together strands of argument from other chapters, we suggest that various apparently unrelated ideas in fact express different aspects of the international market reliance practice and its basic responsibility of structural equity. This gives fairness discourse greater normative unity than it might otherwise seem to have, and it develops our overall framework for the prosecution of specific fairness disputes. Insofar as the structural equity issue is itself an internal issue, any fairness ideas we explain with reference to it can be seen as internal as well: their content will then depend on whatever deeper structural equity principles turn out to be justified. We here mainly assert plausible relationships, returning to a less dogmatic presentation of key issues elsewhere.

Fair Play. As discussed in Chapter 3, fidelity or "fair play" is a matter of doing one's part within a cooperative practice when it comes time to do so.[30] Here the subject of assessment is not the structure of a practice but the conduct of particular agents within a practice. Even perfect "fair play" by all does not ensure structural equity; there can be perfect compliance with a practice whose terms are grossly unfair.

Structural equity does, on the other hand, plausibly shape what "fair play" in a practice requires. In routine policy administration, fair play chiefly involves officials applying and following established rules. Insofar as trade rules are often crafted within open-ended terms, which officials must interpret and apply, fidelity requires good faith efforts to apply rules in the light of their understood purpose, deliberative mutuality,[31] principles for a

---

30. Hart, 1955; Rawls, 1971, p. 112; Simmons, 1979; Klosko, 1992.
31. By "deliberative mutuality" I mean the norms that apply in the context of what Joshua Cohen and Charles Sabel, 2005, call "deliberative polyarchy." These involve "dynamic accountability" to co-deliberators, even or especially in the absence of centralized authority. Given situated uncertainty and openness to mutual learning in the face of open-ended values, parties make shared decisions based on mutual responsiveness to the force of reasons, assumed to be mutually relevant and acceptable to reasonable co-deliberators. The sphere of governance is generally open to demands for transparent explanation and justification of decisions, especially to informed or affected parties, and in comparison to decisions

structurally equitable trading practice.[32] It would be "unfair play," for example, to set policy *simply* according to "national self-interest" whenever rules seems indeterminate (especially when rules, say, for "anti-dumping" measures are rife with indeterminacy).[33] The interests of a given country or its members do matter, but structural equity principles concern how other countries and their members fare as well.

Political Fair Play. Fair play also applies to explicitly political institutions or practices, for instance, to trade negotiations within established bargaining procedures (e.g., the WTO rule of consensus). These can also be structurally equitable or inequitable, quite independent of the underlying structure of trade rules.

Political fairness is partly "procedural": it requires, for its own sake, that negotiations be transparent, that negotiators respect norms of deliberative mutuality, that all affected parties have voice in setting the negotiation agenda, and that technical assistance be available as needed. Negotiators are to abide by such expectations, as a matter of fair play, even when their de facto bargaining power allows them to cheat or simply set rules aside. But political fairness is also "substantive": how political institutions are designed will make a big difference to what market reliance practice emerges over time. Insofar as trading countries share responsibility to steer the practice in the direction of structural equity, the responsibility is equally to establish political institutions that best facilitate that steering role.

Fair Bargaining. In Chapter 3, we argued for much the same conclusion as regards bargaining *within* established procedures.

---

made by similarly situated agents, all as liable to judicial or peer review. Cohen and Sabel argue that such accountability without authority now applies to a relatively autonomous sphere of global administrative law, comprised of formal and informal international institutions and regulatory networks. WTO law and financial institutions and networks present especially clear cases.

32. See the duty of fidelity in Chapter 3.1. We may see the required judgment, in a Dworkinian way, as an interpretive judgment that is appropriately sensitive to the best conception of structural equity. For examples (associated with "constructivism") from judicial rulings in international law, see Koskenniemi, 1989, pp. 223–36.

33. For problems of vagueness in anti-dumping duty rules that encourage unfair application, see Stiglitz, 1977.

The basic responsibility of fair play (what we called the "duty of fair governance") is to negotiate toward trade rules which, in the context of the larger system, are fair to all countries involved, according to basic structural equity principles. For developing countries with limited bargaining power, this may rightly mean zealous advocacy for the "national self-interest." For rich countries in a strong bargaining position, by contrast, to bargain *simply* for the "national self-interest" is a dereliction of duty. Negotiating toward equitable terms is the fair price of the trading system's significant benefits.

Fair Default. Ideas of fidelity also apply *within* markets, for instance, in expectations that voluntarily assumed debts should be repaid. When a government defaults on its debt due to corruption or gross fiscal mismanagement, for example, this is unfair to its (official or private) lenders, who legitimately expected repayment. At the same time, default or debt restructuring may also be fair, for reasons of structural equity, when repayment would be sufficiently onerous (e.g., interest payments in foreign-currency denominated loans suddenly become a large percentage of GDP or export revenue falls due to an unforeseeable exchange-rate fluctuation). The least-developed countries will often require complete debt forgiveness. Emerging markets or middle-income countries will often require significant debt restructuring (with private or official lenders). Instead of leaving the details to bi-lateral negotiations, or even international banks, they would be more equitably resolved in an international bankruptcy facility, or at least by international bankruptcy standards perhaps as interpreted by third-country courts.[34]

From a structural equity point of view, we should not treat loans taken by governments or private parties as a standard transactional promise—"if you give us such-and-such funds, we'll repay with such-an-such interest." Borrowing and lending instead reflect participation in the larger international market reliance practice. Rights and obligations of repayment are to be assessed, not on a loan-by-loan basis, but in terms of the practice's overall consequences, over time. So long as countries and their members or firms adequately benefit from opportunities to borrow or lend, as assessed by structural equity principles, a

---

34. Sachs, 1995; Krueger, 2003; Stiglitz, 2006, p. 233.

particular government that falls on hard times may not necessarily be under a strict duty of fidelity to repay. When a developing country is suddenly faced with massive and unexpected interest outlays, for example, its government will not show infidelity to the *practice* if it defaults on the stated agreement (or unilaterally restructures its terms of repayment), especially when full repayment would seriously threaten its otherwise positive development trajectory. The lenders who lose out this time may still amply benefit from borrowing or lending across other occasions, with this or other countries. (We can assume lenders have a claim against arbitrary treatment, which provides yet another reason for the suggested bankruptcy institutions.)

This adds yet another reason that fidelity should not require repayment of "odious debts" taken on by illegitimate regimes. Illegitimate regimes are presently allowed to borrow in their country's name, leaving heavy debt obligations upon their populations. When the regimes crumble, the country is still expected to repay, no matter how badly the money was spent (e.g., Chile still pays the debts of Pinochet, and South Africa the debts of apartheid). This is arguably a humanitarian disaster, as well as illegitimate (the people never took on the obligations because the illegitimate government never represented them). It is also structurally inequitable: the lenders who generally profit from this arrangement can fairly take the loss. When the legitimacy of a government is unclear, they can play it safe, or simply defer to a public watch list. Although lenders will be concerned with disappointed expectations of repayment,[35] the watch list in effect puts them on notice: "lend as you will, but don't expect to be repaid."[36]

Free and Fair Trade. Structural equity requirements do not tell countries how far they should remove barriers to trade. As we suggest in Chapter 7, fully free trade can be perfectly fair, so long as it is embedded within nonmarket institutions that appropriately distribute the resulting advantages and disadvantages, according to applicable structural equity principles. The question is then whether social insurance institutions can indeed be established and at what cost. If developing countries cannot easily

---

35. See Chapter 7.11 for why "legitimate expectations" do not preclude such fairness measures.
36. Jayachandran and Kremer, 2006.

afford this, but free trade is preferred, then advanced countries will be required to supplement a regime of free trade with social insurance support, as the fair price of involvement in the system. When the social insurance schemes or the support are not forthcoming, well-targeted trade barriers may well be fair.

Free Trade and (External) Moral Values. A common moral argument for trade protection arises when a country takes objection to conditions within its trading partner's jurisdiction, say, on grounds of human rights abuses, environmental degradation, or some other external moral value. Setting aside our working exclusion of external values for the moment, it is plausible to hold that trade protection would be fair on such moral grounds (even if not always wise, given better alternatives). Trade restrictions will presumably be justifiable if they curb genocide, for instance, and there may be a range of cases of less dramatic kinds.[37] The constraint of structural equity will be that action on such values, especially when it comes at an economic cost to other countries, is regularized on roughly equal terms.[38]

In related cases, which we discuss in Chapter 10, the issue *combines* external and internal values. Consider the burdens of environmental protection to developing countries. Why should they be asked to forgo significant economic activity (a relevant internal value) for the sake of environmental preservation (an external value) if they are in effect asked to pay for this? If environmental protection matters, it would seem fairer for industrialized countries to pay, since they incur a smaller economic sacrifice and have often created the major environmental threats in the first place. In such cases, external values support the charge of internal unfairness in conjunction with internal values.

Respect for an external value may also be an *internal* issue if the concern is not *simply* with the objectionable conditions in the partner country but rather with the way members of a country may become *complicit* through those conditions in an unfair economic relationship. If developing-country workers often receive

---

37. For versions of this claim, see Howse and Trebilcock, 1996, as well as Risse, 2007, who limits potential grounds to the violation of negative rights.
38. GATT Article 20 reflects this idea by making action upon various values open to all member countries, subject to non-arbitrariness constraints.

exploitative wages or conditions for work, rich-world consumers may well be complicit in exploitation when they buy the goods those workers produce, in effect keeping exploitative firms in business. In that case, market protection might be a condition of structural equity on internal, purely socioeconomic grounds. (But see Chapter 10.2–10.5 for a qualified defense of "sweatshop" labor.)

Fair Prices. As suggested in Chapter 2.7, the subject of structural equity is not market transactions but the institutional settings that embed markets and shape their overall outcomes (perhaps by setting transactional incentives). The market price may well be the fair price. This will be so, however, only when the market in question is adequately embedded within a system of domestic or international institutions, where "adequacy" is judged with reference to structural equity principles.

As suggested above, a deep rationale of market-oriented society (as opposed, e.g., to a system of bartered exchange) is that any responsibilities of fair exchange can be shifted to the structural level: market actors can simply respect the thinned-out responsibilities of voluntary market exchange (non-coercion, non-deception, and so on), because functionally embedding institutions see to it that the overall gains of market allocation sufficiently redound to the benefit of all, as judged from a structural equity point of view. While advanced economies presumably usually qualify as "adequately" embedded, developing-country markets and the global economy at large are far less well organized. It does not seem that "adequate" international institutions are in place such that, say, investment deals between multinational corporations and developing-country firms can fairly be "left to the market."

Accordingly, in the context of poorly embedded markets, market actors inherit some share of the responsibilities that embedding institutions might under better circumstances have assumed (see Chapter 10.5). So even as the central advanced-country markets approximate "morally free zones,"[39] firms that venture abroad will inherit substantial responsibilities to adopt policies that accord with the larger purposes of developing-country integration, especially as specified by established international "best practice"

---

39. Gauthier, 1986. Although advanced countries arguably face substantial moral limits as well; see Satz, 2010.

norms,[40] but also by more general understandings of what terms lead to structurally equitable outcomes. Consumers, too, arguably have responsibilities to support transnational relationships (e.g., "fair trade coffee" cooperatives, or other certification schemes) that compensate for the structural inequities allowed by poorly embedded labor and development institutions. These "inherited obligations" will no longer apply once countries develop, or once appropriate embedding international institutions have been set up. Yet there is no telling whether that will eventually happen or how long it might take.

Fair Wages. Perhaps the most important issue of price fairness is developing-country wages. Because developing countries have their comparative advantage in labor, one of the main rationales for trade suggests that wages should not be artificially made more expensive. At the same time, to simply leave wages and working conditions to the market can also seem tantamount to allowing systemic exploitation of third-world workers. Unless "sweatshop" labor can be justified, it can indeed seem only fair to developing-country workers to make labor standards (for workplace conditions, collective bargaining, and perhaps minimum wages) a condition for trade, and perhaps the subject of future WTO commitments.

Even from a structural equity point of view, however, it can in principle be fair for the capitalist to "exploit" the worker, in Marx's technical sense of expropriating the surplus of his labor. Setting wages by the market need only be part of a larger fair system of cooperation, whose institutions return real and sufficient benefits to each worker over time. So if it turns out that workers are afforded appropriate levels of benefit, as specified by structural equity principles, then minimum wage labor standards won't be fairly enforced within the WTO. (Which is not to say that "core" standards or other "linkage" is not required; see Chapter 10.4.)

Fair Competition and the Level Playing Field. A quite different concern of fairness, often voiced in advanced countries, pertains to the circumstances of market competition. In many developing countries, labor is cheap, environmental rules are lax, and rules of intellectual property are not established or are weakly enforced. This is often said to create unfair competitive advantages for developing-country economic actors. Advanced-country actors

---

40. Ruggie, 2003, 2004.

then have to compete in a common market environment while saddled with the economic burdens of high wages and strict environment or intellectual property rules. Even if this does not justify outright trade protection, rules that "harmonize" policy across countries can be seen as a fair way to reduce the competitive disadvantage and "level the playing field."

This thought is legitimate in principle, but, as we will see in Chapter 9, it lacks the significance often claimed for it. We do not generally take competitive interactions to be subject to a demand of fairness for a "level playing field" in the sense that no player is allowed to have a competitive advantage over any other. The extent to which ex ante prospects of victory should be equalized depends entirely on the extent to which this would serve purposes assumed in the form of competition going on. The shape of "competitive fairness" depends largely on *instrumental* considerations. In the trade relationship, differential advantages may indeed be part and parcel of its basic mechanism for mutual benefit, and in that sense perfectly fair. Countries are not in competition per se but rather are engaged in a long-term cooperative relationship. Competition among their respective firms merely has a key instrumental role: it is the normal way each country's comparative advantage is "revealed." But if the role is merely instrumental, then we can equally allow competitive advantages when needed for countries to reap levels of benefit required for a structurally equitable practice overall. If freedom from policy harmonization is what it takes for developing countries to appropriately benefit from the system of trade, the resulting competitive advantages for developing-country firms are perfectly fair.

CHAPTER SIX

The Benchmark of Equality

We have argued that the central issue of fairness in the global economy is equitable treatment in the structure of a social practice. The global economy as we know it is embedded within a social practice of a distinctively international kind, a practice wherein different countries rely, mutually, on common markets. The basic subject of fairness is the overall structure of this relationship, or the way its institutions, rules, and expectations distribute advantages and disadvantages across different countries and their respective classes over time. Global commerce is founded on fair terms only when this organizing international practice is structurally equitable—only when it is arranged to distribute its benefits and burdens in a way that can be reasonably accepted by each and all.

But what does fairness substantially require? We have discussed numerous examples, but no answer of any generality—nothing like general principles that might guide a judgment about when going practice is structurally equitable rather than not. In this chapter, we take a further step in this direction, by defending an *equal gain benchmark*: equal distribution of the "gains of trade," adjusted for each country's background endowments, is the benchmark from which inequality of gain must be justified. Roughly, when nations gain from trade in national income to different degrees over time—when some prosper while others stagnate or eke along—the shared trade practice is presumptively unfair. Inequality of gain can be justified for special reasons, but equality of gain is the moral default.

1. A Problem of Fair Division

Why think equality of gain is even presumptively fair? Our answer is that we should view division of the "gains of trade" much as in the basic case of fair division discussed in Chapter 5.2. In that case, again, two parties are to divide a distributable good, such as some amount of money (e.g., $100). We assume the parties' situations are symmetrical—that nether has any special entitlement, or claim of need, or difference in potential benefit—and ask what split would be fair. It is very widely held, and hard to deny, that the fair distribution is equal shares.

Given our constructive method, we cannot automatically conclude that this requirement of equality applies elsewhere, whether to transactions in a modern economy or to the national income gains of international trade. Whatever is true of other contexts, however, we will argue that the trade relation is appropriately modeled as a fair division problem of the same general kind.[1] The case of trade is similar enough, in its relevant fundamental respects, such that an equal gains benchmark applies: trading countries are moral equals and symmetrically interested, and so must receive equal "gains from trade" over time—at least barring special reasons that inequality of gain is justified.[2]

The trade relation is of course often viewed in quite different terms. In one common picture, for example, fairness requires that transactions be voluntary—mutually informed, uncoerced, and so on—along with the institutions of contract and law needed for general circumstances of voluntary market exchange. But it supports no presumption that transactional gains must be equal, presumptively equal, not too unequal, or otherwise "appropriately" distributed. After all, it may be argued, we do not usually think any equal gain presumption is appropriate when you buy something I have at the

---

1. Specifically, we defend the equal division benchmark *as appropriate for the trade context* and not by a direct analogy with the highly suggestive fair division problem formulated in the text. We make no attempt to in a general way rule out alternative proposals of bargaining theory such as Nash, 1950, and Kalai and Smorodinski, 1975, which would imply divergent conclusions for the trade context despite similar symmetry axioms. We do return to the Nash bargaining solution below.

2. Unless otherwise indicated, we provisionally assume that countries are being compared over the same selected period of time (e.g., a decade or two or three). For many purposes, this basic model will need to be complicated by considering intergenerational distribution, within or across countries (e.g., when the current generation must bear the burden of correcting past unfairness to another country allowed by an earlier generation, or when burdens to a current generation are justified in part by future benefits of trade with a developing country).

market price. It is fair, we assume, to let the chips fall where they may, to let voluntary exchange and competition advance the general liberty or welfare, as by Adam Smith's famous invisible hand. But is not international trade *just so many transactions*, except that they happen to cross a state border? Is not the governmental choice to free trade just the choice to allow such transactions to occur, in the name of liberty, or for the sake of transactional welfare benefits? Trade can be justified by concern for the greater liberty or welfare of all. But why, then, should there be any issue of relative gains? Trade, in this picture, advances liberty and the greater good but has no further aim.

This "transactional" interpretation fundamentally mischaracterizes the established practice of international trade. At issue, we assume, is the structure of an international social practice, and how it is best interpreted overall. Even as government officials routinely act from narrowed interests (even, e.g., of mere bureaucratic self-promotion), there is a structure to the practice beyond such particular acts. While motivational tendencies are among the sources of structural interpretation, widely if implicitly understood organizing ideas, in trade theory, mercantilist sentiment, economic history, and contemporary practice, can also be relevant or of greater significance. In that light, we maintain, the suggested transactional conception mischaracterizes the practice of trade. The structure of the global economy as we know is best seen in fundamentally *international* terms: the chief aim of trade is to mutually augment *national* (aggregate or average) income, by way of national market reliance upon a common market, with welfare or liberty as welcome side effects. The transactional picture is at best a revisionary proposal, a *replacement* of going trade practice rather than a moral conception grounded in the structure of the global economy as it actually is.

To be more specific, our internationalist conception involves two central social interpretive theses. First, *the point of international trade is national gain*. The basic organizing rationale for the international practice of trade is not to benefit individuals per se, or to facilitate voluntary exchange for its own sake, but macroeconomic restructuring through the specialization of labor, for the sake of national aggregate or average efficiency gains.[3] Market

---

3. We may regard national income as what Rawls calls a "primary social good," i.e., something one has reason to want, whatever else one wants. Its augmentation can thus be the central, final aim of trade but also be significant for further reasons.

competition and voluntary exchange are primarily *mechanisms* for achieving this larger social purpose. Even if market exchange offers welcome welfare or liberty benefits, to take them as the point of trade is to conflate means with ends. They are not the central justifying, presumed legitimate purpose of maintaining an open economy, but rather welcome side effects. Second, *countries, not individuals, directly participate in this relationship*. Individuals participate in the practice indirectly, through regular economic activity, but it is a society as a whole that relies, mutually with other societies, on a common market. Individuals and firms compete and make voluntary exchanges *in* the common marketplace. But the relevant kind of participation is international construction and maintenance of the marketplace itself, for the larger socioeconomic end of mutually augmenting national wealth.

Once the trade relationship is properly understood in these internationalist terms, we can see why it would present a fair division problem to which the equal gain benchmark applies. This follows provided three further framing assumptions (which we state here and clarify below):

Status Equality: parties to the practice (chiefly, countries) are moral equals;

Symmetry of Interest: each trading country has a relevantly similar interest in greater rather than lesser shares of the gains of trade (national income gains, adjusted for background endowments not created by the trade relationship);

Absence of Special Entitlement: trading countries lack special entitlement to any particular level of gain, independent of what division is fair.

Under these conditions, as in the basic fair division case, the default fair division is equality of gain in (endowment-adjusted) national income.

Our aim in this chapter will be to provide plausible rationales for these assumptions. Our main thought is this: the national gains of trade are socially created by the international market reliance practice. Once we factor out the gains countries would have reaped under autarky, given their background endowments (land, labor, capital, technology, etc.), national income gains can only be understood as the fruit of international social cooperation. In that case, however, co-creating countries have no proprietary claims to any particular shares, short of what division is otherwise fair. Because countries plausibly have both equal moral status and symmetrical interests, the equal gain benchmark follows. Equal (endowment-adjusted) national income gains are the moral default. An unequal distribution of gains would arbitrarily discriminate against countries that receive lesser shares over time. Equality in the gains of trade, to the extent it is feasible, is the benchmark for equitable treatment in a common market reliance practice.

Several qualifications should be noted up front. One is that we offer no general characterization of how to "adjust" for background endowments. And our ability to track the gains of trade, to a reasonable approximation, is admittedly crucial: the equal gains benchmark (and our related principles in Chapter 7) will not qualify as regulative principles for trade practice if the idea of endowment-adjusted gains is hopelessly indeterminate.[4] Here we lean on morally informed economic science. The concept of gains over potentially divergent background endowments is central to international economics, and economic science already offers methods of approximating how much a given country gains from a trade relationship, over some period of time, given an assumed set of productive capacities. Especially as such methods improve, the benchmark of equal gains can fulfill a practically workable if perhaps general regulative role.

We should also emphasize that a mere *benchmark* of equality is quite consistent with special grounds for inequality, which apply in special circumstances, so long as they are not reflective of the general fairness situation, from a moral point of view. We will

---

4. Rawls, 1999, p. 13, calls welfare and capability sets "unworkable ideas" on these grounds. It is worth noting that our benchmark (and resulting principles) is not what Rawls, 1971, pp. 87–88, calls an "allocative" conception of fairness that seeks to meet known desires and needs while tracking complex transactions and changes in class position among particular individuals. As we explain later, we gain the practical advantages of regulative workability by focusing in the general case on the primary social good of national income and representative social positions, in light of temporally extended outcomes shaped by a public system of rules that shapes ongoing production. Moreover, as discussed in Chapter 5, we assume that outcomes matter, not per se, but because they reflect fair or unfair treatment in trade practice. If our account is not quite a case of "pure procedural" justice, we take our broadly procedural account to be appropriate for our distinctive subject matter.

consider several such special grounds in due course, including both special entitlements and special claims of need. Our overall argument is that they should be viewed in either of two ways: either they are out of place in the trade context, for interpretive or moral reasons, or they present legitimate special concerns that may be weighed up separately, without calling the basic equal gain benchmark into question. (The claim is that such concerns are *adequately* captured as special concerns, which means that our full argument depends upon other chapters which take them into account.)

If our argument is correct, fairness in trade is fundamentally egalitarian, but in an international sense. We compare the relative national income gains of whole countries in the first instance, and consider how their respective classes internally compare only as a secondary matter. The fair share for each person is a fair share of his or her country's fair share. There is no scope, then, for "cosmopolitan" comparisons in the relative fates of any two individuals of the world, taken aside from their society of membership over some span of time.

But why not accept a more "cosmopolitan" principle of fair division? If the principle is external, it will not answer our question of whether fairness generates *internal* demands, at least in the sense specified by the constructive method. If a principle of distribution is to be justified, it must be *justified as appropriate for the trade relationship* in light of the best constructive interpretation of what the trade relationship is like. In general, the social relationship in question is to itself shape what the fair division problem is, whether it even arises, and what form any appropriate fairness principles must take. We will in effect be arguing, in this chapter and in Chapter 7, that the best understanding of this shaping role fails to support a fully "cosmopolitan" standard of fair distribution. And yet, we claim, fairness generates the equal gains benchmark, a significant egalitarian presumption.

2. Relative Contribution?

Our main question, then, is whether our best understanding of the trade relationship supports the three framing assumptions stated earlier. We will discuss the three assumptions in reverse order, starting with Absence of Special Entitlement.

A prominent alternative to that assumption is David Gauthier's conception of fair division (or non-exploitation, as Gauthier might put it).[5] Applied to the case of trade, trading countries *would* have a kind of special entitlement to a particular level of gain, according to their relative contribution, where contribution is settled by rationally self-interested bargaining. In an imagined bargaining situation, each party would lay initial "claim" to his or her maximum possible gain (i.e., his or her welfare improvement over non-cooperation when he or she takes the full cooperative surplus). Each then modifies his or her proposed agreement (by "concessions"), optimizing for self-interest, until an agreement is reached. Each gets as much as possible for himself or herself, giving others only enough so that they cooperate rather than walk.

A rational agreement can yield equal shares, but only when all stand to lose equally if cooperation is never established: all must have roughly equal bargaining power. But there is no reason to suppose this is normally the case, especially not in global economic life. Non-agreement prospects will often vary: even when all countries benefit from trade, some countries stand to lose more than others from a situation of general autarky. Insofar as a well-endowed economy such as the United States can expect to do well on its own without trade, its relative benefit from trade cooperation will be less than that of a poorly endowed country such as Japan, which depends (or at least once depended) on trade for prosperity. By Gauthier's accounting, the United States gains much less than Japan when each is imagined to take the entire cooperative surplus for itself. So it rightly takes the lion's share.

We can reject this proposal for both moral and interpretive reasons. On the moral side, each country's initial "claim" to the full cooperative surplus and maximum possible benefit is inadmissible from a moral point of view. No country has a *morally relevant* interest in taking the full cooperative surplus. Each does have an interest in greater rather than lesser shares (discussed later), but that will not amount to a morally relevant interest, or potentially reasonable claim, if it is flatly inconsistent with each other country's interest in also having greater rather than lesser shares. The interest of each in a greater rather than lesser share can at most be a claim to an equal level of gain. We may even grant that participating countries in the trading system have special

5. Gauthier, 1986.

claims as compared to countries not involved in the joint venture, or that special burdens amount to "unequal contribution" and require compensation. Even so, when no such further considerations enter, there is only one initial kind of morally relevant participation-based claim consistent with the morally relevant participation-based claims of all: a (presumptive) claim to equal gains.

Gauthier might of course cite some *further* moral reasons that cooperation is only fair when those who benefit least from cooperation see the largest share of gains. But the case would have to be made, and there is certainly no general moral reason to think that any participant's morally relevant interest in greater rather than lesser shares somehow terminates at the level of gain at which there is prudential reason for him or her to cooperate rather than walk (to prefer trade over autarky). Such matters of prudence depend on too many factors which have no justificatory relevance to questions of what arrangements are fair. If it is unreasonable for someone to ask for more, there must be a *morally relevant* reason for this to be so.

Moreover, the reason cannot be differential contribution, in a more intuitive sense. Those who gain least against Gauthier's benchmark aren't necessarily those who *contribute the most* to the scheme of production. When the notion of relative contribution applies, a given participant's level of contribution will be assessed in terms of what the *other participants* lose if that party were not involved (given the group's perhaps limited opportunities to replace him or her by someone else). Gauthier's benchmark instead tracks what *the given participant would lose* from his or her non-participatory alternatives. There is no necessary connection between these notions. Someone who gains least might offer the least, because he is easily replaced. And someone who gains the most might offer the most, because she is irreplaceable.

But is a notion of contributory fairness even relevant? We will suggest a threshold conception of participation, and we will admit that endowments fairly create differential levels of gain from trade. This, however, is not a notion of contributory fairness but rather a natural way of specifying the goods which *trade* creates, as distinct from background economic conditions. We will also distinguish participants in the trade relationship from non-participants, who have not or will not contribute to the gains, and we can happily admit special considerations of differential contribution that must be weighted up separately (e.g., some countries shoulder more of the cost of maintaining and administering the trading system). We may treat these as special burdens that require compensation, so long as compensation is not already provided indirectly (e.g., U.S. security guarantees stabilize the trading system but also augment its political power). But this is as far as "contributory fairness" goes. This is not to admit that fair relative gains are determined by some general criterion of contribution (and what would it be? degree of "openness"? trade volumes?). Once we identify the endowment-adjusted gains and admit special burdens of participation, no notion of differential contribution seems generally relevant between countries that meet the participatory threshold.

To be sure, the case is different in contexts of fully voluntary association. A stronger idea of contributory fairness might well apply when groups and individuals choose each other for membership against a background of opportunities (for a group to admit different individuals, or for an individual to associate with different groups). Our claim, in effect, is that the trade relation is not a fully voluntary association, at least not in any sense that undercuts the equal gains benchmark. The trade relationship, even if defined by formally voluntary treaties, is relatively unavoidable. Every country of the world is affected by the international economic system (including those that lack formal membership), so no country can be justifiably excluded, except on especially significant grounds. And once involved, no country can afford to leave. A country's presumptive claim to equal gain depends on its full participation but not its total contribution by some measure; the basis of that claim is its equal moral status and its morally relevant similarities and differences as compared to other countries.

The case is similar to domestic society. It is a familiar point that domestic society cannot be legitimated on the grounds that its subjects actually accept it (tacitly or explicitly). While many do emigrate, sometimes in protest, quitting one's country of birth is just too costly for most people (and even if they did leave, it would be to another country, where the same problem will arise). Accordingly, Rawls regards one's state of nature prospects, as set by one's natural talent endowment, as irrelevant (if even coherent) for deciding one's fair share of the social surplus. What is fair won't systematically depend on one's prospects without society or on society's prospects without one. If one must participate, one's fair share can be settled only by independent fairness reasons (which, for Rawls, turn out to reward talent, on the right grounds). Our appeal to the not-fully-voluntary nature of the global economy is similar: it rules out ideas of contributory fairness that might be apt otherwise. Insofar as a country's "autarky prospects" matter, as set by its natural endowments, there must be relevant fairness reasons for this.[6]

3. Are the Gains of Trade Already Owned?

We have now answered a first challenge to Absence of Special Entitlement. A further challenge might arise from entitlement views of a different kind. If countries *own* whatever gains they reap at a given time, for instance, then there may be no reason to suppose that an issue of distribution arises, and indeed reason *not* to presume in favor of any particular distribution of gains. Distribution of gains would be potentially wrongful or unfair *re*distribution, a violation of standing property rights. Even a mere benchmark of equal gain would be out of place.

But why accept this conception of ownership? Specific ideas of entitlement, such as investor or intellectual property rights, will not clearly support this very general concern. Even relatively strong entitlements would merely *shape*, rather than preclude, general distribution concerns, by introducing further considerations (e.g., patents and copyrights will expire, for the sake of general benefit). A *presumption* of equality of gain is not a final conclusion precisely because such special, circumstantial considerations will often arise. Accordingly, we can ask whether or to what extent they do arise as a separate, secondary matter (our task in Chapter 9 as regards intellectual property rights).

A more general idea of entitlement might result from a more sweeping appeal to natural property rights. According to some libertarians, so long as holdings are justly acquired, through just original appropriations or just transfers, the benefits of voluntary market exchange are one's property as a matter of natural right.[7]

---

6. We so defend two main forms of "baseline-dependence." First, our endowment-adjustment reflects the limited, augmentation function of the international social practice of trade. Second, we rely (in Chapter 7) on autarky prospects to identify a relevant form of harm.
7. Nozick, 1974.

The same goes, it may be argued, for the gains from international trade. The legitimate function of the state does not include the regulation of market exchange beyond protection against force and fraud. But there would seem to be no fundamental distinction between domestic markets and international trade. The state's duty is simply to stand aside.

Any such appeal to natural rights would be an "external" argument of the sort we have set aside. Without trying to refute such views, we might emphasize their radical character. Indeed, some libertarians might object that we have largely assumed the legitimacy of state trade policy when the very existence of the state system is equally in question. The first question about the proposed natural property rights is why they do not require anarchy and so many private protection agencies, or at most a minimal "night-watchman" state. A global economy may or may not then emerge. Indeed, to the extent a truly global-sized market constitutively depends on the state system and an international practice of free trade, as argued in Chapter 2, we might expect a world less like our own and much more like Hobbes's state of nature (perhaps, e.g., the weak or non-existent economic relations of the interwar years).

Lockean accounts of natural rights fare best in "state of nature" cases but are not very plausible under the conditions of modern society.[8] Such views are false if one's moral property rights depend on what one gets in a fair scheme of cooperation (as, e.g., according to the "legitimate expectations" principle in Chapter 7.11). And, indeed, modern societies widely assume that one has no natural right against the general modification of holdings through taxation if this is necessary for the provision of public goods such as security, infrastructure, environmental protection, or education. The controversy in public debate is over tax *level*, not the legitimacy of taxation for anything other than the protection of non-interference rights. Trade policy is in effect a form of tax policy aimed at the public good of national income gain, so there should be no special issue of its basic legitimacy.

A different, still broadly libertarian argument might appeal to the presumptive importance of basic economic liberty within any established scheme of property rights. If trade policy is in effect a

---

8. But see Chapter 9.2 for a tempting appeal to natural rights in the case of intellectual property.

kind of tax policy, it may be said to amount to state interference in voluntary transactions and holdings and thus an infringement upon personal economic liberty. Whatever the liberty-based objections to, say, income taxation, however, the argument will have force only insofar as trade policy has a significant bearing on individual choice, and the relation between these is very indirect. The basic function of reducing tariffs has less to do with individual choice than the structure of production in the overall economy: as imports free labor and other resources to do more productive things, and as the division of labor is ever-further refined, national income is increased and average living standards rise. No one needs to have consciously chosen a micro-pattern of transactions that leads to macro-level gain. One tends to gain anyway, as standards of living rise. Distribution of the macro-level gains of trade, from "winners" to "losers," is thus nothing like a case of taking what someone has made with his own bare hands and giving it to someone else. It is more like a case in which a government deposits funds into one's bank account and reserves a right of fairness to give notice and take some of it back.

Even that may overstate the connection between trade policy and economic liberty. Again, the macro-economic aims of trade policy do not require the direction of consumer behavior, by sending implicit messages about the supposed desirability of certain purchases as opposed to others—by "telling people what to buy." And even when trade barriers are removed, people are not "more free" as a result of lower prices. A change in tariff policy will usually entail a change in *relative* prices, as the relative scarcity of goods and services is altered. As imported goods become more abundant relative to other goods, they become relatively cheap. But those other goods also become relatively dear, as now relatively less abundant. If one is somehow given greater liberty to buy the now cheaper goods, one is equally given lesser liberty to buy the now more expensive goods. The total effect on liberty may simply be a wash. One may wind up better off under freer trade but no freer than before.

The general lesson here is that it is a mistake to characterize the trade relation in individualistic terms, either as an issue of individual property rights or of personal economic liberty. At least so long as the state system is admitted as legitimate, the trading system works most fundamentally at the level of national and international public (albeit distributable) goods. It is not, in that sense, a relationship between so many individuals in a common market, each of whom is faced with both opportunities for voluntary transactions and a standing threat of government interference. Such individualism simply misrepresents what the global economy is socially like.

A different entitlement view might grant this point. One might instead defend a *collective* property entitlement at the national level. Gains from trade reaped within a country's borders might count as owned, by a society, as a matter of sovereign property right. (They are owned "by a society," and not by individuals, because the gains might sill need to be fairly distributed within the sovereign collective.) Like its individualistic variant, however, this view is ill-suited to the central issues of distribution that arise in the trade context.

For one thing, sovereignty rights of non-interference, as usually understood, are largely beside the point. Nothing akin to war or coercive diplomacy need be involved. The gains of trade are distributed across societies in large part by *domestic* trade policies that have consequences abroad via economic interdependence. Imposing a beggar-thy-neighbor cost on one's trading partners, for short-term gain, is perfectly consistent with admitting that the imposed-upon country has sovereign rights to close its borders down, or to retaliate with beggar-thy-neighbor policies of its own. A central role of a mutual market reliance practice is to get such policies under control, for the sake of mutual gain over the longer haul. Moreover, to join or to help establish such a practice is precisely an *exercise* of sovereign powers. The Hobbesian argument of Chapter 3 notwithstanding, signing the WTO treaty amounts to the voluntary assumption of associated market reliance expectations, including expectations of fairness, which include, say, refraining from beggar-thy-neighbor policies of certain (perhaps vaguely specified) sorts. There is no challenge to sovereignty here. Although the WTO treaty is an "all or nothing" rather than "a la carte" agreement, member countries remain legally free to leave as their sovereign judgment provides. So long as they do not in fact leave, also as a matter of sovereign choice, a general issue of fair relative gain can arise.

More important than the limits of formal property rights, however, is the essentially international nature of the gains of trade. If the gains of trade are owned at all, they are owned in common by the countries that trade. No person, firm, class, or country can claim to have created the greater level of wealth "with its own bare hands," independent of the international relationship. The gains of trade are essentially socially created. As argued in Chapter 2.4–2.5, an international mutual reliance practice is generally necessary for the gains of trade to arise. Market "reliance" involves not just government removal of trade barriers, but substantial de facto coordination in a common division of labor. The gains of trade are created by a system of joint production if they are created at all.

To see this, consider countries with strictly similar endowments that have become substantially (if partially) integrated over time (e.g., several decades). Under autarky, let us say, each would have the same productive output, yielding the same national income level. But with trade, each has done better still, reaping a national income level that was otherwise unattainable. Why, again, do such "gains of trade" arise? Not from mere market exchange per se. Though presumably beneficial to the transacting parties, mere exchange does not imply any change in the structure of production and the overall level of national income. In theory, factors of production may well do just what they did before. When aggregate gains for one country do arise, they reflect a new deployment of productive resources, which is enabled by the productive activity of another country, and would not have occurred without it. And likewise in the second country: its aggregate gains result from its new deployment of productive resources, as enabled by the productive activity of the first country. The increase in national income for each is, in each case, the product of sustained international cooperation, as the division of labor is mutually refined. The total product, in that case, is not the increase for each country, taken separately, but rather total increase for *both* countries, taken together.

We might add that this point applies only among substantially integrated countries. It applies only to countries that fully participate in a common market reliance practice, where full participation depends on meeting some threshold of economic integration. The threshold will fall well short of the robust integration approximated within many advanced countries (as per what we called "partial economic integration" in Chapter 1.4). But it also need not be met in pairwise comparisons between any two trading countries. A network of interdependence may suffice, perhaps as follows. A set of countries {A, B, C ... n} might constitute a market reliance practice, of full participation, when (1) all are at least open to trade with all others, and (2) a given country is in fact integrated with at least one other country that is integrated with at least one other country in the set. If A is integrated with B, and B integrated with C, then A and C may not be fully integrated directly but none the less fully participate in a common market reliance practice. For, in this case, it may be true that the gains reaped in A, as a result of integration with B, will often be enabled by B's integration with C. Even if A and C are not directly integrated, if B weren't able to import what it imports from C, it may not be able to specialize in ways that allow A to specialize as it does. Thus, we might say, every country in the set is to reap equal (endowment-adjusted) gains over time.

If all of this is correct, it is hard to see how the gains of trade could be "owned" in any conclusive sense before they are fairly distributed. As long as the total gain is essentially the result of international social cooperation, each participant in the system of joint production can rightfully lay claim to greater rather than lesser shares of its fruit. It matters little where the fruit is picked. If you and I are neighbors and cooperatively grow apple trees along our common property line, it makes no difference if most of the apples happen to fall on your side of the fence. I retain the same claim to them as before. Your right of sovereignty over your property might give you legal powers to exclude me from collecting my share. But my share of the apples remains mine as much as your share remains yours, in the sense that we have the same claim of fairness to them. Likewise, a sovereign government has no moral claim to the jointly produced gains of trade simply because they are first reaped within its borders. If a government may well be legally empowered to prevent other countries from recovering their fair shares (e.g., by refusing to pay compensation required by a WTO ruling), that will not change what fairness requires; such measures may simply be a form of cheating.

4. Endowment Adjustment

We have so far assumed that we can isolate background endowments and identify a kind of good that is essentially created through international cooperation. That good, the *surplus* of international cooperation, is not the wealth of nations per se, but the *augmentation* of productive capacities that are by and large there anyway. Even the *degree* of augmentation—the size of the gains, over time—is sensitive to those independent capabilities. We therefore must isolate the improvements created specifically through international cooperation, by factoring out any gains that would have accrued under autarky anyway. The relevant "gains of trade" are *endowment-adjusted gains.* Although we offer no general rule for how background productive capabilities are to be factored out, we will offer some suggestive remarks that develop the intuitive idea.

We implicitly adjust for endowments when we compare similarly endowed countries, as suggested. In a world of similarly endowed countries, the equal gains benchmark requires equality of gain. When similarly endowed countries trade but gain to different degrees over time, the trade relation is unfair, barring special reasons that the inequality should be justified. So, for example, an inequality might arise among similarly endowed trading partners because one of them adopts a beggar-thy-neighbor policy (an exchange rate adjustment, or change in labor standards) that increases its national income at the expense of another country. In that case, if all else is equal, the beggared country would fairly adopt an equalizing policy that generates a comparable gain for it at the first country's expense.[9] Accordingly, it is not presumptively unfair when countries *symmetrically* adopt policies that at once reduce the benefits flowing to their respective trade partners (e.g., both similarly raise labor standards, increasing costs of production in both countries), even if this reduces overall welfare. The gains received need only remain equal, even if at a lower level.

Many countries of course differ in background productive capacities. Indeed, the whole point of trade according to the comparative advantage rationale (unlike the economies of scale argument) turns on mutual benefit from "natural" differences in cost of production that arise from differential endowments in population,

---

9. Because other things often aren't equal, this isn't to recommend "tit for tat" trade policy as on-balance fair; there are often better ways to appropriately adjust trade practice, e.g., as through the multilateral dispute adjudication system. We leave open when unilateral "correction" is both fair and wise when the system is failing to respond to important fairness claims.

climate, quality of land, geography, level of technological development, productive structures and culture, and so on. This is quite consistent with the equal gains benchmark. The case of similarly endowed countries illustrates the idea that the gains of trade are essentially the fruit of international social cooperation. Differential endowments complicate but do not change that fundamental point. For consider cases in which there are ample natural differences in cost of production and yet "relevant similarity" in endowments, say, in *overall* or average productive capacity. Under autarky, such countries perform similarly, overall, in terms of gross income gain. But in that case the situation is much as it is with countries that are strictly similarly endowed. When such countries trade, the gains to each, due to the new deployment of productive resources, are essentially created by productive activity in the other country, and so essentially socially created. An inequality of gain, over time, is presumptively unfair. (The same is true, moreover, for gains reaped due to economies of scale, perhaps among very similar countries. When average production capacities converge overall, as in many advanced countries, the gains reaped due to arbitrarily divided specialization count as socially created and subject to the equality default in much the same way.)

Many countries of course differ even in average productivity. Even so, however, if the difference is not too great, equality of gain may still function as an appropriate rule of thumb, subject to correction as needed. That is, although certain differences in endowment (e.g., a difference in population) might fairly generate unequal gains, equality of gain could be an appropriate working presumption, which we correct as particulars of a given case require (e.g., starting from the equality default, we double expectations of gain for a country whose working population is twice as large). In a world of trading countries that are similarly endowed, roughly and overall, then, equality of gain might still be the (rule-of-thumb) default. Put a different way, as countries increasingly converge in institutional and economic makeup (as many advanced countries have), equality of national gain will increasingly become the mark of a fair global economy (even as inequality of gain might be needed for developing countries to "catch up").

A further complication is that endowments are not fixed over time. Trade itself (along with other domestic policy) has dynamic consequences for productive capabilities. Integration can improve national income over an earlier time in ways that count, at a later time, as "natural" or "background" endowments for trade going forward. However, if we assume rough similarity in dynamic improvements, whether they are automatic or induced by coordinated policy intervention (e.g., by public investment), the case is similar to those above. When there is dissimilarity in dynamic improvement, perhaps because one country adopts interventionist policies that the other does not, inequality of gain is unfair, barring an appropriate explanation for the difference or some further reasons that the inequality should be justified (e.g., a developing country subsidizes industry or adjusts its exchange rate to cheapen exports for purposes of reducing poverty).

Suggestive as these comments are, it is of course a plain fact of international life that countries often greatly diverge in productive capability. Consider examples that at least suggest how this might be generally accounted for. When trading countries gain in unequal measure, but each does as well as could be expected given its respective productive capacities, the inequality in output is presumptively fair. Alternatively, when the countries gain equally over some span of time but differ greatly in underlying productive capabilities, the trade relationship will be presumptively unfair. It will be unfair, at least, when the better-endowed country would have gained more from the relationship under a feasible alternative policy configuration (e.g., it wasn't "beggared" by foreign government policies that took benefits at its expense), and there are no special reasons that the inequality in gain should be fair.

This assumes that we can form expectations about how much each of different countries could gain from trade with one another, given their respective endowments, under feasible policy configurations (e.g., the joint removal of border barriers). This is well within the purview of economic science, which uses various methods—including historical or "peer" comparisons, natural experiments, and computable general equilibrium models—to approximate how much actual countries would or do gain from trade with each other over time given their different endowments.[10]

---

10. Wing, 2004, usefully surveys computerized general equilibrium models. Given our focus on internal distribution in Chapter 7, we might note the importance of models that adjust for risk and unemployment at the sub-national level, especially for poor people, as held by Hertel et al., 2003.

Crucial for our purposes, in particular, are ways of estimating the degree to which inequalities in gains of trade can be explained by differential endowments among the countries and periods of time in question. International economists traffic in such expectations, and while current methods may have to be adopted for our specific purposes, we can safely assume that rough but plausible estimates are within the reach of social scientific possibility.[11]

Estimates of the potential gains of trade (e.g., from liberalization, a change in regulation, or an added tax) indeed already figure prominently in policy and public debates.[12] If anything, the cited numbers are implausibly precise, neglecting both significant benefits and significant costs of economic integration. While social scientific measurement has familiar limitations, global economic governance can hardly do without it, and we can safely assume that relevant methods will develop and improve (in part due to skepticism about current models coming from economists themselves). In any case, great precision is not required for our very general principles to have a correspondingly general role in the governance of trade practice in light of its observed and expected general tendencies over the medium to longer haul.

Of course, in relying on (morally informed) economic theory, we are in effect allowing that laissez-fare trade practice could in theory be most conducive to egalitarian fairness in trade. Still, this is a large empirical thesis; it would at least have to be *argued* that a laissez-faire system reliably yields equality of endowment-adjusted gains (perhaps because it almost always returns appropriate benefits to endowments over time, while interventionist policies almost always upset this pattern). Especially as economies become increasingly similar, we could equally presume that equality of gain is the appropriate rule-of-thumb, taking measures to compensate unduly disadvantaged countries only when this is clearly required (e.g., as with great discrepancies in working population size).[13]

---

11. Kenneth Arrow (in personal communication) expresses confidence that the idea is fully coherent from the point of view of international economics but also emphasizes the persistent difficulty of estimating how much gain different endowments create in practically important terms.
12. For example, the World Bank, 2003, estimated a $500 billion global increase in real income by 2015 from further trade liberalization.
13. Compare Rawls's difference principle, which allows domestic inequality for dynamic productivity gains, so long as it maximizes prospects

A presumption of rough equality of benefit may stand behind the famous charge, mounted by 1960s French Minster of Finance Valery Giscard d'Estaing, that the dollar-based currency reserve system gives the United States an "exorbitant privilege" (of very cheap loans and of payment for imports in its own currency). The disparity in benefit as compared to other roughly comparable advanced nations is, the thought might go, just too large. If special benefits for the United States could once be rationalized as compensation for special burdens, the argument against the resulting disparities has become only more forceful today. Developing countries increasingly hold huge dollar reserves as crisis insurance (given the perceived failures of the IMF in the East Asian Crisis), but at an enormous opportunity cost. Money parked for a rainy day, earning very low interest rates, is money not being invested in potentially far more productive ways. Meanwhile, countries both poor and rich (including the United States) suffer a resulting shortfall in demand and consequent underemployment. Developing countries are presumably better off for being insured against crises but would do much better under an entirely feasible mutual insurance cooperative. One version, for instance, is based in widespread and regular distribution of IMF Special Drawing Rights (or in regional arrangements such as an Asian Monetary Fund).[14] Once established, each government in the cooperative receives an option to buy hard foreign exchange at a specified reasonable rate, allowing each to spend or invest valuable resources and forgo buying what is in effect extraordinarily expensive crisis insurance. Even if the United States loses its exorbitant gains, the relative improvement for the developing world seems only fair.[15]

We should emphasize that the equal gains benchmark applies as a presumptive fairness requirement only insofar as the augmentation of national income is our assumed concern. We have not

---

for the least well-off. While this could in theory permit great inequality, the case would have to be made. We can be skeptical about whether hugely unequal rewards are needed merely to induce risk-taking or hard work (status-conscious strivers will usually do that for much less). The rule-of-thumb would then be in the direction of equality of income with only modest departures for dynamic effect.

14. Stiglitz, 2006, ch. 9.
15. Our principle of International Relative Gains (see Chapter 7) admits special privileges for poor countries. The present point is meant not to invoke that further fairness consideration.

said that the benchmark so applies ultimately or all things considered, a matter that also depends on internal concerns of domestic socioeconomic distribution,[16] as well as a wide range of external concerns that potentially limit the significance or even the permissibility of economic production.[17] So even as economic science gives concrete expression to an economic value that seems relevant for policy, fairness cannot be other than a value-infused matter.

For example, even the question of what counts as a country's relevant "endowments" or productive "capacities" will partly depend on its choice of how far to put factors of production to use. If the French choose leisure over work, while Americans choose work over leisure, then (even with no difference in per-hour productivity) France will not become as rich as it might. Nor will its trading partners such as the United States gain as much as they otherwise would. The opportunity cost to the United States is fair, we may suppose, because Americans are responding to the same value in choosing work over leisure instead: in shaping standard work hours or vacation length, both are defining the basic value of life. But it seems mistaken to describe this as adducing a special justification of a *presumptively* unfair economic opportunity cost for the United States. It is not as though fairness somehow presumptively tells people to work as much as humanly possible, even if it admits special reasons for why they might work less. The Protestant Work Ethic is at most a substantive conception of fairness, an answer to a basic question of value about what kinds of lives are most worth leading. These and perhaps other values are thus not justified bases for relaxing a presumption of equal gain but instead part of the proper social and institutional backdrop against which relevant possibilities of production are to be assessed in the first instance.

5. The National Gains of Trade

We have so far defended Absence of Special Entitlement against various challenges. The equal gain benchmark also depends on further assumptions, including what we are calling Symmetry of

---

16. See Chapter 7.1–7.5.
17. See Chapter 10.

Interest: each trading country must have a relevantly similar interest in greater rather than lesser shares of the gains of trade, understood as *national* income gains. Is there a plausible sense in which this is the case?

Our concern is with internal argument, that is, justification of principles *for* and in part *from* the kind of social structure at hand. The natural place to start, then, is with the point of the practice of trade. The trade relationship is created by human beings for certain purposes. We may therefore ask, Why has it been set up and why is it being maintained? A sociological answer doesn't decisively settle the nature of the trade relation; our best understanding of that relationship might still show that established understandings of its point are significantly misguided. Yet established understandings are at least indicative of its nature. They provide important data points, evidence that must be explained away by an interpretation that largely rejects, rather than largely interprets, implicit or explicit social understandings.

Consider history and practice, then. The basic economic rationales for trade—comparative advantage, economies of scale, the spread of technology—have persuaded governments to gradually relax or remove trade barriers for over two centuries (the two world wars and interwar years being an exception that proves the rule). The rationales are still routinely cited as reasons for greater openness in advanced and developing countries alike. As suggested in Chapter 2.3, each rationale works primarily at the level of whole countries rather than individuals or firms. The value of trade, chiefly, is that imports release resources in a domestic economy to do more productive things. National income is increased by macro-economic restructuring of the economy-wide division of labor. It is not persons or firms, but *countries* that trade to comparative advantage, that specialize, and that gain, in the first instance.

This aim would be irrelevant from a moral point of view if there were no good reason for countries to augment national income. Established social purposes would be of merely sociological interest. But surely countries do have good reason for this, other things being equal, from a moral point of view and otherwise. Why not be richer rather than poorer, other things being equal?

Perhaps one is uncomfortable with the idea that a collective agent— in this case a society represented by its legitimate government—can itself have reasons for action beyond a mere motive or "revealed preference." In that case, the relevant interest can be rephrased as an interest of the individuals living in the society in question which concerns the kind of society they live in. For surely most people have some significant interest in living in a society that sees augmented national income and rising standards of living, and so some significant interest in having their respective societies see greater rather than lesser shares of the gains of trade.[18]

The suggested rephrasing is intended to cite a significant, morally relevant interest that arises from *within* the trade relationship, given the kind of international relationship it in fact is. The relevant interest is therefore not identified as "being made richer rather than poorer" *as such*, in a sense that might well support the abolition or fundamental reorganization of the international system of trade. Our concern is with internal structural equity in that general practice, in light of the advantages and disadvantages it typically creates. So we restrict "relevant" interests to outcomes that are so created by the going trade practice.

At the same time, to say most people have a significant interest in living in a society that sees greater rather than lesser national gains is merely to point to *one* kind of interest. This is hardly to say that such a person's own life, in some narrow sense, will go well *only* when his or her society prospers. Individuals can of course fare poorly as their society prospers, or do well as their society languishes. Nor does our suggestion deny or minimize the fact that individuals clearly *also* have very significant interests in how much of the national gain they ultimately see in their personal lives. This may matter as much as or more than how their society fares overall, and it raises important questions of fairness in its own right, which we address in Chapter 7.5.[19]

---

18. To say that claims about the "national interest" are not fully reducible to claims about the independent interests of individuals is not to say that nations, as such, have interests. (Would that be in virtue of some sort of collective conscious mind?) Indeed, it would be odd to suggest that a whole country somehow had an interest in greater than lesser gains if *no one* in the country had an interest in his or her country seeing such gains.
19. If one remains uncomfortable with the idea that individuals have national economic interests, one can also explain this in instrumental terms with reference to certain still more basic personal economic interests. It need only be added that such interests are properly characterized as a national interest in national level policies, for present purposes of internal justification.

188 FAIRNESS IN PRACTICE

The Symmetry of Interest condition requires not only that trading countries each have *an* interest in greater rather than lesser gains from grade, but also that they have the *same* (relevantly similar) interest in greater rather than lesser national gains. This claim would be clearly false if it implied that country size is irrelevant. Surely size matters; populous countries should reap larger gains than small countries. By virtue of greater numbers, they have a greater interest in greater rather than lesser shares. It would be unfair, absent some special justification, for two countries of very different size, but otherwise the same, to reap the same levels of gain. We have already partly accounted for this by considering only endowment-adjusted gains, where endowments include population size. Then larger countries can be expected to see larger gains, other things being equal. We can also admit that population differences present special considerations. Perhaps a country reasonably limited its population growth for the sake of increasing incomes (whether through incentives or by spontaneous household choices). But now, decades later, it has difficulty financing social support for a larger group of retiring workers. Perhaps a country failed to discourage large families (e.g., for religious reasons). But now, decades later, it faces problems of underemployment. Such countries might have special interests in the benefits that might accrue to income-augmenting trade policy. But this would be a further interest over and above the similar interest in greater rather than lesser shares it shares with all trading countries.

We may say the same of the special interest of developing countries in the gains of trade. Because many of their members are very poor in absolute terms, standard of living gains mean more to them than to most any rich-world citizen. This is not necessarily to deny that all countries have *a* similar interest in augmented wealth, however. Even if poverty presents special fairness concerns, every country can be said to have this more general interest. In that case, the question is how that interest relates to the separate, special interests of poor people—a question we take up in Chapter 7.6.

6. Status Equality

Our final framing assumption is Status Equality: parties to the practice (countries and their members) are moral equals. This idea is rooted firmly in the state system that embeds the system of trade. If any one government enjoys the legal powers of sovereignty, then any other government does so as well—at least provided an adequate record on human rights.[20] The multilateral trading system takes up much the same idea, explicitly in its pronouncements of the formal equality of all member countries, and implicitly in its persistent concern with "arbitrary discrimination." A trade or trade-related policy that gives advantage to some rather than others (whether by favoring nationals over foreigners or one trading partner country over another) requires an appropriate justification. Discrimination *requires* justification, rather than counting as the justified default, because the trade-related interests of all member countries are assumed to count.

If one is skeptical about the idea that *countries* have trade interests, from a moral rather than purely legal point of view, the issue of status equality can again be rephrased in terms of the national interests of individual persons. As stated earlier, we can say that persons have a significant interest in how their respective societies are treated in an international practice of trade. In that case, the interests of all trading countries have to count in order that their members so interested are counted. To suggest that a justification is not needed for discriminatory trade policy, because discrimination is the justified default, would be to suggest that some such interested persons are irrelevant.

7. Participation and Exclusion

We have formulated our framing conditions in terms of "trading countries," that is to say, in terms of *participants* in the market reliance practice, rather than simply countries as such (some of which may not trade). This is a significant difference from our initial fair division problem, in which windfall gain is treated as

---

20. Although international political culture now presumes that sovereignty must be earned, the trading system has perhaps yet to adequately operationalize all that this might mean. It is at least widely believed that human rights violations (of appropriate kinds) in principle mean that trade relations need not go on in the normal way (sanctions, or protection, may be justified, depending on the case). Because these very important issues assume values external relative to the global economy, they are not our present concern.

manna from heaven to which the parties have no special claims. (As the relevant fair division game is usually framed, a third party offers some amount of money divided as a gift.) But why, we may ask, should the fact of participation make a difference? Why wouldn't the equal moral status of all countries, each with an interest in greater rather than lesser income, underwrite a fully universal benchmark of equal national gain? Why are non-participants left out?

The answer is that our argument *does* assume (defeasible) entitlements of a very general kind. The gains of trade are neither a mere gift from God nor a mere stroke of natural fortune, but socially created: they result from a quite deliberate choice to establish a market reliance practice that integrates domestic systems of production across national borders. Even if co-creation generates no special entitlements *within* the system of production, countries wholly outside the system do not enjoy the same kind of claim to greater rather than lesser shares—in this case, a claim to benefit from the activity of others. Countries that participate in the system of joint production have at least *some* claim to its fruit that non-participating countries lack.

The trading system seems to assume the general form of this idea. The system is resolute in its affirmation of the moral equality of each member country but equally limits standing to "member" countries or "contracting parties." Nothing is required as regards countries outside the system. While the system is in principle open to fundamental moral critique, the general claim to enjoy the fruit of one's cooperative labors is also plausible because quite consistent with other moral claims and concerns. The entitlement in question is not necessarily a strong, overriding right to exclude non-participants from benefit, let alone to allow them to suffer harm, or to refuse to pay compensation or provide aid. Non-participating countries can retain equally or more powerful claims against harm done to them, their exclusion from the practice, and to humanitarian assistance.

Reasons of humanity are often external reasons. Harm done to outsiders can, however, be treated as an *internal* fairness concern, insofar as the concern is with the structure of the trade practice in light of the difference it makes in the world. Structural equity is a matter of how the practice treats everyone it affects. Harm certainly qualifies, even if participants in the practice have different, special claims to gain over and above their claims not be harmed.

The same may be said of unfair exclusion. The comparative advantage rationale for trade is strongly inclusive: even a country with an absolute advantage in nothing can contribute to a mutually beneficial division of labor, as each country produces what it does best relative to its own productive options and trades for the rest from abroad. Particularly good grounds are therefore required to exclude any country from such a relationship, precisely because all parties stand to gain. Even so, countries may not enjoy the distinctive claim of participants until they are in fact substantially involved. Supposing one could identify the gains a country *would* reap as a participant, but in fact fails to see, the unfairness may reflect not a failure of fair return but unfair exclusion (or, more specifically, the opportunity cost of unfair exclusion.)

Almost every country of the world has formally joined the multilateral trading system. From a practical point of view, outright exclusion is therefore perhaps of less central importance than lack of substantial inclusion. Many developing countries are formally included but not quite full participants in the system, if only because they have yet to achieve substantial integration. That cannot be said of many middle-income developing countries (e.g., China, India, Brazil, South Africa), which stand in substantial interdependence relations with advanced countries, even as their domestic economies are themselves less than fully integrated wholes. (Consider that, according to the WTO, 11 developing countries were among the world's top 30 exporters in 1997.)[21] For many least-developed countries, however, the central fairness issue would seem to be not relative gains because of substantial interdependence through trade but rather the sort of opportunities they are afforded to *become* so integrated. Failure of integration often reflects lack of development (e.g., inadequate roads, telecommunications, civil instability, weak rule of law). But it may also reflect the terms of integration on offer (terms, e.g., such as the international borrowing and lending privileges that entrench corrupt rulers; expectations of capital and trade liberalization, even when it may well be premature; advanced-country agribusiness subsidies, which severely disadvantage farmers; prohibitions on development-friendly infant-industry protection or industrial policy needed to integrate firms into global supply chain networks;

---

21. Rodrik, 1999, p. 9.

requirements of expensive and disadvantageous intellectual property rules; and so on).

What should be said about such cases, in relation to our benchmark? Here are two suggestions. One is that in the case of developing countries, the appropriate threshold of integration and interdependence can itself be adjusted according to endowments. For example, consider that trade with sub-Saharan Africa is a relatively small and declining share of world trade—now only 1 percent, down from more than 3 percent in the mid-1950s.[22] If trade volumes as compared to the global total are the standard of "contribution," then most countries in sub-Saharan Africa either contribute little or may seem below any plausible integration threshold. On the other hand, integration expectations should arguably be sensitive to local factors. According to Dani Rodrik, African countries trade on average as much as would be expected by international norms once their income levels and the size of their economies are taken into account, and by some measures *more* than should be expected based on their income and size.[23] And despite declining shares of global trade, the ratio of exports to GDP in that set of countries has been relatively stable since 1960, ranging between 26 percent and 30 percent, and even increasing since the 1980s.[24] The decline in relative share of global trade, Rodrik suggests, is better explained by lack of growth, just as East Asia's increased significance in global trade has resulted from its rapid economic expansion and not increasing trade ratios.[25] Thus it is plausible to conclude that many or most African countries have in fact contributed to global trade, in the sense required to count them as full participants. They enjoy the participant's claim to equal endowment-adjusted gains—even if the endowment differential justifies a much lower level of gain than for many better-endowed countries.

A second suggestion applies even when this condition is not met. Even if a developing country fails as yet to qualify as a full participant, it can still properly lay claim to substantial present benefits because of expected *future* contribution. To see the idea, consider any cooperative practice being negotiated de novo—whether

22. Yeats, 1997, p. 1.
23. Rodrik, 1999, p. 113.
24. Ibid., p. 111.
25. Ibid., pp. 110–11.

an automobile ride-sharing scheme, a game of cards, a division of household labor, or a fresh system of international trade (e.g., as undertaken in the wake of World War II). By hypothesis, contributions to the shared activity (by any measure) have yet to be made. Yet it will remain appropriate to ask what rules and expectations are fair, in light of their expected future consequences, on the presumption that each party will do its specified part in good faith, whatever that turns out to be. Knowledge of past misconduct might weaken this presumption for particular parties, just as past cooperation might give assurance of good faith compliance in the future. But claims to present benefit, once the practice is undertaken, are not wholly determined by past contributions. Indeed, the would-be fairness claims may be so significant that the negotiating parties may feel it is wise not to get involved.

Most African countries are involved in the multilateral system, so the prospective demands of fairness for African countries are not mere would-be claims. They now have internal fairness claims, against current arrangements, in light of current and expected future contribution.[26] The temporary cost to advanced countries for present aid or forgone levels of benefit will be "paid back" in future beneficial trade.

8. Individualism as Revisionism

We close this chapter by considering an objection that will help clarify the interpretive component of our argument. One possible objection to our focus on national income and participation argues that only gains to *individuals*, as such, are relevant. Thus, one may argue, either no issue of relative gains arises, or it arises as between all the individuals thereby involved in the common scheme of economic cooperation. The existence of a global economy might itself seem to suggest the appropriateness of such "cosmopolitan" comparisons between any two people it jointly

---

26. If expectations are relevant, one might ask whether we can reasonably expect substantial development in much of Africa given its ongoing problems of ethnic strife, civil war, corruption, and economic decline. We answer that economic development is not impossible, very likely in due course, and that current fairness in trade must make special provisions to facilitate developing countries' best conceivable development path.

affects. Why not compare the plights, say, of a given American and a given Brazilian? Are not both participants in, and deeply shaped by, the same worldwide division of labor?

While an external (e.g., "luck egalitarian") principle could clearly support such "cosmopolitan" comparisons, our question is whether some internal principle of structural equity might do so. There are different ways to press a case for this. Chapter 7.12 will consider whether an internal "cosmopolitan" principle might be justified on substantive moral grounds *despite* our international conception of trade practice. In the remainder of this chapter we consider a quite different social interpretive argument, which seeks to ground an individualistic conception of the nature of trade practice itself. Here our claim is that an individualistic conception represents a significantly revisionary conception of the trade relationship that organizes the global economy as we know it.

As always with social interpretation, the question is which of rival interpretive conceptions best explains the preponderance of the various sources of law and practice. Even as a matter of "constructive interpretation," we cannot simply assert that a "cosmopolitan" conception casts the practice in its best light. The proposal cannot simply be a moral recommendation. It must be grounded in a conception of what the practice is actually like. But, as we will now see, the main sources of law and practice for the global economy—whether in informal social practice, economic law, economic theory, international trade politics, or emergent social understandings—weigh in favor of taking international trade practice in internationalist rather than individualistic terms.

Recall the main reasons for our internationalist conception. As explained in Chapter 1.4, the global economy is marked by partial economic integration. So there is no easy analogy from well-integrated domestic economies. And even if integration were more substantial, a mere general state of affairs of economic interdependence would not be enough, in itself, to support concerns of fair treatment. Any two people are causally related in innumerable ways that do not generate special fairness obligations, if only because they might know very little about each other. Likewise with market relations: without a plausible characterization of the social relationship that gives rise to obligations of fair treatment, a market could in theory be a largely impersonal force beyond any individual or institutional agent's influence or control. No question of fair or unfair treatment in human activity would then arise (even if ideas of "cosmic fairness" apply).

The situation is quite different, however, when economic interdependence reflects an organizing social relationship that is consciously chosen or allowed and subject to human regulatory control. We then do have a site of structural equity assessment. But the global economy as we know it is a fundamentally international social relationship, and not chiefly or even mainly a set of relations between individuals. There are special cases; some special economic arrangements across borders may generate special responsibilities between certain specific parties (e.g., as with "fair trade" cooperatives, or "trade" relations between firms in a supply chain). But no such arrangements generally exist between any two people substantially affected by the global economy, and, again, the bare fact of being causally affected by a common market is insufficient in itself. More important, special economic arrangements exist at all, or to any considerable degree, only because underlying international relationships allow them. The extent and pattern of such relations is ultimately attributable to a state system in which borders can be shut down.

When we consider the organizing international relationship itself, however, the social practice of mutual market reliance does generate responsibilities of fair treatment among the different countries involved, or so we have argued. The particular American and the particular Brazilian participate in this practice, but indirectly; the international social practice is directly sustained by their respective countries, as represented by their respective legitimate governments. They therefore do not, as individuals, enjoy the direct claim to fair national income gains that is held by their respective countries themselves. They *share in* that direct national claim. Accordingly, the equal gain benchmark has an international rather than a "cosmopolitan" form. The first concern is the division of gains across trading countries, and secondarily the division of gains among their members. A difference in prospects for individuals, as such, reflects neither fairness nor unfairness in the international trade practice, from an internal structural equity point of view.

The question, then, is whether more specific sources of law and practice might nevertheless suggest that we are fundamentally mischaracterizing the social nature of the global economy. Do they? Not if we look, say, to international economic law. It adopts a largely state-centered focus. Terms for the regulation of trade policy are addressed to governments. Whether codified as formal rules or left as implicit understandings, they are formulated and addressed as responsibilities for government action on economic and social policy; the relevant addressees are administrators, legislators, or judges, but not individuals or firms, per se. Firms are addressed by various "codes of conduct," as well as the domestic and internal rules that recognize them as legal persons, perhaps much in the way natural persons are addressed by domestic rules of contract and property. But all of this is part and parcel of market relations that are chiefly constituted by the state, and only shaped and modified in international practice and law.

We might instead look to international economic politics and perhaps find deeper assumptions about legitimacy. Much of political argument in world economic politics is about international rules and expectations and what governments should do. Both domestic and international rules and expectations implicitly ask for the support of citizens, and so implicitly give them standing to in turn ask why such support should be justified. Indeed, most anyone would seem to have legitimate standing to complain, on behalf of anyone treated unfairly, whether as an individual or as an NGO. But this is to say that political *accountability* is "cosmopolitan," in a certain sense, and not that the fairness responsibilities being assumed are "cosmopolitan" in some stronger way. Even with many voices, within and beyond the state, most of world economic politics remains about what fairness requires in the internationally constituted global marketplace and its associated domestic and international responsibilities. To be sure, many progressives do share a more deeply "cosmopolitan" conception of fairness, perhaps along with hopes that the state would simply "wither away." But this view, whatever its merits, hardly represents an international political consensus or even the preponderance of moral opinion about fairness in global economic affairs. Most of global economic argument is about a more immediate set of concerns, concerns that do not require fundamental revolution away from a system of states but rather serious and perhaps deep changes.

Perhaps economic theory is the most likely source for an individualistic conception of trade practice. Even so, as we have explained, the case is at best unclear. According to the standard economic rationales for trade, as (perhaps imperfectly) understood in almost two centuries of trade liberalization, the aim of trade is the augmentation of national income through country-level participation in a shared division of labor. The central and essential point of removing trade barriers is *not* to allow people to exchange across borders, per se, but to allow imports that free productive resources for better employments. As the division of labor is ever-further refined, and resources are allocated ever-more efficiently, national income increases and standards of living rise. Exchange across borders is merely a *means* to efficient specialization: the possibility of exchanging for what was previously produced allows ever-further refinement, ever-greater productive output, and ever-greater national-level income gains. If transactional liberty and welfare benefits are welcome, they are beside the point. They do not, in themselves, entail a change in the structure of production that augments national income. Insofar as governments have a different way of so augmenting the national income, without new exchange abroad (e.g., domestic investment in technological innovation), the national case for those measures is much the same.

To highlight the point, recall from Chapter 2.3 that trade gains may or may not translate into welfare for countries overall or for individuals. For countries overall, whether national income gains lead to overall welfare depends on how the gains are distributed. A net welfare loss might result if all the gains go to a few people, while enough "losers" suffer dearly. As for individuals, trade may or may not benefit a given person because trade simply changes relative prices. Whether one is better off overall thus depends on what is in one's overall consumption basket. Even if some prices fall, the price of what one needs most may go up to a degree not covered by savings elsewhere, leaving one a net loser. Nor is liberty clearly advanced in any general sense. As suggested earlier, to the extent one is more "free to buy" a good that has become cheaper because of imports, one is also less "free to buy" those goods that have correspondingly become more expensive, as the relative prices of goods shift. Changes in liberty may often be a wash.

To be sure, economic theory is not especially clear about all of this. Ricardo, like many classical theorists, largely conflated national income and welfare. Modern welfare economics addresses the relation explicitly, but it is hardly a model of clarity, as we saw in Chapter 2.3 and 2.6. Kaldor-Hicks efficiency, which requires only hypothetical compensation, is essentially the classical focus on national income explicitly rephrased in the language of welfare.

Any connection with the welfare of individuals is tenuous at best. In what sense is trade "good for the nation" if, as is strictly possible, a few people may benefit greatly while most people are worse off? Pareto efficiency seems more clearly individualistic. It does bear on actual welfare because compensation is required. But in what sense is trade "good for the nation" if, as is strictly possible, a single person could receive all of the gains, so long as no one is harmed? In fact, economists usually assume that gains from trade will be broadly shared. But this suggests that they are not strict individualists, in any principled or practical sense. Economists are moved by the possibility of widely shared gains, not gains to each individual person, taken by himself or herself. The argument for free trade is *not* that we should free trade, despite real risks of injury, so long as *a single lone soul gains* and chances are good that no one else will be made worse off.

Paul Samuelson, the godfather of neo-classical trade theory, does betray a sort of individualism, and he was no doubt very influential in this. His famous results can seem to suggest that even national gains from trade should be seen as a direct function of gains to different individuals.[27] Yet what this comes to is far from clear. Like most neo-classical economists, Samuelson still took the international system for granted, and not simply as an unfortunate political reality that must be assumed for the sake of argument, despite the theoretical possibility of still greater gains to individuals as a result of global revolution. Indeed, some of Samuelson's major results are important precisely because they show that a prosperous global economy can retain a fundamentally international structure. "Factor price equalization" (the idea that labor/capital ratios in different countries equalize under free trade) is significant in part because it shows that, at least in theory, trade can benefit different countries even if labor is immobile between them. A global economy need not be like a domestic economy in that respect: international trade can be mutually beneficial to different countries (assuming losers are compensated) even if their governments exercise a sovereign right to restrict the movement of people across state borders.

The lesson we should draw from all of this is that neither classical nor neo-classical economics displays a clear-cut individualism

---

27. Especially in light of his skepticism about interpersonal comparisons, which became common among economists.

but rather draws from a variety of normative considerations. Quite different considerations seem to be at work: there are considerations of national income gain, on the one hand, and considerations of harm or relative distribution, on the other. Nations have some significant interests in greater rather than lesser income gains from trade. Or, alternatively, most people have some significant interest in living in a society that sees such gains. But individuals also have significant interests both in not being harmed and in how much of the national income gains they see. In these terms, we might say that Kaldor-Hicks efficiency approximates the national-level interest, while Pareto efficiency explains how trade, for the sake of national income gains, could be a legitimate policy move. Trade is sufficiently fair, so as to not be clearly illegitimate, if national gains are reaped and no one is harmed—especially if the gains are likely to be widely shared. Yet, in the present suggestion, no one conception of "welfare" or "national welfare" functions at once as considerations of both of the above kinds. If the name "welfare" or "efficiency" is used for both, it is simply ambiguous between them.

A further source of confusion is that economists often illustrate economy-level specialization mechanisms in the lives of individuals, where the concepts are easy to grasp. As a matter of comparative advantage, it is said, a sports star does better to spend his time in practice and let the neighborhood teenager mow his lawn, even if he could do a better job mowing the lawn himself. As a matter of economies of scale, a brain surgeon might have been equally good at rocket science, but he does best to let someone else do rockets and stick to brains. Nevertheless, it is a major mistake to assume that *countries* are strictly analogous to individuals or even small groups. The mistake is invited by Adam Smith himself in his famous passage: "What is prudent in the conduct of every family [i.e., specialization] can scarce be folly in that of a great kingdom." The two cases are crucially different, from a distributional point of view. As economist Robert Driskill explains:

> Families are composed of relatively small numbers of intimately connected individuals. A move from autarky to trade might create some "losers," but these could be easily identified and compensated. This is just not the case for a nation with many millions of individuals.[28]

28. Driskill, manuscript, p. 14

As noted in Chapter 2.3, it is clear that Smith was not particularly concerned with distribution; his major advance over prior mercantilist thought was the *national* income benchmark. Smith's objection was precisely that mercantilism was concerned with consequences for particular parties *instead* of the good of the country as a whole, and that specialization in the international division of labor would serve that end.

The mercantilism that Smith rejected was also nationalistic, in the broad sense that it is largely unconcerned with the effects of trade policy on people abroad. Like its contemporary expression (trade negotiators seeking reciprocal "concessions" on market access), the animating concern is not every person of the world, but rather national or sub-national gain or harm. Some "cosmopolitan" critiques of mercantilism—by J. S. Mill or, in our own day, by Jagdish Bhagwati—reject that position of national egoism, suggesting that foreign societies matter as well. But the argument is mainly for mutuality or reciprocity in international relations, not for pure "cosmopolitan" concern for general human welfare. If general human welfare per se were the compelling concern, a country should be willing not just to offer reciprocal or mutual gains, but whatever national self-sacrifice is needed for the greater good of all people—even if that means making most of the country, or even the country as a whole, substantially worse off. Neither Mill nor Bhagwati is willing to press the "cosmopolitan" argument that far.[29] Neither would defend Kaldor-Hicks and Pareto inefficiency in the name, say, of maximizing aggregate human welfare.

The cost of the suggested individualism, then, is revisionism—a revision, that is, of the understood point of international trade. Of course, someone who rejects that point as illegitimate on external grounds might happily grant the charge and argue that current practice should indeed be radically revised. Those seeking to challenge egalitarian fairness (e.g., on libertarian grounds) might go this route. More interesting is whether individualistic *egalitarians* might stage a revisionary argument as well. Though this is open in

---

29. Mill favored an indirect utilitarianism, which he thought remained closer to commonsense morality. Bhagwati, web article, contrasts "cosmopolitan-efficiency" with "national-efficiency" to suggest that free trade should improve every country's welfare rather than one's own. Utilitarian national self-sacrifice isn't entertained.

theory, it is not clear what is to be gained from an egalitarian point of view. Why reject substantial egalitarian responsibilities? If one hankers for a fully "cosmopolitan" principle of just distribution, it can be defended on the basis of external argument. Nothing we have said prevents this; we have merely set that possibility aside, as a way of asking whether internal argument might support egalitarian conclusions as well.

Some might nevertheless find an internal "cosmopolitan" conception especially attractive, and a bit of revisionism may seem a small price to pay for this (especially given possible uneasiness about any talk of national interests and national gain). Here our claim is that revisionism is indeed the price. The price, we may add, is high. Egalitarian responsibilities of internal structural equity are most forceful when firmly rooted in a clear understanding of their grounding social relationships. To the degree that grounding is revised, those responsibilities are eroded at their moorings. To the extent that the point of trade is seen as something like "global welfare", or as another means of global redistribution, perhaps without regard for special domestic responsibilities, it becomes harder to see how fairness could give rise to a substantial presumption of equality in the national gains of trade. Equality comes to seem more like a mere worthy ideal goal and less like a demand. It might be pursued, if all goes well, but it also might be dropped, in order to pursue other worthy values instead. The price of greater egalitarian reach, in short, is attenuated normative force.

CHAPTER SEVEN

Principles of Equity

We now defend three basic principles of structural equity. Each principle governs a different general socioeconomic tendency.[1]

The first principle concerns the socioeconomic harms of trade, such as unemployment, wage suppression, and income volatility that diminishes lifetime savings. According to

Collective Due Care: trading nations are to protect people against the harms of trade (either by temporary trade barriers or "safeguards," etc., or, under free trade, by direct compensation or social insurance schemes). Specifically, no person's life prospects are to be worse than they would have been had his or her society been a closed society.

The second principle concerns the national income gains of trade and how they are distributed among countries.

International Relative Gains: gains to each trading society, adjusted according to their respective national endowments (e.g., population size, resource base, level of development), are to be distributed equally, unless unequal gains flow (e.g., via special trade privileges) to poor countries.

The third principle concerns how shares of national income are distributed domestically.

Domestic Relative Gains: gains to a given trading society are to be distributed equally among its affected members, unless special reasons justify inequality of gain as acceptable to each (as,

---

1. Because the principles apply to a general tendency, they have an implicit "absent special justification" clause that leaves them open to modification or specification as needed for particular contexts of application. We consider such cases later in the chapter.

e.g., when inequality in rewards incentivizes productive activity in a way that maximizes prospects for the worst off over time).

Taking for granted the moral/interpretive claims defended in earlier chapters, our present task is pure moral argument. Each principle, we argue, is a principle that no one can reasonably complain of, as compared to a familiar range of alternative principles for the same specified regulative roles. We focus on principles that are less egalitarian than our three principles, but also consider more egalitarian "cosmopolitan" principles in closing.

1. The Unfairness of Harm

The global economy does significant harm. That is to say, whatever its benefits in the long run, people often suffer serious *specific* forms of socioeconomic injury, over some period of time, as a result of being exposed to global economic forces. For example, many developing-country farmers are further impoverished for their exposure to lavish rich-country agribusiness subsidies. Some are made worse off by a historical baseline: they now fare worse than at earlier times, perhaps having been cast into destitution from an earlier stage of life lived at subsistence levels, with little reasonable hope of compensating gains within their lifetime. (Think of Mexican corn farmers thrown into destitution after NAFTA flooded Mexico with highly subsidized U.S. corn.)[2] Others fare worse in subjunctive-historical terms: many who remain at the same level of subsistence would have been better off had their society instead been closed to trade at some earlier stage of their lives. The choice to free trade worsens their condition; they do not see the standard of living they would have enjoyed had domestic markets been open to them but closed to the outside. Moreover, the parties harmed (in either historical or subjective-historical terms) often have scarce opportunities to avoid injury. They may fare only slightly better, for example, when forced to move to the city, where unemployment may be high. And such cases are hardly rare. In developing countries that lack strong infrastructure

---

2. Stiglitz and Charlton, 2006 p. 197, suggest that real wages fell in Mexico in the decade after the signing of NAFTA.

and social insurance institutions, resources—whether labor or land—are often not readily redeployed.[3]

Although it is especially problematic that such displaced workers are often desperately poor, the harms of trade often befall advanced-country workers as well. Low-skilled, uneducated workers (and especially women) are highly susceptible to repeated and persistent unemployment as trade reallocates resources to higher-skilled, export-oriented industries. High-skilled work is also increasingly affected as firms "outsource" or "offshore" jobs to foreign firms or subsidiaries.[4] Even when the total number of jobs in the economy remains roughly constant, as it does in normal times according to economic theory, this does not imply that displaced workers are readily retrained and reemployed in the industry to which their jobs have moved. Willing workers often face a difficult and perhaps extended period without stable income, along with income volatility that hinders long-term savings and prospects for eventual retirement. They may thus fare worse than at earlier stages of their lives, or simply fail to see gains they would have reaped under greater market protection. By one estimate, displaced U.S. workers see a *permanent* loss of between 8 percent and 25 percent of pre-displacement income, even when continuously employed (with bouts of unemployment bringing additional losses).[5] Wages can stagnate for very long periods of a worker's able-bodied years. In the United States during 1980–2009, for example, huge net income gains, which accrue in part to trade, have been distributed away from the bottom and lower-middle of the income distribution, despite a modest but functioning social safety net.[6]

The harms of trade seem to raise a significant issue of fairness, in developing and advanced countries alike. As we emphasized in Chapter 2.6, even the standard economic argument for free trade

---

3. See the references in Chapter 2.3 in the grounds for protection called "Job Loss" and "Unemployment."
4. Blinder, 2006, warns that this may amount to a third, information-age Industrial Revolution.
5. Kletzer, 1998b; see also 1998a, 2001, 2005.
6. According to Levy and Cochan, manuscript, even as labor productivity increased by 78 percent in the United States between 1980 and 2009, median compensation of thirty-five- to forty-four-year-old male high school graduates (with no college) declined by 10 percent. Median compensation of thirty-five- to forty-four-year-old male college graduates (without

seems to implicitly assume that it would be unfair not to compensate "losers" with some share of the "winners'" gains. But how should we account for this thought? The equal gains benchmark defended in Chapter 6 presumes against harmful policies that would lead to inequality in endowment-adjusted national gain. But this is at most part of the story: the benchmark concerns national income and so says nothing about the harms that might befall "losers" within trading societies. Strictly speaking, a member of a trading society cannot gain or lose in *national* income. And in any case, whether or to what extent any member will share in a national income improvement is a separate question: as our examples suggest, many may mainly see worsened prospects, over considerable periods of time, even when their societies gain from integration overall.

If constructive argument were narrowly limited to the good a practice is intended to create (in this case, national income augmentation), we would have to appeal to an external principle to capture the unfairness of harm. Our characterization of the "internal" is more inclusive. While the central, organizing aim of the practice fixes the primary "currency" of distribution, further consequences can be admitted as relevant for argument about what socioeconomic outcomes are fair. Specifically, we may assess any socioeconomic outcomes of a practice in terms of what those affected could reasonably accept or reject, and so justify a regulative principle for trade practice without assuming any further principles, external or otherwise. Among potential objections to the practice are considerations of harm that lead to a principle such as our principle of (Collective) Due Care. Thus trade practice can be unfair, in fully internal terms, when it creates the good of national income augmentation at the expense of those made worse off.

Consider the suggested argument in greater detail. To begin, suppose certain workers will suffer protracted unemployment, in a weakened import-sensitive industry, *merely* for the sake of giving a comparably sized gain to other workers, for instance, a comparable job in an enhanced export-industry. Assume that the parties are

---

graduate degrees) grew by 32 percent, less than half as much as overall productivity growth. Only the median compensation of thirty-five- to forty-four-year-old men with post-graduate training came close to labor productivity growth, increasing by 49 percent. International trade is cited as a contributory factor.

otherwise similarly situated, that there are no further relevant benefits or costs to society, and that the imposition is entirely avoidable (by trade barriers or, under free trade, compensatory arrangements). The disadvantaged parties can in this case reasonably object that they are made worse off. For it is hard to see how those potentially benefited would have a comparatively powerful objection to protecting the losers from a worsened condition. If trade is freed and losers are compensated, they may still benefit, even if compensation cuts into their gains. And even if the harm is simply prevented, by retaining or imposing a trade barrier, they may be no worse off than before; they simply are not afforded a benefit. Other things being equal, the objection "I am made worse off" is more powerful than "I could have been better off," in which case either market protection or compensation of the loser carries the day. In other words, special presumptive weight is to be accorded to ways someone's condition is worsened, relative to what it was at some previous time (i.e., by a historical baseline of comparison), or what it would have been had the policy change in question not occurred (by a subjunctive-historical baseline). At least when other things are equal, worsenings are not on the same footing as mere opportunity costs, or ways one *could have done better* although one's condition is not worsened in either of the above ways.

This presumption against worsening also seems to retain its force even when other things aren't equal, say, because potential benefits and burdens aren't of comparable significance. It seems unfair to worsen someone's condition by $1,000 simply to give someone else $1,500 (assuming this is a moderately greater and so not strictly comparable gain). This may be fine when the beneficiary would see a dramatically larger gain, when the harmed person is very well-off, or when the would-be beneficiary is very poor. But some such weighty considerations seem required. We return to such special cases momentarily.

These are indeed special cases; the general trade situation does not involve comparable benefits and harms, but in a way that reinforces rather than overturns presumption against harm. The harm to displaced workers is usually *much greater* than the benefits for any other particular affected parties. Low-skilled workers tend to bear severe employment hardships, whether protracted unemployment or permanent income loss while fully employed. Newly employed workers in export-industries see real but smaller employment gains, while each consumer, taken by him or herself, sees only a slow and modest rise in standard of living over time. Although the displaced worker will also benefit as a consumer from cheaper goods and services, this will hardly make up for a life of unsteady employment or stagnating wages, especially when it diminishes income and savings over a lifetime.

Now, none of this is to deny the significance of freed trade to would-be beneficiaries. If compensation can and will be arranged, then losers cannot reasonably object to free trade (at least on grounds of harm; relative gains might remain a concern—of which more later). It won't be reasonable to insist on protection merely to avoid a *specific* compensable injury such the loss of a particular job. Why should others be asked to forgo the benefits of free trade if no one is *ultimately* made worse off? Accordingly, when losers can reasonably complain of having their condition worsened, the objection will be that they are made worse off *over the course of their whole lives* for their society's exposure to the global marketplace. Specific forms of injury are presumptively unfair, but the unfairness can be rectified when suitable compensatory benefits are provided (at earlier or later stages of life).

We thus have an initial argument for our principle of Due Care. The losers from freed trade can reasonably reject any principle weaker than Due Care, which does not demand either market protection or compensation over time. Their complaint against being harmed, we have in effect argued, carries the day. The potentially advantaged parties could reasonably complain of being asked to forgo the benefits of freed trade if no one is made worse off. But they cannot reasonably insist on such benefits at the *expense* of those made worse off.

2. Who are the "Losers"?

This initial argument is forceful but incomplete. Not everyone who suffers a loss as a result of trade would seem to have a claim of fairness to compensation. Should we also compensate the oligarch whose monopoly is undermined by foreign competition, or the rich owner, manager, or shareholder in a threatened import-oriented industry who may lose out from freer trade but remain rich and secure? Pareto efficiency requires that such people be paid off. As a claim of fairness, however, this seems wrong. Less well-off members of society can reasonably object to having lesser gains from trade simply so that the privileged can be made whole. Because they are already very well-off, ways their condition is worsened (they take a "haircut") are less significant for them than the opportunity cost to less well-off fellow citizens, especially to the least well-off, who could be compensated for losses or see still greater gains.

We may account for this as follows. In general, the relatively privileged tend to be not only rich but net beneficiaries of life in an open society. Losses to them may thus leave them unharmed overall. There may of course be exceptional cases in which the privileged are made worse off overall. These can be handled, as just suggested, by supplementary considerations of fairness for extenuating circumstances (under a "special justification" clause implicit in Due Care): the privileged will in any case lack a reasonable objection to being disadvantaged if this provides significant benefits to people who are less well-off, especially given the substantial opportunities for adaptation afforded by their greater wealth. Abolition of the infamous British Corn Laws made wealthy landowners worse off, and they loudly complained, but this was not especially reasonable. They remained in a position of safety and comfort, while poor workers ate cheaper bread.[7]

But who, then, are "losers" of the right sort, and on what grounds? We will suggest three relevant grounds: harm to lifetime prospects, acceptable risk, and burden sharing. The first two are expressed by Due Care, suitably elaborated. The third and perhaps the most important, which we take up separately later, is expressed by the principle of Domestic Relative Gains.

According to Due Care, the trade relationship is structurally equitable only when no person's life prospects are worse than they would have been had his or her society been closed to trade.[8]

---

7. In more difficult cases, different relatively poor people are harmed under either protection or freed trade. Here special considerations have a similar role: we might, e.g., aggregate over comparable benefits and burdens, or place greater weight on (non-comparable) gains to relatively less well-off people.

8. Our model is the normal case in which a person is born into a society where he or she resides for most of his or her life. We can similarly treat cases in which someone immigrates but spends most of his or her life in an adopted society, making suitable adjustments as needed. Cases in which people substantially divide their lifetime between countries, either by moving back and forth or immigrating once, may require special treatment.

We assume it will rarely be coherent (or relevant, if coherent) to ask how a person would have fared in the absence of any society whatsoever. Yet in real-world cases the comparable question about a person's society is all too apt. As suggested, people suffer severe and prolonged disadvantages. Although these might *in theory* be compensated by benefits at other periods of life, the case must be made that this will actually come about. According to Due Care, manifest forms of injury must be directly compensated (to a best approximation), unless the preponderance of evidence suggests that sufficient benefits have been or will be reaped at some other time of life. If we don't arrange direct compensation for the impoverished developing-country farmer, or the advanced-country worker who sees unemployment or stagnating wages over many decades, there must be good evidence that other arrangements will somehow ensure compensatory benefits over the course of their lives.

This is potentially consistent with the familiar argument that the global economy is rarely if ever harmful in the bigger scheme of things, because serious specific injuries are automatically compensated over the long haul. Ultimately, it is sometimes suggested, cumulative gains buoy the general prospects of most every society and class over enough time.[9] As we will understand Due Care, however, this argument is more difficult to sustain than usually assumed.

We agree that policy matters do often require a more general perspective. Although we have so far spoken of disruption in the lives of specific individuals, we take such examples to be relevant insofar as they track (1) representative groups or social classes, rather than specific individuals, and (2) the longer-term, lifetime prospects of those people, rather than shorter-term harm that may befall them, which may in fact be compensated at other

---

9. Driskill, manuscript, p. 19, offers the following "veil of ignorance" thought experiment, which he suggests captures the case for free trade as held by many economists. Imagine two economies, one closed and one which trades freely and meets the conditions for Kaldor-Hicks efficiency. Which would one prefer to be born into if one didn't know *when* one would be born? The answer, it seems, is that one would prefer the integrated rather than the closed society, since one would presumably be better off even without knowing how wealth is distributed in each case.

times. Even so, however, the suggestion of automatic compensation, over the longer haul, only shows that it may be *possible* to adopt a generalized perspective from which everyone benefits. It does not show that this is the *appropriate* generalized perspective from a fairness point of view. The pertinent question is whether some more specific perspective might support a morally relevant notion of harm. And there is such a perspective: even if we allow compensation *over* a person's life, the supposedly compensating benefits must come over *the course of his or her life*, and so not before the person is born, or after he or she dies. Accordingly, at least one relevant benchmark is as follows: given a manifest specific injury, in some particular context, we compare the person's condition with how well his or her life would have gone had his or her society (perhaps gradually) chosen autarky roughly around his or her birthday. (We avoid "non-identity problem" worries insofar as we focus on a given person's social class, whether or not it is the numerically same individual. The person's birthday corresponds to his or her generation's entry into the world.)

So, for example, take a person (or social class) whose condition is materially worsened partly as a result of global economic forces (e.g., the Mexican corn farmer impoverished by NAFTA). We may in theory reach any of three conclusions about how this person fares overall:

1. The injured person's life prospects would have been better under autarky, in which case he or she is made worse off, overall, for life in an open society.

In this case, the incurred material injury is not duly compensated, and special arrangements are required by Due Care. Alternatively, it may instead be true that

2. The injured person would have fared similarly, in which case he or she is no worse off; or
3. The injured person would have been worse off under autarky, in which case he or she has benefited, overall, from life in an open society.

It is only in these last two cases that compensation would not be required.

Now, such grand counterfactuals of course create enormous epistemological difficulties. Setting those aside for the moment, it seems an open possibility *in theory* that some people (some social classes) fare worse than they would have had their society been closed to trade over the course of their lives. It would surely be rash to insist that no one or hardly anyone would have fared better had their country of lifetime residence never exposed them to the vicissitudes of the global economy and instead remained autarkic starting early in their lifetime. Such judgments of overall harm are no less suspect, in theory, than the judgment being assumed when people manifestly harmed by a specific disruptive policy change are said to nevertheless be a net beneficiary from life in an open society. The judgments in both cases are of the same general kind.

Application in practice does matter, however, so the epistemological difficulties are not to be ignored. But the suggested "long view" falls short on epistemological grounds as well. As we have just elaborated Due Care, when someone suffers a specific injury as a result of exposure to the global economy, as people routinely do, the specific harm is justified only when the preponderance of evidence would support (2) or (3); we need pretty good reason to think the incurred injury is in fact being compensated for at some other stage of life. But it won't do, then, to point to gains a country has reaped in the distant past, before the person in question was born, let alone to vaguely presume general benefit or hold solemn faith in free markets. The honest truth is that we will often be at best *uncertain* whether a good case for (2) or (3) can be made, in which case we cannot justifiably conclude, or even safely presume, that the manifest specific injuries are *in fact* being indirectly compensated for. Uncertainty means that *more direct and more certain compensation is necessary*. For when people are manifestly injured by the global economy, their potentially reasonable objection won't be answered by saying: "although we admit compensation is necessary in theory, we can't confidently establish whether you are being indirectly compensated for your injury. So you are on your own." The burden of justification runs the other way around: Due Care requires either market protection or a social insurance scheme, unless compensation is not conjectured but *shown*. That is not to say that the preponderance of reasons won't weigh in favor of (2) or (3) in many cases. The point is that the case must be made for different representative groups and cannot be generally presumed.

3. Social Insurance as a Condition of Fair Trade

When the required case cannot be made, Due Care offers a solution consistent with free trade: simply adopt a compensatory social safety net. In developed countries, feasible arrangements might include direct payments and/or social insurance facilities, in the form of unemployment and wage insurance, pensions, education subsidies, job training and placement, employment-stimulating public investment, and so on. In developing countries, institutional schemes are more difficult to establish and maintain, especially in informal sectors, but appropriate measures nevertheless include public investment, government purchase of goods and services, temporary revenue-generating trade barriers, infant industry protection, and any feasible ways of supporting people directly (e.g., paying families for each day their child attends school).

Of course, developing countries often cannot pay for robust measures by themselves, whether from their own gains of trade or otherwise (especially since tariffs are often a chief source of public revenue). A crucial implication of Due Care, however, is that the responsibility to fund and establish compensatory measures does not stop at a given country's borders.[10] As argued in Chapter 3.5, the international practice of market reliance generates *collective* responsibilities, for all trading countries. So when a country cannot afford the necessary compensatory schemes, this does not show that the schemes are prohibitively expensive; it only shows that trading partners are obligated to shift the cooperative surplus so that the shared market reliance practice leaves no one worse off.[11] Insofar as countries will be unreliable in unilaterally providing the

---

10. In order to help developing countries manage adjustment costs and support infant industries, Stiglitz and Charlton, 2006 pp. 94–102, suggest a scheme that will streamline the intricate General System of Preferences *and* promote trade liberalization, especially "South-South" integration between developing countries: all WTO members give free market access in all goods to all developing countries that are smaller than themselves (e.g., Egypt gets free access to the United States but gives free access to Uganda).

11. As we emphasize later, countries will not as a matter of general fairness be required to part with more than the surplus, though this might be required for different moral reasons.

necessary support, structural equity in trade supports the establishment of relatively autonomous international institutions for the maintenance of domestic social safety nets (as enforced, if need be, within the WTO). If GATT duly provided policy space for each country to bolster social insurance schemes in the face of increasing openness and external risks,[12] fairness also requires that countries both poor and rich stably develop or retain the means for doing so (e.g., through development assistance or special loan facilities). (The appropriate slogan is then not "trade not aid" or "trade as aid" but rather "aid as fair trade.")

When such compensatory schemes are not feasible, free trade will not be fair. Appropriate trade barriers will be justified as a "next-best" solution. Such barriers will presumably often be temporary (e.g., developing countries should rely on tariff revenue only until they have established an adequate alternative tax base). But some barriers may well be permanent fixtures, even in developed economies. As Dani Rodrik explains, "in an economy like the United States, where average tariffs are below 5 percent, a move to complete free trade would reshuffle more than $50 of income among different groups for each dollar of efficiency or 'net' gain created! . . . It's as if we give $51 to Adam, only to leave David $50 poorer."[13] In these cases, compensation cannot be paid from the gains of trade but require the general public purse or international support. When trade is already relatively free, *fully* free and fair trade may or may not be worthwhile.

This highlights the importance of determining what *level* of social protection is required for fairness. If only modest levels of social insurance are needed for fairness, fully free trade will be easier to justify. This is arguably the real force of the epistemic difficulty of establishing who has been harmed and by how much: if that is uncertain, it is hard to say what level of compensation is necessary. Two further considerations do suggest, however, that fair levels of social support will not be modest.

First, Due Care carries a risk premium. Someone who wins $1,000 by betting his house in roulette is not clearly made better off for the gamble; the gain may not be enough to justify the high risk of very significant loss. Likewise, a social insurance scheme

---

12. Rodrik, 2007, ch. 4.
13. Rodrik, 2011, p. 57, 1994.

will not prevent net loss to a person unless the level of benefit is sufficient to justify exposure to significant risks of disruption, instability, and impoverishment. One will not "break even" unless one sees a good measure of gain.

Second, and to anticipate somewhat, our second proposed principle, Domestic Relative Gains, presumptively supports social protection at high levels. Background differences in wealth make a large difference to one's vulnerability to foreign market forces. The affluent will have a much easier time managing disruptions (in employment or savings) than those in the middle and especially the lower classes. If the less well-off bear the burden of a society's overall enrichment, it is not fair for the affluent to enjoy all or most of the gains. That the least well-off so often chiefly bear the burden of societal benefit from trade gives them an especially weighty claim to greater shares. So, for example, because income volatility is more likely to diminish the displaced, low-skilled worker's ability to save and ultimately retire, wage insurance, beyond mere unemployment insurance, is arguably only fair. (One is then guaranteed one's previous wage level, in one's next job, as opposed to mere post-employment pay for a period of time.) In this way, fair social insurance schemes will be generous beyond the requirements of Due Care, even with its suggested risk premium. And for all of our focus on harm, we need not suppose that it is the central or most significant fairness issue: it is the beginning, not the end, of fairness. Even if we found few actual cases in which an idea of "harm" is appropriate, we'd still have to reckon with the way the burdens of social cooperation are being distributed within society. We return to this later in the chapter.

4. Aggregation, Fair and Unfair

We should pause to discuss a familiar alternative principle to Due Care. It is less demanding, in the sense that it would allow trade to irreparably harm workers, whole countries, or even whole regions of the world. According to

> *utilitarianism*: the practice of trade is structurally equitable when, and only when, it is arranged so as to maximize global welfare overall.

According to utilitarianism, compensation of losers might well be necessary in practice, but only insofar as this turns out to be a necessary means of promoting the welfare of people taken as an aggregate. It is not required as a matter of principle.

Yet compensation for serious harm does seem a matter of principle: those who suffer specific injury can at least reasonably insist on substantial mitigation, if not full compensation, even if aggregate welfare is diminished, and especially when this merely cuts into consumers' levels of gain. It is not fair for workers to suffer severe unemployment burdens simply for the sake of small benefits to millions of consumers which add up to a net welfare improvement. Compare the potential countervailing objections. The severe unemployment burden gives the displaced worker a powerful complaint against utilitarianism as a regulative principle for international trade practice, and in favor of a principle such as Due Care. But any given consumer, taken separately, will have relatively slight grounds for countervailing complaint, since a given consumer merely risks seeing a slower rise in standard of living. Much the same point would hold if the full liberalization of capital turned out to maximize overall welfare despite the occasional country's losing a decade of two of growth as a result of a financial crisis (as, e.g., in the "lost decades" in Argentina or Japan). Insofar as capital controls would prevent this, they seem only fair, even if net welfare gains are forgone. Likewise, it could in theory turn out that a highly discriminatory system of trade—for example, high barriers against most of the developing world, but free trade with a few populous developing countries such as India and China—maximizes poverty reduction and welfare overall. The excluded part of the developing world could reasonably object to having its condition worsened, especially if the aggregate welfare gain resulted merely because comparatively poor people see tiny improvements in huge numbers.[14]

---

14. Collier, 2007, recommends similar temporary trade diversion away from fast-rising Asia toward the least-developed countries in Africa and elsewhere, in order to reduce Asia's first mover advantages into skill-intensive and higher-return industry. He suggests utilitarian reasons, writing: "Privileging the bottom billion against low-income Asia is not just or fair; a more accurate word might be 'expedient.' Without such a pump-priming strategy, the bottom billion are probably doomed to wait until Asia becomes rich and is at a substantial wage disadvantage

We have so far ignored pure aggregative reasoning and instead compared the positions of different (representative) people one by one. Although that is in accord with our basic account of structural equity reasoning in Chapter 5.4, it may then seem little surprise that utilitarianism comes out as objectionable. If we have so far cited cases of "unfair aggregation," the relative strength of utilitarianism is that it easily explains other cases of "fair aggregation," that is, cases in which the number of beneficiaries does appear to matter from a fairness point of view. Might such cases show that Due Care is on balance unjustified? Recall, for example, our claim that it is perfectly fair for freer trade to worsen the oligarch's life prospects, by undercutting his monopoly rents for the sake of the public good. We suggested a non-aggregative rationale for this—his plight can be worsened so that less well-off people might gain. But it might also seem to have an aggregative rationale instead: large overall gains, though small to any one but shared by millions, can justify significant losses to an unlucky few. Or to take a still clearer case: when losers cannot be feasibly compensated, and autarky is the only way of leaving no one harmed, we might think trade should be freed anyway, for the public good. But are we not then assuming an aggregative idea of the "public good" which takes into account that fact that so many people are likely to benefit?

We allowed in Chapter 5.4 that pure aggregative reasoning might be appropriate from a fairness point of view when there is an especially compelling case for it. The question, then, is whether we should admit aggregation in a way that grounds an objection to our principle of Due Care. Our answer is that it is at best unclear why we should, and so that we do not have the compelling case required.

The matter is unclear for several reasons. First, harm can be justified in personalistic terms, without purely aggregative reasoning. Even when poor people are harmed by freed trade, this may be justifiable to them if much greater benefits flow to other

---

against the bottom billion" (p. 167). One can also read this as an appeal to substantive equality of developmental opportunity, however. Least-developed countries should not be "doomed" for decades simply because Asian countries "got there first" (entering the global economy without similar competitive hurdles), because significant opportunities are not then equal or even close to equal. We return to this later in the chapter.

comparably poor people. (Assume for the sake of argument that a compensatory scheme cannot be established.) Earlier we said that one can reasonably complain of being harmed merely to give a *comparable* benefit to another comparably situated person. But in the present case, the persons are harmed in order to give a much greater benefit—perhaps even escape from poverty—to other persons. In this case, the would-be beneficiaries do seem in a position to mount a reasonable complaint against autarky. (Though when compensation schemes are in fact feasible, those harmed can also reasonably insist on them, as argued earlier.)

Second, harm can be justified in *aggregative but personalistic* terms. When losses to some are seen as comparable in significance to gains to a larger number of others, the larger number of people "breaks the tie."[15] Although worsenings will not be comparable in significance with mere benefits, per se, the argument can add the further claim that they become comparable under special circumstances, for instance, when the benefit is large and the worsening modest.

Third, we may admit purer cases of aggregation as extenuating circumstances. Our principles concern the fundamental nature of the global economy and its organization over the medium to longer haul. We can conceivably admit more specific, temporary circumstances as extenuating conditions, assuming the relevant "extenuating" versus "normal" circumstances can be plausibly specified (e.g., an urgent national security threat which implicates trade). Utilitarianism presents an attractive alternative to Due Care (or any of our three principles) only when it has divergent implications at our general level of inquiry that seem to tell against our more egalitarian ideas of fairness. But it is hard to see what these implications might be. If anything, utilitarians will tend to downplay such divergence over the longer haul on general empirical grounds. It will be said that protective barriers against a whole continent will not tend to maximally reduce poverty; that the frequency of severe financial crises will hobble an aggregative cost-benefit argument in favor of aggressive capital liberalization; and that growth (and welfare) will tend to be optimized by strong social safety nets (if only for reasons of "diminishing marginal utility").

The key question, then, is our original one: whether losers should also be compensated as a matter of principle. Here utilitarianism

15. Kamm, 1993, pp. 116–17; Scanlon, 1998, p. 232.

diverges from Due Care, but to its peril. As suggested, we would not think free trade could be justified as fair if it irreparably harmed social classes, whole countries, or whole regions of the world. And this just shows that, insofar as we nevertheless find ourselves assuming that free trade is justified "for the good of all," utilitarianism is not our assumed ground.

5. Domestic Relative Gains

We have so far suggested that structural equity requires "compensating the losers" for several reasons: reasons of harm to lifetime prospects, of acceptable risk, and of burden sharing. We saw that the Domestic Relative Gains principle stands behind the idea of fair burden sharing. It does so, we are suggesting, as an internal principle of fairness in trade. Again, considerations of harm count as internal concerns although they are only indirectly related to trade practice's aim of augmenting national income. In much the same way, our conception of internal argument allows us to consider how or whether national income is itself shared among the members of a trading society. The distribution of national gains must be reasonably acceptable to them if international trade practice is to be fair.

Domestic Relative Gains is more demanding than Pareto efficiency. As discussed in Chapter 2.6, Pareto efficiency is indifferent to distribution: so long as no one is made worse off as a result of trade, a few people may take the lion's share of the national gains. Domestic Relative Gains explains how this might be unfair with a presumption of equality of gain. Assuming each society has received its fair share of national gains, Domestic Relative Gains insists that inequality of gain among a society's members is unfair, barring reasons that this should be acceptable to them all.

Why this presumption? If everyone is made substantially better off, who could reasonably complain? Our answer is the domestic analogue of the equal gains benchmark in Chapter 6. The domestic gains of trade reflect the fruit of domestic social cooperation and so cannot be said to be owned by anyone independently of what distribution is fair. Moreover, from a domestic point of view, the gains of trade chiefly result from a national-level choice of policy. The goal is macro-level change in the allocation of productive resources, for the sake of macro-level (average or aggregate) gains across an economy. People contribute by doing what they would do anyway, except insofar as freer trade creates new incentives, which leads market actors to refine what they produce and sell, perhaps buying and selling with different people and on different terms than before. In each case, they by and large promote their personal prospects. Under conditions of substantial integration, and aside from those who suffer special hardships, no general class of market actors makes any special contribution to the gains of trade for society overall, at least none that gives them any proprietary claim to the gains they see, beyond what they would receive in a fair system of cooperation. If this is right, equality of gain is the fair default. Everyone who has had a hand in the socially created augmentation of wealth has the same presumptive claim to greater rather than lesser shares. Unless further reasons for a difference in treatment can be given, equality is the only distribution that recognizes every such participant's full claim; inequality in gains would unfairly discriminate between the different claimants.

If equality of distribution is the fairness default, when, if at all, are departures from equality acceptable? Domestic Relative Gains admits of different versions, depending on our answer. One answer is "never," a principle of

> *strict equality (applied domestically)*: the national income gains of trade are to be distributed equally among the members of each trading society. (The "gains of trade" here are each country's fair share of gains as compared to trading countries, as specified below.)

A different answer admits inequality as acceptable for dynamic reasons (e.g., because greater rewards incentivize productive effort and risk-taking, etc.). Following Rawls, we might so favor a

> *difference principle*: each trading country is to distribute its fair share of the national income gains of trade equally among its members, unless inequality of gain is to the greatest possible benefit to the society's least advantaged.

This interpretation of Domestic Relative Gains follows straightforwardly from Rawls's own difference principle when the gains of trade counted among the "primary social goods" of income and wealth.

The choice between these principles raises familiar questions of domestic distributive justice that we will not pursue. The present claim is that Domestic Relative Gains must be specified in some such way, for the gains of trade, whether or not further principles have any broader application. Thus, even if there are no general requirements of domestic distributive justice, fairness in trade itself generates principled requirements of internal egalitarian distribution of some such kind.

More important for our purposes, domestic distribution of the gains of trade bears on what is fair in the *international* system, since a country's inegalitarian policies can affect the relative gains of other countries and their members. For example, we will argue that developing countries can fairly expect special privileges in the trading system (e.g., freedom from intellectual property, services, investment, or competition rules) on grounds of poverty, even at significant cost to rich countries. But this argument will be considerably weakened if the affluent in those developing countries gain to a degree that is not necessary to maximize prospects for their society's less well-off members. (The practical relevance of this concern is unclear, however: in fact, the very rich in developing countries represent a tiny fraction of the population.) Even if we suppose that everyone in a developing country is made better off, the level of relative gain will matter. Rich countries can reasonably expect limitations on inequality of gain, so that gains flow as much as possible to relatively poor people. It won't be fair to ask rich countries, including their own worst-off, to pay for unnecessary gains to relatively rich people.

6. International Relative Gains

How then are gains across trading societies to be assessed? According to our third principle, International Relative Gains, the default is equality of gain, as according to the equal gains benchmark defended in Chapter 6. The gains of trade are socially created, by the joint practice of market reliance. Because each trading country has a morally relevant interest in greater rather than lesser national income gains, equal treatment requires equal distribution of gains, unless we can specify a relevant difference among participant countries.

International Relative Gains admits two such relevant differences, two possible grounds for inequality of gain. First, gains are to be adjusted according to relevant endowments such as a country's population size, natural resource base, level of development, and any other factor not created by the trade relation that predictably changes how much a country gains from global market integration. Second, inequality of gain is fair if greater benefits flow to people who are worse off in absolute terms (for instance, because developing countries are granted special trade privileges, offered technological and infrastructural assistance, or are released from specific intellectual property, services, investment, or competition rules).

As for the first ground for inequality, we can see the intuitive idea by comparing a large and small country. It would not seem fair to simply sum up the total gain from trade and divide it equally. This would overlook the significant role of prior endowments, which often dramatically shape how much a country will gain from the trade relationship. In domestic society, by contrast, beneficial personal endowments are by and large a product of the very system of cooperation whose justification is in question. In our politically decentralized and partially integrated world, there *is* a meaningful difference between what the trade relation creates and the social cooperation that is there anyway.

Endowments will not necessarily make a difference because they somehow generate independent entitlements. Indeed, we can assume there are no such entitlements, beyond what is independently fair among participants in the practice of trade. Rather, endowment sensitivity simply reflects the limited aim of trade practice, namely, to *improve* upon endowments roughly as given (through specialization and exchange), rather than to redistribute the benefits of those endowments as such. We might still advocate the redistribution of the benefits that flow from differential endowment, for reasons other than internal structural equity. But this is a separate moral issue. Trade itself is legitimate and fair so long as the practice of market reliance is mutually beneficial and the improvements it creates are distributed in a way that is reasonably acceptable to all.

The idea behind our second ground for inequality of gain is that rich and poor countries are not symmetrically situated in at least one crucial respect: they have (often vast) differences in wealth. In that case, while rich countries do have a legitimate interest in ever greater wealth (to support further consumption, public goods, or the arts, and so on), it is less significant than the interests of developing countries in benefiting large numbers of poor or very poor people. It is only fair for rich countries to benefit from trade, but also only fair for developing countries to see greater gains.

To see why this might be so, consider a suggestive analogy. Imagine two friends who regularly dine together and who make a practice of taking turns paying the check. Assuming they are of roughly equal wealth and that they eat and drink at roughly the same expense, taking turns seems perfectly fair. But now vary the case so that one friend is rich, while the other is relatively poor. Holding all else equal, it would then seem only fair for the richer friend to pick up the check more than every other time. (How often might depend on the size of the difference in wealth.) But the goal needn't be the equalization of overall benefit by compensating for a special burden (the poorer diner "pays" more each time given his smaller overall budget). It seems fair for the rich diner to pick up the check even after overall benefits are equalized, simply because she can easily afford it. Nor need this be a consideration of humanity (the extra payments might better reduce poverty if they were given to the beggar outside the door), and in any case the poorer friend needn't be especially poor; it is enough that the size of the gap between the two is sufficiently great.

International Relative Gains similarly reflects a limited form of "priority for the worse off": the benefits of trade matter more, from a fairness point of view, the worse off the beneficiaries are in absolute terms.[16] Here the relevance of poverty is limited to the trade relationship, seen as an international practice. Nothing follows for market transactions or business relationships per se.[17] The present principle applies only among trading countries, taking no account of poverty (absolute or relative) outside of the trade relationship. Even among trading countries, it applies only to the opportunities for benefit that economic integration creates, taking no account of

---

16. We assume what Parfit, 1997, calls the "deontic" rather than "telic" interpretation of prioritarianism, and follow Scanlon, 1998, pp. 226–29, in taking such considerations to apply only within specific types of interaction.
17. But see the "inherited" transnational obligations discussed in Chapter 10.5.

other potential ways poor people might be benefited. In the trading system, poverty is a relevant fairness consideration because it *modifies* the prior and independent claim that trading countries have to enjoy the fruit of their shared practice. It can matter in this way without assuming either general prioritarianism or humanitarian concerns.

An alternative to International Relative Gains would be a principle of

> *strict equality (applied internationally)*: trading countries are to divide (endowment-adjusted) gains equally.

This principle is less demanding than International Relative Gains, in the sense that rich countries will not be required to make special arrangements needed to give poor countries unequal benefits (even if special privileges are still required for humanitarian or other moral reasons). But this seems too permissive for the trade context. While there is no fairness in asking someone to pick up the whole dinner tab simply because he is rich, the global market reliance practice bears little resemblance to one-off interaction or exchange. In the case of the regular diners above, it is fair for the rich dining partner to pay, because their ongoing social practice changes the fairness equation. That is, even if bartered exchanges in a state of nature were subject to a rough equality norm, the situation changes when exchanges are embedded within a cooperative practice of market reliance that extends indefinitely into the future and substantially shapes people's whole life prospects, especially the world's poor. Under these conditions, the relatively advantaged cannot reasonably insist upon equality of gain in the goods created by the shared relationship, for an equal share of the gains of trade will mean very different things to advanced and developing countries. Indeed, developing countries can reasonably object to any principle that treats benefits to rich and poor in comparable terms and so can reasonably expect to be allowed to use trade to advance their development goals, even or especially when unequal gains flow their way.

On the other hand, if equality of gain seems too permissive, strict priority for the worst off can seem too stringent, at least as far as international commerce is concerned. It would not seem fair for rich countries to adopt prohibitive trade barriers against Asia and Latin America in order to divert trade flows to less well-off

African countries (quite aside from the fact of Africa's significantly smaller population). Nor will mere fairness require the degree of self-sacrifice associated with potentially demanding humanitarian obligations. The whole purpose and point of international trade is mutual benefit. Internal structural equity does require, then, that all countries benefit from trade. Economic integration must be significantly worthwhile, over time, even for advanced countries ("over time" because significant temporary disadvantages may still be required, because compensated in future benefits).

The required "priority" for the less well-off may be seen as a standing privilege of special benefit. At least as far as trade policy is concerned, developing countries can reasonably insist on being free to use global economic integration in any way that would advance their development goals. This may cut significantly into advanced-country levels of benefit, so long as global economic integration remains significantly worthwhile, overall and over time. Although rich-world *individuals* are often made worse off, this only implies that "losers" must be compensated. And because rich countries can almost always afford such measures (provided appropriate taxation), they do not justify a cost to developing countries in forgone opportunities for development. Nor is there any real risk at the country level that advanced economies will see little or no gain from trade under feasible domestic or international policy scenarios, especially over the medium to longer term.[18] Over the longer haul, degree of benefit is the only realistic concern.

We might develop the suggested privilege of special development benefit as follows. To say that developing countries should not have this special privilege would be to say that, in some important range of cases, *development goals should, in fairness, be compromised or postponed for the sake of some further economic benefit to developed countries*. But there does not seem to be an important class of cases of this kind. We have already ruled out cases in which advanced and developing countries stand to reap roughly the same level of benefit from different sets of rules or policies. Because members of developing countries will tend to

---

18. Although China's exchange rate peg clearly harms the United States in important respects, the United States is certainly significantly better off for trade in general (and with China in particular).

fare badly in absolute terms, a given level of benefit to them will matter more than it would for absolutely better-off rich worlders. But if that justifies unequal benefit, the point will also hold when policies can shift unequal benefits even further in the direction of developing countries. So long as people in developing countries are significantly worse off in absolute terms, the benefits to them matter more from a fairness point of view. They would matter more, indeed, even than greater benefits to absolutely better-off people.

Though the moral issue here is not merely humanitarian, it is sensitive to the *absolute* state of a person's total condition. As the relatively badly off representative person's condition improves, his or her claim to the smaller level of benefit gradually diminishes (i.e., as according to a graduated scale of urgency rather than terminating at some threshold level). At some (rough) point, then, the greater benefit may fairly flow to the absolutely better-off parties. We may conjecture that this situation arises only after developing countries have developed. That is, a plausible conception of what countries are properly classified as "developing," and what then qualifies as a "development goal," will identify features of a country's condition that preserve their prioritarian claims over time.[19]

7. Further Principles for Trade Outcomes

We have now presented the central rationales for our three principles. We have noted some less demanding principles, but others remain.

A difference principle, applied at the international level, would be less demanding than our principle of International Relative Gains. A difference principle would allow inequality of gain even in a world without absolute poverty; it need only maximize prospects for the least well-off trading partner. International Relative Gains, by contrast, would not allow the relative advantage, without a poverty or development rationale.

---

19. In other words, we conjecture that an appropriate gradual scale of urgency will coincide with plausible classifications of which countries count as "developing."

Despite this abstract contrast, it is not clear that a difference principle presents a real alternative to International Relative Gains, at least not when it is seen as a regulative principle for trade practice and is grounded in its standard incentives-based rationale. That rationale finds no general footing in global economic life as we know it. Rawls's difference principle is apt within a domestic economy because tax and other institutions shape choices of work over leisure, risk over caution. Unequal rewards can thus be potentially justified by the resulting dynamic gains, appropriately distributed. In international trade relations, by contrast, the main rationales for the gains of trade—again, specialization in the overall division of labor, economies of scale, and the spread of technology and ideas—require no appeal to the dynamic consequences of offering greater rewards to individuals or firms. Nor are prospects of unequal reward supposed to somehow incentivize government policy action: the gains of freer trade for each are reason enough.

A true alternative to International Relative Gains would be the Nash bargaining solution, seen as a criterion of fair division. Assuming we can work out an appropriate social welfare function for each trading country (and assuming, perhaps, that Due Care and Domestic Relative Gains are assumed to be satisfied), according to

> *the Nash solution*: the gains of trade are to be divided so as to maximize the product of the welfare improvement for each trading society.

Unlike utilitarianism, this would not call for aggregation which allows for some countries to be made worse off. Nor would it necessarily require equality of gain: inequality might be fair depending on the social welfare functions of different trading countries. Yet, seen as a conception of fairness, the Nash solution goes wrong in key cases. When a poor country sees a large welfare gain with even a small share of the division, while a rich country requires a large share for a modest welfare improvement, the Nash solution will give the *rich* country the lion's share.[20] But surely the poor

---

20. For this point with a different example, see Barry, 1989, p. 15.

country can reasonably expect *at least* half of the product of the shared activity, as under International Relative Gains. While it might be *rational* for a poor country to give up the lion's share in trade negotiations, rich countries surely could not *fairly* insist on this. The Nash solution thus seems better suited (as Nash himself understood it) as a proposal of rational bargaining theory, and not as criterion of equitable division.[21]

We may also object to the assumed welfarism. As we argued in Chapter 6.8, a country's basic presumptive claim to equal gain is not based in welfare in the first instance, but rather in joint creation of certain economic goods through the trade relationship. We have admitted an *aspect* of welfare as a further relevant consideration, in the sense that background conditions of poverty properly shape how much countries should benefit. But treating poverty as a morally relevant aspect of welfare does not necessarily generalize to anything we might want to call "welfare." The background welfare levels of fabulously prosperous people do not have any similarly general significance for what is fair. If a country has expensive tastes, and so gets less welfare from a given bundle of economic goods than countries more easily satisfied, the welfare inequality is not unfair, but tough luck.

8. Equality of Opportunity

If our principles concern the *outcomes* of trade, a different class of fairness principles focuses on *opportunities* instead. On what may be called an

> *opportunity principle*, the practice of trade is fair when, and only when, each relevant agent is afforded a substantial range of economic opportunities, consistent with equality opportunity for all.

In the most restrictive version, the relevant agents are countries, while the "substantial range" of economic opportunities is limited

---

21. The same might be said of Gauthier, 1986, and other bargaining theory proposals that might be adapted as conceptions of fair division, albeit in light of different counterexamples. See Barry, 1989, for general discussion.

to the absence of formal discrimination in established international rules (as, e.g., according to the "most-favored nation" rule, which generally forbids tariff discrimination). According to a less restrictive version, attention is also paid to opportunities for each country's respective citizens or firms, as treated by other market actors or by domestic or foreign government policies that structure market relations (e.g., the rule of national treatment, which forbids trading partners from discriminating between foreign and domestic firms). Finally, beyond such "formal" versions, opportunity principles can be applied more "substantively" to the background conditions (e.g., technological or infrastructural development, institutional flexibility) needed for legal or market opportunities to be effectively used. The common feature of all such views is that some such opportunity set is the *sole* basis for assessment of fair treatment; there is no basis in fairness for regulation of the global economy's outcomes. On all such views, opportunities for choice, not actual benefit, are all anyone can reasonably expect.

Purely "formal" conceptions of opportunity are open to powerful objections in light of the more substantive demands of "fair opportunity." Consider, for example, a system of "static" comparative advantage, in which countries specialize according to their purely "natural" differences in endowment. Assuming a lack of formal discrimination in trade policy among all countries (perhaps as required by non-discrimination norms), such a system might initially seem to treat all countries in the same way: any differences in gain, it may be said, are attributable to *nature* rather than to the system of trade. Yet if the system in effect discourages societies from actively changing their relative position in the emergent division of labor (e.g., through public investment and far-sighted industrial policy), asking them to leave specialization entirely up to the market, this will predictably create substantially unfair inequalities of opportunity. Although any number of countries could initially have created economies of scale in skill-intensive, higher-return industries, once a subgroup "gets there first" the others may become frozen out for a long time. Developing countries that initially specialize in primary products, for example, then suffer a relative lack of opportunity due to largely arbitrary ways the international division of labor is refined. Unless substantial remedial opportunities are created, perhaps by actively facilitating policy flexibility and industrial experimentation, the disadvantaged countries are not being treated "in the same way," not by nature, but by the system itself.[22]

There is, however, a more basic problem with opportunity views, whether formal or substantive: they do not account for unfairness in the harms of trade.[23] A practice aimed at creating certain benefits could be fair without compensating those who will be foreseeably harmed, but only if the parties likely to be harmed have an adequate opportunity to avoid injury. But people rarely have adequate opportunities to avoid the harms of trade, and so they can reasonably complain when compensatory arrangements are not made. As we have emphasized, few can be reasonably expected to leave their country (to where? another trading society?). And it is not as though the people most vulnerable to global market forces are simply not doing enough to gain from market relations; developing-country farmers, for instance, are often doing as well as they possibly can for themselves given their limited options. Like domestic institutions, but unlike a club, university, or game, the international system of trade is not "voluntary" (i.e., reasonably avoidable) in a sense that could appropriately support an opportunity principle.

One might suggest that any *country* can always avoid exposing its people to outside market forces by simply erecting trade barriers, in which case the country alone bears responsibility for compensating its losers when it chooses free trade instead. So long as relevant opportunities for integration are provided, the idea goes, the *international system* is not unfair, whatever its outcomes. Although governments certainly do bear responsibility for their choice of trade policy, it does not follow, however, that other governments (taken individually or collectively) are not liable as well. Much as with individual citizens, the international system is not "voluntary" in the sense that a choice to participate legitimates any outcomes that result, because each country has an adequate opportunity of non-participation. Again, no country can afford not

---

22. Unger, 2007, powerfully argues for developing-country policy flexibility and institutional experimentation on similar grounds.
23. Patterson and Afilalo, 2008, p. 180, suggest the emergence of a substantive norm of "global equality of opportunity," but also call this the new "basic welfare norm" of the trading system. This suggests that equality of opportunity is an instrumental norm rather than a fairness principle that rejects sensitivity to (in this case welfare) outcomes.

to join the trading system, and member countries benefit from greater specialization when other countries sign up. Nor can countries already in the system, and subject to its market reliance expectations, be reasonably asked to leave; the cost of leaving will be too high, whether in terms of future gains forgone or uncompensated costs of past integration.

Moreover, specific choices will legitimate specific outcomes only when clear lines of responsibility can be drawn, and these are just not to be found given substantial economic integration. Especially at our general level of inquiry, but also in many routine matters of trade or financial policy, outcomes arise due to systemic tendencies and the policy choices of many different governments. If people are harmed because their countries abide by internationally established expectations of freed trade, in goods, services, or capital, and the country is a participant in the practice in good standing, then all the countries involved remain liable for the outcome. The burdens of liability must be fairly shared, and a country may, in certain cases, appropriately bear greater burdens in light of some past choices. But such considerations of "desert" are rarely the whole story and indeed often greatly exaggerated in the heat of political argument (e.g., Germany exaggerates Greece's culture of leisure in resisting a "bailout," while underestimating its own gains from the euro).[24] And in any case it is a mistake to think one can finally "place blame" when any policy choice in a global economy is made in light of a thousand other policy choices already decided. As a general and basic matter, all trading countries are together collectively responsible to see to it that compensatory arrangements are set up in each trading country. And, again, insofar as countries tend to be unreliable in providing the necessary support when left to their own devices, structural equity in trade requires the establishment of international institutions that reliably support domestic social safety nets.

---

24. Could considerations of desert systematically neutralize a country's claim to endowment adjusted gains? Not plausibly. Countries plainly do not always or nearly always get what they deserve in the global economy because of purely domestic mismanagement or otherwise. This kind of view is not very plausible in the relatively calm harbors of advanced society markets, and simply incredible on the global economy's high seas. See also Chapter 8 on unruly financial markets.

To be sure, governments cannot assume full responsibility for the welfare of individuals or other governments. They can at most offer goods or resources that one can choose to use or not to use. This follows from our intended "resourcist" interpretation of our principles: each principle is associated with its specified bundle of goods or resources, or its appropriate "currency" of application. Fairness is not concerned with welfare outcomes per se, even as regards the significance of harm, but rather with morally relevant interests in certain goods or resources, which ground reasonable complaints. The concern is then with "opportunities," but only in the trivial sense that any good or resource represents an opportunity for use rather than its use itself. Such "resourcism" is not a reason to favor an opportunity conception over our principles.

To the extent that the harms of trade do matter, one might instead adopt a modified opportunity principle. Fairness might be understood in terms of equality of opportunity, with the exception that a special privilege of compensation or assistance is accorded to poor countries.[25] And to the extent that the harms of trade to advanced-country workers seem unfair, the demand for compensation might be extended to them as well. It would then matter for fairness that trading countries or their members suffer harm, but not in a way that implies equality of gain as the default distribution. So long as compensation of losers is well supported, and so long as certain relevant opportunities are equal, a fair trading system would be insensitive to what economic outcomes otherwise result.

Even so, in focusing simply on harm, this view still ignores one of the central moral issues in trade: the basic reasonable claim that all trading countries enjoy in virtue of being joint participants in the market reliance practice, namely, a claim to the fruit of the joint venture. That claim is not simply to opportunities to gain, but to the internationally created augmentation of wealth itself. The claim is to actually enjoy the fruit (or at least to have it in one's hands, with a choice to eat or not).

The point is especially important in the case of developing countries, who are not mere needy supplicants but full participants in the common reliance practice with rightful claims to equal shares. Indeed, the doctrine of comparative advantage entails precisely that all countries—even those with an absolute

---

25. Brown and Stern, 2007.

advantage in nothing—can contribute to a mutually beneficial division of labor. Insofar as no country has proprietary claim to the intended (endowment-adjusted) gains, each has a presumptive claim to a greater rather than a lesser share of the joint activity. It is thus not the case that conditions of poverty justify a shift from opportunities to outcomes only in exceptional cases. Outcomes are at issue in the first instance: they reflect directly on whether the common market reliance practice treats its participants in an equitable way. The fact that so many contributors are poor is merely a further consideration, which justifies special treatment in the form of greater gains. Insofar as developing countries have themselves historically advocated "special and differential treatment" provisions on something like opportunity-based grounds of status equality, they, too, misrepresent the central socioeconomic fairness issue.[26] Developing countries are active contributors to the mutually beneficial relationship. They can rightfully lay claim, not simply to equality of status as reflected in so many opportunities, but to equality of shares.

9. Reciprocity of Risk

A quite different route to an opportunity view appeals to the idea of reciprocity of chances of benefit or risks of harm. The international market reliance practice might still have the aim of creating national income gains, and yet be seen as fair, with no concern for outcomes, so long as the following principle is satisfied:

> *Risk reciprocation:* trade practice may permissibly offer all countries the opportunity to augment national income, without regulating outcomes, if and only if trading countries impose similar risks upon one another.

To elaborate: I impose a *non-reciprocal* risk upon you when you do not impose the same risk upon me (I build a fusion reactor on

---

26. See Hudec, 1975, on the history of this dialectic. We agree with Hudec that the stated focus on status equality misrepresents the ultimately *instrumental* justification for the non-discrimination norm, but disagree with his skepticism about the applicability of fairness within the multilateral system.

my side of our property line, or put a loaded gun to your head, or run near you with hot coffee in hand, and you fail to do likewise). The risk is *reciprocal*, or reciprocally imposed, when we impose similar risks upon one another (e.g., we both drive, taking only some normal range of driving risks, putting each other at similar risk of injury). There is often a point in allowing such risk imposition instead of simply requiring due care. This can be mutually beneficial; we may both stand to benefit from being permitted to engage in some risky activity (as we both stand to gain from driving). As for why this should be fair, it suffices, it may be said, that the imposition is reciprocal.[27] Our respective ventures may then come to very different results: if your luck is good, but mine bad, it will be no matter for fairness if we each faced similar risks of injury. Any residual unfairness in the unequal outcome is not the unfairness of unfair *treatment*, but of a more "cosmic" kind. We may blame the gods, but not one another.

Applying this to the global economy, the idea would be that trade practice can be fully fair insofar as all countries stand to gain from economic integration, where each country faces similar risks of harm to workers, firms, or overall country prospects. Actual benefit or actual harm is then immaterial. No country can lay claim against the others, in the name of unfair treatment, to either compensation for harm or the redistribution of benefits. Beyond domestic risk management, how each country fares is left for the gods to decide.

Current trade practice is clearly a situation of non-reciprocal risk. Developing countries face special vulnerabilities, whether to increased unemployment or to volatility in commodities markets (which may erode the value of exports, dramatically increase the cost of food relative to tight budgets, and cause riots in the streets). On the principle of risk reciprocation, however, this is not to say that advanced countries must limit the risks they impose upon developing countries; development countries can instead *increase* the risks they impose on advanced countries. What matters is simply similarity of imposition. And indeed advanced countries are already subject to real risks themselves: trade affects employment levels (e.g., in the aftermath of a crisis); rapid developing-country industrialization (e.g., in China or India) can cause especially

---

27. Fletcher, 1972.

painful disruptions to long-standing forms of industry; and so on. If advanced-country risks are nevertheless of lesser and more manageable significance than the risks faced by developing countries, the fair solution, on the present suggestion, can be for developing countries to *ramp up* the risks of harm they create for advanced countries, so that the risk imposition approaches similarity. For instance, they might further amass rich country currency reserves, which flood rich countries with capital and increase the risk of a financial crisis, high unemployment, and protracted budgetary woes.

There is perhaps a macabre sort of fairness here. Perhaps such mutuality makes a situation less unfair than it would otherwise be. But risk retaliation is hardly a recipe for a structurally equitable global economy. The proposed principle of risk reciprocation requires only that the risk imposition be "similar." But the *level* of risk matters greatly as well: similar risks, under some description, can vary dramatically in significance depending on background factors. Two people might face a "similar" risk of automobile accident under some general description—for example, both have the same probability of similar auto damages—but the risk will have much greater significance for one of them if he or she is unable to pay for repairs. Likewise, even if developing countries could somehow impose similar risks upon advanced countries, the risks would not be morally comparable. Developing countries are at risk for far more profound forms of injury, and it will be incredible to suggest that real injurious outcomes to very poor people are wholly irrelevant as grounds for reasonable complaint.

We could instead read the principle of reciprocal risk in a different way, in terms of the *expected overall value* for each party taking and accepting exposure to risks.[28] Fair treatment is then achieved, not when risk levels are similar but when the parties can each expect roughly the same overall value from being allowed to engage in the risk-imposing behavior, being subject to like risk-taking of others. The special vulnerabilities of developing countries might then be justified given their prospects of gain. A route out of poverty is indeed a monumental advance, and insofar as integration supports this, it might go a long way toward justifying

---

28. Coleman, 1992, p. 254.

much if not all of the risks of harm along the way. Could that amount to a rough equivalence in expected gain with advanced countries? Perhaps a case might be made. Advanced countries stand to gain less, but they also face less risk. In theory, the overall expected value of each country's opportunities to integrate could work out as roughly the same.

Yet if we are to consider expected value, why not also consider how benefits and harms actually fall out? All risk assessments assume a particular informational situation, at some time. But the practice of mutual market reliance continues over time, as events play out. The veil of the future is crucial when the risks are of irreparable harm; if compensation ex post will be unavailable, precaution rather than risk-taking may be the order of the day (see Chapter 8.6). When the risks are not of irreparable harm, however, and compensation might well be offered, it is hard to see why fair treatment in an ongoing practice should not require the adjustment of economic outcomes as they become known. Trade practice will be fair, over time, only when trading countries and their members actually enjoy the appropriate gains. For having actually incurred risks of harm for the benefit of others, only *actual benefit* is fair return. It makes little difference if there was, at some earlier time, an epistemic position from which the then-ex ante chances of overall benefit were roughly the same. The actual outcomes, over time, still seem relevant. By asking us to set them aside, the principle of risk reciprocation obscures or ignores an entirely reasonable source of complaint.

Take, for example, a developing country that depends on world commodities markets and suffers extreme boom-to-bust cycles as commodities prices fluctuate. The ensuing hunger, unrest, and budget crisis won't be justified to its members by pointing out that this is of course how risks work, that the gods do not of course play fair, and that the government at any rate could have hedged its bets with precautionary food inventories or by diversifying more during boom times. The question at issue is not how the gods play but whether *trade practice* is fair to those involved, on an ongoing basis, even after certain risks have played out. Perhaps the adversely affected developing country is partly to blame. Even so, it will fairly ask other governments for compensatory finance ex post. Indeed, it will fairly ask for precautionary measures that mitigate the outcomes of risk-exposure over time—measures, for example, such as commodities price stabilization funds, loans indexed to commodity prices, so that the risks of further price fluctuation are shared, and so on. Such measures seem not only desirable but eminently fair.

10. Substantive Libertarianism

An opportunity conception might instead be defended by appeal to the value of liberty. The harms of trade might be defended as an unfortunate but fair result of registering the reasonable demands, of individuals or of countries, to be allowed to make certain economic choices. While we have set aside sweeping external natural rights of non-interference in focusing on internal fairness concerns, one can still so defend libertarianism on more substantive, internal grounds. The opportunity principle stated earlier might thus be supplemented with the following conception of its grounds:

> *substantive libertarianism*: economic liberty (for the relevant economic agents, whether countries, firms, or individuals) is to be presumptively respected. When liberty and other values conflict, liberty is to be protected, even at great cost to other worthy values. Any limitation on economic liberty is presumptively open to reasonable rejection.

Accordingly, when liberty and other values conflict with an attempt to regulate global economic market outcomes, it follows that fairness can at most require the protection and facilitation of the preconditions for voluntary exchange (whether a commercial exchange among market actors or inter-governmental "policy swap"). The preeminent value of liberty undercuts potential objections of harm.

A first question to ask is whether and to what extent liberty actually conflicts with the prevention of harm. Chapter 6.8 suggested that trade law and policy does not bear upon individual economic liberty in any very direct way. Nor can it be plausibly said that any regulation of the harms of trade will threaten basic liberties as usually understood in liberal societies, whether personal liberties (e.g., of speech, conscience, movement, etc.) or the best-established basic liberties of economic life (e.g., choice of occupation, place of work, country of residence, etc.).

We do find a potential conflict in familiar territory, in the tax measures likely to be part of any regulation of the harms of trade (e.g., income taxes for domestic safety nets, securities taxes for crisis prevention, or mandatory country dues for an international social insurance support scheme). People or governments so taxed are not "free to spend" or save money they would have had under lesser taxation. The question, then, is whether this reduction in liberty can be said to have paramount importance of the sort needed to justify the presumptive respect for liberty claimed by our principle of substantive libertarianism. Why respect *that* liberty *even at great cost to other important values*? What possible complaint upon the part of those faced with prospects of having less money could be so powerful as to overrule the complaints of those who would be left to suffer serious and perhaps irreparable harm?

The answer cannot of course appeal to J. S. Mill's famous presumption in favor of liberty, which does not apply when the exercise of liberty is likely to harm others.[29] Nor can one plausibly limit the harm principle to the harms of particular transactions or policy choices, to the exclusion of harmful systemic patterns that emerge from various transactions or policy choices. In the present context, harmful systemic outcomes cannot be defensibly left for fate to decide and charity to rectify. This would arbitrarily exclude a central feature of trade practice, which is all about emergent socioeconomic patterns. Moreover, any proposed way of regulating the overall structure of trade practice will in effect raise questions of taxation in one form or another. To the extent that some pay less through formal institutions, others "pay" in foreseeable income reduction by other means. The question is not whether people pay but who pays and how much.

The issue, then, is one of relative burden. We compare the burden of being left with less money to save or spend under a given tax scheme with the burden of suffering serious and potentially irreparable harm. The losers who stand to gain from a compensation scheme can't reasonably complain of being taxed and so less free to spend the amount of money they would otherwise have had; they may or may not be asked to pay a tax and in any case

---

29. Mill (1859), 1977. Even a libertarian such as Nozick, 1974, ch. 4, allows significant choice-regulation in the name of risk-regulation needed to prevent harm.

stand on balance to gain. A fortiori, the beneficiaries of trade certainly can't complain, especially not the relatively rich and privileged among them. Compared to those who suffer severe and irreparable harm, the relative burden for them is small. The taxes might even command a large share of their income and yet pale in significance by comparison to the major and irreparable disruptions of work and income suffered by losers. So long as the question is one of fair relative tax burden, it is hard to see how it would rule out regulation of the harms of trade in the proposed sweeping way. Those who may be irreparably harmed clearly have the stronger complaint.

11. Legitimate Expectations

One might therefore argue that the relevant considerations are not those of fair relative tax burden but rather "legitimate expectations": promised rewards in an established system of reward (e.g., a low top tax rate, or highly profitable investment terms) must be paid, just as promises we make as individuals must be kept, even at significant cost to worthy values. We might put the idea as the

> *promissory principle*: once expectations of reward for labor or investment are established within a legitimate (even if not fully just) system of cooperation, the promised rewards must be granted, even at significant cost to worthy values.

Although this principle does not say that income and capital gains taxes must be set at any particular level, the fact that they are now set at low levels in many countries would compel institutional inertia. Tax rates could not be fairly raised, even when the goal of doing so is to fund social insurance schemes that compensate for the harms of trade. That would be true so long as the trading system is a legitimate system of cooperation, even if it is not fully fair to allow significant harm.

One line of reply is to argue that the harms of trade delegitimize the trading system. They certainly do delegitimize the system in the eyes of many of those who are substantially harmed, and a high standard of legitimacy might support this verdict. If people are to be legitimately asked to support the system despite their relatively disadvantaged position, then it at least needs to arrange for them not to be made significantly worse off, at least not without offering a real opportunity of avoiding harm and of benefiting to some degree.

This is to deny that the expectations principle helps the cause of expansive economic liberty. A more basic problem lies with the expectations principle itself. Mere expectations of reward do not have the supposed trumping significance, even in a legitimate system. The appropriate principle is as follows:

> *legitimate expectations*: once expectations of reward for labor or investment are established within a legitimate system of cooperation, the promised rewards must be granted, even at significant cost to worthy values, *insofar as this is consistent with a fair overall scheme of cooperation.*

Reasonably formed expectations presumably do generate *some* relevant concerns of fairness in a legitimate system (and little or no claims under illegitimate arrangements). But they will approach the presumptive force of promissory rights *only* within a scheme of cooperation that is fair overall. Reward levels can be adjusted (by raising taxes, or raising costly environmental or labor standards, subject to appropriate procedural constraints of notice, generality, etc.). Even reasonably formed expectations will lack presumptive force when such measures remedy otherwise more significant and unfair burdens created by the system. So, for example, the Multilateral Agreement on Investment, proposed by the OECD (but later dropped), was misguided in allowing transnational corporations hurt by domestic environmental or labor standards to sue for compensation on grounds of expropriation.[30] Firms have no overriding claim of fairness to expected investment returns, provided that the adjustment in level of reward is undertaken for the right reasons, and implemented in the right ways.[31]

---

30. The agreement would have followed NAFTA investment provisions. In 1996, the Ethyl Corporation successfully used NAFTA investor rights against the Canadian government for having banned a gasoline additive that Ethyl produced. Canada settled out of court for many millions of dollars.
31. Stiglitz and Charlton, 2006 p. 133, suggest the need for cross-country coordination of concessionary tax rates in order to limit the large fiscal losses developing countries incur as a result of competing within each other to attract investors.

In other words, given a background fairness demand, the idea of legitimate expectations does not bear a direct analogy with interpersonal promissory rights and obligations, as the promissory principle suggests. One can indeed be obligated to fulfill expectations one has voluntarily created (e.g., one promised to meet someone at a certain time and place), even at significant cost to worthy values (a fine day at the beach). But in the present context this is not the relevant analogy. The relevant analogy is a case in which someone makes a promise he or she had no right to make in the first place (e.g., to be at a meeting when others already had a claim on the person's time). If expectations of gain were created by the system (e.g., with low income or capital gains taxes, or very favorable rates of investment return), there is no unfairness in adjusting the level of reward to make the overall system more fair.

12. Internal Cosmopolitanism?

We have now defended our three principles against various principles that make less egalitarian demands. "Cosmopolitan" principles of various sorts might make greater egalitarian demands: they require us to compare prospects not just for countries and classes within countries, but for all the individuals of the world, taken as so many individuals. We would directly compare how a given group of Americans and a given group of Brazilians fare in light of how the common market reliance practice shapes their respective fates.

As suggested in Chapter 4, the issue here is not "cosmopolitanism" in the bare sense that individuals are the ultimate unit of moral concern. We are assuming that much; the question is what form regulative principles should take, given our constructive method of justification. Moreover, by focusing on internal issues, we have already set aside clearly external cosmopolitan principles (e.g., a "luck egalitarian" principle that requires the elimination of all undeserved misfortune). We have also already challenged arguments for a cosmopolitan principle on internal, social interpretive grounds in Chapter 6.8; any such view, we said, amounts to costly revisionism of the practice of international trade. For all we have argued so far, however, one could still offer a cosmopolitan principle and claim that it can be justified within the confines of internal argument. For example, one might defend:

internal cosmopolitanism about fairness in trade: the benefits and burdens created by the system of international trade are to be distributed equally (or otherwise acceptably) among all individuals involved in the common international practice.

This might be regarded as an internal principle in at least the sense that it assumes the basic international aims and structure of trade practice, and so limits itself to the advantages and disadvantages that trade creates. The question, then, is whether it can be justified on substantive grounds that do not invoke an external principle.

One possibility would be to argue that unless the proposed principle is respected, the trading system would improperly distribute its advantages and disadvantages on grounds that are arbitrary from a fairness point of view.[32] The appeal to what is "arbitrary from a fairness point of view" would not impugn the natural distribution of country endowments, which countries bring to the trade relationship, but only the endowment-adjusted gains that result from international social cooperation. Nor will the argument assume any external principle that precludes the influence of such arbitrary factors (e.g., a luck-egalitarian principle that impugns any influence of undeserved luck per se). Instead, the idea would be that we have an independent sense of what sorts of considerations are relevant or irrelevant within established trade practice, and that anything short of regulation by the proposed cosmopolitan principle allows it to improperly distribute according to some such irrelevant factors. Whether or not luck or misfortune have a role, then, it would matter that distribution is shaped by factors that have no bearing, as relevant considerations, on the justifiability of trade practice, in the same way that it would be objectionably arbitrary to distribute the wealth of a society based on eye color or physical height: such natural factors just don't bear, one way or the other, on whether the distribution is justified, and so shouldn't in fact be the systematic basis for distributing cooperatively produced wealth (even if they do in fact shape how people fare, without being a "systematic basis" of

---

32. Garcia, 2003, 2007, defends principles for the WTO, IMF, and World Bank in light of arbitrary sources of inequality, as informed by the basic workings and assumed purposes of these institutions. His argument is at least partly "internal" for being institution-sensitive in those respects.

distribution).³³ The claim, then, would have to be that for some such specified reasons, we should ignore the country in which an individual lives and works, and instead directly compare how all individuals fare within the common, worldwide division of labor.

But here we may ask, What considerations of relevance or irrelevance within established trade practice would have that upshot, and why should they rule out our international principles in favor of internal cosmopolitanism? What considerations have this particular kind of force? The answer seems at best obscure. We have already precluded the most natural suggestion, namely, that it is arbitrary to allow trade prospects to depend on country endowments. While country endowments are in one sense no less arbitrary than a person's eye color or physical height, the claim here, again, cannot simply be that country endowments reflect natural and largely undeserved fortune or misfortune. And in any case, natural endowments clearly do seem at least *relevant* from the point of view of established trade practice, in the sense that they inform its central understood aim. The aim is precisely for countries to mutually *improve* upon given assets, in part by taking advantage of "natural" differences in ease of production. The aim is not to redistribute endowments or their benefits per se, and insofar as background endowments shape the augmentation function of trade, they *are* relevant to its justifiability in internal terms.

A perhaps more promising route is to deny our international characterization of co-production. Insofar as anyone has a special claim to the gains of trade, it may be argued, it is not countries, but the various individuals who in effect work together around the globe. And so to characterize whole societies as the relevant claimants to fair shares in the internal scene, as we have, is to introduce irrelevant considerations that turn mainly on how individuals just happen to be politically partitioned. That sociopolitical fact, it may be said, is arbitrary from an internal fairness point of view.

---

33. See James, 2005a, pp. 287–90, for this interpretation of Rawls's famous claim that the system of natural liberty allows the improper influence of "factors so arbitrary from a moral point of view." This reading is consistent with Rawls, 1999, on natural endowments, which is chiefly concerned with the "resource curse." Rawls does not assume a need to redistribute natural resource endowments or their potential benefits.

How plausible is this view, understood in light of actual trade practice? The scheme of cooperation that constitutes the global economy must then be understood as itself having a fundamentally "cosmopolitan" structure, with the state system seen a mere superstructure of productive relations. But as suggested in Chapter 1.4 and argued in Chapter 6, this is a fundamental misinterpretation of the global economy as we know it: the worldwide division of labor is fundamentally constituted by an international social relationship, and the gains of trade are only reaped by mutual integration between the overall productive structures of whole societies. Indeed, without major international efforts to construct a global economy in the postwar era, it is hard to say whether or in what sense a global economy would even exist. This line of argument therefore seems either insensitive to social practice or not the fresh sort of internal argument we are looking for.

One might instead deny the relevance of supposed entitlements to the fruit of co-production. All that matters, it may be said, are relative benefits and burdens, gains and losses, to all the various individuals potentially affected. But this unduly narrows the scope of fairness argument (perhaps in much the way a blanket welfarism does). As argued in Chapter 6.7, having a hand in production plausibly does give rise to special claims, even if it is one among many potentially relevant fairness concerns. It would be morally revisionistic and in any case implausible to suppose that our claims or special interests in benefiting from the fruit of our labor have no significance for fairness at all.

No doubt other lines of argument are possible. Since our aim is not to refute cosmopolitanism, we can simply conjecture that the most plausible lines argument will either collapse into an external standard of evaluation or implausibly narrow the range of morally relevant concerns. Cosmopolitanism, we suggest, is best seen as an external rather than an internal principle.

In closing, we might add that an internal cosmopolitan principle would itself bear a significant burden of justification in light of its potential institutional implications as a regulative principle for trade practice. One question we will have to ask, for example, is whether gains to the globally worst off will come *only* at the expense of the worst off in rich countries, rather than those far better off. It is common to worry that global trade liberalization would imply just this: the poorest of the world would gain, the richest of the world would gain, but the worst off in rich countries would lose. Our specifically international principles foreclose that distributive pattern: if the claim of poor country A falls to rich country B, then B would pay from its total income, and not (directly) from gains to its poorest members. Rich countries might both give favorable trade to poor countries *and* protect their own worst off with social safety nets. But would a global cosmopolitan principle also have this crucial implication? It might, or it might not; the case must be made.[34]

---

34. This is not to suggest that we disallow trade-offs between our principles; we are not assuming a lexical ordering. This may bring our view closer to a cosmopolitan position that allows trade-offs. Our point in the text is simply that the acceptability of the principle can't simply be assumed.

PART III

Fairness Issues

CHAPTER EIGHT

Financial Crises

Financial crises have become commonplace. It was not always so. For over two decades after World War II, under the Bretton Woods system of monetary and financial controls, financial crises were relatively rare.[1] Since the early 1970s the number and frequency of financial crises (currency crises, banking crises, sovereign debt crises, or combinations thereof) have dramatically increased, culminating in the enormously destructive Great Recession, the global crisis of 2008–2009. To take banking crises by way of illustration, there were by one count at least 124 crises between 1970 and 2008. During the postwar decades before 1970 the number is—two.[2]

What explains the post-1970 rise? The date suggests a natural explanation: capital liberalization. With the early 1970s breakdown of Bretton Woods, governments increasingly removed controls on private capital movements across their borders. As capital flows dramatically increased, especially in the 1980s, economically integrated countries became markedly more susceptible to financial crises as compared to the postwar years of careful controls. While each crisis has its own local causes and leaves plenty of blame to go around, the general *tendency* for crises to become more numerous and more frequent is substantially (even if not wholly) explained by a major trend in government policy: the

---

1. On twentieth-century and postwar trends, see Eichengreen, 2004a, ch. 2, and Reinhart and Rogoff, 2009, especially pp. 155–56, 204–6, and Appendix A.3.1, pp. 345–47.
2. According to Laeven and Valencia, 2008, during 1970–2007 there were 124 banking crises, 208 currency crises, and 63 sovereign debt crises (42 banking crises were also currency crises, and 10 were crises of all three kinds). The two banking crises cited in the text during 1945–1970 are Brazil 1963 and India 1947 (though one might also count Uruguay 1971 within the same period); see Reinhart and Rogoff, 2009, Appendix A.3.1, p. 346. Even if we include the following decade of increasing capital mobility, there were only seven further crises.

1. The Significance of Crises

choice by governments to remove capital controls has created a global economic environment in which financial crises readily break out.[3]

It is difficult to overstate the profoundly consequential nature of this choice. More than almost any other adverse economic event—an import surge, downturn in the business cycle, a commodity price spike—financial crises cause severe and potentially irreparable harm on a large and often global scale. Developing countries from Argentina to Mexico to Malaysia to Indonesia have become familiar with crisis-induced ravages of high unemployment, reduced tax revenue, exploding public debt, and cuts in social services.[4] The losses often fall hardest on very poor people, though they would be significant for most anyone. The opportunity costs alone are extraordinary: some developing countries have lost as much as a decade of growth, the chief engine of poverty reduction. Yet crises are not merely an unfortunate but necessary part of economic development, mere "growing pains" that end once countries "graduate" into "deep," "sophisticated," and "mature" financial markets. As the Great Recession made plain, major crises can and will befall advanced countries as well. Millions of people lose their jobs and homes, see their savings erode, put off or forgo education, and find little means of restoring the income and retirement trajectory for which they may have hoped or long planned. Indeed, on the high seas of global capital flows, countries rich and poor are in the much same leaky boat. The cost of crises is surprisingly similar

---

3. Which is not to say the absence of capital controls are *the* cause of crises. Depending on the case, other causes may include banking liberalization, debt-fueled consumption, or even regressive tax policy and weakened unions, which lead to inequality and fuel instability. Our essential assumption is that controls on mobility across borders are causally relevant in the sense that their judicious imposition would make crises substantially less frequent and/or severe. Kindleberger, 2005, emphasizes credit-fueled speculative excess but also the enabling role of high capital mobility given the absence of controls (pp. 280–81). Reinhart and Rogoff, 2009, p. 155, concur.
4. See, e.g., Levinsohn et al., 2003, for the case of Indonesia.

across countries of all kinds.[5] And financial crises are highly contagious in an economically interdependent world.[6] A crisis almost anywhere potentially endangers economic neighbors, regions, and the global economy at large.

A cautious course, going forward, would be to establish strong tax-like capital controls. Along with other regulatory measures, developing countries can adopt Chilean or Colombian or Brazilian-style "inflow limits" that curb destabilizing "hot money."[7] Advanced countries can adopt a multilateral securities tax.[8] A modest levy (e.g., .1 percent) on securities transactions would curb short-term, purely speculative capital movements—a large and especially destabilizing share of global financial markets. Market actors then have to adopt longer investment horizons in order to recoup the cost of the tax. By increasing the tax rate, capital flows can be shifted into the medium or long term as needed to reduce the general likelihood that financial crises will erupt. A securities tax is thus sound risk management: it curbs the market activity that creates substantial crisis risk. (In a slogan: "Stop crises, tax banks!") It is also a fair revenue-raising device: because even a tiny tax raises huge revenues (the volume of transactions is very large), governments might recover the public cost of private risk-taking (to "make bankers pay" for social costs of bailouts, fiscal stimulus, unemployment, lost output, etc.).[9]

This chapter will argue that here the question of justifiability is much as it is for any potentially beneficial but highly dangerous activity, whether nuclear fusion, genetic engineering, or sky-diving: To what extent, if at all, are the risks of harm fairly imposed? The ongoing choice of governments *not* to adopt capital controls—to favor capital liberalization instead—creates increased risks of financial crisis: the global economy is then more likely to

---

5. Reinhart and Rogoff, 2009, ch. 14.
6. Eichengreen, 2004a, ch. 6; Reinhart and Rogoff, 2009, ch. 15.
7. For evidence that such controls shift inflows toward less vulnerable forms of liability, see de Gregorio et al., 2000, and Cardenas and Barrera, 1997.
8. Tobin, 1976, who focused on currency exchange. Tobin's arguments also apply more broadly.
9. Although "making bankers pay" would arguably put current banks out of business given the enormity of the costs to society. See Andrew Haldane, of the Bank of England, in "The $100 Billion Question," manuscript.

erupt in financial crises, and people and countries are more likely to suffer the serious injuries that crises tend to inflict. A basic question of fairness is whether or to what extent this imposition of risk could be fair.

As with any question of fair risk imposition, the fact that the activity is beneficial is relevant but insufficient in itself. Even if capital liberalization offers large economic benefits (discussed later), the risks of crisis in a world of high capital mobility still have to be justified as fairly imposed—for instance, because the risk of harm is small, because the risks are voluntarily assumed, or because everyone is made better off over the longer haul. If the risk of crises cannot be justified, in some such way, then capital controls that curb the dangerous activity are morally required— even at significant economic opportunity costs.

Two conceptions of fairness discussed in Chapter 7 might conceivably justify the risks of capital liberalization: fair risk assumption and reciprocal risk. We will find neither appropriate for global finance. A more appropriate fairness conception is our principle of Collective Due Care, applied to questions of risk. Yet it renders capital liberalization difficult to justify. According to that principle, we can allow liberal financial markets only to the degree they can be embedded within institutions that reliably compensate people for the harms financial crises do. But, in fact, governments in our politically decentralized world have limited powers of mitigation and compensation under conditions of high capital mobility. It follows that financial markets must be dramatically scaled back. Even if free (uncontrolled) capital markets could in theory be embedded in robust compensatory institutions, they are unjustifiable unless and until those institutions are in fact set up.

This is hardly to reject capitalism or economic globalization. The issue is what *form* capitalism takes on the international stage. Controls help it take a more justifiable form. The basic function of capital *within* a domestic capitalist economy is to allocate savings in its most productive uses. Free mobility across borders can hinder that allocative role, by inducing manifestly unproductive crises. Insofar as controls inhibit crises, they facilitate the productive social role of capital. There is little reason, moreover, to reject capital markets wholesale. Many longer-term relationships (e.g., foreign direct investment) or even medium-term lending or exchange are arguably justifiable as beneficial and sufficiently safe.[10] Judicious capital market integration may also be crucial for economic growth in some developing countries, where investment incentives are high but capital is scarce. But none of this requires a world of general capital liberalization, without strong capital controls. Nor can free capital mobility be presumptively assumed. The conclusion of our argument is precisely that any such world carries a weighty burden of justification, a burden that is often unappreciated and difficult to discharge.

This is to firmly reject conventional wisdom, which instead operates with a substantial presumption in favor of free financial markets. On its conservative variant, the presumption is rarely relaxed, and, if so, only very reluctantly. On its moderate or left-leaning variant, grounds for regulation are easier to come by, but the initial presumption is made all the same: the case for *regulation* must be made. Regulation bears the burden of justification, it is assumed, because the most important risk is that of missed financial opportunity, not that of another destructive financial crisis. Our argument will show that no such presumption is justified: prohibitive capital controls are the proper justificatory default, while any case for relaxing controls carries a heavy burden of proof. Due Care requires that we allow only those crisis risks that embedding institutions can reliably address. Where those institutions can be expected to fall short, or have yet to be set up, the dangerous markets must simply be stopped. If a securities tax set at a prohibitively high rate would largely eliminate substantial crisis risk, for example, then the burden of justification weighs heavily in favor of establishing the tax and against any reduction in the tax rate.

2. An Allegory

Consider an allegory.

> For at least a century or so humanity has known of a powerful bio-agent. It holds great promise as a source of cheap energy and thus large economic savings compared to alternative

---

10. Safe, that is, from the point of view of crisis prevention. Investment rules (e.g., WTO GATT rules, or the stronger measures found in many regional trade agreements) may still impose unfair risks upon developing countries. For a related general discussion of risk level, see section 8 in this chapter and Chapter 7.9.

energy sources. But it is also highly dangerous: any profitable use of the bio-agent regularly breaks out into a highly contagious and debilitating disease.

Aside from its unpleasantness, the disease has serious social and economic costs. Large swaths of the population become unable to work, often for years on end. Economies contract, public debt explodes, and services are cut—all of which is especially hard for the less well-off. In some cases, a decade of economic growth is lost. Because the disease is highly contagious, even across borders, these effects ramify internationally. The local economic contraction already itself harms other economically interdependent countries, by reducing demand for foreign goods and services. When several countries are infected all at the same time, a downward spiral of mutual economic contraction and trade flow reduction is the inevitable result.

For almost three decades, the disease was largely contained by careful domestic and international controls on bio-agent use. Despite the lost opportunity of cheap energy, this led to an era of unprecedented growth and prosperity among countries rich and poor alike. But in recent decades, as the bio-agent's use was deregulated, the disease has returned in full force. Outbreaks are increasingly common, appearing every few years, and they have recently culminated in a disease pandemic of global scale.

If there were in fact such a bio-agent, the debate about its use would surely presume against the recent deregulation in favor of some sort of return to the safer years of bio-agent controls. The high risk of severe, potentially irreparable harm would not seem worth the economic gains. Or at least respectable arguments for greater liberalization would have to propose strong measures of disease prevention, mitigation, and compensation. Few would take the horrific view that we should tolerate continued substantial risk of disease pandemic just for a cheap energy source.

The allegory, however, is more or less the story of recent financial globalization, where use of the imagined bio-agent is capital market integration, and the disease is financial crisis. The analogous period of crisis-free globalization occurred during the Bretton Woods years of capital controls. Yet world politics is not presuming that our task is to reduce capital mobility to Bretton Woods levels by adopting an updated set of strong controls. But there seems to be no relevant difference from our allegory. Why, then, doesn't the prevalence of financial crises at least raise fundamental questions about the very existence or general extent of international capital flows, much in the way we often raise questions about mixing the market with politics, organ distribution, or sex?

Even in the wake of the Great Recession, it is widely (though not universally) assumed that the chief question for policy is how to strike a certain balance, a balance between preservation of the various benefits of capital liberalization, on the one hand, and protection against various "market failures," on the other (e.g., information asymmetries, herd behavior, adverse selection, moral hazard, asset bubbles, boom-to-bust cycles, and so on). While developing countries may need capital controls, at least for a time, these restraints are not generally necessary for advanced countries, which can take more modest regulatory measures instead (e.g., increase bank reserve requirements). Financial markets, it is assumed, raise no fundamental question of justifiability; we need only "balance" the risks and rewards.[11]

Does this "balanced perspective" have a principled basis? Some apologists of capital liberalization largely ignore questions of principle,[12] or worse, cite the incoherent international economics cliché that we should "maximize the gains and minimize the risks."[13]

---

11. There has been growing support among major players (e.g., Britain, France, Germany) for stronger measures such as international securities taxation, partly for fairness reasons. It is only fair, it is said, for banks and investors to pay the social cost of the risks they take. How far this departs from the pre-crisis conventional wisdom depends on how the tax rate is set. If the tax rate is too small to substantially reduce risk-taking exchange (while perhaps big enough to fund future bailouts), it functions only as a fair revenue-raising device; the tax is then only a way to "make bankers pay" for, or "internalize," social costs rather than a way of limiting the very scope of financial markets and the crisis risks they create.
12. Wolf, 2004, ch. 13, mentions many pros and cons, concluding that the pros carry the day, but he doesn't give a principled reason for why this might be so. Wolf, 2008, goes further in the direction of reform, and his postcrisis columns in the *London Financial Times* (e.g., Wolf, 2010) urge bolder steps.
13. We cannot at once "maximize the benefits" *and* "minimize the risks." The risk-minimizing course—universal financial autarky—forgoes gains. The often presumed gain-maximizing course—full capital liberalization—takes on substantial crisis risk. As far as we know, any liberalization scheme that preserves the gains of integration will substantially increase crisis risk, while any regulatory scheme that largely eliminates crisis risk will forgo would-be gains.

Barry Eichengreen helpfully explicates what is presumably meant: "the task for policy is . . . to maximize the benefits of foreign investment while minimizing the risks—to enhance the resource mobilization, technology transfer, and institution-building roles of capital flows while limiting threats to financial stability."[14] We are to find ways of reducing the risk/reward trade-off as far as possible. But this is to simply assume that we do *not* have to take the properly risk-minimizing course: universal financial autarky. It is to *assume* that the gains somehow justify the risks. The question of principle is why this should be so.[15]

If capital liberalization is ultimately justifiable, there must be *some* principled basis for this conclusion—some basis according to which the risks of crisis, and the harms they often entail, are justified in light of the promised benefits. The job of political philosophy is to clarify what it would take for capital liberalization to be justified as a recommendation for what we ought to do. Though any conclusive policy recommendation requires help from empirical science, the philosopher can examine what principled grounds, if any, could conceivably have this justifying role.

3. Inevitability, Presumption, Overall Benefit

Several standard justifications are remarkably inadequate once they are thought through. Consider three such arguments: an argument from the inevitability of capital liberalization; from a presumption in favor of freedom; and from overall costs and benefits.

Inevitability? According to the inevitability argument, we can justifiably continue liberalization because governments cannot now do otherwise. The operative principle is, "You are justified in

---

14. Eichengreen, 2004a, p. 13.
15. Eichengreen's invaluable work, to which I am greatly indebted, perfectly captures the "balance perspective" we mean to challenge. To cite another example, the "balanced perspective" is largely assumed even among those such as Kotlikoff, 2010, who urge radical institutional change (banks would hold no financial assets, functioning like mutual funds). On the more basic question, he writes (p. 124): we have to "protect ourselves to the maximum extent possible without throwing the baby (economy growth) out with the bathwater (financial malfeasance)." But is forgoing some level of growth for the sake of minimizing crisis risk "throwing the baby out"? No principled answer is suggested.

doing something if you are incapable of doing otherwise." As Eichengreen explains, because "international financial liberalization and growing capital flows are largely inevitable and irreversible," we should seek only to "improve the trade off between financial liberalization and financial stability."[16] "[C]rises will still occur," but we can "minimize their incidence" and "help to resolve them at a lower cost," so that financial integration is "more attractive."[17]

The success of Bretton Woods shows that it is a major intellectual mistake to assume that capital liberalization is just another issue of "free trade," or that it is an inevitable or even "natural" part of capitalism and economic globalization.[18] Eichengreen's inevitability argument is more sophisticated. According to the argument, the rapid development of information and communications technologies, in conjunction with deepening economic integration, means that any regulatory attempts will be increasingly "porous"; restrictions on a government's capital account (lack of "capital account convertibility") will ultimately be unsustainable.[19]

The argument cannot plausibly be that governments are literally *incapable* of sustaining dramatic capital controls. Suppose financial crises became one hundred or one thousand times more common and severe than they already are. In that case governments would surely find the will and the means to dramatically reduce capital flows. (Compare the will and the means found to combat terrorism, which is far less destructive than financial crises.) Even if capital flows became another "black market" they might remain impactful but far less consequential than they in fact are. We will argue below that governments do have limited powers. But they are not limited in the suggested way.

The crux of the argument must therefore be normative: its essential claim is rather that capital controls have become "onerous," "distortionary," or "unacceptably" costly.[20] But in that case the argument is at best incomplete; our question is precisely what costs would be unacceptable in principle. We would accept very

---

16. Eichengreen, 1999, p. 2.
17. Ibid., p. 6.
18. As, e.g., according to the "organicism" arguably found in Adam Smith (1776), 1994.
19. Eichengreen, 1999.
20. Eichengreen, 2004a, refers to controls in these familiar terms.

large costs to prevent a disease pandemic from bio-agent use. Likewise, even if the costs of effective capital controls were also very high, we might think they are required to prevent people from suffering severe and irreparable harm because of financial crises. We are looking for a principled reason why that might not be the case.

Without some such further reasons, the cost of capital controls bears only on *which controls to choose*: we should prefer the least costly among equally effective controls. Exchange rate controls, for example, may be extraordinarily costly compared with equally feasible alternatives. For even full capital account liberalization does not preclude tax-like controls on underlying fundamentals, such as inflow limits (a la Chile or Colombia) or a securities tax. The effectiveness of securities taxation will of course depend on multilateral coordination (in order to prevent jurisdiction shopping) as well as tax enforcement (including an end to offshore banking and bank secrecy, and measures to prevent the smuggling of finance under the guise of goods and services trade). Yet the relevant cost is not that of perfect enforcement. So long as enforced controls dramatically raise the cost of socially unproductive financial transactions, they may have the intended deterrent effect. Tax-like controls are unlikely to be *very* costly if they also generate huge public revenues. But even when they are costly, this has little force without further reasons to explain why the costs are "too high"—too high, that is, even in the name of preventing the profoundly severe damage that financial crises do.

Presumption: liberty? It is often assumed that there should be a strong presumption in favor of free markets, which equally applies to financial markets. Even if the risk of crises requires precautionary regulation, the presumption holds sway—on grounds of liberty, welfare, or both. As Eichengreen puts the thought, "markets allocate resources in socially desirable ways," producing "better outcomes than heavy-handed bureaucratic control," and "there is no obvious reason why this presumption should apply less to financial than other markets. . . . The presumption in favor of markets being so strong, any counterargument had better be based on incontrovertible evidence."[21]

If personal liberty and welfare are supposed to ground this presumption, does either have the requisite force? In the case of

---

21. Eichengreen, 2004a, pp. 280–81.

liberty, if we have in mind the general presumption against interference in personal choices famously defended by J. S. Mill, then it simply does not apply when people are highly likely to be harmed.[22] In our allegory, whether the dangers of bio-agent use are imagined to emerge from a particular choice of use or a totality of such choices, liberty restrictions are manifestly justifiable on Millian grounds: one has no right to use a bio-agent when doing so creates high risks of severe injury to others. And financial transactions do not seem an exceptional case. As basic liberties are usually understood in liberal societies, restrictions on financial transactions do not pose a threat to personal liberties (e.g., of speech, conscience, or movement), or even to specifically economic liberties (e.g., choice of occupation, of place of work, of country of residence, etc.). One might point to unusual circumstances, for instance, when Malaysia imposed strict capital controls during its 1998 crisis (including strict controls on removal of the currency from the country).[23] Even here, however, it is hard to see why liberty should carry the day, provided the relevant capital controls are truly necessary to protect people from high risks of serious harm.[24]

One might argue that the essential function of political liberties is precisely to prevent political authorities from abridging personal freedom for the sake of preventing what are viewed as unacceptable harms, and that economic liberties over financial transactions should have this status. With the standard range of recognized liberties, however, their special weight derives from the fact that the assumed interests are especially important, while authorities are notoriously likely to threaten those interests for inadequate reasons (e.g., the abridgement is simply unnecessary or politically motivated).[25] The liberty to trade in capital markets hardly has this special standing. Not only do benefits of free capital market trade accrue mainly to rich people but governments nowadays tend to err on the side of granting liberty even when regulation would be justified. Proper respect for economic liberty in such cases will mean only that we should favor the less liberty-infringing course in choosing among equally

22. Mill (1859), 1977.
23. Wolf, 2004, p. 284, who cites Hayek, 1944.
24. See, e.g., Krugman, 1999, on Malaysia.
25. Scanlon, 2003, chs. 2, 3, 5.

safe regulatory approaches, not that we should defer to liberty when it is tantamount to allowing serious and potentially irreparable harm.

Presumption: beneficial exchange? A second familiar ground for presumption in favor of market exchange concerns the presumptively *beneficial* nature of voluntary transactions: people exchange only because they believe it makes them better off, and, as Mill explained, they are often more likely to be right about this than about centralized price regulation. Insofar as welfare improvements are desirable, then, we have reason to presume against the regulation of exchange, absent special reasons for intervention. Or put in terms of the fundamental theorem of welfare economics, free exchanges under "perfect competition" lead to a (Pareto) efficient allocation: no one can be made better off without making someone else worse off. Insofar as this is desirable—at least other things being equal, as it presumably is— we therefore need special grounds for market intervention: a "market failure," or some reason we should want something more than mere efficiency (e.g., a social preference for certain distributions).

If this argument is to succeed, then the presumption (1) must apply equally to the relevant financial transactions and (2) must be strong enough to preclude direct regulation even in the name of crisis prevention. Neither assumption is defensible.

International financial market transactions are not mutually beneficial in any particularly significant sense. First, trade in assets generally is not welfare-enhancing in the direct way that trade in goods and services exchanges can be. Assets represent a claim on future goods and services, not the direct consumption of a good or a service. Second, the main private actors in international financial markets—commercial banks, large corporations, non-bank financial institutions, and so on—do not have morally relevant interests themselves; at best, they act on behalf of people with relevant interests. But such people are usually relatively rich, in which case "diminishing marginal utility" of money or its asset equivalents sharply reduces the size of any welfare gain; they will either not see significant welfare improvements from free asset exchange, or the welfare difference between free exchange and capital controls will be insignificant. Third, in any case, not all welfare improvements have clear moral relevance or urgency, in contrast, say, with a person's significant interest in having a decent standard of living or in avoiding the severe hardships of a financial crisis.[26]

Accordingly, the value of international financial markets is largely *instrumental* rather than constitutive: it lies not in the beneficial nature of asset exchange itself but in the general services provided to the real economy, for example, in allocating savings in its socially most productive uses, allowing farmers or firms to hedge against risk on futures markets, enabling people to "smooth" consumption over time, and so on. But the real economy, domestically and globally, may in fact be best *supported* by capital controls that reduce the likelihood of destructive financial crises.

Moreover, even if the relevant welfare gains were significant, this will not generate a strong presumption against market intervention given the inordinate amount of harm that financial markets do. The fundamental theorem generates a presumption in favor of free markets *only* to the extent that conditions of "perfect competition" can be approximated, conditions that include the absence of "negative externalities." But financial crises certainly qualify: many, many people are harmed, often irreparably. Unless some further thesis is advanced, the fundamental theorem generates *no presumption at all* against regulating market exchange for the sake of preventing inordinate amounts of harm.

One might argue that the desirability of voluntary transactions still exerts some presumptive force on the appropriate *form* of regulation. Conditions of "perfect competition" might be restored, or sufficiently approximated, when we can force market actors to "internalize" the full social cost of their actions. The desirability of beneficial exchange then weighs against any further market interventions. In the present context, however, there is simply no feasible way of fully "pricing in" crisis risk to financial market transactions (though securities taxes are perhaps a start). The social costs of crises are simply too high. (By credible estimates, full internalization of those costs would wipe out all bank and investment firm profits.)[27] Addressing the relevant market failures requires nothing less than eliminating substantial crisis risk, which is precisely what we do not know how to do short of a dramatic move in the direction of universal financial autarky.

26. Scanlon, ibid., ch. 4.
27. Haldane, manuscript.

Furthermore, even if we could put a price on crisis risk, this still would not approximate conditions of perfect competition. International finance is replete with "market failures" of other kinds, including information asymmetries, herd behavior, short-term speculative bubbles, boom-and-bust cycles, and systemic risk. And as long as there is more than one market failure in play, there is no presumption that they should be dealt with separately. In the context of goods and services trade one can argue that market intervention (e.g., a tariff) should be used only as a last resort, when less disruptive measures are unavailable. In the present context, the "disruption" is merely to financial market exchanges. Given their limited intrinsic welfare value, we might think it important to target possible sources of crisis risk broadly rather than narrowly, in order to maximally protect people from high risks of severe and potentially irreparable harm. Even if this is not ultimately required, why *presume against* it?

Overall benefit? Whether or not there is a presumption in favor of free capital markets, one might argue that the benefits of substantial capital liberalization render it on balance justified. The "benefits must exceed the costs," one might say.[28] But very different principles can be at work here. In one interpretation, the benefits must exceed the costs *for each person (or class or country) affected*. In that case, however, capital liberalization becomes difficult to justify. As we will see below, it is not clear that we can ensure that no one is made worse off, overall, in a world of high capital mobility.

Utilitarianism offers a more relaxed interpretation: the benefits need to exceed the costs only in the aggregate. So long as that is the case, capital liberalization can impose severe risks of harm. It is doubtful, however, that capital liberalization can be justified by an aggregative cost-benefit analysis given the truly extraordinary fiscal, economic, and social costs of crises.[29] The high probability of huge losses heavily weights any aggregative cost/benefit calculation against liberal capital flows, other things being equal. If sufficient gains could in theory still tip the calculus in capital liberalization's favor, these gains are not typically to be had. The

---

28. Eichengreen, 2004a, pp. 11 and 13, suggests something like this standard.
29. Haldane, manuscript.

benefits to developing countries are limited, and in any case benefits tend to fall in the hands of very few people. Again, because these people are usually very rich, diminishing marginal utility sharply reduces the size of any welfare gain. Nor are gains to country GDP (taken individually or as a global aggregate) sufficiently large, given the relevant alternatives. Many alternative forms of globalization—robust goods and services trade combined with controlled finance—would create large gains as well. In that case, the comparative gains of high-risk capital liberalization are correspondingly small and cannot make up for high crisis risk.

4. The Question of Justification

The standard arguments for the persistent "balanced perspective" in world politics are therefore wanting. That perspective also has a deeper problem: it fails to appreciate the basic question of justification that financial crises raise. Much as in our allegory, capital liberalization is an ultra-hazardous activity, akin to many potentially beneficial but highly dangerous social activities that we may see fit to ban or at least severely curtail (private nuclear fusion, low airplane flight over populated areas). Whether or to what extent the activity should be allowed at all will depend entirely on our ability to regulate the risks of harm it creates. The risks must be either eliminated or justified as fairly imposed. Otherwise, the dangerous activity itself must simply be stopped or scaled back—in the present case, by the imposition of prohibitive capital controls.

Might this thought apply only to acts of risk-taking and not to our overall regulatory framework itself? Perhaps the regulatory framework does not pose questions of risk imposition of the same kind that individual market actors do. In reply, we should make explicit why the activity regulated and the regulatory framework do indeed pose questions of the same moral kind.

Capital liberalization is an international social practice. Although banks and investors are often blamed for crises, the central issue posed by financial crises is not behavioral but structural. Transactions that reduce personal risk (e.g., hedging with derivatives trades) are often perfectly benign taken by themselves. While bad behavior often happens (a firm gambles for redemption, hides risky debt, or culpably ignores key risks), and while this bears on institutional design, it is not essential. Systemic crisis risk can emerge even from a totality of perfectly "innocent" transactions.

Particular government policies also shape the risk climate, but not taken by themselves, independent of international practice. A particular government pursues *policies* of capital liberalization when it substantially eases or removes government controls on cross-border asset transactions—whether currency exchange, borrowing or lending, or direct or portfolio investment (specifically, all official or private transactions registered in the "capital account" portion of its national balance of payments). The *international practice* of capital liberalization involves multiple governments easing or removing such controls, usually (but not necessarily) in a coordinated way. A single government's dropping controls will not suffice to create an international financial marketplace; private banks, investment firms, or commercial businesses residing in a particular country will not have foreign private parties for asset exchange unless enough other governments (at very least, one) ease controls as well. Nor then will a single government's choice generate the crisis risks that have in fact emerged. Responsibility ultimately rests upon the international practice of capital liberalization itself.

The existence and nature of international financial markets is a matter of social choice. If international financial markets are created by a practice of capital liberalization, governments acting in concert can also curb them, or reduce their size, or allow one kind of capital market while stopping another.[30] Any number of controls on private capital flows might be adopted and, if necessary, backed by stronger exercises of state power. If political will for strong measures is lacking, this does not fundamentally change what countries *ought* to choose over the longer haul (though it may change what political tactics leaders might adopt in the short run).

Economic globalization does not require capital liberalization. Economic globalization is fully consistent with strong capital controls. A world of liberal goods and services trade can in theory

---

30. Capital controls are legal for member countries under IMF Article VI (3), but have been discouraged in recent decades. The IMF staff is only recently acknowledging their potential advisability; see, e.g., Ostry et al., 2010.

coexist beside relative financial autarky. The essential social function of financial markets—to allocate a society's savings according to its most productive uses—can be served mainly within each country's borders. Governments could meet their basic budgetary, balance-of-payments needs strictly through "official" government or international bank lending. Only the private finance necessary for well-functioning goods and services trade (e.g., "trade finance") might be allowed. Indeed, an economic order of roughly this kind actually existed not long ago, in the form of the postwar Bretton Woods system—one of the most prosperous eras of capitalism in the history of the world.

Capital liberalization offers limited benefits in practice. If capital liberalization is not required for globalization, then it must be justified on its own terms. Economic theory points to a cornucopia of benefits. Capital-scarce but labor-abundant countries can trade to comparative advantage with countries that are capital abundant and labor scarce, and vice versa. Savings can be put to their globally most productive uses, at home or abroad. Governments can more readily augment domestic savings and investment. Financial market integration tends to spread technology and ideas, as well as encourage institutional discipline. Capital markets allow firms or individuals to manage risk on their returns to wealth through portfolio diversification and hedging techniques (e.g., the judicious use of futures, swaps, and other derivatives). In monetary policy, floating exchange rates give central banks monetary autonomy. Freed from having to defend a currency peg, they have greater ability to regulate inflation and unemployment levels by adjusting the money supply. Moreover, liberalization has the advantage of avoiding controls—for example, "pegged but adjustable" exchange rates—which are themselves destabilizing and-costly to maintain.

However, even setting aside the cost of crises, the benefits are often oversold. According to some studies, there is little or no direct correlation between developing-country growth and capital market integration.[31] Even if some developing countries see indirect benefits (e.g., to institutional quality), these may be necessary only late in the development process, and in any case they require

---

31. Rodrik, 1998.

the careful sequencing of reforms.³² Premature capital market integration may even hinder growth, by altering exchange rates and reducing investment incentives in tradables.³³ In many cases, developing countries see (licit and illicit) net capital outflows.³⁴ And even in the advanced countries the average citizen has tended to see only modest benefits from financial globalization, for example, cheaper credit, smoother consumption, and improved investment opportunities—but nothing as significant, for instance, as steadily rising wages.

Capital liberalization tends to cause financial crises. We began this chapter observing the historical fact that the number and frequency of financial crises dramatically increased as governments freed private capital flows across borders in the early 1970s. From a broader historical perspective, this is but one instance of a larger trend. As Reinhart and Rogoff explain in their magisterial quantitative survey of financial crises dating as far back as twelfth-century China and medieval Europe, "Periods of high international capital mobility have repeatedly produced international banking crises, not only famously, as they did in the 1990s, but historically."³⁵ Correlation does not of course establish causation. Yet history and economic theory strongly suggest that capital liberalization is at least a substantial contributory cause. If controls had not been liberalized, there would be little or no private capital movements across borders to speak of. So the fact that private capital movements usually in some way explain the occurrence of crises equally implicates the choice of liberalization itself.

One might argue that the true cause of financial crises is not capital liberalization but simply weak economic fundamentals. Capital movements merely track this underlying reality and so can be correlated with the cause of crises, but they are not a proper contributory cause in and of themselves. This picture is not borne out by economic models inspired by and used to explain real-world crises, however. The capital outflows that trigger crises—a bank run, a liquidity freeze, a speculative attack

---

32. On indirect benefits, see Kose et al., 2006, but also Rodrik and Subramanian, 2008.
33. Rodrik and Subramanian, 2008.
34. DeLong, 1998; Collier and Gunning, 1999; Collier et al., 2001. On illicit flows, see Baker, 2005.
35. Reinhardt and Rogoff, 2009, p. 155.

against the currency—do not necessarily reflect unsustainable economic fundamentals. Collapses in market confidence—due to information asymmetries, herd behavior, self-fulfilling speculative bets, or contagion effects—have a social life all their own.[36] In game theoretic terms, crises involve "multiple equilibria," as in the assurance or stag hunt game. Each party in the market does best so long as most others stay invested (the "cooperative equilibrium"). But if most others don't, each does best to divest (the "non-cooperative equilibrium"). Without public "confidence," non-cooperation becomes the "risk-dominant" choice for all, even with no change in economic fundamentals.[37]

One might argue, instead, that the real cause of crises is simply the prevalence of government policy mistakes, including a failure to anticipate such collective action failures. This is not plausible, however, on either the outflow or inflow side of capital movements. Capital outflows often cannot be anticipated and prevented by cautious government policy. As Eichengreen explains, "governments that follow traditional conservative policies cannot be assured of insulation against speculative attacks; there are no clearly 'right' policies."[38] If capital inflows enter a domestic economy at a slower and potentially more manageable pace, the risks of crisis are no less grave. Banking crises, for example, tend to erupt after a "capital inflow bonanza" during prosperous times,

---

36. Economic models explain how speculative attacks can precipitate a currency devaluation that would otherwise not have occurred, regardless of economic fundamentals, as well as how controls can prevent such a collapse, e.g., Obstfeld, 1996; Ozkan and Sutherland, 1998. These "second-generation" models contrast with "first-generation" models such as Krugman, 1979, which assume weak fundamentals. So-called third-generation models (e.g., Irwin and Vines, 1999) have similar implications but include effects of currency devaluation on private balance sheets, including private deleveraging and further currency depreciation. On bank runs, see Diamond and Dybvig, 1983, and Allen and Gale, 2007. On public debt, see Calvo 1988. Financier George Soros, 2003, sounds the theme of "reflexivity" from practical experience, a theme found also in Keynes, 1936, and Minsky, 1986.
37. Reinhart and Rogoff, 2009, explain (p. xliii): "Economists do not have a terribly good idea of what kinds of events shift confidence and of how to concretely assess confidence vulnerability. What one does see, again and again, in the history of financial crises is that when an accident is waiting to happen, it eventually does."
38. Eichengreen, 2004b, p. 103.

which generates credit or asset bubbles and excessive risk-taking, often in conjunction with financial liberalization.[39] And as long as governments forswear controls and otherwise adopt liberalization policies, they generally lack the institutional means of ensuring that crises will not eventually come about. Prudential supervision, transparency, international standardization, and exchange-rate management are helpful but of limited effect.[40] Even the stronger measures with a chance of being adopted in advanced countries in the wake of the Great Recession—supervision of derivatives markets, increased reserve and capital requirements, bankruptcy resolution measures, limits on bank or firm size, precautions against systemic risk—are at best uncertain. Indeed, if history is any guide, as memories of the Great Recession fade, folly of epic, Shakespearean proportions will no doubt once again become conventional wisdom. Experts will argue that "this time is different"—as they nearly always have before a crisis erupts.[41]

Might there be some further alternative explanation that wholly displaces capital liberalization as a substantial contributory cause of crises? If there is, it could not simply cite specific causally relevant factors; what is needed is an explanation of the *general prevalence* of crises that does not depend on the larger practice of capital liberalization and its associated policies. And even if we cannot point to a strong correlation between any *particular* policy or institution and crises, this will not disconfirm a causal relation between crises and a *general* liberalization practice, which may take many specific forms. And in any case it suffices for our purposes that controls such as securities taxes will in fact make crises less frequent and less severe, even if by dampening a more proximate cause of crises (such as excess capital accumulation). They need only be causally relevant, in that sense.

---

39. On the prominence of financial liberalization, see Kaminsky and Reinhart, 1999; Demirguc-Kunt and Detragiache, 1998; and Caprio and Klingelbiel, 1996.
40. Eichengreen, 2004b, ch. 4.
41. As Reinhart and Rogoff, 2009, p. xxxiv, explain: "Financial professionals and, all too often, government leaders explain that we are doing things better than before, that we are smarter, and that we have learned from past mistakes. Each time, society convinces itself that the current boom, unlike the many booms that preceded catastrophic collapse in the past, is built on sound fundamentals, structural reforms, technological innovation, and good policy."

Because the practice of capital liberalization makes crises substantially more likely than they would be under capital controls, it thereby creates substantial risks of severe harm. There is no doubting that financial crises cause severe specific injuries, such as extended unemployment or loss of a home. To the extent that capital liberalization makes crises substantially more likely than they would be under controls, it is substantially implicated as a contributory cause of those outcomes. When the injuries have not occurred but might have or might still, it substantially contributes to the risk that such harm will come about.

The question of justification is a question of risk creation under profound uncertainty. Among the numerous ways the manifest risks of crises might be regulated under a general capital liberalization practice, all have the crucial feature of allowing crisis-prone international financial markets to exist, despite the fact that we do know of institutionally feasible alternatives that would make crises far less likely. We know what the maximally cautious course would be: an aggressive move to financial autarky. Full economic autarky is arguably not required. The Bretton Woods system shows that flourishing goods and services trade and prosperous domestic capitalist economies are fully compatible with strong controls and the relative absence of crisis risk. Nor is full *financial* autarky necessary: we can equally allow the international finance (international bank lending, trade finance, foreign direct investment) that has no known, significant correlation with the occurrence of financial crises. Even if we assume for the sake of argument that there is no road back to Bretton Woods,[42] securities taxation stands available as a risk-regulation device. So long as some such scheme of strong controls is indeed feasible, the joint choice of governments to nevertheless retain capital liberalization amounts to the collective imposition of risk: every country and

---

42. There is perhaps a case to be made for regional or global monetary unification—the "hardest" currency peg of all. Yet it also creates trade-offs in terms of the very values at stake in financial crisis risk. If the virtue of monetary union is stability, the vice is loss of national monetary autonomy, which is helpful for the regulation of employment. Accordingly, under Bretton Woods, many countries felt forced to import "excessive" inflation from the United States in defending their dollar exchange rate pegs, being concerned in part with the local consequences for growth and employment. Similar disagreements now create tensions with the European Monetary Union.

class affected by the global economy, so organized, is more likely to suffer the profound social and economic injuries that financial crises tend to inflict.

Capital liberalization thus creates risk, but not in the strict sense that an institutional decision is made between outcomes with known probabilities. Little that is certain is known and likely to be learned about how different arrangements might compare in their tendencies to produce crises; the best analysis will work from highly speculative empirical considerations, drawn from theory and history, about how numerous varying parameters interact. It is a mistake, however, to suppose that such uncertainty supports capital liberalization by default. Should we not wait and see whether crisis risk can be substantially reduced by a targeted fix that leaves capital liberalization largely intact? Would it not be premature to impose strong controls before the specific causes of crises are better understood? Is not the "scientific" course to choose financial autarky only when no more targeted fix will do? This would be fine if financial crises were so much data in a grand global economic laboratory rather than one of the more profound blights on human social life. The stakes are higher only in matters of war and peace, government oppression, and, perhaps, climate change. And in any case we do not know and cannot expect to learn of any such targeted fix. Even if a fix were to ultimately emerge, that would only suggest that an eventual return to capital liberalization might *then* be justifiable. It would not show that it is the place to start.

The basic issue is not policy but regulatory disposition. The situation of uncertainty means that fundamental practical questions are not about specific policy but the overall kind of financial world we should have or at least move toward. The basic choice is between regulatory dispositions of two opposing kinds. A first is tolerant of crisis risk and averse to economic opportunity costs. It presumptively favors capital liberalization, for the sake even of low probability gains, and takes regulatory measures only when they are highly likely to dramatically reduce crisis risk at minimal economic opportunity cost. So, for example, one might thus embrace the regulatory status quo along with measures clearly necessary to manage systemic risk (e.g., increased bank reserve requirements, bank decomposition measures, regulatory supervision). If securities taxes are also necessary, in order to curb the clearest speculative excesses (e.g., due to high-volume, split-second, computer-based trading), they are to be set at the lowest possible effective rate.

A second regulatory disposition is tolerant of economic opportunity costs, but averse to crisis risk. It presumptively favors financial autarky, in order to minimize crisis risk, and permits liberalization only when especially large gains can be expected with minimal additional risk. While it might accept low-risk forms of international finance, such as trade finance, foreign direct investment, and international bank lending, it would presume in favor of establishing an aggressive regulatory system along with international financial "safety net" analogous to that now standard within each advanced country. This might include a mix of aggressive harmonization of regulatory standards; a global systemic risk regulator; the full segregation of banking from investment; international bankruptcy courts;[43] covered bond markets instead of securitization; measures to reduce risks of exchange or interest rate fluctuations to developing countries (e.g., developing countries borrow in their own currency, perhaps as required by G7 or G20 legislation for their members,[44] or issue Argentinean-style GDP-indexed bonds, which pay according to growth, with international banks serving as "market makers"); counter-cyclical lending by international or regional banks to developing countries to offset procyclical private lending; a more effective lender of last resort (e.g., through continued relaxation of IMF loan conditionality); reform of the global monetary reserve system, including wider and more regular international use of IMF Special Drawing Rights[45]—all subject to modifications needed in order to mitigate "moral hazard" risks. Which package of such reforms would be best is up for debate (though there is no need to choose between them when joint implementation is the safest course). As a default, however, the present regulatory disposition would at least insist on securities taxes that curb short- and perhaps even medium-term private

---

43. Sachs, 1995; and Krueger, 2003. Stiglitz, 2006, p. 233, also suggests that developing countries adopt "super Chapter 11" provisions so that domestic firms can quickly default on foreign loans in case of macroeconomic calamity, such as a collapse in the exchange rate, a major recession or depression, or an unanticipated spike in emerging market interests rates.
44. Krueger, 2000.
45. Stiglitz, 2006, ch. 9.

capital flows.[46] The presumption is in favor of a high tax rate, for maximum deterrent effect, unless lower rates are clearly safe. If the first disposition's watchword is "Don't overact!" the second's is "Safety first!"

Because the likelihood of severe and potentially irreparable harm is particularly high in a world of liberal capital flows, the fundamental question is not one of mere regulatory depth but of whether international financial markets should be allowed to exist at all. The latter, risk-averse regulatory disposition accepts this and so proceeds with extreme caution. The former, risk-tolerant disposition is more concerned not to miss a chance of gain and so needs to explain why the risks it countenances should be acceptable.

We have already seen that several standard justifications are wanting. We will now see that no further justification is likely to emerge. Our main argument is an *argument from the limited compensatory powers of governments*. According to the argument, a practice of capital liberalization, beyond that necessary for well-functioning goods and services trade, will meet the standard of due care only if each country and class affected can expect to fare no worse than it would in a global economy with stronger capital controls. But governments lack the powers necessary to meet this condition in a world of high capital mobility. While governments have relatively reliable institutional means of regulating the market outcomes of free goods and services trade, their capabilities of prevention, mitigation, and compensation are sharply limited in the face of large, fast-moving, and profoundly consequential capital flows. The presumption of fairness is therefore strongly against international financial markets of any significance.

5. Due Care and Harm

Our argument turns on a requirement of due care. As characterized in Chapter 7, the principle of (Collective) Due Care chiefly concerns ways one's condition is *worsened* for life in an open

---

46. While securities taxes are a particularly aggressive preventive measure, there is empirical evidence that even when capital controls do not prevent crises, they significantly reduce loss of economic output when crises do break out. Gupta et al., 2007, argue for this in surveying 200 crises, in 90 or so countries, between 1970 and 2007.

society. We are thus to leave aside opportunity costs (or rather leave them for other principles). It will indeed be true that, for any given crisis, caused in part by the absence of capital controls, domestic or world output will be lower than it would have been under its counterfactual path in which the crisis does not occur, or is less severe, and things are otherwise as far as possible equal. In that sense, even those who gain overall from life in an integrated society may not fare as well as they otherwise would have (at least depending on their share of the national gain). Due Care's concern, instead, is specific crisis-induced injuries that leave one either (1) worse off than at some previous time (perhaps one is newly homeless, newly jobless, or both), or (2) worse off than one would have been under an international practice of capital controls (perhaps one would have been better employed or would have retained savings for retirement one has now lost).

Our present question is whether one *version* of global capitalism meets the standard of Due Care. The relevant worsenings will therefore accrue specifically to the choice of capital liberalization over capital controls, quite aside from the benefits or burdens of economic integration more generally. One can gain on balance from free goods and services trade but lose on balance for the absence of capital controls. For present purposes, then, the relevant world for comparison will not be general economic autarky but rather *financial* autarky accompanied by a robust goods and services trade (but along with official lending, trade finance, etc., as suggested above). For someone injured by a crisis under capital liberalization, the question is whether he or she would be better off, overall, under a practice of controls, given otherwise similar conditions of economic integration.

We granted in Chapter 7.1–7.2 that specific worsenings could in principle be compensated by gains received earlier or later in one's lifetime. We also resisted the presumption that general economic integration provides such gains as a matter of course. If that is at least a tempting suggestion, the corresponding thought about liberalized capital has less initial appeal. It seems likely, if not plainly true, that many people, in advanced and developing countries alike, suffer severe crisis-induced injuries, due in part to liberalized capital flows, without also at any point seeing sufficiently large compensatory gains. A crisis-induced "lost decade," as in Argentina or Japan, seems to do irreparable harm, harm that would not have occurred under more careful controls (perhaps those which were removed).⁴⁷

To illustrate, consider someone born into the U.S. working class during Bretton Woods, who lost his job and home in the 2008–2009 crisis, and now faces long-term unemployment with uncertain wage, savings, and retirement prospects. His current prospects might nevertheless be justified if they *would have been no worse, or even worse,* had the governments of the world not abandoned Bretton Woods or refashioned controls that similarly limit capital mobility. (A high Tobin tax might have been adopted when Tobin first proposed it.) He would thus not have been harmed for the turn toward capital liberalization. But if that might be true in theory, the specific injuries he suffers are all too real, and the preponderance of evidence must point toward some real and quite significant compensatory benefits—perhaps a dramatic wage or standard of living gain—which he has already received over the previous years of liberalization, or will receive in the years to come. And given the enormity of the injuries, and the modesty of working-class wage or living standard gains, the argument for this will seem a lot like vague conjecture, solemn free-market faith, or at best a stretch. It seems likely, and perhaps plainly true, that many such people instead now fare worse, overall, than they would have had crisis-dampening capital controls been adopted or retained at an earlier stage of their lives.⁴⁸ Even if they are winners for general economic integration, they are losers for the choice to withhold controls.

---

47. This is of course consistent with the existence of net beneficiaries. Suppose capital liberalization has contributed to poverty reduction (e.g., among some group living under the $2/day line). Other people may still be harmed (e.g., some group living under $2/day in Latin America, or most groups living under the $1/day line).

48. Likewise, it seems likely that many *will* fare worse, overall, by a decision today not to adopt capital controls, given the expected consequences of institutional arrangements going forward. In defending such a judgment, we might project forward from the costs of past crises and their size and frequency under conditions of high capital mobility, making conservative assumptions about future average size and frequency in light of current or expected regulatory changes, and so on.

6. Compensation and Limited Powers

One might quibble about what count as examples of such worsenings and upon what evidence. The argument from the limited powers of governments works at a more general level of abstraction. Due Care will permit harmful liberalization, but only provided institutional arrangements that *reliably* compensate for the harm it does. In that case, if there are general reasons of institutional feasibility why no assurances against irreparable injury can be provided, capital liberalization is in trouble.

To develop the point, we might restate Due Care as the

Compensation Principle: absent special justification (e.g., fair risk assumption or reciprocal risk), a set of social arrangements fairly imposes risk of harm on some party A if and only if the arrangements also reliably ensure that A will be fully compensated should the harm come about.

(It is plausible to add that "full" compensation includes a risk premium: A's net expected gain must be large enough to justify A's exposure to risks of being made substantially worse off, *whatever* the outcome. We will not assume this, for the sake of keeping the argument's normative assumptions modest.)

Assume for the moment that the international market reliance practice lacks an appropriate "special justification." In that case, it has only two options for meeting the standard of due care:

Compensation: adopt the socially beneficial practice (capital liberalization) but establish a scheme that reliably compensates people for any harm that results.

Precaution: give up the practice (impose capital controls) in order to eliminate the risks of harm (or at least to reduce them to a level at which compensation will be reliably provided).

These options are exhaustive. If compensation is not feasible, because the harms in question tend to be irreparable, then due care requires precaution: the risks must be eliminated, or at least reduced to a level such that reliable compensation becomes feasible.

According to the argument from limited powers, capital liberalization is in exactly this situation. Because governments have limited powers to regulate financial market outcomes, the damage financial crises do tends to be irreparable. The Compensation Principle cannot be reliably fulfilled. The only remaining course for a structurally equitable global economy, then, is to scale back international capital markets—to take whatever precautions are needed to rein in crisis risk. The safest scheme is financial autarky. If any degree of capital liberalization is to be justified as fair, it can create only those risks that established measures of prevention, mitigation, and compensation can effectively address. If free capital markets can in theory be justifiable—embedding institutions that either reliably help limit crisis risk or reliably compensate people when crises occur—they are justifiable in practice only *after* such institutions have been set up. Until then, strong capital controls are morally required.

The philosopher cannot settle empirical matters of what the powers of governments are like in any conclusive way. Several observations will at least suggest that governmental powers are often quite limited in the face of substantial capital mobility, at least under the general kinds of institutional conditions likely to exist in the foreseeable future.

For starters, we might ask whether the Compensation Principle would rule out globalization generally, and so be too strong, or at least present no special problem for financial globalization. But it wouldn't seem to, as far as goods and services trade is concerned. Another lesson of Bretton Woods, in conjunction with the rise of social insurance schemes, is that there is no general reason of institutional feasibility that appropriate mitigation and compensation cannot be arranged. Governments do have the means to ensure, reasonably well, that all will fare better under liberal goods and services trade than under economic autarky. Adjustments (e.g., in employment) due to changes in import or export markets are usually relatively predictable and slow paced. They can often be feasibly addressed in several different ways: by ex ante measures (wage insurance, basic income and health care), ex post measures (unemployment payments, job retraining, paid retirement, direct compensation), or combined measures (public education, progressive taxation). Even in a food crisis spurred, say, by a commodity price spike, governments often have effective remedies (precautionary inventories, well-timed interventions into domestic supply, inter-government coordination to prevent hoarding and other beggar-thy-neighbor interventions, countercyclical compensatory finance, perhaps from an international commodities stabilization scheme).[49] Although governments have often not taken the full compensatory means at their disposal, we can credibly envisage embedding institutions that ensure general net benefit all around. We can move from questions of basic harm to questions of relative gains.

In a world of high capital mobility, by contrast, the damage wrought by large-scale financial crises tends to be swift, sure, severe, long-lasting, and of enormous scale. For many if not most of the specific injuries resulting from financial crises, we cannot reasonably expect financial globalization to somehow automatically compensate people provided enough time: compensation for the harm in question has to be arranged and provided, if it is ever to happen. But the measures of compensation, mitigation, and prevention typically available to governments are not up to the task. Purely ex post compensation measures are often too little too late. Nothing will repair a decade of lost growth to a developing country. Even in advanced countries, modest gains often will not come in time or sufficient measure to rectify long-term unemployment, loss of a home, or retirement savings loss, especially when the losses come later in life.

But might not large cash payments be paid out? Perhaps funds are raised through securities taxation, held in trust until a crisis erupts, and then distributed as it becomes clear what harms result. If this is possible in theory, it is not (yet?) feasible in practice. It would not be enough, for example, for each government to receive aggregated payments, unless the appropriate share was reasonably certain to reach each representative person affected. Might a more direct scheme of compensation do the job? Perhaps payments are deposited into a transnational bank to which affected parties have direct and unfettered access, by way of an internationally enforced agreement. If this is possible, however, substantial capital liberalization would meet the Compensation Principle only when the necessary scheme is actually established. Until that time, precaution would be the only permissible course: capital markets would have to be scaled back and could be opened again only when the scheme is tested and reliably in place.

---

49. Different measures will be appropriate for other causes of food crises (e.g., bio-fuels, animals as food, speculation, hoarding, adverse supply, and natural disasters).

We might then look instead to crisis prevention or substantial mitigation. Could appropriate precaution be taken without the imposition of capital controls? Perhaps, but it is not clear what measures would suffice. Standard measures of crisis mitigation, such as monetary or fiscal stimulus, tend to be hobbled by the deteriorating budgetary situation which crises themselves bring on. Countries can print money or borrow, but global markets have limited tolerance for high inflation or high debt. An international lender of last resort, such as the IMF, can make funds available at a reasonable cost (and the IMF did indeed aggressively help many countries in the Great Recession). Though such measures provide valuable mitigation, we cannot be reasonably assured they will prevent significant crises from breaking out. Indeed, some would argue that tacit guarantees dramatically increase the risk firms or countries take.

There are, finally, fairly reliable measures of crisis prevention short of curbing the market, but these can equally increase overall crisis risk. One of the more reliable measures of "self-insurance" is for governments to amass foreign reserves, to be spent when severe balance-of-payments problems arise. Though reliable, this tends to be extremely costly, especially for developing countries, who suffer massive social opportunity costs (the funds could instead be invested for social returns, in education, public health, or infrastructure). Even if they are a bargain compared to the cost of a crisis, however, large reserves also add to the very macro-economic imbalances that fuel crisis risk in the first place (e.g., Chinese dollar reserves, held as "insurance" in the wake of the 1990s Asian financial crisis, partly caused the Great Recession). Risks are not reduced but are shifted on to others.

7. Fair Risk Assumption

Returning to the Compensation Principle, we now consider whether some "special justification" might allow the risks of capital liberalization without a corresponding demand to compensate for crisis-induced harm. We noted ideas of fair risk assumption and reciprocal risk, which we discussed in Chapter 7.8–7.9. We now argue that neither is appropriate in the context of global finance.

It may be argued that the international market reliance practice has a further way to make the crisis risks of capital liberalization fair, beyond compensation and precaution.

Risk assumption: it may adopt the socially beneficial practice (capital liberalization) so long as it ensures that resulting risks are voluntarily assumed only by people who have a reasonable option to do otherwise.

We allow a construction worker to face risk of death on a building project because or insofar as we think he has voluntarily assumed it, against a background of reasonable opportunities to take on less dangerous work. If he does die, he of course cannot be compensated. But assuming the risk of death was fairly assumed, we take this outcome to be merely horrible and unfortunate rather than unfair. Similarly, one may argue, especially in a postcolonial era, sovereign governments only integrate into global financial markets because they have themselves chosen to drop capital controls. Accordingly, it may be said, they thus "enter at their own risk" and are alone liable for any harmful crises that result. A version of this view adds that "the market is (almost) always right" (perhaps a la the Efficient Markets Hypothesis), in which case crises must reflect domestic economic mismanagement. Crises are thus a country's "own fault."

As emphasized in earlier chapters, however, even formally "voluntary" government choice does not necessarily generate full liability, or, what comes to the same thing, a lack of fairness claims upon others. Many governments choose to liberalize their capital accounts without having had a reasonable, "real option" of doing otherwise, at least not in the sense that implies full liability for harm that results.[50] International social pressures to liberalize, and to adopt a particular form of liberalization, can be significant even among advanced countries, and developing countries face pressures that are stronger still. There are tremendous asymmetries in expertise and bargaining power (rising powers such as China being exceptions that prove the rule). Developing countries often must liberalize in currently favored ways to be seen as a

---

50. Reddy, 2005, pp. 229ff, emphases this point, along with the limited control of developing countries over their debt adjustment burdens.

"good student," or to receive promises of "trade as aid." Because trendy policies may even have a chance of working (despite great risks), developing-country officials often feel compelled to comply.

Even if we grant for the sake of argument that liberalizing governments do have a reasonable option of doing otherwise, it does not follow that the *citizens* likely to be harmed have such an option as well: citizens normally have no alternative to the choices their officials make on their behalf. Even if those choices are legitimately made, this does not mean that those hurt by an ensuing crises have no claim to compensation. They retain such claims against their own government. But if so, they also have some claim against the other agents that have substantially contributed to the outcome, chiefly, the set of countries engaged in the common liberalization practice that helped to bring the crises about—though of course countries bearing some share of collective responsibility will not all be responsible to the same degree.

This suggests that the international market reliance practice is generally not the kind of context in which voluntary choice triggers full liability, even provided a reasonable alternative. Compare other contexts. We assume that a skydiver has voluntarily accepted the risk of serious injury or death when it is clear that any injury will be self-imposed. Although others may have causally contributed to the outcome (someone piloted the plane), so long as the skydiver takes due care not to injure others, his decision to jump means that he has taken his fate into his own hands. Many contexts of ongoing interdependence, relationships, or social practices are not like this, however. Suppose a married woman asks her husband to pay more attention to her likes and dislikes; he does not plausibly address her claim in replying, "Sorry, but you didn't have to marry me, and you knew what you were getting into." This may be quite true—she had real marriage options, and she knew that sensitivity was not the man's strong suit. Yet this is not a relevant reason that greater sensitivity is not now required, as a matter of marital obligation or of reciprocity. The international context is more like this than the skydiver case: voluntary risk assumption does not necessarily displace standing fairness obligations arising from relationships that are anyway in place.

So even if a government has a real alternative to capital liberalization, and officials knowingly take crisis risks, this is not to say the society in question cannot reasonably press claims against other governments, either to curb risky policies or to provide mitigation or compensation when crises strike. For suppose the structure of international finance could be adjusted so as to substantially reduce the risk of crisis for a particular set of countries, perhaps at small cost to others. (Suppose, for example, that lender of last resort facilities are increased, while loan conditionality is relaxed, with no new "moral hazard" problem created. Or perhaps the dollar-based reserve system is reformed, by wider and more regular use of IMF Special Drawing Rights.) The countries may, it would seem, fairly lay claim to this. And if this kind of claim is even eligible in principle, then the issue of structural equity is *not* simply foreclosed, as it would be on the present proposal: the risks of harm are not already fully assumed. Rather, others can be asked to take greater care. The basic question of fairness, then, is not one of fair risk assumption but of what terms of the social practice of capital market reliance would be fair to all countries involved.

We might instead take an example more favorable for advanced countries. Consider again how developing countries have "self-insured" against crises by amassing currency reserves for ready use when a threat to domestic macro-economic stability arises. As suggested earlier, this further fuels crisis risk for the advanced countries (again, Chinese dollar reserves, amassed in the wake of the East Asian crisis and recirculated through the U.S. economy, became housing and asset bubbles that partly caused the Great Recession). Thus risk is reduced domestically (in China), but also shifted on to others. It is presumably fair for developing countries to have considerable special privileges for such measures of self-protection. Yet there is also presumably *some* limit on the risks they can fairly impose on other countries—even if these countries, too, voluntarily assumed these risks. It is fair for the United States or other affected countries to ask China to reduce its reserve holdings (provided it also provides a credible alternative, whether a truly trustworthy lender of last resort or a Special Drawing Right-based mutual insurance cooperative.)

There may well be cases in which governments take on "unnecessary" risks, which are indeed "their own fault." Our claim is that such conditions will involve exceptions to background of fairness expectations generated by the general market reliance practice. Governments do not bear full liability for the risks of crisis simply because they chose capital liberalization with full formal powers of sovereignty.

8. Reciprocity of Risk

We close this chapter considering a second and final potential "special justification." In this suggestion, risks may be fair because they are reciprocally imposed.[51] That is, the international market reliance practice might set aside the Compensation Principle for reasons of

> *Risk reciprocation:* it may adopt the socially beneficial practice (capital liberalization) so long as it ensures that the risks are imposed only among those who the risks are imposed only among those who impose similar risks upon one another.

Thus, so long as countries impose similar crisis risks upon one another over time, they bear no obligation to compensate one another when crises break out. A liberalization practice that involves non-reciprocal risks—some countries are at greater crisis risk than others—can be made fair simply by reforms that make all countries subject to similar risks of crisis. Countries now imposing non-reciprocal risks on other countries might adopt less risky polices. Or the countries imposed upon might *ramp up* their risk-taking so that the imposition is mutual.

Intriguing as this possibility is, it does not represent a substantial alternative to a compensation-based conception. Compensation will still be required for any harm that results from a non-reciprocal imposition, and this seems largely unavoidable in the context of international finance. Most developing countries will not ever impose similar risk levels upon major advanced countries (notwithstanding special cases such as China). Even in a "two track" system, in which developing countries adopt controls (e.g., Chilean inflow limits) while advanced countries retain liberalized capital, developing countries will be subject to non-reciprocal exposure. So long as developing-country macroeconomic prospects depend on goods and services trade with advanced countries, rich-world crises that reduce trade may significantly contribute to developing world crisis risk.

More important, even if crisis risk could be imposed reciprocally, this would not be sufficient for fairness. On its most plausible

---

51. See Chapter 7.9.

interpretation, fair risk imposition is sensitive to risk *levels*, not mere mutuality. In that case, measures of risk reciprocation collapse into measures either of compensation or precaution, leaving capital liberalization no more justified than on our original compensation-based argument.

As discussed in 7.9, risk levels matter because similar risks can vary dramatically in significance depending on background factors. We therefore suggested an alternative proposal: equality of expected benefit. Fair reciprocity of risk is achieved, on this suggestion, not merely when risk levels are similar but when there is a rough equivalence between the parties in the expected overall value of being allowed to engage in the risk-imposing behavior, given that each is also subjected to those same risks. This seems an improvement, but it will not help capital liberalization. Developing and advanced countries are simply too differently situated. Even if advanced countries could expect overall gain from capital liberalization (at least provided the gains are well distributed among their members), developing countries can expect to gain very little, and indeed can expect a great deal of pain. They are simply better off in a world of capital controls.

CHAPTER NINE

The Level Playing Field
Intellectual Property

The global economy is now subject to a more or less universal system of intellectual property (IP), as set and enforced within the WTO. This is troubling, for the standard arguments for IP rights—arguments from social utility, piracy, and natural or human rights—are remarkably inadequate. Indeed, as we will see, the arguments are so weak that it is natural to conclude that the emerging global system should simply be abolished. Or if the system is not abolished, it should at least be *eviscerated*: developing countries should be exempted from WTO IP rules (TRIPS),[1] by an unlimited grace period. (In a slogan: "eviscerate TRIPS.")

There is, however, a different, less well understood line of argument that at least has a fighting chance of supporting the emerging system, an argument from the idea of a "level playing field." If developing countries were granted the special privilege of having any or no IP laws, many would presumably grant their citizens and firms free use of the plethora of rich-world intellectual creations, be they drugs or fertilizers or videos. But according to the argument, such usage—now commonly referred to simply as "piracy"—amounts to unfair competition. A global rather than national-level IP protection is needed if the market actors of different countries are to compete on a "level playing field" in the global marketplace. Without global-level IP protection, the creators of drugs, fertilizers, films, software, and other products of the mind suffer unfair disadvantages when they seek market profit and must compete with those who are left free to appropriate and capitalize on such intellectual goods without having to seek permission or pay compensation. In particular, developing-country market actors—pharmaceutical producers in

---

1. Or "Trade-Related Aspects of Intellectual Property Rights."

India, video distributors in Taiwan—gain real but unfair competitive market advantages over developed-world innovators, enjoying the fruit of their intellectual labors for free.

One might argue, in reply, that such competitive market advantages for developing countries are *unfair, yet fully justified*, say, because they advance the cause of humanity or basic justice. In this chapter, we develop a stronger line of reply: competitive advantages for developing-country market actors are *perfectly fair*, given requirements of fairness *internal* to the system of trade. Our ideas of "competitive fairness" and "level playing fields" are themselves highly sensitive to larger demands of structural equity in the international trading system. It is with the global economy as it is with most games: the very content of our ideas of "fair competition," and the degree to which we should "level the playing field," if at all, depends on aims and principles associated with the particular sort of competitive interaction going on. Applying this "instrumental" conception of competitive fairness to trade in particular, competitive advantages for developing-country actors turn out to be perfectly fair, because they are necessary for developing countries to reap a fair level of gain from the larger market reliance practice that organizes the global marketplace. What is commonly called intellectual "piracy" is thus in fact fair play.

1. The Emerging IP Regime

Consider the WTO IP regime and its consequences. In general, to have a legal IP right, such as a copyright or patent, is to have legal right to exclude access to and use of one's intellectual creation (e.g., an original artwork, a computer program, a drug), usually for a specified period of time. Before the 1990s, such rights were granted only within limited legal domains. If I had such a right against you, we either shared the same domestic IP-endowing legal system, or we were members of a limited number of different countries that had signed a special IP treaty. As of the 1994 Uruguay Round of negotiations, however, standards concerning a wide variety of intellectual creations[2] were included within the

---

2. A wide variety of items are now commonly bundled as "intellectual property," including copyrights, patents, trademarks, geographical indications, trade secrets, industrial designs, integrated circuits, breeders'

multilateral trading system and became enforceable within the newly formed WTO.³ As a result, legal IP rights are now poised to become global in reach. Because the WTO has a large and growing membership—indeed, no country can afford not to join—a single set of demanding IP rights have been or will soon be granted to authors of intellectual creations (nearly) worldwide. Soon enough, if you wish to use my copyrighted drawing or recording, or my patented chemicals or drugs, I will have legal claim against you almost no matter where in the world you and I happen to be.⁴

The emerging system is chiefly troubling from a moral point of view because of its consequences for developing countries: large numbers of poor people in developing countries are made worse off than they would be under feasible alternative arrangements. The controversy over South Africa's use of HIV/AIDS drugs highlighted how the current patent rules raise the cost of death- or disease-preventing pharmaceuticals.⁵ But the untoward consequences reach far beyond complications for public health protection. IP rules tend to slow economic development.⁶ They transfer resources from developing countries to rich-country authors, away

---

rights, and "traditional knowledge." In general, an item of each kind is authored by way of intellectual activity, and its use or expression can be exploited for commercial gain. Unless otherwise noted, I focus on what rules concerning such items tend to have in common. We happily concede modifications where specific forms of IP have relevant peculiarities.
3. TRIPS rules have two main functions. First, they require non-discrimination between citizens of different member countries; foreigners are to be treated the same as nationals ("national treatment"). Second, the new rules both require and "harmonize" minimum standards across all countries involved. Earlier agreements (dating as far back as the Berne Convention of 1886) also required non-discrimination, but left it up to each country what IP standards, if any, to have.
4. As of 2011, a *global* system can only be said to be "emerging." Current rules apply only to WTO member countries. Moreover, the "least developed" WTO countries still have until 2016 to implement their IP systems. In other member developing countries, enforcement remains weak.
5. This is true despite "compulsory licensing" provisions, since developing countries still have to compensate patent holders, even when they could instead save another life. For discussion of the complexities of implementation, see Correa, 1998.
6. Even pro-globalization economists such as Bhagwati, 2004, pp. 182–90, raise this objection, along with more critical economists such as Stiglitz, 2006, ch. 4.

from where they do the most good. They slow the transfer of technology to developing countries—one of the chief benefits of trade—by making it more expensive. They limit the imitative innovation that was crucial for advanced countries when they industrialized, as well as the policy flexibility that has been a hallmark of almost every development success story.[7]

None of these consequences are inevitable. They would be mostly avoided if developing-country governments instead had a free hand to have any or no IP rules, according to what best serves their development goals.[8] This privilege could be easily added to the current system: we simply grant all developing countries in the trading system an unlimited grace period to comply with current rules.[9] The rules would become applicable and enforceable only when societies cross an appropriate threshold of development.[10]

2. Why Supernational Protection?

How, then, could it be reasonable to ask developing countries to accept such adverse outcomes? There are reasons on the other side, yet at least the three standard arguments for legal IP rights—from social utility, piracy, and natural or human rights—are remarkably inadequate. What is needed is some compelling reason that IP protection cannot simply be left to domestic governments—why certain IP rights should have "supernational" protection. But the three standard arguments barely offer an adequate rationale for this, let alone a compelling justification.

---

7. Rodrik, 2007.
8. Should we further specify what types of policies or institutions would promote appropriate "development goals"? The agreed failure of the "Washington Consensus" tells against any such effort, and less rigid "diagnostic" approaches (e.g., Rodrik, 2007) merely outline a framework for country-specific analysis.
9. This is not to say other measures concerning IP aren't also necessary. A general exemption won't by itself create incentives for poverty-targeted innovation, for example. For that we need a supplementary institutional scheme, such as a publicly funded system of rewards (as, e.g., according to Pogge, 2005, and Stiglitz, 2006, p. 124).
10. Though specification of the threshold between "developing" and "advanced" country status might be not be uncontroversial, we assume plausible characterizations can be provided.

Consider first the argument from social utility. Does "supernational" protection of certain IP rights promote welfare overall? In fact, there is little empirical evidence that required "harmonization" of standards across all countries yields aggregate global gains, precisely because a domestic IP regime can be of little overall benefit, and indeed detrimental, to many developing countries.[11] Why suppose that twenty-year patent protection, now a matter of international law under TRIPS, should be optimal for developing countries, as opposed to, say, fifteen or five? Might it be best to have no IP protection for a time? The answer is a delicate empirical matter, depending on a given country's particular circumstances, its stage of development, its particular "binding growth constraints," its distinctive institutional complexities and quality, and so on. It would be very surprising then if any blanket rule were optimal.

We can even grant that an IP regime can be helpful in some cases. Perhaps it encourages certain technology flows (e.g., because foreign exporters or investors are reassured that their IP will not be used).[12] Still, it does not follow that establishing and maintaining IP protection is the optimal course. This is expensive in itself, and scarce resources may be better used elsewhere. Even if some flows of technology are encouraged, they may not be well timed, or of the best kind, or in any case justifiable if the cost is limitations on what may be more important forms of technological imitation and use.

It is commonly argued that temporary monopolies on intellectual works create incentives for socially beneficial innovation. Even if this is so in and across the advanced countries, such incentives are poorly targeted for poor and relatively poor people in the developing world. There is little market incentive to create potentially expensive drugs for people who cannot afford them, for example. Poverty-targeted innovation is far more likely to emerge from a publicly subsidized system of rewards. The resulting gains to the developing-world poor would yield much larger welfare improvements than gains to rich-worlders, even including the relatively better off rich-world poor. Other moral

---

11. Chin and Grossman, 1988, suggest global aggregate welfare gains from global IP rules (especially regarding patents) but *only* when special compensatory provisions are made for developing countries.
12. Maskus, 2002, pp. 369–81.

considerations being equal, then, the welfare-promoting course seems clear: stop the damage being done by the current IP system, by granting all developing countries an unlimited grace period, and set up a public, non-market system of incentives for poverty-targeted innovation.

Of course, other moral considerations may not be equal. The piracy or rights arguments claim that they are not. According to the argument from piracy, by stopping or at least slowing the unauthorized and uncompensated use of patented, copyrighted, or otherwise protected intellectual products in developing countries, the current global IP system polices a modern form of international piracy. As Jack Valenti, then president of the Motion Picture Association of America, colorfully put the claim:

> Keep in mind that the U.S. film industry does about $24 billion a year. Forty-one percent of that comes from international markets, so it is increasingly crucial and important that those markets remain open and that our IP is protected from thievery. We are constantly vigilant because, like virtue, we are every day besieged.[13]

This argument is plainly inadequate if it is meant (as intended) as a reason to create international IP laws where they do not yet exist. When the piracy argument was at the height of its influence in the early 1990s, during the Uruguay Round trade negotiations, the copying of foreign videos or drugs in, say, China or India was not illegal, and so not "thievery" or "piracy" in any legal sense. Voiced in that context, the piracy argument was merely a convenient rhetorical construct—a way of presenting normal commerce *as though* it is illegal, in order to demand police action. It provides no rationale for making foreign use of intellectual creations illegal in the first place.

Valenti may have instead meant to argue from pre-legal, natural, or human rights. If the author of an intellectual creation has a natural or human IP right to control or at least benefit from its use, then *any* unauthorized or uncompensated use, anywhere in the world, would count as an infringement, regardless of whether those rights are legally protected. Global IP rules can be seen as a

---

13. Quoted in Devereaux et al., 2006, p. 44.

necessary way of respecting innovator rights, by giving them a credible threat of lawsuit against unwanted use and, if need be, their day in court. Fortunately or unfortunately, IP rights have indeed made it into numerous international human rights agreements, including, most notably, the Universal Declaration of Human Rights (Article 27.2): "Everyone has the right to the protection of the moral and material interests resulting from any scientific, literary or artistic production of which he is the author."[14]

Do such "rights" really justify global-level protection? The answer will depend on how the proposed rights are understood. Rights can be understood as either morally relevant interests, which have no essential priority or weight over other relevant interests, or as overriding moral claims, which normally "trump" other moral considerations.[15] On either interpretation, however, the argument is open to serious objection.

Understood in the former, "relevant interests" sense, IP rights are relatively easy to motivate and defend. One can claim that creators have *some* interest in benefiting from their intellectual works without staking any claim about what has to be given up when conflicts with other interests arise. As "human rights," then, they are simply factors to be balanced against other human rights considerations.[16] Precisely because such IP rights are readily open to balancing, however, they provide no clear, general argument even for *domestic* IP protection, let alone for inclusion within international law. A society seeking a robust public intellectual commons could conceivably protect many of the "moral and material interests resulting from any scientific, literary or artistic production" by lavishly funding creative production, rewarding and recognizing achievement, but otherwise having no copyright regime.

---

14. Similar provisions are found in the United Nation's International Covenant on Economic, Social and Cultural Rights (1966), Article 15.1 (c) and General Comment No. 17 (2005); the American Declaration of the Rights and Duties of Man (1948), Article 13.2; and the Additional Protocol to the American Convention on Human Rights in the Area of Economic, Social and Cultural Rights (1988), Article 14.1 (c).
15. For the former view, see Thomson, 1990. For the latter view, see Dworkin, 1977, as well as Nozick 1974, who regards rights as "side-constraints" rather than goals to be promoted. For a general, critical discussion of appeals to natural IP rights, see Shiffrin, 2001.
16. This is emphasized and advocated by WTO secretariat counselors Anderson and Wager, 2006.

In developing countries, the trade-offs are starker still: IP protection can come at the cost of famine relief, the elimination of disease, the promotion of basic literacy, and any number of other recognized human rights. If the author's IP rights are little more than relevant interests, it is hard to see why such other morally relevant interests should not normally hold sway.

The second, "trumping" interpretation avoids this difficulty. An author's IP right, if it could be justified, would *by definition* normally override even the strongest of countervailing claims. But such strong rights are not easy to defend on their own terms. Authorization of use is not plausibly always one's right, in the present strong sense. For it is not as though *no* amount of compensation, no matter how large, could legitimate use without one's permission. Authors who are not asked, or who deny permission, will at most have an overriding right to fair compensation, at some reasonable level.[17]

If only reasonable compensation is required, this suffices to undercut the argument for global rather than domestic IP protection. Perhaps each country will have to set up some IP scheme within its own borders, providing compensation to some substantial degree. Let us assume for the moment that each does so. If the compensation is substantial, even if varying across different systems, why should anything more be necessary? Why wouldn't the rewards granted within one's own country's IP scheme be fair? Why suppose that, having reaped substantial gains, one retains a residual claim to reap *still further gains* from foreign usage, let alone an *overriding* claim to those gains? The point is especially clear in large industrialized economies, where creators may profit handsomely from domestic opportunities for commercial exploitation. They do not then seem to have an overriding right to *still further gains*, especially when their provision comes at great cost to developing countries. Fair compensation has already been provided.[18]

---

17. This is implicit in TRIPS recognition of "compulsory licensing," which requires reasonable or fair compensation (as decided by the expropriating country). Is even this a violation of natural rights when authorial permission is not granted? To suppose that it is would be a quite radical view. It would preclude even "fair use" by individuals, for non-commercial purposes.

18. One might object that although creators can only demand so much

Indeed, if strong, "trumping" IP rights cannot be defended, then global-level IP protection violates the rights of *potential users* abroad. For so long as fair compensation is provided by domestic protection, any potential benefits to foreigners count as morally free positive externalities. It is then the foreign users, not the authors, who are deprived of what is rightfully theirs to use.[19]

3. The Argument from Competitive Fairness

There is, however, a more plausible but less well-understood argument for the emerging IP system, an argument from competitive fairness. According to the argument, global IP rules are needed if authors of intellectual creations are to compete with foreign market actors in the global marketplace on a "level playing field." The sole function of global-level rules, on this view, is to "level" certain competitive advantages, so that authors are not forced to compete in the global marketplace under conditions that are unfair.

---

from any *given* user, there is no benefit threshold that prevents them from commanding unlimited overall gains from *an unlimited number of users* (e.g., the billions of potential users in the developing world). If a large number of people pay (what may for each be a small amount) the total compensation will be correspondingly large. But there is no threshold of benefit beyond which the next users no longer have to pay; each simply pays the individually fair compensation rate. This radical view is not plausible. It is inconsistent with *any* time limit on the creator's monopoly rights (except, perhaps, at the creator's death). For to say the monopoly should last, say, for only twenty years would be to say that use after that time comes free, and so the creator need not be paid.

19. The larger point made in the earlier section holds even in the most plausible cases of rights violations, such as the expropriation of "traditional knowledge" from indigenous peoples. When, for example, a traditional medical remedy is wrongfully expropriated for development of new, rich-world pharmaceuticals, this is often wrongful because reasonable compensation has not been provided. Perhaps the indigenous group even consented, failing to appreciate the market value of their innovation. Domestic governments can take measures to prevent this, for instance, by educating the group. If this is insufficient, domestic IP rights would provide further protection. Though further, "supernational" protection might also be desirable, there is no easy and direct rights argument that it should be necessary. Lesser measures may often suffice.

Unlike the standard arguments we have considered, this kind of argument explains why, in a globalizing world, domestic-level protection might be inadequate. In the global marketplace, the "playing field" is global or nearly global in scale. But no appeal to natural or human IP rights is assumed. And because the argument is an appeal to fairness, it is the kind of argument that could in principle justify significant welfare losses to developing countries. The argument can marshal powerful deontological intuitions: development should proceed apace, but only within the moral constraints of fair play.

To appreciate the force of the argument, consider an analogy. Suppose that your neighbor grows apple trees, allowing them to grow over your common fence. The trees in turn drop apples into your yard. Though the apples only exist because of your neighbor's intellectual and other labors, the fallen apples seem, at least for certain purposes, morally free for your use. You could, for instance, use them to make delicious apple pies, for the enjoyment of your family and friends. Your neighbor is within his rights to cut back his tree, to be sure. But one reason he does *not* have for doing so is that your use of the apples is unfair. For your limited purposes, your benefit from the apples is a positive externality of his creative activity and in no way unfair. In order to emphasize intellectual creation, let us add that the trees only exist because the neighbor has innovated new breeding and nurturing techniques that allow the trees to grow in an otherwise unfavorable climate. Still, it seems, your use of the apples, for your own enjoyment, is a positive externality of his creative activity and morally free.

Let us now vary the case. Suppose you use the apples, not for personal enjoyment, but to make pies that you sell in the local marketplace, in competition with your neighbor's own pies. You have a lower cost of production than your neighbor—unlike him, you get your apples free—so you sell at a cheaper price. This cuts into his profits. In this case, because your use of his apples gives you a competitive advantage over him, it becomes relevant; it is morally "internalized," no longer a mere positive externality. The neighbor can now cut back his tree in the name of fair competition. You can now, in the name of fair competition, offer to compensate your neighbor for your use of his apples (perhaps in the amount that your free use entails a cost to him). The community can, in the name of fair competition, ask you and your neighbor to work out a deal.

One might wonder whether such talk of "fair competition" is really apt. For the moment, however, we need only grant that *if* it makes sense to talk about fair competitive arrangements, then it is fair to adopt measures that level or remove the advantage you gain over him. This would make the circumstances of competition fairer than they were before.

If all of this is right, the case of global IP may seem analogous. If countries were not substantially integrated economically—if globalization did not exist—inventors in one country could not lay claim against use of their creations in other lands. For this causes them no disadvantage. As with the spread of technology generally, the benefits to users are positive externalities, morally free, and in no way unfair (as in our first variation on the apples case). But these are not the circumstances of our world. In a global economy, market actors in each country are often, or often enough, in market competition with one another (as in our second variation of the apples case). And unless special arrangements are made, firms that copy and sell software or drugs not only benefit from the prior creation of those intellectual products but they also gain competitive market advantages over their authors, potentially cutting into their market share. Indian firms that copy drugs or software innovated by U.S. firms, for example, can sell them at a cheaper price. The U.S. firms potentially lose not just in India but also abroad, in the United States or third markets such as the EU. Thus, as above, assuming it makes sense to talk about fair competitive arrangements, we can say that it is fair to adopt measures that level or remove the competitive advantage that such users have over authors. This can be the sole function of global IP rules: they make the circumstances of global competition fairer than a situation in which trade flourishes but IP protection is confined within so many domestic spheres.

If the analogy is to hold, it must of course be appropriate to speak of "fair competitive arrangements" in the global commerce. This is quite plausibly the case, whatever we say about the apples case. Any market interactions at least give rise to basic requirements of good faith: one is not to gain market advantages over a competitor by, say, sowing confusion about his or her products, by discrediting his or her reputation, or by otherwise misleading the public. We make the circumstances of global commerce fairer by adopting laws or social customs that assure wide compliance with such norms. In the same way, we can also adopt any number of feasible rules or expectations that shape the relative prospects of parties to competition, including, for example, global-level antitrust and competition rules. The present argument, in these terms, is that global IP rules are needed, beyond these other forms of market regulation, if relative market prospects are to be distributed in an appropriate way.

Since the argument is specifically for IP rules, it is important that the analogy turn on claims arising specifically from *intellectual authorship*, quite aside from any claims to fair return on investment of labor, time, or other capital. The analogy is robust in this way. In the apples case, we can imagine that the neighbors incur the same capital expenditure in bringing their pies to market. Though they thus have equal investment-based claims, the innovator's objection of an undue competitive disadvantage seems to remain. It seems to matter that the technique for growing the trees was his idea. In the global economy case, we can imagine (in a somewhat different but more realistic way) that the owners of drug patents or software copyrights have merely *purchased* their IP rights from the original innovators. Assuming a fair price was paid, no claim deriving from intellectual authorship is then in play. We can also assume that no global IP rules exist, that the purchasers knew or could have known that their locally patented content might be used and commercially exploited abroad, and that they had the option of keeping it secret. If our analogy is apt, we should see no corresponding claim of undue disadvantage when the IP holders choose market exploitation and incur the relative losses in our original example. And this seems right. It is more plausible to say that the purchasers might have invested poorly than to say that their market disadvantage is unfair.

Having now presented the argument from competitive fairness in an intuitively plausible form, we will now refute it. The question we need to press is, Why can't the circumstances of competition be fair even if authors *do* suffer real competitive disadvantages? Only two kinds of answer seem possible. Either the elimination of such disadvantages is *intrinsically* fair, or it is not. If it is, we should be able to appreciate this with plausible examples. If not, there must be substantive reasons (which do not mention intrinsic fairness or unfairness) that it is unreasonable for authors to suffer competitive disadvantages when the playing field could be level instead. In the remainder of this chapter, we see that neither sort of answer justifies the IP constraints currently being placed on developing countries.

4. When is Leveling Fair?

Begin with the appeal to intrinsic fairness. The idea is that global IP rules are justified on the grounds that the competitive advantages they remove are intrinsically unfair. The system then needs no further raison d'etre. If this is right, however, we should be able to find competitive arrangements in which we level competitive advantages for this reason. But as we will now explain, we almost never, if ever, level competitive advantages because they are intrinsically unfair, and there is no reason to think economic relations are an exception.

There are cases in which a level playing field can seem intrinsically fair. Consider golf, a most egalitarian of contests given its elaborate and widely practiced system of "handicaps." As a statement by the United States Golf Association explains, "The USGA Handicap System enables golfers of all skill levels to compete on an equitable basis."[20] An "equitable basis" in the system amounts to roughly equal ex ante chances of success. By adding "strokes" to the scores of the better players, and deducting strokes from scores of the lesser players, the deliberate aim is to eliminate as far as possible any measurable benefit of greater skill, giving each player an equal chance to win on the particular occasion of play. "Equitable Stroke Control" even caps the maximum per hole stroke count. This limits the score damage of unfortunate contingencies that arise in the course of game play (e.g., being caught in the rough and stroking freely to get free). Thus it may be said that, in this and perhaps other cases, reducing or eliminating competitive advantages is intrinsically fair, because ex ante prospects of winning a particular contest are thereby equalized among the competitors, and because a situation of equal prospects is fair in and of itself.

Notice that the issue here is quite distinct from the indisputable issue of intrinsic unfairness that arises when parties are

---

20. See http://www.usga.org/playing/handicaps/handicaps.html.

treated differently under rules that do not formally or informally call for differential treatment. Intrinsic unfairness of this kind does not necessarily require that competitive advantages or disadvantages be leveled. Differential ex ante prospects can, for instance, reflect the explicit or unstated rules of the game. They do not then flow from an intrinsically unfair difference in how the rules of the game are applied, which has no basis in the game's structure.

Why do we sometimes remove or reduce a competitive advantage? This is often *instrumentally* justified, because competition is thereby more likely to serve the larger goals of the kind of interaction in question. In chess, yacht racing, or golf, a contest in which ex ante prospects of winning are relatively equal might be the most enjoyable to watch or play; it might make for more interesting betting; it might be most likely to "bring out the best" in the contestants; and so on. The concern is not necessarily that unequal prospects are intrinsically unfair. When such purposes are the only factors in play, we remove or reduce advantages only to the degree that those purposes are well served. In competitive surfing, one usually simply wants the best possible surfing done in the wave conditions of that day. No one sees any reason to handicap the surfer who everyone expects to win. Even more obviously, in a dog show, we see no reason to shear the prize poodle in order that the neighborhood mixed-breed has a chance to win Best in Show. The operative interests—to call forth the best specimens of their kinds—are best served when all prior advantages of nature and good grooming carry the day.

Indeed, the case of golf may seem similar, at least if professional golf is any indication. In a well-publicized U.S. Supreme Court case, *PGA TOUR v. Casey Martin*, the PGA Tour denied Casey Martin use of a golf cart intended to mitigate the walking-induced pain caused by his special disability. It was argued on the PGA Tour's behalf that removal of Martin's disadvantage is inconsistent with the competitive nature of professional golf play. To level the playing field would not make for a fairer version of the game being played but rather change its very nature. While that may or may not be a correct view of the metaphysics of Golf, or of what is fair, it does suggest that, even in golf, the assumed purposes of a competitive interaction—those that partly make up the game, or the version being played—can determine whether or to what degree leveling is required for competitive fairness. The issue is not what is intrinsically fair.[21]

Is the global marketplace an exception because concerns of intrinsic fairness somehow come up that are absent in other competitive relations? It does not seem so. In a state system, a global marketplace only exists to any substantial degree because governments reduce trade barriers, allowing market exchange and competition across borders. According to economic theory, the aim of allowing competition is wholly instrumental. As we have emphasized in previous chapters, the final goal of trade is mutual national gain. Popular misconceptions notwithstanding, countries are not ultimately in competition; only their respective firms or other market agents compete.[22] Such market competition has a wholly instrumental role: competition between Chinese and U.S. firms, say, is simply the *mechanism* through which the comparative advantage of each country is "revealed." Market competition, in sum, is simply a means to country-level mutual gain.

If this is the whole story, then there is no intrinsic unfairness if we alter the circumstances of competition—whether by leveling, allowing, or even *creating* competitive advantages, for example, by eviscerating current IP rules, to the advantage of developing-country firms. There is at least nothing illegitimate in such measures, in the sense that they are quite compatible with, and perhaps required for, the presumed legitimate goal of trade: mutual gain. In this kind of situation, as in the games considered above, we normally at least regard the resulting circumstances of competition as "not unfair." And this is just to say that the disadvantages involved are not intrinsically unfair.

One can of course argue that this is not the whole story because competitive disadvantages *are* or at least can be intrinsically unfair. Indeed, even if it could be shown that fairness in the larger system of trade requires them, one could insist that this merely shows that fairness requires intrinsically *unfair* competitive advantages. But how plausible is this view if it is contrary to our usual social understandings and few, if any, plausible examples

---

21. Other fairness issues can also of course be at play. The American Disabilities Act, which was at issue in the case, is concerned with access in society generally.
22. Krugman, 1996, repeatedly emphasizes this point.

are forthcoming? It seems, instead, that there is no issue of intrinsic fairness. If indeed fairness in the larger system of trade requires developing countries to have certain competitive advantages, as we will now argue, then they count as perfectly fair.

5. Structural Equity

Even if some advantage-altering measures are not unfair as such, they may still be unfair for some special reason. To return to the apples case, for example, the circumstances of competition seem unfair because standing arrangements (or the lack thereof) allow the neighbor to suffer an undue disadvantage. The level of disadvantage seems undue, because we can think of practicable ways of avoiding it that impose only reasonable costs on the user of the apples. In a similar way, one might argue that some common IP rules should govern advanced country economic integration, for the users of foreign IP in advanced countries will tend to be well-off and therefore able to pay moderate or even substantial compensation. The competitive disadvantage innovators suffer without common rules may then seem undue.

Let us grant that this may justify common IP rules for *advanced* countries (though perhaps weaker rules than those we now have).[23] The case of developing countries is quite different. In countries populated with very poor people, the cost of common IP rules will often be paid in terms of forgone medicines, school books, or provision for any number of other basic human needs. It is harder to argue that the market disadvantages rich-country authors suffer, without such rules, is undue. They seem quite reasonable.

One might object that a general appeal to poverty is beside the point. Why, one may ask, should it be fair for a developed country author to lose out to an *equally rich or richer* competitor just because he or she happens to live in a poor country? The answer, we take it, is that the cost of leveling the advantage usually falls not only to the rich user but to the many poor or poorer people in

---

23. Even here we concede this tentatively, remaining open to countervailing arguments for IP anarchy that override the considerations of competitive fairness we have described.

his or her family, employment, or industry. Global IP rules are not fair to them.

A different and more significant objection grants that poverty relief is indeed precisely the issue. It may be said that global IP rules raise no issue of fairness in economic relations as such but are simply a humanitarian problem. We grant that the emerging global IP system is a humanitarian disaster. Our claim is that there is *also* an important moral issue of fairness in economic relations as such, which should not be ignored or minimized. Our remaining task is to explain why this should be so.

We can assume that any IP system in a globalized world will be part of a larger system of international economic cooperation, if only because one of its basic functions will be to create incentives for economically advantageous innovation. Payment of promised rewards to innovators will be a matter of economic fairness, but only in the "legitimate expectations" sense defined in Chapter 7.11; fair reward will be subject to the demands of fairness elsewhere in the larger cooperative practice. The question of fair reward for innovation is thus subject to the demands of structural equity in the global economy's organizing market reliance relationship. But in that case, competitive advantages for developing-country firms will count as perfectly fair so long as they are necessary for developing countries to reap a fair level of gain from the larger trading relationships that create and organize the global marketplace. If, as we will now argue, developing countries must have special IP privileges in order to reap a fair level of gain from this larger set of relations, then any cost those gains entail to innovators in advanced countries is both legitimate and fair. The argument from competitive fairness can thus be answered in terms of the fairness of economic relations themselves.

In claiming that developing countries should in fact have special IP privileges, we partly defer to economists who urge greater policy flexibility for developing countries, with little sympathy for the current IP regime.[24] At the same time, whether special IP privileges are "necessary" as an empirical matter partly depends on what they are necessary for. While economists often focus simply

---

24. Rodrik, 2007. See also Bhagwati, 2004, who is less concerned with policy flexibility than with keeping "trade-related" issues out of the WTO, though with a similar upshot.

on social utility, the philosopher can add the conception of fairness that would make special IP privileges seem required. The International Relative Gains principle suggests the following answer: if the system of trade is to be fair, developing countries must be afforded special development benefits, in this case, those flowing from being exempted from the IP system.

Here one may object that a fair set of trade rules is simply that which treats all countries in the same way, in which case special accommodation for developing countries is unfair. At best, the objection continues, we can say that the unfairness is justified, on balance, for independent reasons of humanity or global justice. This is, however, an implausibly narrow view. As argued in Chapter 7.1–7.3, fairness surely at least concerns the harms of trade, which may not befall all countries in the same way. Special accommodation in the form of transitional protections, and technological and financial assistance to support them, seems a clear demand of fairness in trade. Yet even if special accommodation for developing countries is not unfair per se, it does not follow that developing countries can in fairness use the economic benefits of discretion over intellectual property rules to advance their development goals, quite aside from what would otherwise be fair. Why should that be fair? Our answer is that developing countries stand to gain much more, and in much more important ways, than developed countries.

Here we assume that the advanced economies are not harmed by this, overall, for the sake of benefits elsewhere. At worst, they may suffer diminished gains from global economic integration. And while rich-world *individuals* may well be made worse off than they would otherwise be for lack of global IP protection, rich countries can afford to compensate them if they do not sufficiently benefit from IP-protected markets. In that case, however, the question is merely one of level of benefit, and there will be a strong moral pressure for benefits to flow in greater measure to absolutely worse off people. As argued in Chapter 7.6, for reasons of "priority for the worse off," a given level of benefit has greater importance when it goes to an absolutely worse-off person, from a fairness point of view. Indeed, even smaller benefits to badly off people mean more than greater benefits to well-off people. This justifies as fair levels of gain that would otherwise be unfair, along with any special accommodations—such as freedom from IP rules—needed for those benefits to be realized.

6. Conclusion

In sum, the best argument for the emerging global IP system, the argument from competitive fairness, can be answered on its own terms. The demands of competitive fairness in the global economy are properly sensitive to and depend on the larger demands of structural equity arising from the practice of market reliance that organizes the global economy as a whole. Those very general demands require developing countries to have a free hand with respect to IP. Considerations of competitive fairness may give the emerging regime some rationale as between developed countries. Even so, there is no excuse for leaving the current system intact. We must, in fairness, eviscerate TRIPS.

CHAPTER TEN

Exploitation, Degradation, and Other Moral Concerns

Much of the "free trade" versus "fair trade" debate is about a range of moral values that have not been our central focus—values such as health, safety, environmental conservation, human rights, dignified work, domestic social justice, and the bonds of community. The "fair traders" charge that globalization is being governed by "free market" ideology that places economic interests above these or other more important concerns. They argue, for example, that GATT/WTO panel judges have favored commercial interests even when the protection of the environment or public health is perfectly legal (e.g., under GATT Article 20), or that "free trade" with Third World countries has made advanced countries complicit in exploitative "sweatshop" labor or environmental degradation facilitated by lax regulation. The "free traders" insist that such fears are overblown. Mass politics animated by moral values, they say, fails to understand the limited and purely economic purposes of the system of money, finance, and trade. Proper governance within that limited purview, in their view, can only be based in "value-free" economic science administered by technocrats sheltered from reactive and unruly politics.[1]

At issue in such debates is the extent to which economic governance should take account of what we are calling "external" moral values. Although we have so far set these to one side, our argument concerning internal fairness indirectly undermines the "free traders'" claim that such values should be excluded. We have argued that global economic relationships *themselves* generate significant socioeconomic fairness requirements, with no assumption of external values that would equally apply in the global economy's absence. If that is right, international economic law

---

1. For helpful discussion and critique, see Howse, 2002.

and policy can never be a mere matter of "value-free" economic science as administered by technocratic elites; the fairness issues generated by economic relations can only be settled by value-infused political judgment. And if that is true of internal, socioeconomic values, it would be arbitrary for economic governance not to include consideration of external values as well. That isn't to say that we shouldn't divide governance labor—between the WTO and ILO, say—and it isn't to say that trade measures are always or often the best way to handle a given moral concern. It is to say that moral considerations rather than supposedly "value-free" economics properly bear on both the division of governance authority and its exercise in any specific governance forum.

This book chiefly offers an internal critique: global capitalism, we have argued, generates substantial egalitarian responsibilities, without reference to external values, from modest ideas of fairness bound up with economic relations themselves. Yet this cannot be the whole story, even on our own conception of fairness as structural equity. The question of what economic social relationships might be "reasonably acceptable" on all sides surely depends on more than socioeconomic outcomes. The aim of this chapter is therefore to show that our account of socioeconomic fairness in no way prevents us from saying sensible things about how external moral values bear on global economic governance.

1. Conflicts of Value?

Humanitarian values, for instance, present no special difficulty for our account. They either call for similar institutional measures, albeit for different reasons, or require further measures (e.g., further levels of aid) with no threat of unfairness. The different forms of moral responsibility simply have different but partly coincident implications.

At the same time, it is easy to feel that the global economy presents important threats to social life that aren't readily justified in the name of economic enrichment. Indeed, people often feel uneasy about the very existence of a global economy for such reasons, whether or not it takes a form that is structurally equitable from a purely socioeconomic point of view. When it is argued that multinational firms exploit desperate Third World workers, or that globalized commerce forces governments into a "race to the bottom" in environmental standards, the objection is sometimes meant to call the very existence of a capitalist global economy into question. And if the different moral values in play are not themselves fundamentally at odds, they at least seem to point in conflicting directions. Concerns of labor exploitation or environmental degradation could in principle require us to close down the global economy, or at least dramatically reduce its significance, instead of allowing it to flourish while making it fairer.

Among the moral values potentially of fundamental significance, concerns of labor exploitation and environmental degradation are especially challenging. We therefore focus on them. If they can be plausibly accounted for, our account would hopefully apply to other moral concerns in similar ways.

Our answer to the question of basic legitimacy is admittedly conventional: while concerns of labor exploitation and environmental degradation rightly shape global economic arrangements, neither undermines its basic legitimacy as a major force in human social life. Specifically, we take a capitalist global economy to be at least presumptively legitimate given its great power as an engine for reducing and eventually eliminating absolute poverty. If only for that reason, we aren't morally required to close down borders. We can instead work to make the global economy fairer.

That is not to accept the standard apologia for "gung-ho globalization," which takes the global economy to be fully legitimate in any or most any form so long as poverty numbers are in decline. This standard view is too easily pleased; the presumption of legitimacy is not so easily met. While bare legitimacy is a much lower bar than full justifiability to all, we will assume that legitimacy at least requires the global economy to be organized and governed with a good and sufficient measure of sensitivity to both socioeconomic fairness and independent moral concerns. Our suggestion is that there is no general reason—short of limited political will—that various governance arrangements cannot give the full range of relevant moral values their due.

More specifically, we will treat labor exploitation and environmental degradation in quite different ways. Concerns of labor exploitation are partly socioeconomic—workers seem underpaid. So the issue can be at least *partly* addressed in terms of internal, socioeconomic fairness and the institutions that might advance the economic prospects of developing-country workers. Insofar as there are residual moral concerns, say, of degrading or inhumane treatment, we suggest that they either may be addressed with issue-specific regulatory efforts (such as support for "core" labor standards), or that the remaining moral issues aren't quite weighty enough to de-legitimize a global economy organized as a (sufficiently) internally fair engine for poverty reduction.

Environmental degradation, by contrast, cannot be justified in this way. The natural world is not a beneficiary of economic activity in any straightforward sense (unlike workers in the exploitation case), and in any case the natural world will not somehow fare better on balance for human economic activity, not least because of the grave risks of catastrophic climate change. At the same time, it is also less clear that environmental threats should wholly swamp the human benefits of economic life. Due preservation, rather than economic autarky, seems the reasonable demand, even as that may require deep reform.

2. Labor Exploitation

Consider, then, the exploitation of workers. On one plausible view, exploitation, in the most basic, morally problematic sense, arises in bargaining situations: one party exploits another party only when it uses its superior bargaining position to win terms favorable to it in the agreement being made between them. (The resulting unfair *agreement* can also be said to be exploitative, in a secondary sense, if it resulted, or could only have resulted, from a wrongfully exploitative bargaining process.) What distinguishes morally problematic exploitation from morally innocent ways of "taking advantage of an opportunity" (e.g., sitting outside on a fine day) is the breach of certain fairness expectations: the exploiting party uses its superior bargaining position to get the other to accept an unfair agreement, *in breach of an obligation to instead offer and cooperatively negotiate toward fair terms*. Regardless of what is fair, the party with the upper hand doesn't budge.[2] Consider, for

---

2. This characterization has much in common with Wertheimer, 1996, and Valdman, 2009. Both allow exploitation to be fully voluntary (unlike libertarians and Marxists) and mutually advantageous. Our additional emphasis on the duty to negotiate toward fair terms provides a clearer characterization of the normative significance of exploitation. This meets Feinberg's challenge, 1988, p. 176, to explain why an exploited person

example, the "grand bargain" of the Uruguay Round trade negotiations. The terms of the deal were structurally inequitable (as argued in Chapter 9), and offering them violated a duty of fair governance (as specified in Chapter 3.1). Even so, developing countries had little choice but to agree, having little reason to hope for a better deal. Rich countries wouldn't budge.

Labor relations can also qualify as exploitative in this sense. Consider negotiations between a multinational firm in search of cheap labor and Third World workers for hire. The worker is expected to toil in "sweatshop" conditions—working long hours, at the edge of his or her physical limits, in dangerous conditions, while subject to intimidation and physical or sexual abuse, all for a subsistence wage. Easily replaced by someone else, and without collective bargaining rights, the terms of employment reflect the market price of labor. Since there's scant hope in holding out for better conditions or pay, the worker has little choice but to agree. If the resulting terms are unfair, in breach of an obligation on the part of managers to offer fair remuneration and decent conditions for work, the resulting agreement is or reflects exploitation in a basic, morally objectionable sense.

The question, then, is, Do firms or managers have such an obligation to offer better terms? Economists, as well as some journalists from the left, often suggest that they do not, since "bad jobs at low wages are better than no jobs at all."[3] As Paul Krugman

---

who gains from the transaction can nevertheless bear a grievance against the exploiter: the exploited person, we are suggesting, was subjected to a wrongful bargaining process. Our suggestion is also consistent with the emphasis in Satz, 2010, p. 157, on "weak agency," and the similar focus in Miller, 2010, p. 60ff, on weak bargaining position that cripples agency due to urgent conditions (such as poverty).

We assume that hard bargaining, innocent haggling, or market exchange can be permissible in many cases. The duty to cooperatively negotiate toward fair terms will apply when the structure of a social practice is to be fairly governed, or when there are real risks that inequalities in bargaining power will lead to domination or preying upon agential weakness and/or circumstantial misfortune. The duty might also apply in interesting cases in which people cooperatively negotiate toward what would or should be the market price, when that is unclear, on the assumption that this is fair. The duty would be violated, for example, when a seller raises prices in light of particularities of a buyer that aren't reflected in "local" supply or demand.

3. Krugman, 1997b.

explains, before multinational firms found it worthwhile to set up operations in Third World countries, limited and largely protected manufacturing wasn't creating a lot of jobs, while farm work and wages were under pressure from rising populations. The jobs are bad by our standards, but often better paying than any most people would otherwise have.

As we now explain, there is an element of truth here, but we have to dig pretty deep through the standard economic arguments to see what it is. Initially, the economist's reply seems to misunderstand the kind of moral concern being addressed. In general, to say someone has been made better off isn't to say that he or she hasn't been wrongfully exploited. Suppose, for example, that, when you are stranded along a seldom traveled road, imperiled by the impending freezing nighttime cold, I could save your life by selling you my spare tire. I would wrongfully exploit you if my price is, say, $10,000. If you happen to have the money and pay, you will be better off overall; $10,000 is cheap if you do indeed avoid likely death. Similarly, the sweatshop laborer can be made better off than he would otherwise be and still be wrongfully exploited, because his or her work is not safe enough, or because he or she isn't better paid.

Another common argument for sweatshops also fails to appreciate the charge of exploitation. It is commonly noted that workers enthusiastically accept sweatshop jobs as they are and even compete to be hired. But this isn't to say workers aren't being exploited, since exploitation usually involves voluntary agreements. When you bought my spare tire, you could have freely chosen our mutually beneficial arrangement, in the sense that you were free to take or leave my proposed deal. I didn't hold a gun to your head or even try to persuade you to accept. Yet the deal could still be wrongfully exploitative if my obligation was to ask only for a fair price (perhaps the cost to me of replacing my tire, and some compensation for my troubles).

The same point holds for another standard economic argument. The economist will suggest that if too many demands on the multinational firm are made, it will have no incentive to stay. When it packs up and leaves, many, many people, usually very poor, will be deprived of jobs that pay substantially better than any they would otherwise have. But, again, the firm's departure may simply mean that there will be much less wrongful exploitation going on. Nor will it necessarily help to add that the people not being benefited are desperately poor. This may only explain why it is so easy to exploit them, not why seemingly exploitative relations are ultimately justified.

The question, then, is, What more needs to be said if a defense of sweatshop labor is to address, rather than simply dismiss, the exploitation charge? Two further economic arguments are more promising, yet similarly incomplete. The first is that sweatshops raise standards of living over time, because of systemic spillover effects. When sweatshops draw people away from rural areas and thereby reduce the rural labor supply, rural wages tend to rise. In urban areas, as employment and productivity levels rise, firms must compete for a shrinking pool of workers, at higher and higher wage rates.[4] Empirical studies do seem to confirm consistent wage increases over time.[5] Nevertheless, everything still depends on *how quickly* and *how high* wages rise. You can't tell a sweatshop worker that her wage is not exploitative because, although *she* will never see more than modest benefit, her child will have a substantially better life. The benefit of rising wages must accrue to her, in a sufficiently short period of time, or at a sufficiently rapid rate of increase, if the current burdens of arduous work are to be justified.

The second argument is that as firms share information about problem solving and best practices, the health and safety threats usually associated with sweatshops tend to diminish over time. Again it matters how quickly conditions improve. But there are also limits on how bad workplace conditions can be. If the risks of serious injury or death are very substantial, some workers will be irreparably harmed. If the risk imposed upon workers is grave enough, it will not be justified by future gains, even when workers are lucky enough not to get hurt.

Now, the force of these concerns does seem to depend on the larger context of economic development. By relying on sweatshop labor, developing countries can reduce or eliminate poverty across large numbers of people, while at least mitigating the worst health and safety threats. Several development success stories could be cited as cases in point. While the reality of poverty and the possibility of its end do help the argument for sweatshops, it is important to examine the form these considerations

4. Krugman, 1997b.
5. Bhagwati, 2004, ch. 10.

take. According to "negative utilitarianism," for example, sweatshop labor would only have to minimize poverty in the aggregate. Huge costs could still fall to an unlucky few, and many poor workers might be left worse off or no better off over the course of their lives. But if our concern is to answer, rather than simply dismiss, the charge of wrongful exploitation, then this is precisely what we cannot say. We presumably aren't prepared to accept what negative utilitarianism would recommend: that a state regime of child labor and child prostitution could be justified if only it could be shown to cause a steady rise in living standards. Harnessing market forces in this way, whether for poverty reduction or any other goal, is a paradigm case of wrongful exploitation.

We do respond to the exploitation charge on its own terms, however, if we instead say this: market-oriented labor policy is a necessary measure for poverty reduction, and such measures are not unfair, at least when suitably embedded in supporting social institutions. The idea might be developed as a basic thought implicit in the social contract tradition (especially Rawls's theory of justice) and its implicit answer to Marxist concerns with labor exploitation. The idea is that it is or can be fair for the capitalist to "exploit" the worker (in Marx's technical sense of expropriating the surplus of his labor) if, but only if, this is allowed as part of a larger, society-wide fair system of cooperation, whose institutions return real and sufficient benefits to that worker over time. Society assumes responsibility for fairness, taking responsibilities of fair labor remuneration off the labor negotiation table.

Since the story of the social contract is usually told of a closed economy, it must be extended if it is to explain why Third World workers are not exploited by multinationals and the rich-world consumers that keep them in business. The idea might be as follows. While responsibility for fairness to the worker receiving the market wage will partly remain in his society's hands, it does not stop at societal borders; it also falls to the international economic institutions of trade, investment, and aid that shape his or her country's terms of integration into the international market reliance practice, especially insofar as those terms shape the representative worker's life prospects.

Apologists of globalization often defend sweatshop labor against the charge of exploitation on economic grounds and yet remain skeptical about whether any talk of fairness applies either within market relations or in governance of the global economy.⁶ But this, once again, fails to take exploitation seriously. The terms of integration on offer to developing societies themselves shape how workers fare over the course of their lives. A developing country's exposure to global markets is not simply so much good or bad weather, which it can use for good or for ill, much as it might adapt as weather patterns change. While the most successful developing countries have carefully and opportunistically shaped their own terms of global economic integration, how well any country can do is also set by the terms given by other countries in a range of ways. These include a country's degree of policy flexibility under trade, intellectual property, investment, services, and competition rules; its degree of access to rich-country markets (e.g., given rich-country subsidies, anti-dumping protections, etc.); and its degree of access to affordable loans, debt relief, technical assistance, and so on. So long as developing countries can be offered better rather than worse terms, in ways that shape the plight of their workers, the question is simply how much other societies can be asked to sacrifice. But this is a question of fairness—a question of what terms of integration are fair, given the advantages and disadvantages they imply for rich and poor countries alike. Developing-country workers are not exploited only when their countries are offered terms of integration that are themselves fair.

So if we are to answer the charge that "sweatshops" are wrongfully exploitative on its own terms rather than simply dismissing it out of hand, we have to consider fairness at the international level. In particular, we have to worry about a further but related kind of exploitation—rich countries self-interestedly exploiting their bargaining power in international negotiations.⁷ This is one of the main obstacles to international economic fairness of the kind needed to answer the labor exploitation charge. As the case of the Uruguay Round suggests, international negotiations over such terms can be exploitative in our basic, morally objectionable sense. Even if there is a social contract rationale for lifting fairness expectations from the wage bargaining table, they are not eliminated but rather *shifted* to international expectations and the negotiations that shape them.

6. Bhagwati, 2004, ch. 10.
7. See also Miller, 2010.

3. What Terms are Fair?

The question, then, is, What terms for developing countries would be fair? For all we have said so far, the laissez-faire approach suggested by standard economic arguments might be defended *as fair* on the grounds that feasible alternatives are worse from the point of view of poverty relief, and so from the point of view of any conception of fairness that supports trade to that end. If traditional "top-down" regulation based on uniform standards is the only policy alternative, for example, then the economic objections (e.g., of an ensuing labor aristocracy rather than widely shared gains) might yield a conclusion of fairness in our terms: we can't do better for developing-country workers by regulating global labor relations, so laissez-faire is fair.

This argument relies on crude assumptions about the available policy responses, both domestically and internationally. While the best conception of what is fair might recommend market-friendly measures, it arguably requires much more than a policy of laissez-faire.

For one thing, there are some forms of treatment that no worker could reasonably be asked to bear, including physical abuse, sexual intimidation, serious imposed risks of injury, slavery and servitude, and perhaps other conditions ruled out by "core" or "minimum" labor standards.[8] We can regard these as "external" requirements of decent or humane treatment, or even as demands of "non-exploitation" in a sense more basic than exploitation in bargained exchanges or relationships. Some such forms of treatment should simply be stopped, as far as possible, at great socio-economic opportunity cost. Even when enforced standards are unwise (e.g., because they push workers into black market labor, such as prostitution), governments seem required to take up other available measures. They can provide meals at schools, or payments for school attendance to families, in order to reduce family incentives for child labor. They can facilitate coordinative measures such as pooling of information and knowledge of best practices that make basic workplace improvements happen as fast as they possibly can. Where developing countries cannot afford aggressive measures, trading countries are obligated, as a

---

8. See, e.g., Satz, 2010, ch. 8, on bonded labor, which workers and especially children still "voluntarily" adopt in large numbers.

condition of non-exploitation, to offer any necessary and feasible institutional support (whether through ILO technical assistance, low-interest loans, or aid).

This would not automatically preclude a market-oriented labor policy, including the absence of any legally mandated minimum wage (at least before an appropriate stage of development). So we might narrow our question: Are there conditions under which market wages can be non-exploitative and fair?

To answer, consider a closed economy and a talented worker who would be well employed under any labor policy, whether a market-oriented or directly managed scheme that hires the most qualified workers. Suppose he would see greater pay under any managed scheme than under any scheme that leaves wages to the market; he'd get the job even if regulated wages created a privileged labor aristocracy. Call the difference in pay his *market wage disadvantage*. A given level of market wage disadvantage would be justifiable to him, as part of an organized system of cooperation, under any of the following circumstances:

1. The worker could expect future increases in the market wage at a rate and level that compensate for his present wage disadvantage. The increase, for example, might equal or improve upon his total wage income, spread smoothly over the course of his life.
2. The worker could expect future non-wage benefits (such as public health) which compensate for his present wage disadvantage. Such goods may, for example, equal or improve upon his total life prospects (measures in both income and non-income based terms).
3. Other people, who are equally poor or poorer, could expect comparable benefits, in wage or non-wage terms. The benefit might be, for example, employment in a sweatshop that, despite paying the market wage, pays substantially better than other jobs (given the need to draw people from rural areas). It may well be reasonable not to legally mandate a minimum wage so that as many as possible are gainfully employed.

It may seem in this last case that the talented worker could reasonably object that he is being exploited for the gain of others. Yet if the gain to others is large enough, or the others are sufficiently badly off, it is hard to find this very plausible. So long as there really is no other feasible way to benefit equally poor or poorer others, this might justify smaller benefits for everyone, over the course of each person's life. It may slow everyone's rise.

This suggests that equitable poverty reduction can justify sweatshop labor in a closed economy, in a way that answers the charge of labor exploitation on its own terms. Our concern is globalization, so we should now ask: What difference does it make that many (but not all) sweatshops are in fact run by multinational firms and the rich-world consumption that keep them in business?

We've already suggested that global integration has to make *some* difference, if only because developing countries can thereby be offered better or worse terms. Still, one might object that this needn't be a question of fairness but merely a humanitarian question of why and how to aid people who are often desperately poor. While humanity is of course a paramount external moral concern, the present arguments can also be restricted to the benefits and burdens jointly created by the international market reliance practice. Because its benefits are jointly created, no society can lay proprietary claim to them, and because burdens are distributed in different ways, according to different terms of integration, there is a distinct question of what distribution is fair to all parties involved. In principle, a developing country's fair share of gains may or may not bring all or many of its workers out of poverty, in which case developing-country workers cannot necessarily claim freedom from poverty as a right of fairness, even if they could still press humanitarian claims to aid. And even if fair terms of integration would relieve poverty, we cannot assume workers are no longer being exploited. Their societies still may not have received terms of integration that would have made them still better off, and which were only fair.

One might instead object that in that case, the demands of fairness are modest; perhaps the terms of integration on offer need only be of *some* benefit to developing societies as compared to economic autarky. Again, however, mere benefit will not necessarily answer the exploitation charge. Our question is when the developing-country worker is no longer exploited in being asked to labor for the benefit of rich-world consumers, for the market wage. But as we argued in a similar connection in Chapters 7.6 and 9.5, it seems the sweatshop worker can reasonably demand the best possible terms of integration for his or her society, as assessed in terms of its development goals, including those that improve labor conditions.

This is so unless there is some reason that advanced countries can reasonably demand something less, so that rich people see even greater gains. But it is not clear that there are cases of this kind. Since the "losers" from trade in rich countries can usually be compensated directly without trade protection of a kind that hurts the developing world, the question is only the level of advanced country gain, in terms of cheaper goods and services, rising levels of real income, and ever higher living standards. But it seems that rich people can be reasonably asked to gain less if this improves terms of economic integration for developing countries, provided the benefits are well distributed within developing countries over time. Greater relative benefits fairly flow to people who tend to be badly off in absolute terms. This is the element of truth in the rich-world consumers' willingness to pay more for sneakers, televisions, or soccer balls so that those who have labored to produce them can have what amounts to more than a few cents of each item produced. It is not the pay per item that matters but rather that the worker's society integrates into the global economy on terms that advance his or her working conditions and pay.

4. Trade and Labor Linkage

What "terms of integration" might be called for? Should we, say, add a "social clause" to the WTO so that labor standards become enforceable against developing countries by threat of trade sanctions?[9] Developing countries strongly resist an enforceable "social clause." Rich countries, it is reasonably feared, will have yet another pretext for denying access to their markets by developing-country producers, while enforced standards may be insufficiently sensitive to local context and potentially counterproductive.

As Christian Barry and Sanjay Reddy have explained, however, these and other standard objections do not apply to a trade and labor linkage based in "carrots" rather than "sticks."[10] On an incentives-based linkage scheme, advanced countries would make

---

9. For discussion of legal issues, see Leary, 1996, and Howse, 1999.
10. Barry and Reddy, 2008, carefully show that "linkage" would not be self-defeating or inconsequential, clearly inferior to more modest measures, unfair in the distribution of burdens, or context-blind and imperialistic.

a standing offer of tariff cuts in exchange for credible increases in developing-country labor standards. The offer would stand within a larger voluntary system, administered with both the ILO and WTO, which sets standards and provides peer review, technical assistance, and dispute adjudication. As "policy swaps" are made, perhaps in conjunction with normal WTO negotiations, the trading system would thus exert a strong upward pressure for developing countries to increase labor standards as quickly as their specific economic circumstances allow.

To see why this is necessary, compare a more modest "within country linkage" proposal by trade economists Bagwell, Mavroidis, and Staiger (on which Barry and Reddy build).[11] The proposal starts from the observation that a change in a developing country's labor standards can have untoward distributional effects either on its own producers (because higher standards raise cost of production) or on their trade partners (e.g., lower standards in "large" countries may create "terms of trade externalities"). But governments can also *neutralize* these outcomes by making appropriate further adjustments to their own trade policies (with further subsidies or tariffs). The idea, then, is that if governments were allowed and expected to take such neutralizing measures (with minor changes to WTO law),[12] this would correct perverse incentives of at least two kinds.

First, it would remove a standing "race to the bottom" incentive to *lower* standards in order to give domestic producers competitive advantages over foreign firms. For any loss in market access to foreign producers (e.g., relative to previously negotiated commitments) would have to be neutralized by a compensating reduction in tariffs (or equivalent subsidies, etc.). Second, it would also remove a "regulatory chill" disincentive faced by developing countries considering *raising* labor standards. Faced with prospects of increasing domestic cost of production and injury to some of the very workers whose prospects they are trying to improve, developing-country governments would be allowed to shelter

11. Bagwell et al., 2002; Bagwell and Staiger, 2001, 2002.
12. As suggested in Bagwell et al., 2002, p. 68, this requires a modest extension of GATT Article 28, amended as, "If they so decide, WTO members wishing to raise their labor standards and implement the standards reflected in the ILO Conventions will be allowed to raise the level of their bound duties without incurring the obligation to compensate the injured WTO members."

import-competing industries with appropriate tariff or other barriers. The trade partners affected could accept this because they would, in theory, be no worse off overall: they would lose from the new trade barrier but also see compensating gains as improvements in the developing-country labor standards improve the competitive position of their firms.

Is such "within country linkage" sufficient? Or is there a fairness rationale for the more ambitious "across country linkage" scheme that Barry and Reddy defend? There is insofar as fairness requires "terms of integration" that improve wages and working conditions in developing countries as much as possible. For mere expectations of neutralization will not create an *upward* pressure on labor standards; they only remove obstacles to improvement by eliminating perverse incentives that arise at any level at which standards are set (by sovereign preferences, which are simply assumed to include a preference for standard increases). By contrast, a cross-country "trade for labor" linkage system, in conjunction with neutralization measures, creates powerful *economic* incentives for labor standard improvement over time. Developing countries would receive market access they often want anyway, and, no less important, the burden of managing distributional outcomes would fairly fall chiefly to advanced countries. Developing countries often lack the resources to fund optimal neutralization measures (e.g., export subsidies).[13] But even when better-off, middle-income developing countries do have the funds, advanced countries will still more readily afford to manage internal distributive concerns (e.g., those hurt by rising labor standards may not be those who are helped by the neutralizing trade policy change).

On the present suggestion, then, a trade and labor "linkage" would supplement what may be less reliable ways of creating incentives for labor standard improvement (e.g., in exchange for

---

13. In defending the neutralization proposals, Bagwell (in Barry and Reddy, 2008, p. 110) mentions the desirability of relaxing WTO restrictions on export subsidies in order to facilitate "within country linkage"; he also points out that developing countries may well lack the necessary resources. He suggests that this may require measures of support (e.g., cash transfers or low-income loans) but does not treat this specifically as a fairness concern. We are suggesting that it is a fairness concern and that it supports a system that tends to give rich countries the role of making neutralization adjustments. On the more general value of export subsidies, see Bagwell and Staiger, 2006.

low-interest loans, debt relief, or aid). Indeed, the trading system is a natural place to address the labor exploitation issue, since concerns of labor exploitation are at least partly *internal* to the socioeconomic relationship. The question is why the issue of labor exploitation *shouldn't* be addressed in the trading system, not why it should be. If the concern were a purely external (e.g., humanitarian) issue, it could perhaps be handled equally well through independent channels. But concerns with labor exploitation are only partly an external human rights or humanitarian concern; the concern, again, is also in part whether workers are fairly paid.

5. Transnational Action and Inherited Obligations

All of this is of course subject to potentially serious concerns about the limits of traditional top-down government regulation. Especially in weak regulatory environments, improvements in legal standards may or may not mean improvements in actual working conditions or wages of the desired kinds. What is wanted, ideally, are measures that nudge and encourage markets to themselves improve productivity, wages, and working conditions as broadly and as quickly as possible, under prevailing circumstances, without untoward side effects.

Fairness requires governments to adopt such measures as they become available. That will at least mean supporting transnational initiatives and movements based in ethical consumerism, as promoted by numerous civil society organizations (including transnational social movements, coalitions, activist campaigns, formal nongovernmental organizations).[14] Consumers now support workers by paying slightly higher prices for goods imported through various "fair trade" cooperatives and certification schemes. Due mainly to consumer pressure, multinational firms now routinely adopt codes of conduct related to their treatment of

---

14. This is emphasized in the "ratcheting" proposal offered by Fung et al., 2001. The proposal is offered as an alternative to "conventional top-down regulation based on uniform standards," but as distinct from laissez-faire "reliance on voluntary initiatives taken by corporations in response to social protest." For discussion of the nature and importance of the larger trend, see Ruggie, 2004.

developing-country workers, with independent performance review by an emerging reporting and certification industry, which is increasingly able to verify desired features of the entire production and distribution process. To the extent that firms sincerely seek to live up to their promises, as many do, they can often exert enormous influence down through their supply chains, all the way to the factory floor. This leads to real material improvements within contracting firms and local enterprises in the same sector.

International institutions have already begun to support such measures.[15] Along with a collaborative initiative between the ILO and the World Bank's International Finance Corporation, the UN Global Compact has an increasingly wide membership, including many developing-country firms that join the initiative to enhance their ability to enter into supplier relationships with larger global firms. The Global Compact specifies obligations for firms (including annual reporting on progress and participation in learning networks aimed to identify and disseminate good practices) but also provides active support of public/private partnerships in developing countries (e.g., through micro-lending, HIV/AIDS awareness programs for employees, alternatives to child labor, initiatives on eco-efficiency). The effort is not a purely humanitarian venture but is explicitly founded upon principles established by governments, through international agreements (especially ILO conventions). We are suggesting that such measures are also required for reasons of fairness internal to the internationally organized global economy.

Those same reasons require particular governments to directly support transnational measures as much as possible, in whatever ways seem to work. Belgium, France, Netherlands, Sweden, and the UK are already encouraging or requiring firms to engage in non-financial reporting. Other governments should follow suit, with additional policies to support firms in adopting the measures that best advance worker prospects (e.g., measures to encourage collaborative information sharing and problem solving rather than police-like inspections, and technical and organizational assistance with management systems).[16] This should become standard

---

15. For the developments mentioned in the text below, see Ruggie, 2004.
16. Evidence from Nike's aggressive voluntary regulatory efforts suggests that monitoring helps, but with considerable variation across regions and factories, and not to a large and sustained degree (Locke et al., 2007).

international practice, as a condition of fairness in trade with developing countries.

Still, if we have so far focused on governmental responsibilities, one might wonder whether our sense of fairness in shared economic relationships is fully captured in specifically international terms. Might it instead reflect a "cosmopolitan" market relationship of a direct kind that our international approach is unable to account for? Indeed, the transnational movement among civil society organizations and multinational firms began independent of government initiatives, and it is at least partly motivated by a sense of complicity in potentially exploitative wages or conditions for developing-country workers. Many consumers feel this way, but many owners and managers of firms share the sense as well, even as they also adopt codes of conduct to minimize marketing risks (perhaps many express their underlying ethical motivation in such economic terms; a *morally legitimate* public relations fiasco seems especially embarrassing).

We can happily admit that market actors *inherit* transnational obligations of fairness as a result of economic relationships created by a basically international market reliance practice. That is, in principle, the global economy could be sufficiently well embedded within domestic and international institutions such that market actors would have minimal fairness responsibilities (not to coerce, deceive, monopolize, and so on), much as within the central domestic markets of advanced countries. But, in fact, the global economy is so far only weakly embedded in institutions that support developing countries and their workers. It is not producing the outcomes required by principles of structural equity (in no small part because of lacking political will). As a consequence of this larger regulatory failure, we may say, actors inherit obligations to take more direct action. Thus consumers and managers moved by a sense of complicity rightly sense that too little is being done to fulfill international obligations of structural equity and so seek ways of taking matters into their own hands. The

---

Nike has now shifted from policing to sharing knowledge of best practices among suppliers, and further evidence suggests that ongoing communication, information sharing, and joint problem solving is more effective than regular "inspections" (Locke et al., 2009). Still more effective is technical and organizational assistance in implementing management systems (Locke et al., 2007).

obligations could well turn out to be temporary, falling away when or if functionally embedding institutions take on a more robust form. But even if the day of equity takes a very long time, or never comes, they remain ultimately of an international kind.[17]

It is a further, more difficult question what our inherited obligations include. They at least require us to hold leaders accountable for their acts and omissions (as many civil society organizations now do worldwide), as well as to advance structural equity in quasi-political roles (e.g., corporations that assume state-like governance functions). They also require us to promote structurally equitable outcomes directly, at least as far as we reasonably can within our limited powers. The matter is unavoidably uncertain for any particular market actor and requires good faith efforts even within established international or industry expectations and best practices. Beyond that, rough guidelines for multinationals might include things such as erring in the direction of costly improvements, insisting only on the part of the surplus needed to stay profitable, and otherwise seeking profit margins at around the rough level needed to generally induce production relations that do the most good for the developing country over time.

Such obligations seem to vary in stringency depending on one's relation to the relevant outcomes. Multinational firms directly involved in setting the terms of production—even if from far up the supply chain—have an especially direct relation to the worker's plight, and so especially stringent obligations. As consumers, our relation to developing-country workers is more indirect. When I buy coffee that partly originates from a producer who is poorly paid, I may in some sense be complicit in his unfair treatment, but I am not engaged directly in an unfair exchange, if only because a vast network of supply chains, intermediate inputs, consumers, and workers stands between my act of purchase and his act of sale. When the coffee farmer is treated unfairly, it is by the larger system of domestic and international market relations that together give him less than his due.

17. Perhaps the responsibility to promote domestic structural equity will never be removed completely from the market actor's plate in advanced countries. The suggested contrast with advanced-country markets only marks a difference of degree in regulatory embedding. In either the domestic or international case, the general point is that principles are justified for the social structure in question, and only secondarily as obligations for market actors with a system.

This internationalist conception of transnational obligations makes no essential reference to obligations of fair exchange. This is a considerable advantage given how difficult it is to specify such obligations in any generally applicable way.[18] Inherited obligations of structural equity do not apply in virtue of specific transactional circumstances but in virtue of the overall economic relationship. If we are to promote the outcomes required for a structurally equitable international practice, at least as far as we reasonably can within our limited information and resources and the going efforts of other actors, what that entails is not a question of transactional fairness but a question for the "ethics" of complicity. The question, that is, is what and how much I must do given my particular role in the going unfair system of cooperation. My obligation is not something as simple as "stop taking advantage of the farmer," as though we are involved in a direct exchange. The moral question is more complicated, being sensitive to a broader range of questions arising from my more indirect role in the larger economic practice (e.g., Shall I sometimes buy certified coffee? Or always do so? At what cost? Even at a cost to other moral issues, e.g., money sent to direct foreign aid?). Most important, my inherited obligation is sensitive to what consumption behavior would support domestic or international efforts to make the global economy fairer to developing countries, especially as they seek to improve their position in the international division of labor.[19]

---

18. Miller, manuscript, sympathetically examines different ideas of fair exchange and their limitations. Our general appeal to structural equity can readily absorb elements of those ideas, such as basic entitlements to a "living wage," though that may or may not support state-enforced minimum wages. See also Miller, 1987, p. 162, and discussion by Wolff, 1998.
19. Economists often object that "fair trade" coffee and other cooperatives are perhaps of humanitarian significance but otherwise inefficient: if producers are "underpaid," that is a market signal to shift into more profitable enterprise, all as part of refining the generally beneficial division of labor. Here a basic fairness issue is whether developing countries are afforded the opportunities and support to shift away from raw materials and other low-income production and toward higher-skilled, higher-return industry; this is the road out of poverty and may involve putting farmers to work doing different things from what they do now. But cooperatives can also support such government efforts if only by providing crucial transitional support.

In sum, then, the socioeconomic advantages created by global economic integration seem to justify what might otherwise be objectionably inhumane or degrading treatment of workers. We can rightly give developing countries fair terms instead of simply closing down the global economy.

6. Due Preservation

Concerns with environmental degradation cannot be answered in this way. The natural environment is not somehow *itself* better off for the emergence of a global economy among human beings. The global economy largely exacerbates (but sometimes mitigates) the plunder of nature.[20] And in any case, it is not the essential source of our major environmental problems. A world of isolated industrialized societies could equally have generated the carbon emissions that now threaten to trigger potentially catastrophic climate change, and each society would still face familiar local questions about how far to use its natural setting for the sake of human and economic benefit. The existence of a global economy merely poses the problem of the value of nature on a grand scale. We therefore face a starker question, about the significance of nature and its potential conflict with economic value generally speaking.

This problem becomes less interesting if we treat environmental degradation as ultimately about the interests or claims of people. It is quite true that one cannot ultimately separate questions of how we treat "nature" from how we treat each other. Human life is too profoundly affected by the conditions of the natural world. And it is at least arguable that people have a right of property (perhaps held by humanity in common) over how nature is used. Familiar anthropocentric views see no further issue of environmental preservation, beyond such human interests or claims. But this is to

---

20. Bhagwati, 2004, pp. 139–40, notes examples of both exacerbation and mitigation. On the one hand, the rapid expansion of coastal shrimp farming since the 1980s in Asia and Latin America, in part due to increasing trade, has destroyed mangrove forests and depleted fish stocks. On the other hand, freed trade can also mitigate environmental harm, as when the removal of automobile quotas in Japan reduced pollution. The quotas made it most profitable for Japanese automakers to export larger, more consumptive cars given their greater profit margin as compared to smaller, fuel-efficient autos.

sidestep the deepest potential conflict between the value of human benefit and the value of nature. For insofar as we have weighty reasons to preserve or respect the natural environment (whether trees, eco-systems, or nature as a whole) for its own sake, we may well be required to adjust or abandon basic economic arrangements, and perhaps give up entirely on an economy of global size.

The basic question, then, is the value of preservation (as opposed to mere "conservation," for human benefit). To pose this question in its sharpest form, we can assume for the sake of argument that our natural environment (somehow specified) gives us good reasons of due preservation and respect, taken simply by itself.[21] The question is what these reasons require. In the remainder of this chapter, we offer remarks on various aspects of the potential conflict between human and environmental value—not to somehow settle the issue, but, again, simply to suggest that sensible conclusions are fully consistent with the overall argument of this book. We conclude by considering a conflict of a deep and potentially revolutionary kind.

A conflict with economics? Economic theory itself provides no reason to deny or minimize the intrinsic value of environmental preservation, quite aside from its service to human interests.[22] While economists have often treated nature as part of a country's capital stock, to be exploited for the benefit of people, they increasingly assume that our relation to the environment is an irreducibly ethical question. Many economists suggest that growth rates should be calculated in light of their environmental impact, by deducting environmental costs.[23] Moreover, even consummate market apologists happily admit that, when it comes to nature, the political economy of laissez-faire is fundamentally misplaced.[24]

---

21. Nature is "valuable" in the sense that we have reason to value it, as according to Anderson, 1993, and Scanlon, 1998, ch. 2.
22. As noted in Chapter 8.3, perfectly competitive markets require the absence of "negative externalities." Environmental degradation manifestly qualifies.
23. For proposals, see Nordhaus and Tobin, 1973; Daly, 1989, chs. 6 and 7; Arrow et al., 2004.
24. When Bhagwati, 2004, p. 145, explains why a pollutant such as sulfur dioxide initially increases with economic development but then declines as incomes rise, he mentions the essential role of environmental regulations spurred by increased public consciousness and environmentalist activist groups.

The question is not whether to regulate but what form regulation should take. For there is no reason at all to think that markets left to themselves will somehow reliably balance commercial interests and the real value of preserving the natural world for its own sake (whatever it is). Even when the question is not a matter of domestic or international law, because resource use is well regulated by informal social practice,[25] it is still a question of how governments might have a supporting role.

Unfair conservation burdens. One question, then, is how global economic governance might show appropriate sensitivity to external environmental values *and* internal socioeconomic fairness concerns when they interact. The basic rationales for major international environmental arrangements, whether for cross-border pollution or climate change, are not necessarily socioeconomic. But because any serious arrangements will regulate economic activity or at least have economic consequences, the form they take will often raise questions of socioeconomic equity in a straightforward way. In particular, it seems unfair to ask developing countries to forgo economic gains (the gains of trade, or otherwise) when rich countries can bear the economic sacrifices of environmental conservation instead.

This is true for any of several reasons.[26] First, very poor people require economically beneficial uses of natural resources (through pollution or carbon emissions) in order to work their way out of poverty, or even just sustain material subsistence. Second, even if relatively (even if not absolutely) poor countries were to forgo economic activity at the same level (or even the same percentage of GDP) as advanced countries, they would still bear the greater sacrifice. The forgone level of activity will be a greater loss for those less well-off. Third, industrialization has largely created the problem in many important cases (as with global climate change). So it seems fair to ask advanced countries to "clean up their mess." Developing countries should of course take care not to make the problems unnecessarily worse (e.g., through deforestation), let alone insist on making the needless mistakes advanced countries made (because it is "our turn"). And larger emitters (e.g., China and India) can perhaps be fairly asked to address their own contribution to the problem, taking into account the two further fairness

25. Ostrom, 1990.
26. Shue, 1999.

considerations just mentioned. Otherwise, however, it seems unreasonable to ask developing countries to bear very much if any of the cost of advanced countries' historical process of enrichment. The case is much like this one: a gold prospector pollutes the nearby farmer's stream, striking it very rich. He then brazenly asks the farmer to pay for costly repairs.

Competitive fairness? More complicated is the question of how such considerations should shape specific governance arrangements. A relatively autonomous environmental agreement is clearly required; trade law and policy are plainly unsuited to establish the large-scale market arrangements needed for credible efforts to curb carbon-induced global warming trends, whether by regulation (e.g., carbon taxes) or market creation (e.g., a cap-and-trade system)—although the WTO judicial system could potentially help with enforcement of an independent agreement. Insofar as distinct regulatory systems are established, they can of course come into conflict, as they would, for example, if carbon taxes were illegal under WTO law, or if economic integration generally triggered an environmental "race to the bottom" as governments reduce environmental standards in order to compete for foreign investment.

These last two concerns are apparently not real conflicts.[27] Yet a similarly general conflict might arise from worries about "unfair competition." Insofar as relatively lax environmental standards in developing countries give domestic firms a significant and unfair advantage over their foreign rivals in cost of production, trade barriers might be required to remove the disadvantage and "level the playing field."

We argued in Chapter 9.4 that concerns of "competitive unfairness," though valid in principle, are highly sensitive to their embedding social context of competition—in this case, a relationship in which competitive market relations are used to mutual country advantage. So if competitive advantages for firms result from different environmental or other standards, and this is concordant with the purposes of the trading system and its overall demands of structural equity for countries, they are perfectly fair.

---

27. Carbon taxes would not be illegal so long as they are applied in non-discriminatory ways or founded in the values specified in GATT Article 20. For evidence that there is no "race to the bottom," and indeed considerable "trading up," see Vogel, 1995, Garcia-Johnson, 2000, and Elliott and Freeman, 2003.

We suggested that there is no competitive unfairness when developing-country firms benefit from different or lower regulatory standards and lower costs of production, since developing countries fairly receive unequal gains from trade. But developing countries and their firms can also fairly benefit from competitive advantages that accrue to regulatory difference; everything depends on its grounds. For example, a regulatory difference may credibly fall under a legitimate social purpose open to all governments (e.g., as specified in GATT Article 20 under general headings such as the "conservation of exhaustible natural resources" or the protection of "human, plant, or animal life or health"). When regulatory differences grounded in such values create market advantages for domestic firms over firms abroad, they may not be unfair but rather part and parcel of a larger international economic relationship that is itself structurally equitable because duly sensitive to a range of legitimate internal and external social concerns.

Moralistic protectionism? It is of course precisely here that developing countries often complain of moralistic protectionism. In the infamous Dolphin/Tuna case, for example, the U.S. prohibited import of tuna caught in tropical oceans with dolphin-killing nets with the clear intent of regulating economic activity and conservation abroad. When Mexico formally complained, arguing that the U.S. had in effect illegally discriminated between different goods based on their process of production, they won. GATT rules, the panel of judges argued, sought precisely to constrain such cases of de facto discrimination, even when supposedly based in moral preferences. Ultimately, however, the U.S. prevailed. On appeal, under the new auspices of the WTO, the Appellate Body affirmed the legality of measures aimed at "sustainable development," on the grounds that it is mentioned in the preamble to the WTO treaty.

Neither the WTO preamble nor the Appellate Body offers a specific definition of what "sustainable development" would include or exclude, and herein lies the chief source of frustration for "free traders." Given such vague value-laden terms, it seems almost any "beggar-thy-neighbor" policy, whether a tariff or regulation "behind the border," can be rationalized under some moral value or other. Why aren't advanced countries thus given yet another opportunity to moralistically raise regulatory standards while in effect imposing an impossible burden upon small, developing-country producers?

For the "free trader," the open-endedness of moral language seems ripe for protectionist abuse and so would be better handled by a technocratic application of trade rules.

The real threat, however, is not the specter of values, per se, but rather *unfairness* in the system of trade. As discussed above, it is unfair for any number of reasons to ask developing countries to bear the economic cost of conservation when rich countries could shoulder much of that burden instead. At the very least, rich countries initiating environmental action can provide accompanying measures of mitigation and compensation for the economic activity forgone. To adopt a fully legal trade restriction in the name of environmental concern without such supportive measures is not simply to insist that developing countries do their part. It is to force them to carry the onerous load of poverty *and* shared environmental concerns. Legal "fair play" does not amount to fairness per se.

Preserving what is. While WTO law is at least broadly consistent with such fairness concerns, it does not clearly register the value of preserving natural forms for what they already are. It does register concerns to prevent harm to plants and animals, for instance, by pests, toxins, or disease that spread through international trade. But if a trade measure for that end is not already recognized by established international standards, it can only be justified on a strictly precautionary basis, according to the scientific evidence about the potential threat.[28] A society is not expected to risk real health or environmental injury when the evidence is incomplete and time is needed for scientific study and debate (say, over the consequences of genetically engineered, pest-resistant crops).[29] When the jury returns without scientific evidence, however, discriminatory trade restrictions are forbidden. They aren't allowed, for example, simply as a way of preserving natural life forms for what they already are, aside from the risks of scientifically specifiable harm.

Is this fair? Many people value growing and eating fully organic corn or soybeans instead of genetically modified versions (whose

---

28. According to WTO sanitary (human and animal health) and phyto-sanitary (plant health) rules (SPS), measures to protect the spread of pests, toxins, and disease must be founded either on (1) established international standards or (2) on context-specific scientific evidence of a threat to a natural form.
29. SPS, Article 5.

chief purpose is to reduce farmer pest control costs). Health fears aside, the preference may simply be for received objects of value, whether natural or artificial. There is nothing unreasonable in wishing to preserve an existing fine sculpture instead of destroying it for a slightly better replacement (even with assurances, let us suppose, of the increase in quality): the valuable things we already have may be worth preserving simply for their own sakes.[30] In that case, especially with valued foods, one can reasonably be concerned when chances are good that one's favored object of preservation will go largely extinct or become significantly altered, for instance, because engineered crops will drive organic products out of the market (because farmers save so much growing the engineered plants). If a society is already adapting to a good deal of technology-induced change, can't it draw some kind of line?

To be sure, the harder question is how to politically define such special protected categories. Accountability to evidence does seem appropriate to discourage purely fabricated value concerns aimed *simply* to protect domestic producers from market competition. The present concern needn't be of this kind (indeed, the preferred organic products may need to be imported). Nor should we deny that "nature" and "artifice" deeply intermingle, or fail to appreciate the impressive history of technological intervention in increasing crop yields, reducing long-term food prices, and increasing incomes, especially for poor people with food-heavy budgets (as in the Green Revolution in Asia). One can generally welcome such economic gains, and yet insist that certain valuable things should in any case be preserved for what they already are. Nor need preservation come at any economic cost. Developing countries that stand to reap large gains from production in genetically modified crops should presumably go ahead with them, and rich countries (even or especially in the EU) may well be obliged in fairness to support this by removing market barriers, because it is still more important to support the economic development of poor people.[31] Still, this is only to say that the needs of poor people may *override* the value of conserving organic crops and food. It is not to say that the preservation value is of no significance or properly excluded from consideration in trade policy.

30. Cohen, 2011.
31. Anderson and Jackson, 2006.

332   FAIRNESS IN PRACTICE

7. Fundamental Challenges

We have been considering ways that the value of nature might shape economic relations. We close by considering the further possibility that it could not only shape but override the human benefits of global economic life, leaving the very existence of a global economy unjustified. One version of this fundamental challenge simply attaches little or no significance to human benefit, except as part of larger nature. We will not try to answer this view.[32] We simply assume that people matter, for their own sakes, independent of any role they may have in the natural order of things, in order to focus on a more plausible but also potentially radical challenge.

Even if environmental protection is not all important, it could still override the human benefits of global economic activity because those benefits are relatively insignificant. Consider, in this light, Rawls's cautions about wealth:

> It is a mistake to believe that a just and good society must wait upon a high material standard life. What men want is meaningful work in free association with others, these associations regulating their relations to one another within a framework of just basic institutions. To achieve this state of things great wealth is not necessary. In fact, beyond some point it is more likely to be a positive hindrance, a meaningless distraction at best if not a temptation to indulgence and emptiness.[33]

Rawls makes these remarks while discussing a society's obligation to save for future generations, in order to suggest that a given generation needn't be saddled with an onerous burden to save. A given generation can justly consume a good measure of the social product, since "Justice does not require that early generations save so that later ones are simply more wealthy." Rawls emphasizes that this is merely a point about justice, admitting that "further wealth might not be superfluous for some purposes." Still, his

---

32. And in any case, how many environmentalists—even the most "romantic" among them—would truly advocate a wholesale return to the pre-industrial world of subsistence living, as opposed to more environmentally conscious ways of living and aggressive environmental regulations of economic life?
33. Rawls, 1971, p. 290.

comments suggest a challenge to our assumption that all countries have a significant interest in greater rather than lesser shares of the fruit of international social cooperation.

We suggested in Chapter 6.5 that while developing countries (or future generations) have a special interest in augmented shares, rich countries also have a more general interest in the standard of living increases that the global economy creates. But if ever-greater wealth is "a meaningless distraction at best if not a temptation to indulgence and emptiness," as it surely can be, then that assumed interest may seem of insufficient significance to permit any real degradation of nature. In other words, a global economy that threatens nature might need to have only certain limited roles. It might be justified *only* to the extent that it is necessary to help reduce absolute poverty and secure what Rawls calls "decent" social conditions, for current societies and future generations. That may or may not leave us with a global economy of any significance.

This argument will have considerable force if the global economy substantially contributes to global ecological ruin (e.g., as on entirely possible doomsday outcomes of climate change) merely for the sake of further enriching the affluent in rich countries. On the other hand, the moral situation substantially improves insofar as the global economy contributes to the reduction of poverty on an enormous scale. It improves still further to the extent that the global economy is structurally equitable, offering widely shared benefits. Indeed, the remaining question, it would seem, is then simply whether the real risks of ecological ruin can be aggressively addressed with regulation and measures of "sustainable growth." And this is arguably the case: the costs of aggressive measures of prevention, mitigation, and compensation are, in fact, relatively trivial in overall cost-benefit terms.[34]

This reasoning assumes that advanced countries have a legitimate interest in ever-greater wealth. Why would that be so? Our answer is that, for all the dangers of materialism, even advanced country wealth can support purposes that are, in Rawls's terms, "not superfluous." Men and women reasonably want more than

---

34. Even a skeptic such as Lomborg, 2001, p. 323, equates the total cost of managing global warming to forgoing one in fifty years of economic growth (e.g., so that we reach the prosperity we would have enjoyed in 2050 in 2051.)

"meaningful work in free association with others," including such things as the arts, architecture, sports, and science. An interest in wealth, for such purposes, does not seem illegitimate, or simply morally irrelevant, in and of itself.

That is not to say the interest has paramount significance, in and of itself, and it is certainly less important than is usually assumed. Indeed, the unmitigated pursuit of ever-greater wealth could well de-legitimate the global economy if this threatens the institutional moorings needed for its basic justifiability. Sufficient measures in the direction of structural equity and environmental conservation are a condition not just of the global economy's full justifiability, but its very legitimacy as a human social form. So if the cunning of history cannot soften the current resistant state of political will, a move to autarky could well be morally required.

Works Cited

Abbot, Kenneth. 1996. "Defensive Unfairness: The Normative Structure of Section 301." In Jagdish Bhagwati and Robert Hudec, eds., *Fair Trade and Harmonization*. Cambridge: MIT Press.

Abdelal, Rawi, Mark Blyth, and Craig Parsons, eds. 2010. *Constructing the International Economy*. Ithaca: Cornell University Press.

Abizadeh, Arash. 2007. "Cooperation, Pervasive Impact, and Coercion: On the Scope (not Site) of Distributive Justice." *Philosophy and Public Affairs* 35(4): 318–58.

Allen, Robert and Douglas Gale. 2007. *Understanding Financial Crises*. Oxford: Oxford University Press.

Anderson, Elizabeth. 1993. *Value in Ethics and Economics*. Cambridge: Harvard University Press.

Anderson, K. and L. A. Jackson. 2006. "Transgenic Crops, EU Precaution, and Developing Countries." *International Journal of Technology and Globalisation* 2(1/2): 65–80.

Anderson, Robert D. and Hannu Wager. "Human Rights, Development and the WTO: The Cases of Intellectual Property and Competition Policy." *Journal of International Economic Law*, Vol. 9, Issue 3 (September 2006): 707–747, 2006. Available at SSRN: http://ssrn.com/abstract=1096880 or doi:10.1093/jiel/jgl022.

Arrow, Kenneth, Partha Dasgupta, Lawrence Goulder, Gretchen Daily, Paul Ehrlich, Geoffrey Heal, Simon Levin, Karl-Goran Maler, Stephen Schneider, David Starrett, and Brian Walker. 2004. "Are We Consuming Too Much?" *Journal of Economic Perspectives* 18(3): 147–72.

Arrow, Kenneth and Gerald Debreu. 1954. "The Existence of an Equilibrium for a Competitive Economy." *Econometrica* 22(3): 265–90.

Axelrod, Robert. 1985. *The Evolution of Cooperation*. New York: Basic Books.

Bagwell, Kyle, Petros C. Marvroidis, and Robert W. Staiger. 2002. "It's a Question of Market Access." *American Journal of International Law* 96(1): 56–76.

Bagwell, Kyle and Robert Staiger. 1990. "An Economic Theory of GATT." *American Economic Review* 89(1): 215–48.

———. 2000. "The Simple Economics of Labor Standards and the GATT." In Alan V. Deardorff and Robert M. Stern, eds., *Social Dimensions of U.S. Trade Policy*. Ann Arbor: University of Michigan Press, pp. 195–231.

———. 2001. "The WTO as a Mechanism for Securing Market Access Property Rights: Implications for Global Labor and Environmental Issues." *Journal of Economic Perspectives* 15(3): 69–88.

———. 2002. *The Economics of the World Trading System*. Cambridge: MIT Press.
———. 2006. "Will International Rules on Subsidies Disrupt the World Trading System?" *American Economic Review* 96(2): 877–95.
———. 2009. "The WTO: Theory and Practice." *National Bureau of Economic Research Working Paper Series* No. 15445.
Baker, Raymond W. 2005. *Capitalism's Achilles Heel: Dirty Money and How to Renew the Free-Market System*. Hoboken: Wiley Press.
Baldwin, Robert E. 1969. "The Case against Infant Industry Protection." *Journal of Political Economy* 77 (May/June): 295–305.
Barry, Brian. 1989. *Theories of Justice: A Treatise on Social Justice*. Berkeley: University of California Press.
———. 1999. "International Society from a Cosmopolitan Perspective." In David R. Mapel and Terry Nardin, eds., *International Society: Diverse Ethical Perspectives*. Princeton: Princeton University Press.
Barry, Christian and Sanjay Reddy. 2008. *International Trade and Labor Standards: A Proposal for Linkage*. New York: Columbia University Press.
Beitz, Charles R. 1979. *Political Theory and International Relations*. Princeton: Princeton University Press. (Revised edition, 1999.)
———. 2009. *The Idea of Human Rights*. New York: Oxford University Press.
Bhagwati, Jagdish. 1971. "The Generalized Theory of Distortions and Welfare." In J. Bhagwati and J. Vanek, eds., *Trade, Balance of Payments, and Growth*. Amsterdam: North-Holland.
———. 1991. *The World Trading System at Risk*. New York: Simon and Schuster.
———. 1993. "Fair Trade, Reciprocity and Harmonization." In A. Deardorff and R. Stern, eds., *Analytical and Negotiating Issues in the Global Trading System*. Ann Arbor: University of Michigan Press.
———. 2002a. *Going Alone: The Case for Relaxed Reciprocity in Freeing Trade*. Cambridge: MIT Press.
———. 2002b. *Free Trade Today*. New Jersey: Princeton University Press.
———. 2004. *In Defense of Globalization*. New York: Oxford University Press.
———. "Protectionism," *Concise Encyclopedia of Economics*. Available at http://www.econlib.org/library/Enc/Protectionism.html (accessed May 2011).
Bhagwati, Jagdish and V. K. Ramaswami. 1963. "Domestic Distortions, Tariffs, and the Theory of Optimum Subsidy." *Journal of Political Economy* 71(February): 44–60.
Bhala, Raj. 1990. "Clarifying the Trade-Labor Link." *Columbia Journal of Transnational Law* 11(17): 11–56.
Binmore, Ken. 1994. *Game Theory and the Social Contract*, Vol. 1: *Playing Fair*. Cambridge: MIT Press.
Blake, Michael. 2001. "Distributive Justice, State Coercion, and Autonomy." *Philosophy and Public Affairs* 30(3): 257–96.

Blinder, Alan S. 2006. "Offshoring: The New Industrial Revolution." *Foreign Affairs* 8(2): 113–24.
Brander, James A. and Barbara J. Spencer. 1985. "Export Subsidies and International Market Share Rivalry." *Canadian Journal of Economics* 14(February): 83–100.
Bratman, Michael. 1999. *Faces of Intention*. Cambridge: Cambridge University Press.
Brigden, J. B., D. B. Copland, E. C. Dyason, L. F. Giblin, and C. H. Wickens, 1929. *The Australian Tariff: An Economic Inquiry*. Melbourne: Melbourne University Press.
———. 1925. "The Australian Tariff and the Standard of Living." *Economic Record* 1(November): 29–46.
Brock, Gillian. 2009. *Global Justice: A Cosmopolitan Account*. New York: Oxford University Press.
Brown, Andrew and Robert Stern. 2007. "Concepts of Fairness in the Global Trading System." *Pacific Economic Review* 12(3): 293–318.
Buchannan, Allan. 2000. "Rawls's Law of Peoples: Rules for a Vanished Westphalian World." *Ethics* 110(4): 697–721.
Calvo, Guillermo. 1988. "Servicing the Public Debt: The Role of Expectations." *American Economic Review* 78(September): 647–61.
Caney, Simon. 2006. *Justice beyond Borders: A Global Political Theory*. New York: Oxford University Press.
Caporaso, James A. 1978. "Dependence, Dependency, and Power in the Global System: A Structural and Behavioral Analysis." *International Organization* 32(1): 13–43.
Caprio, Gerald Jr. and Daniela Klingelbiel. 1996. "Bank Insolvency: Bad Luck, Bad Policy, or Bad Banking?" In Boris Pleskovic and Joseph Stiglitz, eds., *Annual World Bank Conference on Development Economics*. Washington, DC: World Bank, pp. 79–104.
Cardenas, Mauricio and Felipe Barrera. 1997. "On the Effectiveness of Capital Controls: The Experience of Colombia During the 1990's." *Journal of Development Economics* 54(4): 27–57.
Carmichael, Calum M. 1987. "The Control of Export Credit Subsidies and Its Welfare Consequences." *Journal of International Economics* 23(August): 1–19.
Cass, Ronald A. and Richard D. Boltuck. 1996. "Antidumping and Countervailing-Duty Law: The Mirage of Equitable International Competition." In Jagdish Bhagwati and Robert Hudec, eds., *Fair Trade and Harmonization*, Vol. 2: *Legal Analyses*. Cambridge: MIT Press.
Chan, Kenneth S. 1985. "The International Negotiation Game: Some Evidence from the Tokyo Round." *Review of Economics and Statistics* 67(3): 456–64.
Chayes, Abram and Antonia Handler Chayes. 1995. *The New Sovereignty: Compliance with International Regulatory Agreements*. Cambridge: Harvard University Press.
Chin, J. and G. M. Grossman. 1988. "Intellectual Property Rights and North-South Trade." *Research Working Paper Series No. 2769*. Cambridge, MA: National Bureau of Economic Research.

Chipman, John S. 1965. "A Survey of the Theory of International Trade: Part 2, The Neo-Classical Theory." *Econometrica* 33(October): 685–760.

Cohen, G.A. 1995. *Self-Ownership, Freedom, and Equality*. Cambridge: Cambridge University Press.

———. 2000. *Karl Marx's Theory of History*. Princeton: Princeton University Press.

———. 2008. *Rescuing Justice and Equality*. Cambridge: Harvard University Press.

———. 2011. "The Truth in Conservativism." In R. Jay Wallace, Rahul Kumar, and Samuel Freeman, eds., *Reasons and Recognition: Essays on the Philosophy of T. M. Scanlon*. New York: Oxford University Press.

Cohen, Joshua and Charles Sabel. 2005. "Global Democracy?" *NYU Journal of International Law and Politics* 37(4): 763–97.

Coleman, Jules. 1992. *Risks and Wrongs*. Cambridge: Cambridge University Press.

Collier, Paul. 2007. *The Bottom Billion: Why the Poorest Countries Are Failing and What Can Be Done about It*. Oxford: Oxford University Press.

Collier, P. and J. W. Gunning. 1999. "Explaining African Economic Performance." *Journal of Economic Literature* 37(1): 64–111.

Collier, P., H. Hoeffler, and C. Pattillo. 2001. "Flight Capital as a Portfolio Choice." *World Bank Economic Review* 15(1): 55–80.

Correa, Carlos. 1998. *Implementing the Trips Agreement: General Context and Implications for Developing Countries*. Penang: Third World Network.

Cournot, Augustin. (1838) 1927. *Researches into the Mathematical Principles of the Theory of Wealth*. Translated by Nathaniel T. Bacon. New York: Macmillan.

Cutler, Claire. 2002. "Private International Regimes and Interfirm Cooperation." In Rodney Hall Bruce and Thomas J. Biersteker, eds., *The Emergence of Private Authority in Global Governance*. New York: Cambridge University Press.

Daly, Herman. 1989. *Beyond Growth*. Boston: Beacon Press.

de Bres, Helena. 2011. "The Cooperation Argument for Fairness in International Trade." *Journal of Social Philosophy* 42(2): 192–218.

de Gregorio, Jose, Sebastian Edwards, and Rodrigo Valdes. 2000. "Controls on Capital Inflows: Do They Work? *Journal of Development Economics*, 63(1): 59–83.

DeLong, J. Bradford. 1998. "Helping Countries Prepare for International Capital Flows." *USIA Economic Perspectives*, August 5.

Demirguc-Kunt, Asli and Enrica Detragiache. 1998. "The Determinants of Banking Crises in Developing and Developed Countries." *IMF Staff Papers* 45: 81–109.

Devereaux, Charan, Robert Z. Lawrence, and Michael D. Watkins. 2006. *Case Studies in US Trade Negotiation*, Vol. 1: *Making the Rules*. Washington, DC: Institute for International Economics.

Dewan, Sabina. 2010. "Let's Rise to the Challenge on Labor Standards." Center for American Progress. Available at http://www.americanprogress.org/issues/2010/08/guatemala_labor.html (accessed May 2011).

Diamond, Douglas and Philip H. Dybvig. 1983. "Bank Runs, Deposit Insurance, and Liquidity." *Journal of Political Economy* 91(3): 401–19.

Dixit, Avinash and Gene Grossman. 1986. "Targeted Export Promotion with Several Oligopolistic Industries." *Journal of International Economics* 21(November): 233–49.

Dixit, Avinash and Albert Kyle. 1985. "The Use of Protection and Subsidies for Entry Promotion and Deterrence." *American Economic Review* 75(March): 139–52.

Driskill, Robert. "Deconstructing the Argument for Free Trade." Unpublished manuscript. Available at http://www.vanderbilt.edu/econ/faculty/Driskill/DeconstructingfreetradeAug27a2007.pdf (accessed May 2011).

Dworkin, Ronald. 1977. *Taking Rights Seriously*. Cambridge: Harvard University Press.

———. 1986. *Law's Empire*. Cambridge: Belknap/Harvard University Press.

Easterly, William, Roumeen Islam, and Joseph Siglitz. 2001. "Shaken and Stirred: Explaining Growth Volatility." In *Annual Bank Conference on Development Economics*, 2002. Washington, DC: World Bank, pp. 191–212.

Edgeworth, F.Y. 1894. "The Theory of International Values." *Economic Journal* 4 (March): 35–50.

———. 1908. "Appreciations of Mathematical Theories." *Economic Journal* 18 (September): 424–43.

Eichengreen, Barry. 1999. *Toward a New International Financial Architecture*. Washington, DC: Institute for Advanced Economics.

———. 2004a. *Capital Flows and Crises*. Cambridge: MIT Press.

———. 2004b. *Financial Crises: And What to Do about Them*. Oxford: Oxford University Press.

Elliott, Kimberly Ann and Richard B. Freeman. 2003. *Can Labor Standards Improve under Globalization?* Washington, DC: Institute for International Economics.

Ellsberg, Daniel. 1961. "Risk, Ambiguity, and the Savage Axioms." *Quarterly Journal of Economics* 75(4): 643–69.

Elster, Jon. 1985. *Making Sense of Marx*. Cambridge: Cambridge University Press.

Feinberg, Joel. 1968. "Collective Responsibility." *Journal of Philosophy* 65(21): 687–88.

———. 1988. *Harmless Wrongdoing*. New York: Oxford University Press.

Finger, Michael J. 1992. "The Meaning of "Unfair" in United States Import Policy." *Minnesota Journal of Global Trade* 35: 35–56.

Finger, Michael J., Ulrich Reincke, and Adriana Castro. 1999. "Market Access Bargaining in the Uruguay Round: Rigid or Relaxed

Reciprocity?" World Bank Working Paper no. 2258. Washington, DC: World Bank.
Flanagan, Robert J. 1993. "European Wage Equalization since the Treaty of Rome." In Lloyd Ulman, Barry Eichengreen, and William T. Dickens, eds., *Labor and an Integrated Europe.* Washington DC: Brookings Institution, pp. 167–87.
Fletcher, George P. 1972. "Fairness and Utility in Tort Theory." *Harvard Law Review* 85(3): 537–73.
Fox, Craig R. and Amos Tversky. 1995. "Ambiguity Aversion and Comparative Ignorance." *Quarterly Journal of Economics* 110(3): 585–603.
Freeman, Samuel. 2006. *Justice and the Social Contract: Essays on Rawlsian Political Philosophy.* New York: Oxford University Press.
Friedman, Milton. 1953. "The Case for Flexible Exchange Rates." *Essays on Positive Economics.* Chicago: University of Chicago Press.
Fuller, Lon. 1964. *The Morality of Law.* New Haven: Yale University Press.
Fung, Archon, Dara O'Rourke, and Charles Sabel. 2001. In Joshua Cohen and Joel Rogers, eds., *Can We Put an End to Sweatshops?* Boston: Beacon Press.
Garcia, Frank J. 2003. *Trade, Inequality and Justice: Toward a Liberal Theory of Just Trade.* Ardsley: Transnational.
———. 2007. "Global Justice and the Bretton Woods Institutions." *Journal of International Economic Law* 10(3): 461–81.
Garcia-Johnson, Ronie. 2000. *Exporting Environmentalism: U.S. Multinational Chemical Corporations in Brazil and Mexico.* Cambridge: MIT Press.
Gauthier, David. 1986. *Morals by Agreement.* Oxford: Oxford University Press.
Gibbard, Allan. 1991. "Constructing Justice." *Philosophy and Public Affairs* 20(3): 264–79.
Gilbert, Margaret. 1989. *On Social Facts.* Princeton: Princeton University Press.
———. 2006. *A Theory of Political Obligation: Membership, Commitment, and the Bonds of Society.* Oxford: Oxford University Press.
Goldstein, Judith. 1988. "Ideas, Institutions, and American Trade Policy." *International Organization* 42(1): 179–217.
Goodin, Robert. 1988. "What Is So Special About Our Fellow Countrymen?" *Ethics* 98 (4): 663–68.
———. 2010. "Global Democracy: In the Beginning." *International Theory* 2(2): 175–209.
Graham, Frank D. 1923. "Some Aspects of Protection Further Considered." *Quarterly Journal of Economics* 37(February): 199–227.
Grieco, Joseph. 1993. "Understanding the Problem of International Cooperation: The Limits of Neoliberal Institutionalism and the Future of Realist Theory." In D.A. Baldwin, ed., *Neorealism and Neoliberalism: The Current Debate.* New York: Columbia University Press.
———. 1988. "Anarchy and the Limits of Cooperation." *International Organization* 42(3): 485–507.

Grossman, Gene M. 1986. "Strategic Export Promotion: A Critique." In Paul Krugman, ed., *Strategic Trade Policy and the New International Economics*. Cambridge: MIT Press.

Gupta, Poonam, Deepak Mishra, and Ratna Sahay. 2007. "Behavior of Output during Currency Crises." *Journal of International Economics* 72(2): 428–50.

Haberler, Gottfried. 1936. *The Theory of International Trade*. London: Wm. Hodge.

Haldane, Andrew. "$100 Billion Question." Unpublished manuscript. Available at http://www.bis.org/review/r100406d.pdf (accessed May 2011).

Harsanyi, John. 1965. "Measurement of Social Power, Opportunity Costs, and the Theory of Two-Person Bargaining Games." In J. David Singer, ed., *Human Behavior and International Politics*. Chicago: Rand McNally.

———. 1969. "Measurement of Social Power, in N-Person Reciprocal Power Situations." In Roderick A. Bell, David Edwards, and R. Harrison Wagner, eds., *Political Power*. New York: Free Press.

———. 1975. "Can the Maximin Principle Serve as a Basis for Morality? A Critique of John Rawls's Theory." *American Political Science Review* 69(2): 594–606.

Harsanyi, John and Reinhard Selton. 1988. *A General Theory of Equilibrium Selection in Games*. Cambridge: MIT Press.

Hart, H. L. A. 1955. "Are There Any Natural Rights?" *Philosophical Review* 64(2): 175–191.

———. 1961. *The Concept of Law*. Oxford: Oxford University Press.

Hassoun, Nicole. 2012. *Globalization and Global Justice: Shrinking Distance, Expanding Obligations*. New York: Cambridge University Press.

Hausman, Daniel and Michael McPherson. 1996. *Economic Analysis and Moral Philosophy*. New York: Cambridge University Press.

Hayek, F. A. 1944. *The Road to Serfdom*. Chicago: University of Chicago Press.

Held, David. 1995. *Democracy and the Global Order: From the Modern State to Cosmopolitan Governance*. Palo Alto: Stanford University Press.

Held, Virginia. 1970. "Can a Random Collection of Individuals Be Morally Responsible?" *Journal of Philosophy* 68(July): 471–82.

Henrich, J., R. Boyd, S. Bowles, C. Camerer, E. Feher, H. Gintis, and R. McElreath. 2001. "In Search of Homo economicus: Behavioral Experiments in 15 Small-scale Societies." *American Economic Review* 91(2): 73–78.

———, eds. 2002. *Foundations in Human Sociality: Experiments and Ethnography from 15 Small-scale Societies*. Oxford: Oxford University Press.

Hertel, T., M. Ivanic, P. Prekel, and J. Cranfield, 2003. "The Earning Effects of Multilateral Trade Liberalization: Implications for Poverty in Developing Countries." GTAP Working Paper 16, version 2. West Lafayette, IN: GTAP.

Hertel, T. and W. Martin. 2000. "Liberalizing Agriculture and Manufacturing in a Millennium Round: Implications for Developing Countries." *World Economy* 23(4): 455–69.

Hicks, John R. 1939. "The Foundations of Welfare Economics." *Economic Journal* 49 (December): 696–712.

Hobbes, Thomas. (1651), 1996. *Leviathan*. Edited by Richard Tuck. Cambridge: Cambridge University Press.

Howse, Robert. 1999. "The World Trade Organization and the Protection of Workers' Rights." *Journal of Small and Emerging Business Law* 3(1): 131–72.

———. 2002. "From Politics to Technocracy—and Back Again: The Fate of the Multilateral Trading Regime." *American Journal of International Law* 96(1): 94–117.

Howse, Robert and Michael Trebilcock, 1996. "The Fair Trade-Free Trade Debate: Trade, Labor, and the Environment." *International Review of Law and Economics* 16(1): 61–79.

Hudec, Robert E. 1975. *The GATT Legal System and World Trade Diplomacy*. New York: Praeger.

———. 1990. "'Mirror, Mirror on the Wall': The Concept of Fairness in United States Foreign Trade Policy." In D. Fleming, ed., *Canada, Japan and International Law*. Proceedings of the 1990 Canadian Council of International Law 88.

Hume, David. (1896), 1975. *A Treatise of Human Nature,* 2nd ed. Edited by L. A. Selby-Bigge, revised by P. H. Nidditch. Oxford: Clarendon Press.

Irwin, Douglas A. 1996. *Against the Tide*. Princeton: Princeton University Press.

———. 2002. Free Trade Under Fire. Princeton: Princeton University Press.

Irwin, Gregor and David Vines. 1999. *A Krugman-Dooley-Sachs Third Generation Model of the Asian Financial Crisis*. Working Paper. London: Center for Economic Policy Research.

James, Aaron. 2005a. "Constructing Justice for Existing Practice: Rawls and the Status Quo." *Philosophy and Public Affairs* 33(3): 281–316.

———. 2005b. "Distributive Justice without Sovereign Rule: The Case of Trade." *Social Theory and Practice* 41(4): 533–59.

———. 2006. "Equality in a Realistic Utopia." *Social Theory and Practice* 32(4): 699–724.

———. 2011. "The Significance of Distribution." In R. Jay Wallace, Rahul Kumar, and Samuel Freeman, eds., *Reasons and Recognition: Essays on the Philosophy of T.M. Scanlon*. New York: Oxford University Press.

———. Forthcoming(a). "Global Economic Fairness: Internal Principles." In Chi Carmody, Frank J. Garcia, and John Linarelli, eds., *Global Justice and International Economic Law: Opportunities and Challenges*. Cambridge: Cambridge University Press.

———. Forthcoming(b). "Moral Assurance Problems in Global Context." In Sharon Lloyd, ed., *Hobbes Today: Insights for the 21st Century*. New York: Cambridge University Press.

Jayachandran, Seema and Michael Kremer. 2006. "Odious Debt." *American Economic Review* 96(1): 82–92.

Johnson, Harry. 1950–1. "Optimum Welfare and Maximum Revenue Tariffs." *Review of Economic Studies* 19: 28–35.

Kalai, E. and M. Smorodinsky. 1975. "Other Solutions to Nash's Bargaining Problem." *Econometrica*, 43(3): 513–18.

Kaldor, Nicholas. 1939. "Welfare Propositions of Economics and Interpersonal Comparisons of Utility." *Economic Journal* 49 (September): 549–52.

———. 1940. "A Note on Tariffs and the Terms of Trade." *Economica* 7 (November): 377–80.

Kaminsky, Graciela L. and Carmen Rienhart. 1999. "The Twin Crises: The Causes of Banking and Balance-of-Payments Problems." *American Economic review* 89(3): 473–500.

Kamm, Francis. 1993. *Morality, Mortality*, Vol. 1. Oxford: Oxford University Press.

Kant, Immanuel. 1797. *The Metaphysics of Morals.* Edited by Mary J. Gregor, 1996. Cambridge: Cambridge University Press.

Kapstein, Ethan B. 2006. *Economic Justice in an Unfair World.* Princeton: Princeton University Press.

Kavka, Gregory S. 1995. "Why Even Morally Perfect People Would Need Government." *Social Philosophy and Policy* 12(1): 1–18.

Keck, Margaret and Kathryn Sikkink. 1998. *Activists beyond Borders.* Ithaca: Cornell University Press.

Kemp, Murray C. 1962. "The Gain from International Trade." *Economic Journal* 87(December): 803–19.

Keohane, Robert O. 1986. "Reciprocity in International Relations." *International Organization* 40(1): 1–27.

———. 1993. "Institutional Theory and the Realist Challenge after the Cold War." In D. A. Baldwin, ed., *Neorealism and Neoliberalism: The Current Debate.* New York: Columbia University Press.

———. 2002. *Power and Governance in a Partially Globalized World.* New York: Routledge.

Keohane, Robert O. and Joseph S. Nye. 2001. *Power and Interdependence*, 2nd ed. New York: Addison Wesley Longman.

———. 2002. "The Club Model of Multilateral Cooperation and the World Trade Organization: Problems of Democratic Legitimacy." Visions of Governance in the 21st Century, Working Paper no. 4. Cambridge: Harvard University, J. F. Kennedy School of Government.

Keynes, John Maynard. 1921. *A Treatise on Probability.* London: Macmillan.

———. 1936. *The General Theory of Employment, Interest, and Money.* Cambridge: Macmillan/Cambridge University Press.

Kindleberger, Charles. 2005. *Manias, Panics, and Crashes.* New York: Basic Books.

Kingsbury, Benedict, Nico Krish, and Richard Stewart. 2005. "The Emergence of Global Administrative Law." *Law and Contemporary Problems* 15 (Summer/Autumn).

Kletzer, Lori G. 1998a. "Trade and Job Displacement in U.S. Manufacturing: 1979–1991." In S. Collins, ed., *Imports, Exports, and the American Worker*. Washington, DC: Brookings Institution.

———. 1998b. "Job Displacement." *Journal of Economic Perspectives* 12(1): 115–36.

———. 2001. *Job Loss from Imports: Measuring the Costs*. Washington, DC: Institute for International Economics.

———. 2005. "Globalization and Job Loss, From Manufacturing to Services." *Federal Reserve Bank of Chicago Economic Review*, 2nd qtr.: 38–46.

Klosko, George. 1992. *The Principle of Fairness and Political Obligation*. Lanham, MD: Rowman and Littlefield.

Knight, Frank H. 1924. "Some Fallacies in the Interpretation of Social Cost." *Quarterly Journal of Economics* 38 (August): 582–606.

Koremenos, Barbara, Charles Lipson, and Duncan Snidal. 2001. "The Rational Design of International Institutions." *International Organization* 55(4): 761–99.

Kose, M. Ayhan, Eswar Prasad, Kenneth Rogoff, and Shang-Jin Wei. 2006. "Financial Globalization: A Reappraisal." Available at http://www.economics.harvard.edu/faculty/rogoff/files/Financial_Globalization_A_Reappraisal_v2.pdf (accessed May 2011).

Koskenniemi, Martti. 1989. *From Apology to Utopia: The Structure of International Legal Argument*. Helsinki: Lakimiesliiton Kustannus: Finnish Lawyers' Publishing Company.

Kotlikoff, Laurence J. 2010. *Jimmy Steward Is Dead: Ending the World's Ongoing Financial Plague with Limited Purpose Measures*. Hoboken, NJ: Wiley.

Krueger, Anne. 2000. "Conflicting Demands on the International Monetary Fund." *American Economic Review* 90(2): 38–41.

———. 2003. "Proposals for a Sovereign Debt Restructuring Mechanism." Available at www.imf.org (accessed May 2011).

Krugman, Paul. 1987. "Is Free Trade Passe?" *Journal of Economic Perspectives* 1 (Fall): 131–41.

———. 1992. "Does the New Trade Theory Require a New Trade Policy." *World Economy* 15(July): 423–41.

———. 1993. "The Narrow and Broad Arguments for Free Trade." *American Economic Review* 83(2): 362–66.

———. 1996. *Pop Internationalism*. Cambridge: MIT Press.

———. 1997a. "What Should Trade Negotiators Negotiate About?" *Journal of Economic Literature* 35(1): 113–20.

———. 1997b. "In Praise of Cheap Labor." *Slate*. Available at http://www.slate.com/id/1918/ (accessed May 2011).

———. 1999. "Capital Control Freaks," *Slate*. Available at http://www.slate.com/id/35534/ (accessed May 2011).

———. 2010. "Chinese New Year." *New York Times*, January 1, 2010, Opinion section. Available at http://www.nytimes.com/2010/01/01/opinion/01krugman.html (accessed May 2011).

———. "Trade and Wages, Reconsidered." Unpublished manuscript. Available at http://www.princeton.edu/~pkrugman/pk-bpea-draft.pdf (accessed May 2011).

Krugman, Paul and Maurice Obstfeld. 2003. *International Economics: Theory and Policy*, 6th ed. New York: Addison Wesley.

Kurgjanska, Malgorzata and Mattias Risse. 2008. "Fairness in Trade II: Export Subsidies and the Fair Trade Movement." *Politics, Philosophy, and Economics* 7(1): 29–56.

Kutz, Christopher. 2000. *Complicity: Ethics and Law for a Collective Age*. New York: Cambridge University Press.

Laeven, Luc, and Fabian Valencia. 2008. "Systemic Banking Crises: A New Database." IMF Working Paper. Washington, DC: International Monetary Fund.

Langille, Brian Alexander. 1996. "General Reflections on the Relationship of Trade and Labor (Or Fair Trade Is Free Trade's Destiny)." In Jagdish Bhagwati and Robert Hudec, eds., *Fair Trade and Harmonization*, Vol. 1: *Economic Analysis*. Cambridge: MIT Press.

Leary, Virginia A. 1996. "Workers' Rights and International Trade: The Social Clause (Gatt, Ilo, Nafta, U.S. Laws)." In Jagdish Bhagwati and Robert Hudec, eds., *Fair Trade and Harmonization*, Vol. 1: *Economic Analysis*. Cambridge: MIT Press.

Levinsohn, J. S. Berry and J. Freidman. 2003. "Imports of the Indonesian Economic Crisis: Price Changes and the Poor." In Michael Dooley and Jeffery Frankel, eds., *Managing Currency Crises in Emerging Markets*. Chicago: University of Chicago Press.

Levy, Frank, and Tomas A. Cochan. "Addressing the Problem of Stagnant Wages." Unpublished manuscript. Available at http://www.employmentpolicy.org/sites/www.employmentpolicy.org/files/field-content-file/pdf/Mike%20Lillich/EPRN%20WagesMay%2020%20-%20FL%20Edits_0.pdf (accessed June 2011).

Locke, Richard, Matthew Amengual, and Akshay Mangla. 2009. "Virtue Out of Necessity? Compliance, Commitment, and the Improvement of Labor Conditions in Global Supply Chains." *Politics and Society* 37(3): 319–51.

Locke, Richard, Fei Qin, and Alberto Brause. 2007. "Does Monitoring Improve Labor Standards? Lessons from Nike." *Industrial and Labor Relations Review* 61(1): 30–31.

Locke, Richard and Monica Romis. 2007. "Improving Work Conditions in a Global Supply Chain." *MIT Sloan Management Review* 48(2): 54–62.

Lomborg, Bjorn. 2001. *The Skeptical Environmentalist*. Cambridge: Cambridge University Press.

Mangabeira, Roberto Unger. 2007. *Free Trade Reimagined: The World Division of Labor and the Method of Economics*. Princeton: Princeton University Press.

Manoilescu, Mihail. 1931. *The Theory of Protection in International Trade*. London: P.S. King.

Markusen, James. 1990. "The Microfoundations of External Economies." *Canadian Journal of Economics* 23(August): 495–508.

Marx, Karl. (1859), 1968. Preface to *A Contribution to the Critique of Political Economy*. In Karl Marx and Frederick Engels, *Selected Works in One Volume*. London: Lawrence and Wishart.

Maskus, Keith. 2002. "Benefiting from Intellectual Property Protection." In Bernard Hoekman, Aaditya Mattoo, and Philip English, eds., *Development, Trade and the World Trade Organization: A Handbook*. Washington, DC: World Bank.

McCallum, John. 1995. "National Borders Matter: Canada-U.S. Regional Trade Patterns." *American Economic Review* 85(3): 615–23.

Meade, James E. 1995. *Trade and Welfare*. London: Oxford University Press.

——. 1995. *The Theory of International Economic Policy, Trade, and Welfare*. New York: Oxford University Press.

Meckled-Garcia, Saladin. 2008. "On the Very Idea of Cosmopolitan Justice: Constructivism and International Agency." *Journal of Political Philosophy* 16(3): 245–71.

Metzler, Lloyd. 1949. "Tariffs, the Terms of Trade, and the Distribution of National Income." *Journal of Political Economy* 62 (February): 1–29.

Mill, James. 1821. *Elements of Political Economy*. London: C. & R. Baldwin.

Mill, J. S. 1825. "The Corn Laws." *Westminster Review* 3 (April): 394–420.

——. 1844. "Of the Laws of Interchange between Nations; and the Distribution of the Gains of Commerce among the Countries of the Commercial World." In *Essays on Some Unsettled Questions of Political Economy*. London: Parker.

——. (1848), 1909. *Principles of Political Economy: With Some of their Applications to Social Philosophy*. Edited by Sir William Ashley, 1987. Fairfield, NJ: Augustus M. Kelley.

——. (1859), 1977. *On Liberty*. In J. M. Robson, ed., *Collected Works of John Stuart Mill*. Toronto: University of Toronto Press, pp. 213–10.

Miller, David. 1987. "Exploitation in the Market." In A. Reeve, ed., *Modern Theories of Exploitation*. London: Sage.

——. 2004. "Holding Nations Responsible." *Ethics* 114(2): 240–68.

——. 2007. *National Responsibility and Global Justice*. New York: Oxford University Press.

——. "Fair Trade: What Does It Mean and Why Does It Matter?" Unpublished manuscript, Oxford University.

Miller, Richard W. 2010. *Globalizing Justice: The Ethics of Poverty and Power*. Oxford. Oxford University Press.

Milner, Helen. 1991. "The Assumption of Anarchy in International Relations: A Critique." *Review of International Studies* 17(1): 67–85.

Milner, Helen and B. Peter Rosendorff. 2001. "The Optimal Design of International Trade Institutions: Uncertainty and Escape." *International Organization* 55(4): 829–57.

Minsky, Hyman P. 1986. *Stabilizing an Unstable Economy*. New Haven: Yale.

Moehler, Michael. 2009. "Why Hobbes' State of Nature Is Best Modeled by an Assurance Game." *Utilitas* 21(3): 297–326.
Moellendorf, Darrel. 2002. *Cosmopolitan Justice*. Boulder, CO: Westview Press.
———. 2005. "The World Trade Organization and Egalitarian Justice." *Metaphilosophy* 36 (1–2): 145–62.
———. 2009. *Global Inequality Matters*. Basingstoke: Palgrave Macmillan.
Morgenthau, Hans. 1946. *Scientific Man Vs. Power Politics*. Chicago: University of Chicago Press.
Nagel, Thomas. 2005. "The Problem of Global Justice." *Philosophy and Public Affairs* 33(2): 113–47.
Nash, John, 1950. "Equilibrium Points in N-Person Games." *Proceedings of the National Academy of Sciences* 36(1): 48–49.
Newbery, David, M. G. and J. E. Stiglitz. 1984. "Pareto Inferior Trade." *Review of Economic Studies* 51(1): 1–12.
Nickel, James. 2007. *Making Sense of Human Rights*, 2nd ed. Oxford: Wiley/Blackwell.
Nordhaus, William and James Tobin. 1973. "Is Growth Obsolete?" *Income and Wealth* 38, *National Bureau Economic Research,* pp. 509–532.
North, Douglas C. 1990. *Institutions, Institutional Change, and Economic Performance*. Cambridge: Cambridge University Press.
———. 2005. *Understanding the Process of Economic Change*. Princeton: Princeton University Press.
Nozick, Robert. 1974. *Anarchy, State, Utopia*. New York: Basic Books.
Nussbaum, Martha C. 2006. *Frontiers of Justice: Disability, Nationality, Species Membership*. Cambridge: Belknap/Harvard University Press.
Nydegger, R.V. and G. Owen. 1974. "Two-person Bargaining: An Experimental Test of the Nash Axioms." *International Journal of Game Theory* 3(4): 239–49.
Obstfeld, Maurice. 1996. "Models of Currency Crises with Self-Sustaining Features." *European Economic Review* 40(April): 1037–48.
Obstfeld, Maurice and Alan Taylor. 1998. "The Great Depression as a Watershed: International Capital Mobility over the Long Run." In Michael D. Bordo, Claudia D. Goldin, and Eugene N. White, eds., *The Defining Moment: The Great Depression and the American Economy in the Twentieth Century*. Chicago: University of Chicago Press.
Ohlin, Bertil. 1931. "Protection and Non-Competing Groups." *Weltwirtschaftliches Archiv* 33(1): 30–45.
Ostrom, Elinor. 1990. *Governing the Commons: The Evolution of Institutions for Collective Action*. New York: Cambridge University Press.
Ostry, Jonathan D., Atish R. Ghosh, Karl Habermeier, Marcos Chamon, Mahvash S. Qureshi, and Dennis B. S. Reinhardt. 2010. "Capital Inflows: The Role of Controls." IMF Staff Position Note, February 19. Washington, DC: International Monetary Fund.
Ozkan, F. Gulcin and Sutherland, Alan. 1998. "A Currency Crisis Model with an Optimizing Policymaker." *Journal of International Economics* 44(2): 339–64.

Panagariya, Arvind. 1981. "Variable Returns to Scale in Production and Patterns of Specialization." *American Economic Review* 71 (March): 221–30.
Pareto, Vilfredo. 1894. "Il Massim di Utilita dato dalla Libera Concorrenza." *Giornale degli Economisti* 9 (July): 48–66.
Parfit, Derek. 1997. "Equality and Priority." *Ratio* 10(3): 202–21.
———. 2011. *On What Matters*, Vols. 1 and 2. Oxford: Oxford University Press.
Patterson, Dennis and Ari Afilalo. 2008. *The New Global Trading Order: The Evolving State and the Future of World Trade.* New York: Cambridge University Press.
Pogge, Thomas W. 1989. *Realizing Rawls.* Ithaca: Cornell University Press.
———. 1992. "Cosmopolitanism and Sovereignty." *Ethics* 103(1): 48–75.
———. 2002. *World Poverty and Human Rights: Cosmopolitan Responsibilities and Reforms.* Cambridge: Polity Press.
———. 2005. "Human Rights and Global Health." In Christian Barry and Thomas Pogge, eds., *Global Institutions and Responsibilities: Achieving Global Justice.* Oxford: Blackwell.
Polanyi, Karl. (1944), 1971. *The Great Transformation: The Political and Economic Origins of Our Time.* Boston: Beacon Press.
Pollard, Naomi, Maria Latorre and Dhananjayan Sriskandarajah. 2008. *Floodgates or Turnstiles? Post-EU Enlargement Migration Flows to (and from) the UK.* London: Institute for Public Policy Research.
Postema, Gerald J. 1987. "'Protestant' Interpretation and Social Practices." *Law and Philosophy* 6(3): 283–319.
Rawls, John. 1971. *A Theory of Justice.* Cambridge: Harvard University Press.
———. 1993. *Political Liberalism.* New York: Columbia University Press.
———. 1999. *The Law of Peoples.* Cambridge: Harvard University Press.
Reddy, Sanjay G. 2005. "Just International Monetary Arrangements." In Christian Barry and Thomas W. Pogge, eds., *Global Institutions and Responsibilities.* Malden: Blackwell, pp. 218–34.
Reinhart, Carmen M. and Kenneth S. Rogoff. 2009. *This Time Is Different: Eight Centuries of Financial Folly.* Princeton: Princeton University Press.
Ricardo, David. (1817), 1951. "On the Principles of Political Economy and Taxation." In Piero Sraffa, ed., *The Works and Correspondence of David Ricardo.* Cambridge: Cambridge University Press.
Ripstein, Arthur. 2009. *Force and Freedom: Kant's Legal and Political Philosophy.* Cambridge: Harvard University Press.
Risse, Mathias. 2005. "How Does the Global Order Harm the Poor?" *Philosophy and Public Affairs* 33(4): 349–76.
———. 2007. "Fairness in Trade I: Obligations from Trading and the Pauper Labor Argument." *Politics, Philosophy, and Economics* 6(3): 355–77.
———. 2012. *On Global Justice.* Princeton: Princeton University Press.
Robinson, Joan. 1933. *The Economics of Imperfect Competition.* London: Macmillan.

———. 1937. "Beggar-my-Neighbor Remedies for Unemployment." *Essays in the Theory of Employment.* New York: Macmillan.

Rodrik, Dani. 1994. "The Rush to Free Trade in the Developing World: Why So Late? Why Now? Will It Last?" In S. Haggard and S. Webb, eds., *Voting for Reform: Democracy, Political Liberalization, and Economic Adjustment.* New York: Oxford University Press.

———. 1997. *Has Globalization Gone Too Far?* Washington, DC: Brookings Institution.

———. 1998. "Who Needs Capital-Account Convertability." In Peter Kenen, ed., *Should the IMF Pursue Capital-Account Convertability?* Princeton Studies in International Finance no. 207 (May). Princeton: International Finance Section. Department of Economics, Princeton University.

———. 1999. *The New Global Economy and Developing Countries: Making Openness Work.* Washington, DC: Overseas Development Council.

———. 2007. *One Economics, Many Recipes: Globalization, Institutions, and Economic Growth.* Princeton: Princeton University Press.

———. 2011. *The Globalization Paradox.* New York: Norton.

Rodrik, Dani and Arvind Subramanian. 2008. "Why Did Financial Globalization Disappoint?" Available at http://www.iie.com/publications/papers/subramanian0308.pdf (accessed May 2011).

Rodrik, Dani, Arvind Subramanian, and Francesco Trebbi. 2004. "Institutions Rule: The Primacy of Institutions over Geography and Integration in Economic Development." *Journal of Economic Growth* 9(2): 131–65.

Rodriquez, Francisco and Dani Rodrik. 2001. "Trade Policy and Economic Growth: A Skeptic's Guide to the Cross-National Evidence." In Ben Bernanke and Kenneth S. Rogoff, eds., *Macroeconomics Annual 2000.* Cambridge: MIT Press.

Ronzoni, Miriam. 2009. "The Global Order: A Case of Background Injustice? A Practice-Dependent Account." *Philosophy and Public Affairs* 37(3): 229–56.

Rousseau, Jean-Jacques. (1754), 1997. "Discourse on the Origin and the Foundations of Inequality among Men." In Victor Gourevitch, ed., *The Discourses and Other Early Political Writings.* Cambridge: Cambridge University Press.

Ruggie, John G. 1982. "International Regimes, Transactions, and Change: Embedded Liberalism in the Postwar Economic Order." *International Organization* 38(2): 195–231.

———. 1998. "What Makes the World Hang Together? Neo-Utilitarianism and the Social Constructivist Challenge." *International Organization* 52(4): 855–85.

———. 2003. "Taking Embedded Liberalism Global: The Corporate Connection." In David Held and Mathias-Archibugi, eds., *Taming Globalization: Frontiers of Governance.* Cambridge: Polity Press.

———. 2004. "Reconstituting the Global Public Domain—Issues, Actors and Practice." *European Journal of International Relations* 10(4): 499–531.

Sachs, Jeffery D. 1995. "Do We Need an International Lender of Last Resort?" Available at http://www.earthinstitute.columbia.edu/sitefiles/file/about/director/pubs/intllr.pdf (accessed May 2011).

———. 2003. Institutions Don't Rule: Direct Effects of Geography on Per Capita Income." *National Bureau Economic Research*, February. Working Paper Series, Vol. w9490. Available at SSRN: http://ssrn.com/abstract=379271

Samuelson, Paul A. 1939. "The Gains from International Trade." *Canadian Journal of Economics and Political Science* 5 (May): 195–205.

———. 1962. "The Gains from International Trade Once Again." *Economic Journal* 82 (December): 820–9.

———. 1964. "Theoretical Notes on Trade Problems." *Review of Economics and Statistics* 46 (2): 145–54.

———. 1981a. "Summing Up on the Australian Case for Protection." *Quarterly Journal of Economics* 96 (February): 58–73.

———. 1981b. "Bergsonian Welfare Functions." In Rosenfeld, ed., *Economic Welfare and the Economics of Soviet Socialism*. Cambridge: Cambridge University Press.

Sangiovanni, Andrea. 2007. "Global Justice, Reciprocity, and the State." *Philosophy and Public Affairs* 35(1): 3–39.

———. 2008. "Justice and the Priority of Politics to Morality." *Journal of Political Philosophy* 16(2):137–64.

Sassen, Saskia. 1996. *Losing Control? Sovereignty in an Age of Globalization*. New York: Columbia University Press.

———. 2002. "The State and Globalization." In Rodney Bruce Hall and Thomas J. Biersteker, eds., *The Emergence of Private Authority in Global Governance*. New York: Cambridge University Press.

Satz, Debra. 2010. *Why Some Things Should Not Be for Sale: The Moral Limits of Markets*. New York: Oxford University Press.

Scanlon, T.M. 1998. *What We Owe to Each Other*. Cambridge: Harvard University Press.

———. 2003. *The Difficulty of Tolerance*. Cambridge: Cambridge University Press.

Searle, John. 1995. *The Construction of Social Reality*. New York: Free Press.

Sen, Amartya. 1992. *Inequality Reexamined*. Cambridge: Harvard University Press.

———. 2009. *The Idea of Justice*. Cambridge: Harvard University Press.

Shapiro,

Shiffrin, Seana. 2001. "Lockean Justifications of Intellectual Property Rights." In Steven Munzer, ed., *New Essays in the Legal and Political Theory of Property*. Cambridge: Cambridge University Press.

Shue, Henry. 1999. "Global Environmental and International Inequality." *International Affairs* 74(3): 531–45.

Sidgwick, Henry. 1883. *Principles of Political Economy*. London: Macmillan.

Simmons, John. A. 1979. "The Principle of Fair Play." *Philosophy and Public Affairs* 8 (4): 307–37.

Singer, Peter. 1972. "Famine, Affluence, and Morality." *Philosophy and Public Affairs* 1(1): 229–43.
Skyrms, Brian. 2004. *The Stag Hunt and the Evolution of Social Structure*. Cambridge: Cambridge University Press.
Slaughter, Anne-Marie. 2004. *A New World Order*. Princeton: Princeton University Press.
Smith, Adam. (1776), 1976. *An Inquiry into the Nature and Causes of the Wealth of Nations*. Edited by Edwin Cannan. New York: Modern Library.
Soper, Philip. 1984. *A Theory of Law*. Cambridge: Harvard University Press.
Soros, George. 2003. *The Alchemy of Finance*. Hoboken, NJ: Wiley.
Sreenivasan, Gopal. 2005. "Does the GATS Undermine Democratic Control over Health." *Journal of Ethics* 9(1–2): 269–81.
Stiglitz, Joseph E. 1977. "Dumping on Free Trade: The U.S. Import Trade Laws," *Southern Economic Journal* 64(2): 402–24.
———. 2006. *Making Globalization Work*. New York: Norton.
Stiglitz, Joseph E. and Andrew Charlton. 2006. *Fair Trade for All: How Trade Can Promote Development*. New York: Oxford University Press.
Stopler, Wolfgang and Paul Samuelson. 1941. "Protection and Real Wages." *Review of Economic Studies* 9(1): 58–73.
Suro, Robert. 2005. *Attitudes toward Immigrants and Immigration Policy: Surveys among Latinos in the US and Mexico*. Washington, DC: Pew Hispanic Center.
Tan, Kok-Chor. 2004. *Justice without Borders: Cosmopolitanism, Nationalism, and Patriotism*. Cambridge: Cambridge University Press.
Taussig, Frank W. 1893. "Recent Literature on Protection." *Quarterly Journal of Economics* 7 (January): 162–76.
Thomson, Judith Jarvis. 1990. *The Realm of Rights*. Cambridge: Harvard University Press.
Tobin, James. 1976. "A Proposal for International Monetary Reform." *Eastern Economic Journal* 3(1): 153–9.
Torrens, Robert. 1815. *Essay on the Corn Trade*. London: Hatchard.
———. 1821. *An Essay on the Production of Wealth*. London: Longman, Hurst, Rees, Orme, and Brown.
———. 1844. *The Budget: On Commercial and Colonial Policy*. London: Smith, Elder.
Trebilcock, Michael J. and Robert Howse. 2005. *The Regulation of International Trade*. New York: Routledge Press.
Unger, Roberto Mangabeira. 2007. *Free Trade Reimagined*. Princeton: Princeton University Press.
Valdman, Mikhail. 2009. "A Theory of Wrongful Exploitation." *Philosopher's Imprint*, 9 (6): 1–14.
Valentini, Laura. 2011. "Global Justice and Practice-Dependence: Conventionalism, Institutionalism, Functionalism." *Journal of Political Philosophy* 19(4): 399–418
Viner, Jacob. 1929. "The Australian Tariff: A Review Article." *Economic Record* 5 (November): 306–15.

———. 1937. *Studies in the Theory of International Trade.* London: Harper and Brothers.
Vogel, David. 1995. *Trading Up: Consumer and Environmental Regulation in a Global Economy.* Cambridge: Harvard University Press.
Wallerstein, Immanuel. 1979. "The Rise and Future Demise of the World Capitalist System: Concepts for Comparative Analysis." In Wallerstein, *The Capitalist World Economy.* New York: Cambridge University Press.
Waltz, Kenneth N., 1970. "The Myth of National Interdependence." In Charles P. Kindlerberger, ed., *The International Corporation.* Cambridge: MIT Press.
———. 1979. *Theory of International Politics.* Reading: Addison-Wesley.
———. 1986. "Reflections on Theory of International Politics: A Response to My Critics." In Robert O. Keohane, ed., *Neorealism and Its Critics.* New York: Columbia University Press.
Walzer, Michael. 1983. *Spheres of Justice.* New York: Basic Books.
Wapner, Paul. 1995. "Politics beyond the State: Environmental Activism and World Civic Politics." *World Politics* 47(3): 311–41.
Weinrib, Ernest. 1995. *The Idea of Private Law.* Cambridge: Harvard University Press.
Wenar, Leif. 2008. "Property Rights and the Resource Curse." *Philosophy and Public Affairs* 36(1): 2–32.
Wendt, Alexander. 1992. "Anarchy Is What States Make of It: The Social Construction of Power Politics." *International Organization* 46(2): 391–425.
Wertheimer, Alan. 1996. *Exploitation.* Princeton: Princeton University Press.
Wing, Ian Sue. 2004. "Computable General Equilibrium Models and Their Use in Economy-Wide Policy Analysis." MIT Joint Program on the Science and Policy of Global Change, Technical Note 6. Available at http://web.mit.edu/globalchange/www/MITJPSPGC_TechNote6.pdf (accessed May, 2011).
Wolf, Martin. 2004. *Why Globalization Works.* New Haven: Yale University Press.
———. 2008. *Fixing Global Finance.* Baltimore: Johns Hopkins University Press.
———. 2010. "Why Cautious Reform Is the Risky Option." *London Financial Times*, April 28.
Wolff, Jonathan. 1998. "The Ethics of Competition." In G. Parry, A. Qureshi, and H. Steiner, eds., *The Legal and Moral Aspects of International Trade, Freedom and Trade*, Vol. 3. London: Routledge, pp. 82–96.
World Bank. 2003. *Global Economic Prospects.* Washington, DC: World Bank.
World Trade Organization (WTO). 2003. *Adjusting to Trade Liberalization: The Role of Policy Institutions and the WTO Disciplines.* WTO Special Studies 7. Geneva: World Trade Organization.

Wright, Erik Olin. 2010. *Envisioning Real Utopias*. London: Verso.
Yeats, Alexander J., with Azita Amjadi, Ulrich Eincke, and Francis Ng. 1997. *Did Domestic Policies Marginalize Africa in World Trade, World Bank?* Directions in Development series. Washington, DC: World Bank.

Index

Abstraction, 104–5, 113, 126–27, 141n9, 275
Accountability
  as cosmopolitan, 196
  to evidence, 331
  of firms, 21, 320–21
  from global civil society, 22
  in international governance, 113, 118, 156n31
Aggregation
  as fair or unfair, 215–19
  as precluded, 142, 143
  as "tie breaking," 142
Arbitrariness
  in bargaining power, 97
  in the division of labor, 229
  from a fairness/justice point of view, 94–96, 101–2, 242–44
  in trade or financial policy, 81, 149, 160n38, 189
  See also luck egalitarianism
Autarky
  as basis for comparison, 20, 58, 153–55, 168, 171–72, 174, 178, 180–81, 269, 308, 316, 334
  financial, 255n13, 256, 261, 265, 269–73, 276
  and formal agreements, 54
  and harm, 174n6, 199, 211, 217, 276,
  as objectionable, 218
Availability/unavailability
  of alternative to state system, 117–22
  of compensatory measures, 236, 262
  epistemic, 113–14, 124
  as required, 124

Arrow, Kenneth, 41, 183n11, 326
Assurance
  in bargaining, 87, 88n24
  basic problem of, 56, 59, 80, 82, 92, 103, 117, 193
  and Hobbes, 4, 77–78, 80, 82n9
  and the human condition, 14, 45, 104
  and ideal theory, 103–4, 106
  and moral motivation, 103, 107–8, 111, 115, 127
  relevance to principle, 106, 111, 114n12, 123–25
  and trade practice, 54–59, 81
  and the international system, 103, 121
  and Kant, 112
Assurance game
  formulation of, 55–57
  significance of, 54–55, 81, 104
  as contrasted with Prisoner's Dilemma, 55–57, 105n4

Bagwell, Kyle, 45, 53, 57n48, 318, 319
Beggar-thy-neighbor. *See* externality
Beitz, Charles, xi, 16n21, 25n39, 113n11, 114n17
Bhagwati, Jagdish
  on capital controls, 8
  on competitive fairness, 69n60
  on direct policy response,
  on the environment, 325n20
  on fairness discourse, 35, 70n61
  on intellectual property, 74n64, 287n6, 301n24
  on reciprocity, 45, 54n43, 60n51, 200

Bhagwati, Jagdish (*continued*)
  on wages, 50n35, 311n5
  on governance, 50n32, 301n24, 313n6, 326n24
Blake, Michael, 9, 94, 98–99
Bretton Woods system
  rationales for, 151–52
  and free trade, 257, 264–65, 269
  and financial crises, 249, 254, 269, 276

Capital controls
  absence of, 100, 150, 250, 251, 253, 273, 279
  and capability, 257–58,
  as cautious, 251, 254, 255, 261, 263, 269, 272–76, 278, 283
  as fair, 3, 8, 216, 252, 253, 259
  and free trade, 264
  as legal, 264n30
  and liberty, 259
Capital liberalization
  and unfair risks, 251–53, 269–70, 275–83
  justifiability of, 256, 262–63, 264, 272
  limited benefits of, 8, 252, 255, 265
  as a cause of crises, 249, 266–70
  as separate from economic globalization, 257, 264–65, 269, 273–74
  and social pressures and practices, 100, 264
Capital markets
  in allocating savings to most productive uses, 252
  as only instrumentally valuable, 259, 261
  as market reliance practice, 150–52
  as unfair (*see* capital liberalization; capital controls)
Clean trade, 154
Climate change
  significance of, 270, 308, 325, 327, 333

  responsibilities for, 108–10, 113, 117, 327, 328
Coercion
  and compliance, 86n19
  and coercion-based views, 94, 98, 100
  as a moral concern, 29, 71, 95, 97–100, 102, 161
Cohen, G. A., 16n19, 24n35, 27n43, 124–25
Collective
  bargaining, 147, 309
  and individual interests, 123n28, 186–87
  ownership, 94, 177
  power, 100, 101,
  principles, 101, 111, 125–26,
  regulatory position, 111, 114–16
  See also collective responsibility
Collective responsibility
  nature of, 15, 92–93, 97, 101, 125, 153
  required as, 20, 92, 93, 131, 153, 203–4, 213
Constructive interpretation, 17, 26–30, 41, 157n32, 170, 194
Constructive method, 3, 25–31, 166, 186, 170, 241
Contribution
  nature of, 171–73
  responsibility for, 110, 327
  to trade practice, 192–93, 220
  See also participation
Comparative advantage
  and capital markets, 150, 265,
  characterization of, 46–47, 186, 199,
  dynamic versus static, 7, 21, 148, 229
  and fairness, 68, 69, 70, 73, 75, 162, 180, 191, 229, 232
  as revealed by competition, 163, 299
Compensation
  and intellectual property, 285, 292–93, 300

of losers, 17, 50–51, 60, 65,
    132, 197–98, 203, 204–15,
    216–19, 232, 234, 238,
    280–81, 330
  principle of, 275–76, 278,
    282–83
  strategies of, 72, 147, 173,
    213–14, 276–78, 236, 252,
    254, 272, 276–77, 333
  See also harm; Principle of
    Due Care
Competition
  in environmental policy,
    328–29
  instrumental value of, 163, 168,
    299–300
  in tax policy, 240n31
  See also fair competition
Complicity, 93n33, 113n11,
    160–61, 305, 322, 323, 324
Corporations. *See* firms
Cosmopolitanism
  characterization of, 11, 113, 105,
    123n28
  as not inevitable, 6, 9, 17, 94, 105
  as internal moral principle,
    241–45
  limitations of, 13–14, 26n42,
    105, 110, 113, 114n12, 124
  as precluded by principles, 18,
    170
  about trade practice, 104,
    193–201, 322
  See also individualism
Currency of fairness
  as opportunities, 223, 228–29,
    230, 232, 236, 279
  in political argument, ix
  as resources, 152, 232, 206,
    232–33
  as welfare, 232

Default, as fair, 158–59
Developing countries
  least-developed, 24–25, 90, 158,
    191, 216n14
  middle-income, 24–25, 158,
    191, 319

Development
  aid, 214, 117–18, 190, 214, 306,
    312, 315–16, 320, 324
  causes of, 12, 47, 121, 192, 216,
    218, 250, 253, 265–66, 277,
    289
  and environmental policy, 326,
    329, 331
  and labor policy, 49n26, 162,
    163, 311, 315–16
  and policy flexibility, 7, 21, 79,
    148–49, 191, 229, 287–89
  and intellectual property, 99,
    287–88, 300, 302
Difference principle, 139, 183n13,
    220, 226, 227
Discrimination
  in trade rules, 74, 75n65, 147–48,
    189, 229, 233n26, 287n3,
  moral issue of, 148, 169, 189,
    220, 329
Distribution
  debate over, 5, 9–12, 17, 255
  domestic, as relevant to
    international fairness, 185, 221
  see also equality; equity;
    structural equity
Doha Round, 75, 83
Driskill, Robert, 66, 199, 210

Economies of scale, 18, 47, 180,
    181, 186, 199, 227, 229
Egalitarianism
  individualistic. (*See* individualism)
  luck, 194, 241, 242
  parochial, 6, 9, 10, 11, 14, 15, 17
  See also cosmopolitanism
Efficiency
  as avoiding waste, 63–64
  instrumental, 62–63
  Kaldor-Hicks, 51, 60, 65–67, 70,
    197, 199, 200, 210
  normative assumptions about,
    63, 36, 60–68, 136, 143,
    208, 260–63
  Pareto, 51, 60, 67–68, 70,
    198–99, 200, 208, 219, 260
  as preference satisfaction, 63

Eichengreen, Barry, 8n5, 249n1, 251n6, 256, 256n14, 257, 258, 262n28, 267, 267n38, 268n40
Endowments
    natural, 46, 174, 243
    in relation to fairness, 172, 174, 179–85, 222, 242–43,
    gains of trade adjusted for, 20, 165, 168–69, 179–85, 180–83, 203, 222
    and resource curse, 154, 234n33
    as subject to choice, 185
Entitlements
    absence of special, 20
    to cooperative surplus, 170, 174, 190, 244
    as not independent of fairness, 222
    to a living wage, 324n18
Environment
    degradation of, 160, 325
    and economics, 326–27
    and economic fairness, 327–30
    preservation of, 325–26, 330–31
    in trade law, 146, 305
Equal gain benchmark, 165, 168–70, 185, 195
Equality
    of status, 20, 136–37, 168–69, 173, 188–89, 190, 233
    substantive, political, 157
    of opportunity,
        formal, 189, 228–31, 229–30
        substantive, 217n14, 229–30, 237–39
    as a rule of thumb, 181–84
    See also equity; distribution; relative gains
Equity
    consequentialist view of, 135–6
    deontological view of, 136–38
    in fair division, 20, 135
    over time, 138–40
    transactional, 138–39
    See also structural equity
Exclusion, 59n50, 189–93

Exploitation
    of bargaining position, 171, 308–9, 310, 313
    definition of, 308
    moral relevance of, 71, 98, 100, 102, 145, 161, 314, 320
    of workers, 68n59, 162, 306–8, 309–13, 316–17
Externality
    and the need for assurance, 56
    as a basis for regulation, 42, 261, 326n22
    as imposed, 40, 44, 51, 52, 177, 180
    positive, 294
    terms of trade, 44, 45, 48, 50–53, 56, 57, 60, 64, 318
    See also harm

Fair competition
    as uncontroversial, 5
    argument from, 7, 69, 71, 73, 75n65, 162, 285–86, 294–95, 328, 331
    as sensitive to structural equity, 162–63, 168, 296, 298, 300
    See also competition
Fair play
    and assurance, 4, 78, 80, 82
    and agreements, 79n3
    in bargaining, 88
    duties of, 79, 92, 156
    and national interest, 77, 82–87
    in politics, 157
    as requiring good faith, 156,
    and structural equity, 156, 158, 330
Fair trade cooperatives, 162, 195, 320, 324n18
Fair division
    basic problem of, 135, 137, 138, 139, 189, 190
    and the gains of trade, 19–20, 30, 139, 165–70
    and Gauthier, 171–74, 228n21
    as Nash bargaining solution, 227–28

INDEX 359

Fair risk assumption
  and equality of opportunity, 230–31
  in capital markets, 252, 278–81
  See also voluntariness
Fair risk imposition, 234–35, 251–52, 263, 283
Fair wages
  and stagnation 7, 11, 17, 49, 50, 145, 203
  as market wages, 68, 315, 316
  as minimum wages, 68, 162, 315, 324n18
  and volatility or uncertainty, 143, 274
  and competition, 73, 216n14
  and insurance, 213, 215, 276,
  and improvement, 311, 315–16
Fairness
  discourse, 4, 146
  emergent responsibilities of, 3, 8, 13, 15, 17, 18, 78, 125, 161, 162, 195, 201, 306, 312, 322
  of prices, 68, 71, 154, 161–62, 167, 331, 309n2, 310
  political, 9, 156n31, 157
  procedural, 5, 157
  socioeconomic, 6, 8–12, 17, 94–98, 113, 145, 146, 161, 185, 203, 206, 233, 305–7, 314, 320, 325, 327
  of trade barriers, 17, 20, 132n2, 159–60, 213, 214, 216, 224, 230, 319, 328, 331
  transactional, 15, 71, 154, 161, 166–67, 223, 260–62, 264
  types of, 156–63
  See also equity; structural equity; fairness in international political morality; fair competition; fair prices; fair wages; fair risk assumption; fair risk imposition; collective responsibility; reciprocity
Fairness in international political morality
  definition of, 6

  explanation of, 17, 105
  as ideal theory, 13–14
  issues of, 8
  modest nature of, 12
Financial crises
  increasing number of, 249
  causes of, 249, 250n3
  caused by capital liberalization, 266–69
  causes as structural, 263–64
  cost of, 8, 250–51, 258, 261
  and regulatory disposition, 270–72
  See also harm; compensation; Principle of Due Care
Financial globalization. See capital liberalization
Firms, 22, 196, 321–24
Free trade argument, 35–37, 46–51, 60–66

Gains of trade
  as adjusted for endowments, 169, 180–83
  and the aim of trade practice, 19, 201
  distribution of, 20, 30, 65–68, 165, 169, 177, 203, 219–28, 232–33
  in economic theory, 17–18, 35–36, 46–48, 227
  as national in nature, 17, 29, 46–48, 168, 185–88
  as owned, 174–79, 219, 220
  as a fair division problem, 19–20, 30
  as primary goods, 220
  as socially created, 17, 44, 54, 178, 190, 244
Gauthier, David, 161n39, 171, 172, 228n21
Global basic structure, 11–12, 113
Global economy
  as embedded in international market reliance practice, 17, 19, 30, 37–41, 41–45, 54–59, 81, 82, 165, 167, 194–200
  and internal values, 144–46

Global economy (*continued*)
  legitimacy of, 23, 239–40, 301, 306–8, 332–34
  as consistent with financial autarky, 264–65, 273
  as partially integrated, 22–23, 39, 58, 153–54, 178, 194
  as politically decentralized, 21–22, 77, 91–93, 97
  as produced by state system, 9–10, 13, 23, 30, 224
  as a political choice, 8–9, 15
  scope of, 152–55
  significance of, 5, 12–13
  as we know it, 13, 16, 18, 21, 24, 26n42, 58, 144, 194
General Agreement on Tariffs and Trade
  and developing countries, 74, 148, 253n10
  and larger trade practice, 150n25, 151,
  and legal rulings, 146–47, 305, 329
  and policy flexibility, 214
  rational reconstruction of, 53
  and values, 160n38, 318n12, 328n27, 329
  and trust and assurance, 56, 81, 86
  See also World Trade Organization
Governance
  by corporations, 22, 40, 321–24
  duty of fair, 79, 80, 87–88, 91, 93, 157
  by governments, 40, 88–90, 165
  by international organizations, 21–22, 40, 165n31
  as politically decentralized, 21–22, 77, 91–93, 97
  principles for, 125, 183,
  as incoherent, 151–52
  as value-laden, 75n66, 305–6, 327–8

Harm
  and aggregation, 64–65, 142, 216–19

  characterization of, 174n6, 204, 211
  and efficiency, 143, 64–68, 71
  as an internal concern, 190, 206, 219
  and liberty, 238
  to lifetime prospects, 209–12, 219
  and opportunity views, 230, 232
  as requiring compensation, 17, 20, 72, 204–8, 208–14
  and risk, 233–37
  from trade, 17, 48–49, 68–69, 71–73, 203
  See also financial crises; capital liberalization; exploitation
Hobbes, Thomas, 4, 14, 24n37, 27n43, 77, 78, 80, 83, 103, 104, 105, 110, 135
Human rights
  significance of, ix
  as external values, x, 3, 8, 9, 18, 20, 94, 144n17, 145
  and intellectual property, 288, 290–92
  as related to fairness, 160–61, 305, 320, 315
  in relation to status equality, 189
  as motivating states, 84
Human condition
  and assurance, 44–45, 58, 105, 114–15
  and circumstances of justice, 24
  and economic models, 44
  within ideal theory, 16–17, 103–4, 124–27
Humanitarian values
  appeals to, 70, 159, 301–2, 306, 324
  as external, 8, 9, 144–45, 223, 320
  and self-sacrifice, 225
  See also human rights
Hume, David, 24n36, 27n43, 58, 59n49, 111

Impersonal/personal reasons, 101, 142
Ideal theory/non-ideal theory
  characterization of, 16–17, 103–4
  as normative for us, 104, 113–16, 124–27
  Rawls's version of, 111–12
  and the human condition, 16–17, 103–4, 124–27
  and the international system, 13–14
  See also abstraction; human condition
India, 24, 65, 89, 191, 216, 234, 249, 286, 290, 295, 327
Individualism
  definition of, 123
  as revisionism, 193–201
  about trade practice, 117, 177
  See also cosmopolitanism
Inequality
  across societies, 9–12, 18, 203, 221–26
  of relative gains, 18, 20, 180–84, 203, 226
  significance of, 5, 10, 206
  socioeconomic, 9, 206
  special reasons for, 165, 169–70
  within societies, 9, 18, 139, 203–4, 219–21
  See also equality; equity; equal gain benchmark; distribution
Intellectual property
  exemption, 21, 285, 302, 303
  rules as inhibiting development, 221, 300, 302
  in international agreements, 74, 79, 89, 99, 155, 285, 286–87, 291
  in Trade Related Aspects of Intellectual Property Rights, 285
  as natural rights, 290–93
  as relevant to fair competition, 162–63, 293–97
Integration
  of developing countries, x, 59n50, 189–93, 225, 253, 312–13, 316
  between developing countries, 213n10
  partial, 22–23, 39, 58, 153–54, 178, 194
  systemic nature of, 11, 178–79, 220
  dynamic consequences of, 181
  See also global economy; gains of trade; capital liberalization
Internal values
  and basic fairness question, 8, 145, 187
  cosmopolitan appeal to, 104, 193–201, 241–45, 322
  as contrasted with external values, 8, 144–46, 185, 307
  fairness issues as, 146–50, 156, 187n19, 193, 206, 222, 225, 286, 320, 321
  libertarian appeal to, 237–39
  as related to external values, 160–61, 305–6, 307–8, 327–29
  See also constructive method
International trade
  aim of. (*see* gains of trade)
  classical theory of, 42n9, 47, 52, 63, 197–98
  as a market reliance practice, 19, 37–41, 41–44, 59, 81
  neo-classical theory of, 43, 44, 47, 197–98
  in relevant organizing sense, 39–40, 153–54
  see also global economy; free trade argument
Interpersonal morality, 15, 110, 111, 125
Interwar years, as non-cooperative, 9, 56, 58, 80, 81, 82n9, 88, 93, 151, 152, 153, 175, 186
Investment
  agreements on, 150, 240, 240n30, 253n10

Investment (*continued*)
  and developing country
    integration, 266, 312–13, 328
  limited rights of, 239–41, 251, 296
  public, 118, 182, 197, 213, 229
  regulation of, 161, 221–22,
    252–53, 256, 269, 271
  See also legitimate expectations;
    capital liberalization
Irwin, Douglas, 42n9, 43n11,
  46n14, 46n15, 47n20, 53,
  53n41, 59n50, 63n54, 74n65

Kant, Immanuel, 4, 112, 120
Keynes, John Maynard, 49n28,
  118n20, 119n21, 139,
  267n36, 118, 119n21
Krugman, Paul, 8n5, 36, 36n2,
  43n11, 46n16, 48n25, 49n26,
  50n31, 69, 259n24, 267n36,
  299n22, 309–10, 311n4

Labor
  and market wages, 68, 315, 316
  and minimum wages, 68, 162,
    315, 324n18
  mobility, limited nature of,
    22–23, 118
  standards
    as linked with trade, 21, 162,
      317–20
    core, 314–15
  See also fair wages; exploitation;
    harm; compensation;
    unemployment; social
    insurance
Laissez-faire
  assumptions of, 5, 42n9
  as fair, 183, 314
  as fictional, 42
  as insufficient, 72, 139, 161,
    314, 320, 326
Legitimacy
  and debt repayment, 159
  basic demands of, 23, 196, 239,
    307, 334
  as fundamental challenge to
    global economy, 332–34
  of state system, 23, 176, 146
  and taxation, 175
Legitimate expectations, 159n35,
  175, 239–41, 301
Level playing field. *See* fair
  competition
Libertarianism, 16n19, 174–76,
  200, 237–39
  See also principle of substantive
    libertarianism
Liberty
  and the aim of trade, 167–68
  basic, 175, 237, 259
  economic, 175, 176, 237, 240
  as unaffected by trade, 176, 197,
    240, 259
  as not permitting harm, 238, 259
  presumption in favor of, 258–60
  See also libertarianism;
    principle of substantive
    libertarianism
Locke, John, 4, 16

Marx, Karl, 16, 23n32, 162, 312
Market failure
  as broadly targeted, 262
  as constitutive or functional, 42
  as grounds for intervention, 260
  See also laissez-faire
Mercantilism, 36, 46, 46n15, 69n8,
  75n65, 167, 200
Mill, J.S., 22n30, 47n18, 48n21,
  48n22, 50n33, 52, 53,
  53n39, 59n50, 63, 200,
  238n29, 259, 259n22, 260
Mutuality
  deliberative, 156–57
  basis for free trade, 37, 45,
    51–59
  nature of, 38, 51
  of risk. (*See* fair risk imposition)
  role in trade practice, 41, 51–59,
    200
  supposed irrelevance of, 35–36
  See also reciprocity

Nagel, Thomas, 9n6, 94, 94n35,
  95–97

Nash
　equilibrium, 54, 55, 58,
　solution, 166n1, 227–28,
Natural duty of justice, 113, 125n32
Natural rights
　in contrast with human rights,
　　144n17
　as external values, 15–16,
　of intellectual property, 290–93
　of property, 174
　and taxation, 175–76
National interest
　egoism about, 83–86
　and discrimination, 188–89
　and fair play, 77–78, 82, 88–90
　and the gains of trade, 17–18,
　　35–36, 43, 46–48, 185–88, 227
　and reciprocal benefit, 83, 86
　in trade cooperation, 52–59
Negotiations
　cooperative, 88–89, 157–58
　as legislative, 88, 91–93
　given rule of reciprocity, 84, 90
　See also fair play
Net food importers, 70, 133
Non-ideal theory. *See* ideal
　theory/non-ideal theory
Normative political philosophy, 14,
　110, 113, 114, 122, 123, 126
Nozick, Robert, 11n9, 16n19, 174n7,
　238n29, 291n15, 16n19

Opportunity, equality of. *See*
　equality.
Opportunity principle,
　formulation of, 228
　as formal, 229
　as insensitive to harms of trade,
　　230
　as insensitive to participatory
　　claims, 232
　as modified to require
　　compensation, 232
　as substantive, 229

Participation
　and claims to fair shares, 44,
　　172, 190–93, 232
　and exclusion, 189–93, 191
　as primarily national, 19, 96,
　　168, 195
　threshold conception of, 40,
　　172–73, 178–79
Personal/impersonal reasons.
　See impersonal/personal
　reasons
Piracy
　as fair play, 286, 288, 297, 302
　as theft, 290
　as unfair competition, 285, 293–97
Pogge, Thomas, xi, 11n9, 113n11,
　117n16, 118n18, 288n9
Power
　bargaining, 77, 78, 80, 89–70,
　　308–9
　and exploitation, 171, 308–9,
　　310, 313
　relations, 101–2
　See also coercion
Poverty
　significance of, ix, x, 10
　as addressed by public system
　　of rewards, 288n9, 289
　as relevant to fairness, x, 18,
　　20, 121, 133, 148, 182, 188,
　　216–18, 228, 235, 250–52,
　　300–301, 307, 311–13,
　　315–16, 327–28
　as separate from fairness, 10, 12,
　　145, 188, 223–24, 226, 228,
　　233, 289–90, 316–17
　rural versus urban, 24, 65, 70,
　　133, 311, 315
Practice-based justification. *See*
　constructive method.
Priority for the worse off,
　characterization of, 223–24
　and unequal national gains,
　　224–26
　and environmental regulation,
　　316–17
　and intellectual property, 302
Principle of Collective Due Care
　argument for, 204–8
　formulation of, 17, 203
　interpretation of, 208–13

Principle of compensation, 275
  See also compensation; harm
Principle of International Relative Gains
  argument for, 221–26
  application of, 20–21, 225, 302, 316–17
  in contrast with difference principle, 226–27
  in contrast with Nash solution, 227–28
  formulation of, 18, 203
Principle of Domestic Relative Gains
  argument for, 219–21
  formulation of, 18, 203
  and social insurance, 215
Principle of risk reciprocation, 233, 234–36, 282–83
Principle of strict equality (applied domestically), 220
Principle of strict equality (applied internationally), 224
Principle of substantive libertarianism, 237
Principle of utility. *See* utilitarianism
Promissory principle, 239
  See also legitimate expectations
Protectionism
  in agriculture, 132–33
  in manufacturing, 132n2
  moralistic, 329–30
  through rules of origin, 133n2
  through anti-dumping duties, 69, 71, 81, 149, 157, 333
Publicity, 58, 104, 110, 111, 112, 115, 117–18, 127

Rawls, John
  on allocation, 169n4
  and the difference principle. (*See* difference principle)
  and circumstances of justice, 24n36, 27n43
  and fair play, 92n31, 156n30
  on making a lot from a little, 6
  as a parochial egalitarian, 9, 15
  on a high standard of living, 332–33
  and human rights, 144n17
  on ideal theory, 111–12
  on justification, 15n17, 16n20, 16n21, 21, 26n41, 97, 114n14 (*See also* constructive method)
  on moralized interpretation, 28n47, 29n49,
  on natural endowment, 173–74, 243n33
  and political philosophy, x
  on primary social goods, 167n3, 169n4
  on reciprocity, 86
  and resources, 243, 33
  and social contract tradition, 4, 312
  on the dangers of wealth, 332–33
  on world government, 120
  See also natural duty of justice
Reasonable
  confidence, 80, 93, 115–16, 117, 119, 120, 169, 212
  complaints as, 55, 66, 98, 132, 136, 143, 171, 184, 204, 208, 209, 218, 232, 235, 236, 237, 278, 279, 280, 288, 292, 293n19, 300, 308, 315
  rejection/acceptance, 96, 131–32, 135, 137, 138, 156
Reciprocity
  in negotiations, 36, 87, 90
  of benefit, 45, 52–54, 74, 75n65, 78, 86, 200,
  as a motive, 83, 86
  of risk, 233–37, 282–83
  See also mutuality
Rectification, 145–6
Regulation
  difficulty of, 256–58, 275–76
  dispositions of, 270–72
  principles for, 14, 19, 101, 125, 126, 134, 169, 241
  as value-laden, 305–6

INDEX 365

Resources. *See* endowments
Revisionism, individualism as a version of, 193–201
Risse, Mathias, xi, 9n6, 94, 101n46, 118n19, 123n27, 160n37
Risk
  assumption. (*See* fair risk assumption)
  dominance, 55, 105, 267
  of moral opportunity cost, 108
  reciprocity of, 233–37, 282–83
  fairness of imposing. (*See* fair risk imposition)
Rodrik, Dani, 7, 8n4, 16n22, 42n10, 72n62, 81n8, 121n23, 148n22, 191n21, 192, 214, 265n31, 266n32, 266n33, 288n7, 288n8, 301n24
Rousseau, Jean-Jacques, 4, 14, 27, 55n44
Ruggie, 22n27, 81n8, 82n9, 83n11, 162n40, 320n14, 321n15,

Samuelson, Paul, 43, 47, 49n26, 49n27, 49n28, 51n38, 66n55, 198,
Scanlon, T. M.
  on aggregation, 142n12, 218n15
  on interpersonal morality, 15n16, 125
  on welfare, 143n14, 260–61
  on priority for the worse off, 223n16
  on reasonable rejection, 14, 137
  on rights and liberties, 259n25
  and "what we owe to each other," 25, 101, 125, 134
  as within social contract tradition, 4
  on value, 326n21
Security
  and bargaining, 89
  as an extenuating condition, 218
  as a fairness consideration, 173
  as increasing, 81, 82, 85–86
  interests in, 123n28

  as an internal value, 145
  as a market pre-condition, 41
  and state identities, 83
  and state system, 117, 120–21
  as swamping trade relations, 155
  and taxes, 175
  as trumping opulence, 62, 85
Smith, Adam
  on advocacy, 63
  on family/kingdom analogy, 199
  on national income benchmark, 41, 46, 200
  as nationalistic, 200
  on public good by private gain, 24
  on security, 62
  on social nature of markets, 42n9, 257n18
  on specialization, 46
Social insurance
  as fair, 7, 213–15
  types of, 213
  collective responsibility for, 213
Social justice
  and power relations (*see* power)
  and social practice (*see* constructive method)
Social practice
  and assurance. (*See* assurance)
  as beyond individual powers, 15, 101
  definition of, 37–38
  as embedding markets, 3, 19, 41–42, 151–52
  of mutual market reliance, 19, 37–41, 88, 93, 131, 263,
  as organizing economic life, 15–17, 194–95
  See also constructive method; structural equity
Sovereignty
  and assurance, 77, 81–82
  as decentralized, 9, 77
  and justice, 94–98
  process view of, 86n19
  and property rights, 177, 179
  and voluntariness, 100, 279
  See also clean trade

Special Drawing Rights, 184, 271, 281
Stag hunt game. *See* assurance game.
Stiglitz, Joseph, 7n2, 133n3, 148n22, 157n33, 158n34, 184n14, 204n2, 213n10, 240n31, 271n43, 271n45, 287n6, 288n9
Structural equity
  characterization of, 3, 19, 131–32, 138–40
  and competitive fairness
  and efficiency, 67, 68, 70, 143
  normative force of, 140–44. (*See also* equity)
  as priority for the worse off. (*See* priority for the worse off)
  principles of, 17–18, 203
  reasoning about, 132–35
  scope of, 44, 150–55, 156–63
Subsidies
  farm, 7, 70–71, 132–33, 148, 204
  export, 7, 21, 79, 148, 319

Technology
  as distinct from trade, 68, 71–72
  as spread through trade, 47, 227, 229, 265, 288, 289, 331
Tobin, James, 8, 251n8, 274, 326n23
Trade diversion
  from bi-lateral agreements, 149
  as correcting first mover advantages, 216n14, 224–25
  and utilitarianism, 65

Ultimatum game, 84, 87, 137, 138
Unemployment, due to trade, 49, 204–5

Uruguay Round, 74–75, 89, 99, 286, 290, 309, 313
Utilitarianism
  definition of, 215
  and efficiency, 64
  negative, 312

Values
  internal/external, 8, 144–46, 305–6
  as basis for governance, 305–6
  as basis for trust, 81
  as shaping production, 185
Veil of ignorance, 25–26, 97, 210n9

Welfare
  diminishing marginal value of, 260
  moral relevance of, 143, 260–61
  See also currency of fairness
World Trade Organization, 7, 21
  as "all or nothing," 81, 100, 177
  and conservation, 329–30
  and global governance, 151
  as inflexible, 7, 21, 148, 253, 301
  judicial system of, 89, 146–48, 305, 329
  rational reconstruction of, 53
  reform of General System of Preferences in, 213n10
  and rule of consensus, 87, 157
  and Trade Related Aspects of Intellectual Property, 285–88
  and trade/labor "linkage," 306, 317–19
  with a "transfer round," 90
  See also General Agreement on Tariffs and Trade

Made in the USA
Coppell, TX
05 March 2021